NEWGATE NARRATIVES

CONTENTS OF THE EDITION

NEWGATE NARRATIVES

Edited by Gary Kelly

Volume 5
The Autobiography of Jack Ketch

Routledge
Taylor & Francis Group

LONDON AND NEW YORK

First published 2008 by Pickering & Chatto (Publishers) Limited

2 Park Square, Milton Park, Abingdon, Oxon OX14 4RN
711 Third Avenue, New York, NY 10017, USA

Routledge is an imprint of the Taylor & Francis Group, an informa business

First issued in paperback 2017

Copyright © Taylor & Francis 2008
Copyright © Editorial material Gary Kelly

BRITISH LIBRARY CATALOGUING IN PUBLICATION DATA
1. Newgate (Prison : London, England) – Fiction 2. Newgate (Prison : London, England) – History – Sources 3. Prisons – England – Fiction 4. Prisons – England – History – 19th century – Sources 5. Crime – England – London – Fiction 6. English fiction – 19th century
I. Kelly, Gary
823.8'0803556[F]

ISBN-13: 978-1-1387-5564-2 (hbk)
ISBN-13: 978-1-138-11296-4 (pbk)
ISBN-13: 978-1-85196-812-1 (set)

Typeset by Pickering & Chatto (Publishers) Limited

CONTENTS

INTRODUCTION

The Autobiography of Jack Ketch

Or, mon abjection était mon désespoir. Et le désespoir la force même—et en même temps la matière pour l'abolir. Mais si l'œuvre est la plus belle, qui exige la vigueur du plus grand désespoir, il fallait que le poète aimât les hommes pour entreprendre un pareil effort. Et qu'il réussît. Il est bien que les hommes s'éloignent d'une œuvre profonde si elle est le cri d'un homme enlisé monstrueusement en lui-même.[1]

Charles Whitehead's *The Autobiography of Jack Ketch* (1835) is perhaps the most original of the 'Newgate narratives'. Certainly it is the most disturbing. For it brings together humour and horror in order to represent Whitehead's vision of the ironic and abject nature of the human condition. In doing so Whitehead's novel anticipated the theme of some of the most powerful fictions of the modern age. In fact, however, Whitehead's vision applied specifically to the social milieu from which he himself came and which he turned to literature in order to transcend – with little material success. Whitehead spent his literary career on the fringes of London commercial writing and publishing and ended his career, and his life, in a distant outpost of the empire. Though not exactly a hack writer, he lived – or rather barely subsisted – by his writing, while aspiring to what he considered higher literary achievement. His literary output was modest but creditable and included his Newgate novel, *The Autobiography of Jack Ketch*, as well as two respected historical novels, two plays that were mounted on the London stage, a volume of poems, and a few dozen tales, poems and essays in magazines and literary annuals. But he struggled to make ends meet, was repeatedly reduced to asking for charity, considered himself constitutionally incapable of achieving popularity and eventually sought a better life for himself and his wife in Australia, where he died in miserable circumstances. What is known of his life reveals something of the often desperate world of the margins of literary production and the business of literature in the middle third of the nineteenth century. Whitehead experienced and observed abjection and he wrote about it almost obsessively, but in his writing he generalized his favourite topic into an ironic vision of human life.

The following pages provide a more comprehensive than usual introduction to Whitehead's Newgate novel. This is for several related reasons. Whitehead and his work have rarely been discussed and are now almost unknown. His writing seems to arise from his own social experience and cultural aspirations, in complex and contradictory ways. Much of the literary and intellectual context of Whitehead's work is now little known. Finally, *The Autobiography of Jack Ketch* forms an important link between earlier and later literature of crime and social abjection and it responds in complex ways both to the long tradition of 'Newgate narratives', or the literature of crime and punishment and to the political and literary debate on crime and punishment in his time. Accordingly, the introduction that follows first examines Whitehead's life and literary career, then elucidates the central themes and ideological implications of Whitehead's writing and finally examines *The Autobiography of Jack Ketch* both in itself and in relation to its principal literary and cultural contexts, as a distinctive contribution to 'Newgate narratives' in the key period of the first half of the nineteenth century.

Life and Literary Career

Like most writers, Whitehead came from the middle ranks of society, though from the commercial rather than professional middle class. One of his important contributions to literature in his time was his fictional portrayal of the world of these people, in both lightly humorous and darkly Gothic modes, or through what he called, in the title of his 1847 collection of such fiction, 'smiles and tears'. Whitehead was born at 86 Great Tower Street, London[2] on 4 September 1804,[3] the eldest of the seven children of a wine merchant, John Whitehead, and his wife. Tower Street, renamed Great Tower Street, led to Tower Hill and the Tower of London, and was in the heart of the City of London, with houses and shops of well-to-do merchants, near the wharves and the old Custom House and so well situated for a man in the wine trade. In the 1810 Post Office Directory, a firm of Means and Whitehead, wine and brandy merchants, were located at 10 Rood Lane, which connected Tower Street to Fenchurch Street. According to the writer Hall Caine, the family were in 'easy circumstances' and Whitehead's father died at age seventy-six from an accident, leaving 'a considerable sum' to his children.[4] Someone who knew the family reported in 1852, however, that John Whitehead 'was a highly respectable merchant in London and, until reduced by misfortune, was an encourager of Literature and collected an excellent library'.[5] At that time the wine business, though one in which a good living could be made, would have been considered a rather low line of trade, in which a man with 'an excellent library' would be considered unusual, indicating cultural aspiration and interests above his station and more usual for a man in the upper or professional middle class. Whereas a man in the professions, especially the 'learned' professions of the clergy, law and so on, could, like a man in the landed gentry, be considered a gentleman, a man in trade usually could not. Like other class distinctions of the time, this was an important one: much of Whitehead's fiction, including *The Autobiography of Jack Ketch*, is about class difference, aspiration, mobility and – more darkly – failure, such as Whitehead's own.

Whitehead was well educated, or in his phrase 'brought up', at a Dr Green-law's school at Brentford, near London.[6] This was Syon House school, which offered a 'gentleman's' education, mainly to the sons of local families in busi-ness, though the poet Percy Shelley, who was the son of a landed gentleman, had attended Syon House in 1802 for two years. Unlike many or most gentle-man's sons, Whitehead did not go to university. Suitably and predictably for a young man of his background, he was employed in a commercial firm – its line of business is not known – and apparently in a position of trust which he could have abused without fear of detection, but which he executed faithfully.[7] Never-theless, the frequency in his fiction of situations of petty deception to outright fraud suggests that Whitehead was well aware of the line between legal and ille-gal conduct and the fascinating and dangerous grey area of the dishonest but not necessarily illegal, especially for those in the lower middle class who never had quite enough money to put on the trappings of social respectability and genteel status for which they strove. Since the late eighteenth century at least, literature or the 'belles-lettres' had become associated with more genteel mid-dle- and upper-class culture and in his mid-twenties Whitehead moved to leave commerce behind and achieve upward social mobility, if not a greater income, as a writer of such serious literature.

His first book clearly asserted his claim. This was *The Solitary: A Poem* (1831), in three parts totaling over 1300 lines and 153 stanzas.[8] The volume was published by Effingham Wilson (1785–1868), bookseller and publisher – the two functions were commonly combined at the time – of a range of literature of interest to urban middle-class people, including literary, social and political satire with a reformist bent; pamphlets on issues of the day such as Catholic emancipa-tion, abolition of slavery, the banking system and paper currency, penal reform, British financial and political interests in South America and the state church; a few handbooks for middle-class cultural interests such as gardening; guides to physical health; advice on fashionable dress; education manuals; a literary peri-odical; pamphlets on urban development and administration of London; and a few poems. In short, Wilson's main market was the tax paying, small investment holding, politically interested, reform minded, socially and culturally aspiring, self-consciously independent London middle classes – the kind of people whom

Whitehead grew up among, but most of whom were unlikely to be interested in a high Romantic autobiographical poem of social alienation such as *The Solitary*. Whitehead's poem sticks out in Wilson's list and it may be that Whitehead's connections with the commercial middle class led him to Wilson or induced Wilson to undertake publication, probably with no financial risk and perhaps to add a little prestige to his list. At the same time, the poem's subject could have appealed to those in the middle classes, like Whitehead himself, of ungenteel middle-class social location but genteel middle-class cultural aspirations. Such aspirations could be realized in one way by demonstrating 'high' literary interest and ability, especially when exhibiting a 'romantic soul', or subjectivity self-consciously alienated from the commercialism and social competitiveness of the day.

It is worth dwelling on *The Solitary* because it was obviously important to Whitehead's sense of himself and of his vocation as a writer and because its central theme of inherently afflicted subjectivity struggling against the degraded and degrading character of modern society and culture recurs again and again in his work. This is a well wrought poem, designed to display its author's participation in 'high' literary culture and to demonstrate his command of 'high' literary discourse. Each of the poem's three parts has a verse epigraph – from Coleridge's historical drama *Remorse*, Milton's Christian epic *Paradise Lost* and Gray's 'Ode on the Spring', respectively. Together these references invoke what was by this time being established as the English national literary canon spanning the seventeenth, eighteenth and nineteenth centuries, and the high poetic genres of verse drama, epic and public lyric. *The Solitary* is in the nine-line Spenserian stanza, a form revived and much used in Romantic poetry and one that by allusion served several purposes. In general the verse form would suggest to the well read and cultivated reader the form of the romance, or quest journey that 'proves', in the sense of tests and affirms, the character of the protagonist. In particular, the stanza form would recall Edmund Spenser's renaissance national romance, the *Faerie Queene* (1590–6), much admired in the late eighteenth and nineteenth centuries and after which the stanza form was named. Nearer to hand, Whitehead's use of the Spenserian stanza, along with elements of his poetic language, would invoke other major Romantic poems of subjective, moral and intellectual quest, such as Byron's manifestly autobiographical descriptive and meditative poem, *Childe Harold's Pilgrimage* (1812–18), Keats's richly descriptive love romance, *Eve of St Agnes* (1820) and Shelley's pastoral elegy for Keats, *Adonais* (1821). *The Solitary* incorporates elements of all of these poems, particularly the descriptive, meditative and elegiac, in fact near the end of the last part of the poem there is an apostrophe to Shelley as a damaged and lost genius. At the same time, as an account of the poet's reflection on self and world from the evening of one day to the dawn of the next, with a theme of religious consolation, the poem invokes a longer tradition of 'night thoughts', or meditative-descriptive poems, in particular Edward Young's widely read Sentimental poem, *The Complaint; or, Nights Thoughts on Life, Death, and Immortality* (1742–5).

The Solitary takes up this line of Romantic poetry by being, in a sense, the poet's elegy for himself as a soul lost from the beginning. Though the poem's mode is lyric, or self-expressive and autobiographical, the poet in *The Solitary* is a figure constructed in and by the poem rather than the poem's author in an unmediated and direct way. The image that Whitehead acquired in his lifetime, and especially later, as a stricken almost-genius, was probably partly informed by the poem and also instrumental in shaping the reading of the poem as autobiographical. Further, there are references in the poem to events in Whitehead's life, in particular the death by drowning of his brother at age seventeen (this information is conveyed in a footnote). The poem's first part opens with a lush description of dusk, when 'All things beauteous more beauteous appear' (l. 23), a description that then precipitates the poet's reflections on 'This world's infinity of ill' (l. 58). The opening establishes a contrast between, on the one hand, the beautiful in nature and poetry's rendering of it and, on the other hand, the degradation and misery of life and the world. This contrast is carried through the rest of part one in relation to the poet's representation of himself as inherently disqualified for the fallen world and its desires, ambitions and competitiveness. The poet declares, 'Let be the baser drudgery of life / To those that toil for plenty, or increase . . .' (ll. 379–80) and turns to the now well established refuges of the Romantic afflicted soul – nature and poetry:

> Meanwhile, of cities and the crowded mart
>   I take my welcome leave; and faint, and tir'd,
> Fall back on nature, and the glorious art
>   Which my young soul so ceaselessly desir'd,
>   Begun too late—alas! too soon inspir'd!
> Yet not too late, if, of that eager flame
>   One spark remain which my sad bosom fir'd,
> With weak but steadfast hand, and measured aim,
>   I fling it to the stars—oh, waft it hither, Fame!
> (stanza 44, ll. 388–96)

Beyond these, there is only the shadowy prospect of life hereafter as a kind of classical Elysium or paradise for beautiful souls: 'Oh, for eternal shores, and fields for ever green!' (l. 513).

Part two further develops the theme of the opposition between subjective sensibility and a materialistic world and the consequences of that opposition for the poet's vocation. At moments, the poet attributes the dislocation of self and society to his own weaknesses and strengths, declaring that to have no will or subjective desire unfits one for the world and that 'we ourselves seek our own miseries' (l. 118), especially if cursed 'With sensibilities too finely cast' (l. 191). Nevertheless, the poem seems to envision an ameliorative and reformative social role for the poet:

> To kindle soft humanity—to raise,
>   With gentle strength infus'd, the spirit bow'd;
>   To pour a second sunlight on our days,
>   And draw the restless lightning from our cloud;
>   To cheer the humble, and to dash the proud;
>   What heav'n withholds more largely to supply,
>   And fringe with joy our ever-weaving shroud;
>   Besought in peace to live, and taught to die;
>   The poet's task is done—Oh Immortality!
> (st. 47, ll. 415–23)

Part three is more directly elegiac, with its opening reference to the poet's fraternal loss, eliciting a meditation on grief and perhaps guilt:

> Oh! that the spade had delv'd my early tomb
>   Instead of thine—for I was to the worm
> A closer kinsman, weaker from the womb,
>   Windfall of glory, canker'd from the germ,
>   Of baser earth, and less resisting form—
> Thou had'st disdain'd the weakness that o'ercame
>   My nature, and, undaunted by the storm,
> Had'st thrown away the vizor of false shame,
> And with unglaiv'd hand struck out thy way to fame!
> (st. 8, ll. 64–72)

The rest of the poem carries forward this sense of some original sin, loss, or trauma, which is not overcome even by the closing description of dawn and the pious hope to do God's will and be rewarded in life after death. Thematically, *The Solitary* represents Whitehead or the poet as abjected from the world, yet the poem symbolized for Whitehead what he should and might have become but, for reasons of personal weakness combined with unfavourable social and cultural circumstance, could not. Poetry, especially an ambitious work such as *The Solitary*, if well received, was a major social and cultural indicator of intellectual cultivation, implying claims to intertwined cultural and social status. Whitehead continued to refer to the poem and even to send copies to people for years after, when he thought it might obtain favourable consideration on some matter. In 1849 he used the poem, along with a collection of his magazine verse, to raise money by publishing a volume by subscription. When Whitehead first published *The Solitary* in 1831, however, the heyday of the market for narrative poems had been over for a decade and poetry was a very unpromising resource for a writer who had to earn a living.

This necessity became more pressing after Whitehead married Mary Ann Loomes on 23 October 1833, though they did not have children. Nothing is known of the couple's married life except for the picture put together much later by the often unreliable H. T. Mackenzie Bell, who had never known Whitehead, from accounts of those who did:

> His wife is described by an acquaintance, as a very retiring lady; a friend, however, who knew both husband and wife for years, says that she was not without a temper of her own, and was a little inclined to shrewishness. Though not what may be described as an amiable woman, and not by any means one of education, she seems to have been a woman of some force of character, and, as such, a very suitable wife for a man so deficient in practical resolution. There is evidence that she exercised a salutary control over her husband. It would appear, also, that in his better moments his conduct towards her was exemplary. At other times he doubtless gave way to the irritation peculiar to men of his habits, but on the whole it may be said that his domestic relations were all that could be desired.[9]

Whitehead persisted in publishing poetry through the rest of his career. One important venue was the literary annual, or gift book. These were elegantly produced pocket-sized volumes with fine engraved plates and accompanying verse or prose pieces, published late each year for the market in Christmas gift books. Though disdained by many writers and critics as merely commercial publications for middle-class aspirants to cultural status, the literary annuals paid authors well and consequently attracted leading writers of the day. Whitehead published poems from 1833 to 1835 in one of the more prestigious of the annuals, *Friendship's Offering*, from the upmarket firm of Smith, Elder and Co. 'Viola', by 'Charles Whitehead, Author of "The Solitary"', uses the same stanza form as 'The Solitary' for a verse tale of love, death and mourning.[10] 'Ippolito: A Chimera in Rhyme' recounts the protagonist's attempts to gain his love through necromancy, with disastrous consequences.[11] In the 1835 issue of *Friendship's Offering*, Whitehead published six sonnets, including one that recapitulates the central theme of *The Solitary* and that later became anthologized, though badly misquoted:

> As yonder lamp within my vacant room,[12]
> With arduous flame disputes the darksome night,
> And can, with its involuntary light,
> But lifeless things that near it stand, illume;
> Yet all the while it doth itself consume;
> And, ere the sun commence[13] his heavenly height
> With courier beams that meet the shepherd's sight,
> There, whence its life arose, shall be its tomb.
> So wastes my light away. Perforce confined
> To common things, a limit to its sphere,
> It shines on worthless trifles undesigned,

With fainter ray each hour imprisoned here.
Alas! to know that the consuming mind,
Shall leave its lamp cold, ere the sun appear![14]

The same issue of *Friendship's Offering* also included a longer poem by White-head, 'The Riddle of Life'. This poem reviews the successive stages of a man's life and asks the philosopher to tell whether that course is shaped by nature or circumstance – a recurring theme in the nineteenth-century debate on crime and punishment and other social ills.[15]

Meanwhile, Whitehead had already sought out the more profitable but less prestigious line of prose fiction and for much of the 1830s produced such work for the publishing firm of Bull and Churton and its successor, Edward Churton. Bull and Churton published miscellaneous literature and in this line commissioned Whitehead to revise and re-organize an established popular classic. This was the *Lives and Exploits of English Highwaymen, Pirates, and Robbers, Drawn from the Earliest and Most Authentic Sources, and Brought Down to the Present Time* (2 vols, 1834[16]), with illustrations by the 'Messrs. Bagg'.[17] As Whitehead acknowledged in his preface he adapted, updated, and arranged chronologically earlier eighteenth-century compilations by Charles Johnson and Alexander Smith. Yet this piece of hackwork would become Whitehead's most reprinted work, translated into French and Dutch and republished on both sides of the Atlantic into the late nineteenth century. As well as elegantly produced popular works such as this, Bull and Churton also published for a more decidedly literary market. In particular, they published *The Court Magazine and Belle Assemblée* (1832–6[18]), a fashionable monthly literary miscellany edited by the society figure Caroline Norton, and the *English Annual* (1834–8), another of the literary Christmas gift books, also edited by Norton.

Whitehead began contributing prose fiction to the *Court Magazine* in 1832, when his friend Samuel Laman Blanchard (1803–1845) was editor and continued until the end of 1837 (see Bibliography), usually under the pen-name 'Omega'. Omega is the last letter in the Greek alphabet, perhaps suggesting already something of Whitehead's at times sardonic, at times despairing sense of himself as a failure. Nevertheless, much of 'Omega's' fiction is a humorous though at times rueful representation of the schemes, shifts, subterfuges and minor triumphs and disasters of people, ranging from the lesser gentry to the lower middle class, struggling to maintain, achieve, or affect gentility. For example, in 'My Father's Legacy', Whitehead's first tale in the *Court Magazine*, Dick Gossamer relates his farcical attempts, after squandering his small inheritance, to retrieve his financial and social position by marrying an heiress.[19] 'The History of the Decline and Fall of Little Felstead', by 'Gibbon Redivivus' (a reference to Edward Gibbon, controversial author of the monumental *History of the Decline and Fall of the Roman Empire*, 1776–88), recounts the attempt of two would-be cultivated city types, Tresillian Twaddler and his friend Heartsease, to improve the village of Little Felstead by introducing elements of modern genteel culture such as a circulating library. The heroes court two newly arrived fashionable ladies, Amaranth Evergreen and Barbara Snowdrop, but two socially vulgar and culturally undiscriminating men arrive, mock the gentility of Twaddler and Heartsease, marry the ladies and move away with them, causing Heartsease to pine and die and Twaddler to leave. Little Felstead returns to its ungenteel insignificance.[20] 'The Miniature' tells of the conjugal jealousy of Diaper Garnet, London jeweller, in a burlesque, lower middle-class version of the fashionable and often melodramatic novel of upper-class amorous rivalry and intrigue.[21] 'The False One: A Tale of Russell Square' recounts humorously the disastrous consequences of a domestic servant, James Lovelace, aping the airs of his employers as a man of fashion.[22] 'The Clever Young Man', Whitehead's last piece in the *Court Magazine*, is another fictional autobiography in brief, in which Thomas Wilkins, an only child, is told so often that he is a 'clever young man' that he believes it to be true. He is discomfited, however, when he courts Una Purple:

> She was devoted to polite literature, and was well acquainted with the works of the great authors of the last twenty years. Dryden and Pope, she told me, were gone out of fashion, and Shakespeare was not much thought of since Mr. Serjeant Talfourd's 'Ion.' She had met the Serjeant, and Sir Edward Lytton, and other great ones whose names I forget, at a literary conversazione; and had a lock of Mrs. Hemans's hair.[23]

Trying to be clever, Wilkins offends Miss Purple by inscribing a verse in her album on the death of her spaniel. 'The Clever Young Man' seems to have been intended as the first in a series, but Whitehead published no more on this character.

Nevertheless, this line of magazine fiction would remain Whitehead's mainstay through his career and similar material comprises much of his novel, *The Autobiography of Jack Ketch*, published late in 1834 and dated 1835, which will be discussed separately. In 1835, Whitehead's success in humorous fiction apparently secured him the editorship of the *Squib Annual*, a short-lived gift book published by Chapman and Hall, and a year later the editorship of Chapman and Hall's almost as short-lived literary periodical the *Library of Fiction* (1836–7). Chapman and Hall were located in the Strand and active since the mid-1820s and at this time published mainly plays (especially farces and comic drama), maps, some educational books, a small amount of literature, a few novels, some German literature in translation and, most notably, the books of Thomas Carlyle, major social and cultural critic of the nineteenth century. *The Squib Annual* and *The Library of Fiction* seem to have been attempts by Chapman and Hall to break into the burgeoning market for periodicals containing mainly 'light' fiction. To *The Squib* Whitehead contributed the ruefully humorous first-person narrative, 'A Word or Two About Geoffrey Gooch'. The story has elements that seem to allude to Whitehead's own life. Gooch is the son of a shopkeeper in the hosiery and woolens line. When he inherits the family business, he is defrauded by his store manager, sells up and engages as secretary to a miserly man of letters. Here he witnesses some farcical episodes and, now wishing to have no employer, takes up the profession of letters. His notions are too high, however:

> ... experience speedily taught me that the most popular literature is a sort of barnacle, which, dropping from the tree of knowledge into the current stream, swims away in triumph, and yet is but a goose after all. Was it my fault that monthly magazines were blind to my merits? was I to blame because hebdomadal editors were obtuse? could I be chargeable with the deafness to the voice of genius evinced by proprietors of the diurnal broad-sheets? I was beyond my age.[24]

He briefly tries school teaching, with equal lack of success, and ends up writing advertisements for shoe blacking, razor strops and hair oil, concluding, 'Nor do I think the present remuneration for my labours (in this golden age for authors)— averaging, as it does, half-a-crown a-day—more than the want, or beyond the deserts, of Geoffrey Gooch' (p. 276). To the *Library of Fiction* Whitehead contributed a character like the petty fraudsters found in the *Autobiography of Jack Ketch*. The eponymous protagonist of 'Some Passages in the Life of Francis Loosefish, Esq.' – a 'loose fish' is a person of irregular habits – recounts his various schemes to live on other people's money.[25] The Loosefish type would be one of Whitehead's favourites, a humorous version of the marginalized middle-class character, like Whitehead himself, trying almost any means to keep body and soul together and especially to keep up the appearances on which depended a person's social and, more important, financial credit.

Later a story circulated that Whitehead's skill at these humorous sketches led to an offer from Chapman and Hall to write similar pieces to accompany the artist Robert Seymour's planned series of 'cockney sporting plates'. According to this story, Whitehead felt incapable of the task and suggested Charles Dickens instead, who made it his huge success, the *Pickwick Papers* (1836–7).[26] It seems, however, that Whitehead merely identified Dickens as the author of prose sketches in the *Monthly Magazine* that Edward Chapman deemed similar to what Seymour wanted.[27] Certainly Whitehead could have used the work. For in June 1836 he made his first application to the Royal Literary Fund, a charity established by David Williams in 1790 to assist (respectable) authors through temporary financial distress. The establishment of this charity indicated both the increasing professionalization of authorship and its continuing precariousness. Whitehead's application identified himself as the author of *The Solitary*, *The Autobiography of Jack Ketch* and 'many articles in the "Monthly" and "Court" Magazines'. 'Unfortunately for myself', he admitted, 'my literary exertions hitherto, whether from a defect of capability, a want of opportunities, or an inaptitude to please the popular taste, have not enabled me to make any way in the world of letters'.[28] Whitehead would refer again in his career to his 'inaptitude' to satisfy the 'popular taste'. The Fund awarded Whitehead twenty pounds, about enough to live on for a month or two. He continued his precarious literary work with pieces in the *Court Magazine* and turned to the potentially lucrative field of dramatic writing.

Whitehead was an admirer of seventeenth-century drama and set his play *The Cavalier* just after the Restoration of the monarchy in 1660. By Whitehead's day this period had come to be seen as one of intertwined moral decadence, political corruption and ruthless self-interest and was regarded by many as similar to the early nineteenth century in these respects. The play opens with discussion between Maynard, a virtuous and benevolent London merchant and his brother-in-law, Hargrave, a royalist gentleman who has had his estate confiscated during the Civil War and who has sued in vain to the King to have it restored to him. A letter is brought from a Lord Moreton, offering to help and requesting a meeting. Hargrave meets young Moreton and his older friend and follower, Beauchamp. Moreton offers help and some money, which Hargrave reluctantly accepts and leaves Hargrave with Beauchamp. Beauchamp insinuates that Moreton's secret interest is in Hargrave's wife and when Moreton re-enters and he and Beauchamp praise Mrs Hargrave's beauty, Hargrave haughtily returns the money, rejects Moreton's assistance and leaves. Hargrave returns to his brother's house and tests his wife's willingness to do anything to help his cause, but when she realizes what he means, she is shocked and rebukes him, whereon he assures her he was but trying her. The act closes with Hargrave's declaration that now he realizes the blessings that remain to him.

When act two opens, however, Hargrave is agitated at his wife's failure to return from another attempt to plead his cause before the royal council and he again begins to suspect her. The scene then changes to Moreton's house, where Beauchamp and Moreton discuss having abducted Mrs Hargrave, and Moreton's intention to force himself on her is revealed in an interview with the woman servant, De Grave. After Moreton leaves, Hargrave bursts in, demanding to know where his wife is, but De Grave tells him that his wife has often been there, implying that she and Moreton are lovers, and Hargrave seems to be convinced by her story. When he returns to his brother's house, the Maynards are dismayed by his jealous stifled rage. Then Mrs Hargrave rushes in and recounts how she was abducted, stabbed Moreton when he attempted to rape her and then escaped. Hargrave remains doubtful, but Beauchamp enters with officers to arrest Mrs Hargrave for murder, closing act two.

The final act opens with Hargrave and Mrs Maynard awaiting the outcome of Mrs Hargrave's trial, when Maynard brings news she was condemned based on Beauchamp and De Grave's testimony that she and Moreton had been lovers and she murdered him when he refused to give her more money. Hargrave leaves to see his wife, after which De Grave rushes in and, conscience-stricken, confesses to the Maynards that she lied; together, they leave to save Mrs Hargrave. The next scene opens in prison, where Hargrave contemplates his sleeping wife. When she awakes, he urges her to a suicide pact with him, but she protests the sinfulness of the act and of presuming to forestall divine will. Hargrave is about to take poison when the Maynards rush in, declaring that De Grave has confessed, Beauchamp has been arrested and a king's pardon will soon follow for Mrs Hargrave. The play closes with Mrs Hargrave's pious moral:

> Let none with impious doubt,
> Suggest to Providence the way to guide him
> Which when he least perceives, and would defy her,
> Is then most prompt to serve him.

This ending was apparently imposed on Whitehead by the audience of the first production; originally he intended the play to end tragically, with the death of the Hargraves.

The play was presented from 15 September 1836 at the Haymarket theatre and was neither a failure nor a success; it received some negative reviews, but was revived several times in the following decades, including a production in New York. Meanwhile, the failure of the *Squib Annual* and the *Library of Fiction* ended Whitehead's career in periodical editing. He had to continue relying on the *Court Magazine* and the annuals, but the launch of a major literary magazine by the important firm of Richard Bentley opened another venue for his writing – *Bentley's Miscellany*, edited initially by Charles Dickens. Richard Bentley (1794–1871) was apprenticed as a printer by his father, a newspaper proprietor, and in 1829 joined forces with Henry Colburn, one of the most enterprising upmarket publishers of the day, specializing in fashionable fiction and publishing such works as Edward Lytton Bulwer's Newgate novel *Paul Clifford*, as well as Thomas Gaspey's two Newgate novels (see volumes 2 to 4 here). The fiction reprint series they started, known as Bentley's 'Standard Novels' – 'standard' meaning something like 'classic' – was one of the most important of the nineteenth century, eventually including most novelists of note. Colburn retired in 1832 and Richard Bentley carried on the business, which would become one of the major London publishing houses of the nineteenth century, eventually incorporated into the firm of Macmillan in 1898.

It was Dickens who advised Bentley to take Whitehead as a contributor to the *Miscellany* from the outset, describing Whitehead as 'a man who has more in him than three parts of the writers alive. In humourous and grave sketches he is equally admirable. He wants training, but I think I can make him of great use.'[29]

Bentley would be Whitehead's mainstay for the rest of his literary career in England, publishing most of his magazine pieces and his two remaining novels. In *Bentley's Miscellany* Whitehead continued to rely on humorously ironic sketches of middle-class and lower middle-class life. But this fiction also contained elements of the lugubrious or grim, and intimations of personal failure and disaster, edging into the melodramatic and the Gothic. Such was Whitehead's first contribution to the *Miscellany*, in February 1837, a gloomy tale of betrayal and forgiveness in private life entitled 'Edward Saville: A Transcript'. It is the first-person narrative of the eponymous protagonist, recounting his courtship and marriage, betrayal by his friend and his wife, revenge on the friend and eventual forgiveness of friend and wife.[30] The story appeared in the same issue of the magazine in which Dickens's Newgate novel, *Oliver Twist*, began serialization. Whitehead's next two *Miscellany* pieces were in a new line, humorous poems. 'The Youth's New Vade-Mecum', purporting to be from a friend, is a doggerel verse burlesque of the kind of counsel offered to middle-class youth by conduct manuals of the day. The poem urges the youth to virtuous conduct in business and private life, but also notes that this may clash with self-interest:

> Be honest,—not as fools or bigots rave;
> Your honest man is often half a knave.
> Let Justice guide you; but still bear in mind
> The goddess may mislead,—for she is blind.[31]

'Rather Hard to Take' is a comic narrative poem about an artist engaged on an ambitious painting on the Biblical subject of 'Dives and Lazarus', in which a rich man spurns a poor one. Called away to paint a portrait, the artist finds that the subject is dead and has already been buried; he asks the man's relations for a description to work from, but receives such contradictory accounts that he cannot proceed.[32]

The next month, September 1837, Whitehead turned back to the darker side of his repertory and began publishing his major piece of fiction of these years, 'The Narrative of John Ward Gibson'.[33] It is a three-part novella of criminal and paranoid psychology, in which Gibson retrospectively recounts his crimes. In the first part, he tells of his childhood of brutal mistreatment by his father and lack of sympathy from his mother. Working as an errand boy for a picture dealer, he educated himself about art and became very useful to his employer, Bromley, who nevertheless treated him as a lower being. Gibson fell in love with Bromley's sympathetic daughter, Louisa, but she was married off by her father to a German art dealer, Steiner, who also treated Gibson with disdain and even beat him. Gibson plotted his revenge and one night set fire to Bromley's premises, apparently arriving just in time to save Louisa and her son from the blaze. In part two, published seven months later, Gibson recalls his defiance of

Steiner's and the neighbours' suspicions and, revelling in his successful vengeance, his indulgence in a period of dissipation. Then he discovered by accident
that Bromley, Louisa and her son, apparently abandoned by Steiner, were destitute; Gibson took them in and educated the son, Frederick, whom he loved
as his own and they lived together in seclusion for some years. But Steiner suddenly re-appeared and demanded money and after a violent struggle in which
Gibson was knocked out, he regained consciousness to find Steiner dead. In the
third and final part, Gibson tells how he himself became the victim of a schemer.
He attempted to dispose of Steiner's body, but it was discovered by Louisa and
the shock deranged and killed her. He eluded the suspicions of Steiner's friend,
Hartwell, for a time and refused Hartwell's attempts to lure him into a dishonest
money-making scheme. But Hartwell succeeded in alienating young Frederick
from Gibson. After Gibson confessed his crime to Frederick, the youth killed
Hartwell in a duel and then killed himself, leaving Gibson to spend the rest of
his life in remorse, as he declares:

> What I feel—if I feel aught now—may be best expressed in the words of an
> obscure author, whose name I have forgotten, but whose lines I remember.
> 'But we are strong, as we have need of strength,
> Even in our own default, and linger on,
> Enduring and forbearing, till, at length,
> The very staple of our griefs is gone,
> And we grow hard by custom—'tis all one.
> Our joys, deep laid in earth, our hopes above,
> Nor hope nor joy disturbs the heart's dull tone;
> One stirs it not, nor can the other move,
> While woe keeps tearless watch upon the grave of love.'[34]

The lines are in fact from Whitehead's *The Solitary*.[35]

    The gloomy tone of 'The Narrative of John Ward Gibson', the despair in the
quoted lines and the self-reference of quoting them may indicate that Whitehead
was experiencing personal and professional difficulty. Part two of 'The Narrative
of John Ward Gibson' was accompanied by a notice that its appearance had been
'unavoidably postponed in consequence of the Author's indisposition' and in
November 1837 Whitehead again applied to the Royal Literary Fund, stating
that he had to vacate his accommodation, leaving his furniture as security. He
confessed:

> I have been, long ago, unable to conceal from myself that my talents, such as they are,
> and as they have been hitherto directed, are not of that popular character which will
> recommend me to Publishers; and I have for some time past, in spite of my former ill
> success, determined upon trying my fortune once more as a Dramatic writer; but you
> are well aware that this branch of literature is even more precarious than writing for
> Magazines, of which my experience has taught me the instability.[36]

The Fund voted Whitehead fifteen pounds. Perhaps his former publisher Bull and Churton also came to his rescue, for in 1838 they published his *Victoria Victrix: Stanzas Addressed to Her Majesty the Queen*, on the accession a year earlier of young Victoria to the throne. Nevertheless, between autumn 1838 and spring 1841 Whitehead published only two pieces, 'The Stock-Broker' and 'Tavern Heads', in *Heads of the People; or, Portraits of the English* (2 vols, 1840–1), edited by his friend Douglas Jerrold and illustrated by another friend, Joseph Kenny Meadows. There may have been several reasons for this inactivity, including his own physical and psychological illness, difficulties experienced by members of his family and work on more substantial works than magazine pieces.

When he did resume publishing, it was with renewed vigour. The next half dozen years were his most prolific, with some of his best and also his most sustained humorous writing, another attempt at drama and two ambitious historical novels. Whitehead also kept up his fictional excursions into the margins of middle-class life. His short story 'Wanted—A Widow', appearing in the March 1841 *Bentley's Miscellany*, recounts what happens when a middle-aged bachelor of small independent means tires of his boarding house, takes a small house and advertises for a respectable widow to be his housekeeper. His advertisement brings so many widows that they fill the street outside his house and he has to be extricated by his neighbour, who also by chance furnishes him with a wife, in the form of the neighbour's widowed sister. 'Eleanor Bingley', like many of Whitehead's short stories, seems like the sketch for a novel. It recounts the history of the eponymous protagonist who, spoiled as a child, weds the more dashing of two suitors but discovers that he has a lower-class mistress and tricks this woman into poisoning him. The woman is hung for the crime, but Eleanor Bingley passes years in remorse before she confesses and dies. 'Old Green, Offley's Regular Customer' is a humorously told but grim account of a retired businessman with no family or friends who is fond only of eating and, when his appetite fails, simply disappears. 'Orlando Griffin' humorously recounts the genteel but naïve protagonist's misadventures at the hands of a vulgar family of confidence tricksters, who inveigle him into marriage with their daughter, leaving him trapped until a fortunate encounter discloses that the woman is already married and Orlando is free. 'Five-and-Thirty or Thereabouts' similarly recounts the misadventures of a man who passes as younger and wealthier in order to marry a wealthy young woman, who turns out to be a confidence trickster. 'Miss Jifkins's Benefit' tells the story from the confidence trickster's viewpoint. 'The Confessions of De Loude Chisleham', as the protagonist's name suggests, continues the swindling theme as 'Chisleham', in fact the self-renamed scapegrace Francis Loosefish of Whitehead's earlier story, humorously recounts his shifts and tricks to get by on the fringes of middle-class London. Whitehead gave another twist to the theme of deceit with 'Mr. Yellowly's Doings', in which the eponymous protagonist uses trickery to inveigle a proudly genteel young artist into being helped out of a fix caused by one of Francis Loosefish's petty frauds.

Something is known of Whitehead's working methods in producing such pieces. The unreliable Mackenzie Bell, blaming Whitehead's weakness for drink, asserted that he 'was very dilatory in his habits of work' and that 'he made but few alterations in his proofs, and rarely an erasure in his MS., unless he took the trouble to re-copy the whole passage'.[37] Whitehead gave his own account of his manner of composition in a note to Bentley's assistant, J. T. Marsh: 'I am getting on with a tragic article for the Miscellany – that is to say, I have arranged it all (the chief work with me) and filled in such parts as are to be written up to, so that I can faithfully promise the whole by this day week.' He added, 'If the paper I am about should chance to be somewhat longer than a light article, I presume Mr. Bentley will not object, as I shall make it, I think, something he will like.' With these assurances, he noted that his rent was due and asked Marsh for an advance of five pounds on 'a paper to be written for him, called "The Revenger's Tragedy."'[38]

According to accounts collected by Mackenzie Bell from those who knew Whitehead around this period, he was living the semi-bohemian life of a professional author. He frequented 'a tavern which has since been pulled down, called the Grotto, in Southampton Buildings, Holborn', where there was a company of 'the usual Bohemian order', including 'young literary men, artists, and some few actors'. Whitehead 'was the leading spirit of the place, being there every night' and known for 'his great geniality of manner and remarkable brilliance of conversational wit and humour'. Some of these characters formed a group called the Mulberry Club, ostensibly dedicated to celebration of Shakespeare, and met at various taverns in and around Holborn. One of the group was Douglas Jerrold (1803–1857), former sailor, drama critic, miscellaneous writer and humourist and popular author of farces, nautical melodramas such as *Black-Eyed Susan* (1829), and so-called 'domestic drama' of middle- and lower middle-class life. In the 1840s Jerrold became an important contributor to the long-lived humour magazine, *Punch* and edited the *Illuminated Magazine* and *Heads of the People*, to which Whitehead contributed. Another of the group was the poet and magazine and newspaper editor, Samuel Laman Blanchard (1803–1845), who edited the *Court Magazine and Belle Assemblée* when Whitehead was a contributor; in 1845 Blanchard committed suicide after a bout of depression following his wife's death. There was the self-taught artist and illustrator Joseph Kenny Meadows (1790–1874), who illustrated *The Autobiography of Jack Ketch*; the novelist and editor Charles Dickens, who published pieces by Whitehead in *Bentley's Miscellany* and *Household Words*; Thomas Noon Talfourd (1795–1854), lawyer, dramatist, proponent of penal reforms such as abolition of the pillory, and social figure; the novelist William Makepeace Thackeray; the painters Charles and

Edwin Landseer and others.[39] While all were cultivated and intellectual or artistic, none of this group had been to university and all had a middle-class social background. Among such company, Whitehead was noted for his story-telling and the kind of wit and wordplay that are features of his humorous fiction. Mackenzie Bell reported:

> One of his early friends tells me that, were he now able to recall a number of Whitehead's puns, they would give him distinction in that lower department of humour; he remembers Whitehead telling him that he hoped *Jack Ketch* would not be considered 'a Ketch-penny[40] publication'! As a young man, one of Whitehead's whims was to project ridiculous works with impossible titles. He once informed the friend to whom I refer that he intended to write a book to be entitled *The Flash Cove's Vade Mecum: or Every Man His own Vagabond*, the volume to consist of short whimsical rules for the performance of various peccadilloes. As might be expected of a man of his temperament, he had a keen appreciation of the ludicrous, and could amuse his friends with felicitous sallies of wit, and could recount his own experiences with great point and comicality.[41]

The proclivity for puns and wordplay is a feature of Whitehead's *Autobiography of Jack Ketch* and shorter humorous fiction, but it has a serious aim, to suggest the instability and relativity of meaning and communication.

With this indication of the continuing relation between the author and his text, it seems appropriate that Whitehead soon began publishing a historical novel about a real-life character who had many similarities to himself. *Richard Savage: A Romance of Real Life* was, in the opinion of many, Whitehead's major work. It was first serialized in *Bentley's Miscellany* from July 1841 to December 1842, with illustrations by John Leech (1817–1864), a well known and popular artist who was a major factor in the early success of a new and soon to be famous humour magazine, *Punch*. As Bentley liked to do, the novel was republished in familiar three-volume format (1842), 'By Charles Whitehead, Author of "The Solitary"', even before serialization had been completed. *Richard Savage* was an ambitious work, significantly longer than *The Autobiography of Jack Ketch* – a fact that may help account for the paucity of Whitehead's published work between autumn 1838 and spring 1841. Those who knew Whitehead asserted that he read widely and deeply in the eighteenth century to write the novel. It was based on the real Richard Savage (1697–1743), known to literary history through Samuel Johnson's sympathetic biography (1744). Savage claimed he was the illegitimate son of the Countess of Macclesfield by Earl Rivers but that his mother, remarried as Mrs Brett, not only refused to acknowledge him but relentlessly persecuted him. Savage became a miscellaneous writer, publishing verse satires and other works and writing plays. He was patronized for a time by his mother's nephew, Viscount Tyrconnel, and was befriended by prominent literary men such as the essayist Sir Richard Steele, the theatre manager Robert

Wilks and the poet Alexander Pope. But Savage quarreled with all of them, and lost their support. He left London to escape his creditors but was eventually imprisoned for debt in Bristol, where he died.

Whitehead's novel purports to be Savage's own account of his life and the story follows closely the then-known facts and assertions about Savage. By using the form of a fictitious autobiography, however, Whitehead was able to retell the story from the 'inside', as it were, bringing the historical character into the Romantic and early Victorian interest in marginal or extreme subjective experience. In a sense, Whitehead's Savage was his Francis Loosefish writ large and long. *Richard Savage* is also a Newgate novel in that it contains prison scenes, portrays crime and, more importantly, represents the subjectivity of a character existing on or beyond the margin of respectability and even the law. To this end, Whitehead added to the biographical facts a story of requited but obstructed love, devoted much of the novel to Savage's description of his feelings and motives and structured the novel as a succession of episodes depicting the way Savage's sense of injustice, persecution and alienation drives him to self-destructive and criminal acts, to abjection, social exclusion and death. *Richard Savage* was, after *Lives and Exploits of English Highwaymen, Pirates, and Robbers*, Whitehead's most successful work, with a further edition in 1844, an edition in Bentley's Standard Novels (1845), editions from the cheap reprint firms of Henry Lea in the 1860s and John Dicks in the 1880s, a further edition from Bentley in 1896 and an edition from the mass market publisher George Newnes in 1903.

Whitehead quickly followed *Richard Savage* with a historical novel again based on a well known figure, Robert Devereux, Earl of Essex (1567–1601). Whitehead signed a contract with Bentley for the new novel on 19 November 1840, even before he had begun the serialization of *Richard Savage*. He was to receive £150 six months after delivery of the novel – perhaps enough to live on frugally for the better part of a year – with a further fifty pounds if reprinted.[42] Whitehead had a different historical subject in mind when he signed the contract, however: the title 'Sir Thomas Overbury' was originally written in, but crossed out and replaced with 'Robert Devereux, Earl of Essex'. Overbury (1581–1613), victim of one of the most famous crimes in English history, was involved in political intrigue at the court of James I and was poisoned by his enemies. He was connected with an earl of Essex, but it was with the third earl (1591–1646) rather than his father, the second earl, subject of the novel that Whitehead published.

The Earl of Essex: A Romance, was not serialized in *Bentley's Miscellany* but came out in three volumes in 1843. It deals with the rebellion of the title character against Elizabeth I. Essex, formerly a favourite of the queen, held a variety of military and naval posts, but appeared to disobey orders when he returned to court, without permission, from his assignment to crush a Catholic rebellion in

Ireland. He seemed to be forgiven, but his haughtiness and defiance led to his house arrest. Soon his pride in his own rank and lineage, his resentment against the queen's advisers Cecil and Sir Walter Raleigh and knowledge that he was popular with the citizens of London led him to over-reach himself. At the head of an armed troop he tried to force an interview with the queen, but the populace failed to support him and Cecil's quick action defeated the move. Essex was convicted of treason and executed on 25 February 1601.

Essex was a familiar figure in English and European literature, having been represented on the stage in La Calprenède's *Le Conte d'Essex* (1638), Thomas Corneille's play of the same title (1678), John Banks's frequently reprinted heroic drama *The Unhappy Favourite; or, The Earl of Essex: A Tragedy* (1682), Henry Jones's often produced and reprinted *The Earl of Essex: A Tragedy* (1753), Henry Brooke's tragedy of the same title (1761) and Jacques-François Ancelot's *Elisabeth d'Angleterre* (1829). Various European critics had commented on these stage characters and Essex had also been a central figure in Thomas Birch's *Memoirs of the Reign of Queen Elizabeth* (1754) and included in Robert Southey's *Lives of the British Admirals* (5 vols, 1833-40). Whitehead's immediate inspiration for the novel seems to have been theatrical and operatic, specifically *Roberto Devereux: Tragedia lirica in tre atti*, music by Gaetano Donizetti and libretto by Salvatore Cammarano, first produced at Naples in 1837 and based on Ancelot's play. This opera was translated into English and produced in London. In English and European literature, the figure of Essex and the relationship between him and the queen were used to represent the interconnected amorous and political intrigues of the monarchic and court systems of government that prevailed in the times when most of this literature was written and also regarded by Whitehead's contemporaries as characteristic of despotic governments across much of early nineteenth-century Europe.

Whitehead's direct purpose was to counter the favourable or sympathetic view of Essex presented in the opera, the heroic drama and elsewhere. The narrator clearly states the novel's view of Essex:

> Robert Devereux has been one of the spoiled children of history. His virtues have been magnified, and his vices sometimes kept carefully out of sight; and not seldom (which is worse) speciously disguised and made to pass for virtues. Thus, his reckless profusion has been termed magnificence; his violent and causeless resentments, outbreaks of a noble and generous nature; and his impatience of the recognition of any other merit than his own, a love of glory.
>
> (vol. 2, p. 180)

Whitehead's Earl of Essex, like his Richard Savage though on the public rather than private stage of life, is a gifted but undisciplined and hence self-destructive character. Whitehead's larger purpose was to show that history is not heroic drama, or grand opera, or even tragedy, but more often farce or crime. In literary and political terms, Whitehead used the form of the Romantic historical novel to counter the optimistic and progressive tendency of most such fiction. Like other Romantic historical novelists dealing with real personages and important events, Whitehead fictionalizes those personages and also sets them among historically marginal and entirely fictitious characters. These minor characters form the context and illustrate the consequences of the actions of the actual historical figures depicted. Whitehead introduces for this purpose a number of minor characters, especially Williams, a sturdy soldier and follower of Essex, and Lambert, a broken soldier who is a drunkard and abuser of his meek and virtuous daughter Maud. Like other historical novelists, too, Whitehead alternates his narrative between 'high' and 'low' worlds, between the world of the shapers of history and the world of history's victims. Likewise, his omniscient third-person narrator portrays the private thoughts and feelings, as well as the outward speech and actions, of characters in both these worlds.

One purpose of this approach is to show history from the perspective of subjective experience and private life – almost entirely unavailable to the historiographer, who has to rely largely on public documents, records of affairs of state and similar material. Another purpose of giving the same narrative treatment to both 'great' and 'small' characters is to suggest that their lives are equally important, if only to themselves. In effect, this narrative strategy implies the irrelevance, or at least the questionable nature, of traditional and historical social hierarchies. As with most Romantic historical novelists, too, Whitehead's use of a third-person omniscient narrator represents the characters in history from a transhistorical perspective, outside of history. Together, these perspectives from 'inside' (the subjective and private) and 'outside' (the transhistorical) aim to give a 'truth' to historical fiction that is unavailable or only partly available to historiography as such. But what is the 'truth' about history that Whitehead wants to convey?

Romantic historical novelists used the form for different purposes, but all did so implicitly or explicitly as a reflection on the novelists' and readers' present. In one major line of development, originating with women historical novelists such as Jane Porter and her bestseller *The Scottish Chiefs* (1810), the purpose was twofold: to critique long established structures of social hierarchy and court government and to construct the protagonist of the historical fiction as an anticipation in the past of the sovereign subject called for in European Romantic political ideology. This was the independent, self-commanding subject who would, with others, form the 'political nation' or electorate of modern constitutional states. Another, more conservative but highly influential development of the Romantic historical novel originated with Walter Scott and his series of Waverley novels. The purpose of this form was also twofold: to show the limitations of historic hierarchical social and governmental structures, but also to suggest that historical actors lacked full understanding of the events in which they were engaged and that understanding of history's meaning and direction was available only to the transcendent consciousness, such as the historical novel's implied author, communicated to and participated in by the readers, as a self-conscious cultural elite, unacknowledged legislators of humanity. In these and other developments of the historical novel, the interest was less the past than the present in which the novel was published and the presumably better future that the novel implicitly or explicitly called for. In its faith that such a better future was possible and could be brought about by human agency, the Romantic historical novel can be seen as generally progressive.

Whitehead's purpose in his second historical novel, as in his first, was to deny this progressive trend promoted to a greater or lesser degree in most historical fiction. History as Whitehead presents it is driven by the selfish human passions of the powerful and powerless alike, overwhelming individual loyalty, virtue and love. The historical protagonist, Essex, though surrounded by scheming rivals and enemies, yet has his loyal followers, including the sturdy soldier, Williams. But Essex's downfall is clearly due to his own pride and ambition, not only destroying himself but also alienating his loyal followers and involving them in his disaster. Though Williams remains loyal to the end, he is severely wounded in the fighting around Essex's attempted coup and collapses and dies at Essex's execution. Lambert's daughter Maud, who loves Williams, is left alone at the end of the novel and enters a convent. History, Whitehead seems to say, is not a way forward but a dead end. The lesson of this pessimistic plot is reinforced by the narrator's depiction of the relentless selfishness of characters both 'high' and 'low'. The nobleman Essex, in his self-elation, vanity, ambition, impulsiveness and appetite for violence, resembles and is no better than the commoner Lambert in his drunkenness, touchy pride, self-interested scheming, vengefulness and readiness for physical violence. Such instructive paralleling of characters 'high' and 'low' is common in Romantic historical fiction and is part of such fiction's social critique. In Whitehead's novel, perhaps the most suggestive of such parallels is that between the 'high' character, queen Elizabeth, and the 'low' character, Maud; the one unmarried for reasons of state, the other unmarried from paternal oppression; the one swayed by personal feeling and even love but in the end ruled by self-interest, the other reluctantly giving in to offered kindness and love and rising to acts of heroism and willing to sacrifice herself for that love. But neither Elizabeth nor Maud, neither ruler of the realm nor domestic servant, can turn back the course of violent men and both end life alone.

Whitehead did not receive fifty pounds for a reprint of *Robert Devereux, Earl of Essex*, for there was none and in October 1843 he was again applying to the Royal Literary Fund, stating that he was living in temporary accommodation and under threat of arrest by his creditors; he was granted twenty pounds.[43] Soon after this, he began working as an editorial assistant and reader for Bentley, as Whitehead put it, 'revising and correcting MSS. and giving my opinion upon works submitted to him'.[44] He received no salary but was paid by the piece. The editing work for Bentley must have provided Whitehead with some security and perhaps a literary circle. It may be this period that George Bentley (1828–1895), son and successor of Richard Bentley, later recalled:

> Whitehead had a rather piquant humour. We had a fashion in Burlington Street, in those old days of candles which required snuffing, of sitting round the fire at 7 o'clock (we didn't close until 8 then!), and Father Prout, or Charles Whitehead, or Hamilton Maxwell, or Albert Smith would take a bowl of tea with us—big cups. The talk was then very good, and I, a youngster, greatly enjoyed it. I remember even then thinking how intimately Charles Whitehead seemed to know all of the men of the time of Sir Richard Steele.[45]

The 'Father Prout' referred to here was Francis Sylvester Mahony (1804–1866), former Jesuit and Catholic priest and author of a series of humorous pieces in *Fraser's Magazine* (1834–6) about a simple rural Irish priest named Prout; from 1837 Mahony contributed to *Bentley's Miscellany*. William Hamilton Maxwell (1792–1850) was a clergyman and writer, author of adventure fiction. Albert Richard Smith (1816–1860) was a medical doctor, miscellaneous writer and humorous novelist, especially satirizing social pretentiousness. George Bentley also provided Mackenzie Bell with a verbal portrait of Whitehead:

> I wish I could tell you of a portrait of Charles Whitehead, but I know of none but what rests on the retina of my eye—the portrait of a refined, scholarly man, with a shy, retiring way of his own, with thoughtful, almost penetrating eyes, good and white brow, standing about 5 ft. 10 1/2 in. I should say, slightly and rather elegantly built, stooping somewhat from the shoulder, otherwise straight set up. He frequently, while talking, had his right elbow resting in the palm of his left hand. I quite associate him with that attitude. He was always in black, and looked, as did John Leech,[46] a perfect gentleman. He spoke carefully, not abusing words, and was, it appeared to me, moderate in statement, and not excitable, or, at least, not easily excited.[47]

Mackenzie Bell gathered descriptions from others who knew Whitehead and composed this portrait:

> He was tall, and of a dark complexion, with a hollow chest and stooping gait, giving the appearance of great fragility. He had a long, careworn face. His voice was pleasant, but very low-pitched, and sometimes in conversation he spoke so low as to be scarcely audible. His manner was modest and diffident; so diffident indeed, that except to his intimate friends he appeared almost too shy and sensitive. One of his favourite attitudes when talking was to stand with arms folded across his chest, and he sometimes seemed awakened by a remark, as if his thoughts had previously been far away. One

who knew him slightly tells me that Whitehead looked to him 'the personification of one of the authors of Grub Street.'[48]

'Grub Street' had long been the proverbial term for the world of hack writers, suggesting poverty and a hand-to-mouth existence.

The editing work for Bentley may have provided Whitehead with a steady subsistence but it also slowed down his own writing and seems to have been irksome: he later referred to the eight years he spent on this work as 'thraldom'.[49] To raise money, in 1845 he tried to promote sale by subscription of a volume of poetry and wrote to Charles Dickens. Dickens agreed to subscribe, but asked to do so anonymously and warned Whitehead:

> I am unwilling to damp your ardor by suggesting that Poetry is a dangerous pursuit better laid aside than encouraged in the position you occupy, of all others most unlikely ever to lead you to fame, happiness, or profit. But this is a grave truth; and one, believe me, which you will do well to consider.[50]

It seems that this project came to nothing. In 1845 Whitehead did publish four prose pieces in *Bentley's Miscellany* and a Gothic narrative poem of parental tyranny and doomed love in the *Illuminated Magazine*, a lavish but short-lived periodical edited by Douglas Jerrold. The following year he provided 'notes and additions' for and also 'revised' a new edition of Charles Dickens's *Memoirs of Joseph Grimaldi* and he wrote a drama, 'Woman's Worth; or, The Three Trials: A Play in Four Acts', apparently for the Royal Surrey Theatre.[51] The Surrey was located in Lambeth, south of the river Thames. Originally a circus theatre, it had been rebuilt after a fire to mount plays and at this period was the venue for popular melodramas by Douglas Jerrold, Charles Dickens, Edward Fitzball and others; Whitehead's play belongs to that type.

In 'Woman's Worth', the Count Carmagnola has secretly married Bianca, a country girl he has fallen in love with, because his mother, wanting him to have a brilliant career, presses him to marry the Lady Juliana. Juliana, however, loves Belvidere, who owes his education and position to Juliana's father, the Marquis Orsini. The villain Luigi, the Countess Carmagnola's servant, plots to murder Bianca and have it appear that Carmagnola approved the deed. Luigi pretends to lead Bianca to a meeting with Carmagnola, but stabs her on a stormy seashore and leaves her for dead. Bianca is saved, however, by the good fisherman Giuseppe and disguises herself in male attire. While Luigi is fleeing from the scene of his crime he is seized by some brigands, led by Bernardo, a Robin Hood figure who exercises justice in his territory, especially against those who betray a vow or a trust. Luigi identifies Carmagnola as one such and Carmagnola is imprisoned by Bernardo's men and destined for punishment but Bianca, disguised as a page, appears and rescues Carmagnola from his prison. Back at Orsini's palazzo, the real intentions and loves of the characters are revealed to the audience through soliloquies and dialogues, but the wedding of Carmagnola and Juliana is to proceed. In the final act, Bernardo and his men seize the palazzo and expose Luigi's plot; the true loves of the characters are revealed to all and the Countess and Orsini gladly recognize Bianca as Carmagnola's wife and sanction the marriage of Juliana and Belvidere. Bianca urges that Luigi be forgiven, since she owes her happiness to his misdirected machinations, and Bernardo and the brigands are given pardons.

'Woman's Worth' has characteristic features of the melodramas put on at the Surrey Theatre: lavish use of dramatic irony, in which the audience knows what the play's characters do not; love at cross purposes; the possible 'dishonour' of a young woman; 'cliff-hanging' scene endings to enhance suspense; stark confrontations between characters; a diabolical villain; onstage violence and even (apparent) murder; settings suitable for spectacular effects (a stormy seashore; a cavern dungeon); and especially a rousing closure with revelations, reconciliations and rejoicings. At the same time, Whitehead was able to incorporate in his play major elements and themes of his writing more generally, such as the indecisive and malleable male character, the persevering female character, the thoroughly vicious villain, the damage caused by social difference and hierarchy, and the constraints (including imprisonment) imposed on individuals by familial and social obligations. Despite his efforts to follow the conventions of the genre and his modest success with his earlier melodrama, *The Cavalier*, Whitehead's 'Woman's Worth' seems to have failed on stage and it remained unpublished.

In 1846 Whitehead also began publishing a series of reviews and essays, many embellished with engraved portraits, on a wide variety of topics, but often referring directly or indirectly to a book recently published by Bentley. The topics included 'Flora Macdonald: The Heroine of the Rebellion of 1745'; Pizarro, the sixteenth-century Spanish conqueror of Peru; the British navy; the rebellion of 1825 at St Petersburg in Russia; General Sir Harry Smith; the publisher Bohn's library of inexpensive 'serious' literature; 'Caricatures and Caricaturists'; the sailor and novelist Frederick Marryat (1792-1848); the liberal German dramatist Friedrich von Schiller (1759–1805) and his contemporaries; the American critic William Ellery Channing (1780–1842); a history of banking; some social novels; the archeologist Austen Henry Layard (1817–94); the craze for railway speculation; the Swedish women novelists Frederika Bremer (1801–65) and Emilie Flygare-Carlén (1807–92); and John Lingard (1771–51), the Roman Catholic priest, translator, historian and apologist.[52] These articles show an acute critical acumen, liberal views and values, broad range of information and simple, direct style, indicating a larger career as essayist was within Whitehead's powers. He published these pieces regularly until 1851, when his career began to disintegrate.

Meanwhile, in 1847, Whitehead collected most of his various prose fiction magazine pieces and published them with Bentley as *Smiles and Tears; or, The Romance of Life* (3 vols). But he had signed the contract with Bentley as far back as November 1841, selling the copyright for thirty pounds and receiving ten pounds on signing. According to the documents appended to the contract, the volume was to be called 'Odd Days' Doings' and to include 'Light Papers' and 'Serious Papers', the former far outnumbering the latter. Whitehead also contributed a memoir to a small elegant edition of *The Poetical Works of William Cowper*, published by the obscure firm of W. H. Reid. Cowper was known in English literature as the poet of 'sensibility' or refined and even excessively refined feeling, as a poet of domestic life and piety and also as a man afflicted by paranoia and mental disease – all traits to interest Whitehead. The book went through several further editions published by J. Kendrick. Otherwise, apart from essay-reviews, the year saw just one story by Whitehead in *Bentley's Miscellany*, 'The Suburban Retreat', in which a man ruefully recounts how his wife nagged him into moving from the city to the rural suburbs, which turned out to be disagreeable to both of them.[53] Modest as this year's output was, Whitehead would not equal it again.

In 1849 Whitehead collected his poems and his drama *The Cavalier* in a volume published by Bentley and sold by subscription to raise money for his brother, who suffered from mental illness, to stay in an asylum. Whitehead approached Dickens for a subscription and Dickens then took on the task of filling out the subscribers list.[54] The volume was dedicated to Francis Leveson Gower, Earl of Ellesmere (1800–57), politician, poet and supporter of the arts, and the subscribers' list spans an extraordinary range of London aristocratic, fashionable, professional, artistic, literary and commercial society. Noble subscribers included Ellesmere; the reform politician George Howard (1802–64), earl of Carlisle; Helen Selina Sheridan Hay (1807–67), Lady Dufferin, sister of the writer and editor Caroline Norton and herself an author and song writer; Lady Angela Burdett-Coutts (1814–1906), wealthy heiress and philanthropist, advised by Charles Dickens; Byron's daughter, Ada King (1815–52), countess of Lovelace and an accomplished mathematician; Chandos Leigh (1791-1850), baron Leigh, friend of Byron and a poet and literary patron; and Sir Edward Lytton Bulwer (1803–73), poet, novelist and politician and author of several Newgate novels. In addition to Bulwer, other literary men included Charles Dickens, editor and novelist; William Makepeace Thackeray, essayist and novelist; Thomas Carlyle, essayist, historian and social critic; and Gilbert Abbott A'Beckett (1811–56), prolific playwright, editor of journals of gossip and humour, author of a series of *Comic Histories* burlesquing well known works such as William Blackstone's summary of English law and Edward Gibbon's history of the Roman empire and appointed a Police magistrate in 1849. Scholarship was represented by the historian Thomas Babington Macaulay, the historian Henry Hallam and the political economist Thomas Ricardo. Subscribers from the medical world included Francis Ramsbotham (1801–68), obstetrician; Benjamin Travers (1783–1858), surgeon; and others. The theatre world was represented by William Macready (1793–1873), the 'eminent tragedian' and leading actor of his time, and others.

By the early 1850s, however, Whitehead seems to have been in difficulties and perhaps had lost some of the friends who had helped him thus far. He published nothing more with Bentley after 1851. The following year he was apparently contributing a serial fiction entitled 'The Orphan' to a new weekly newspaper, but he had difficulty keeping up with the assignment, making repeated apologies for delay and in any case the periodical failed and Whitehead was unable to complete the work.[55] In December 1852 he again applied to the Royal Literary Fund. In his application he stated that he had been employed for almost eight years by Bentley as a literary advisor and editor and corrector of manuscripts; that this had prevented him from publishing his own work; that he had been engaged to write a work for a weekly newspaper but that the young editor had insulted him and the work was lost; and that Bentley had dismissed him when the first number of his new work appeared. At just that time, he wrote, his mother had died.[56] The weekly newspaper was probably the *Home Companion* (1852–56), a penny-an-issue paper consisting mostly of serialized reprints of 'standard' English fiction, such as Goldsmith's *The Vicar of Wakefield*, alongside new original fiction, such as Harrison Ainsworth's novel, *The Star Chamber*. The Fund granted Whitehead twenty pounds. It must have been this period that the painter Cornelius Pearson referred to years later. Pearson had written a supporting letter for Whitehead's 1852 application to the Royal Literary Fund, but in 1884 he wrote to Mackenzie Bell after reading the proofs of the latter's biography of Whitehead:

> That he had genius must I think be admitted by all impartial critics; but it was tinged by so much morbid feeling, that it is painful to read many of his serious works, as he seemed to delight in dwelling on the darkest side of human nature. I fear his propensity to indulge in drink greatly added to that morbid tendency, which he inherited I believe, and which at times bordered on insanity. You know that I was obliged to break with him on account of his violent outbursts, and my life was hardly safe at times, so vindictive were his feelings towards me, when he accused me of being false in my friendship towards him. This being so, it is no wonder that he depicted some of his heroes in such gloomy tints.[57]

In 1854 Whitehead managed to produce a *Life and Times of Sir Walter Ralegh* with 'copious extracts' from his *History of the World*, published by the firm of N. Cooke, which published miscellaneous literature, books for children and manuals on various subjects. Whitehead was now being given work by friends such as Charles Dickens, who published Whitehead's 'Off! Off!', an essay on theatre audiences in *Household Words* and two years later a grim tale entitled 'Nemesis: In Four Chapters'.[58] But in 1854 Whitehead was again applying to the Royal Literary Fund, though he declared that it was for the last time. He stated that he had some small debts and had sold some of his furniture, had written a tragedy, published a life of Raleigh and published a piece in the *Illustrated London News* and a couple of pieces in the *Home Companion* and was once again employed by Bentley, but was considering a suggestion to emigrate to Otago, New Zealand and set up as a schoolteacher. The Fund granted him twenty-five pounds.

In 1856 his early drama, *The Cavalier*, was revived at the Lyceum Theatre and he managed to publish a piece in *Household Words*, but on 16 November he and his wife left for Australia on the ship Diana. They arrived on 17 March 1857 and settled in Melbourne, where Charles may have had a prior offer of work on the *Argus* newspaper. James Smith, who knew the couple after they arrived, later gave this account of Whitehead's situation:

> Accompanied by his faithful wife, he came out here in 1857, being then fifty-three years of age; and it would be difficult to imagine a man more utterly disqualified for a plunge into the rough and tumble life of the period than Charles Whitehead. He was a man of letters to his fingers' ends; refined, scholarly, sensitive, delicate-minded, and but scantily equipped with worldly wisdom. He was devoid of self-assertion, aggressiveness, adaptability to the circumstances of a new country, impudence, and push; and was therefore foredoomed to failure. He was overflowing with talent; but it was talent of that kind which is only marketable in an old and highly civilized community. He was a poet, but he did not know how to write songs to be sung in a goldfield's concert-hall. He was a novelist of more than ordinary ability, but he was not the sort of man to manufacture sensational clap-trap out of a murder in a hansom cab.[59] He was a humorist, and *Melbourne Punch* published and paid for many of his clever contributions, but they were 'caviare to the general.' He was an historian, but he settled down in a colony which had no history, and was only just beginning to make one. He was a writer of sketches, but the only medium of publication open to him was some struggling magazine, which depended upon gratuitous contributions to fill its pages, and usually died in its infancy. He was a child of genius for whom men like Charles Dickens, 'Christopher North,' Dante Gabriel Rossetti, and Douglas Jerrold conceived a high admiration, and who numbered among his friends the (first) Lord Lytton and William Makepeace Thackeray, and he was as much lost in Melbourne thirty years ago as he would have been if he had been suddenly dropped down in Timbuctoo.[60]

This account may be romanticized, but the Whiteheads certainly had a hard time of it.

Whitehead did publish some work. He contributed to various Australian magazines, including the *Examiner* and Melbourne *Punch*; he began serializing a novel, 'Emma Latham; or, Right at Last' (1858), in the Melbourne magazine *My Note Book*; and he published the first part of a verse drama, 'The Spanish Marriage', in the *Victorian Monthly Magazine* (July 1859). It seems he was not paid for some of this work, however, and early in 1860 was reduced to pawning part of his dictionary.[61] Another immigrant British author, Richard Hengist Horne, planned to publish an essay in London holding Whitehead up as an example of the literary author's fate with the uncultivated colonial reading public; Whitehead was shamed, alarmed and angered, but managed to prevent the publication. Mary Ann Whitehead seems to have disintegrated psychologically and was confined in the Yarra Bend Asylum, where she died of pulmonary consumption on 21 August 1860. Whitehead himself was destitute and obviously very ill. According to a local paper, he was brought to the Police Bench 'as a dangerous lunatic, his insanity being the effect of habitual intemperance'.[62] In early 1862 he applied unsuccessfully for admission to the Benevolent Asylum, but was instead admitted to the Immigrants' Home. Friends then took him in, but he left them and was picked up after collapsing in the street. He died on 5 July in the Melbourne Hospital from liver disease and bronchitis. Since he seemed to be without friends or relations, he was given a pauper's burial.

Humour and Horror: Whitehead's Fiction and the Irony of Middle-Class Life

Whitehead wrote in a wide range of discourses and genres, including poetry, drama, biography, critical essays and prose fiction. Most of his work, however, was narrative fiction, in prose or verse, which he himself categorized as either 'light' or 'tragic', designed to evoke either 'smiles' or 'tears'. The former predominates in his shorter fiction, the latter in the longer, which he seems to have regarded as his more legitimately literary work. Even in his 'light' fiction, however, the 'tragic' and 'tears', or worse, often seem nearby, narrowly escaped, or probably inevitable. Most of Whitehead's fiction, whether 'light' or 'tragic', depicts characters powerfully motivated by self-interest, social ambition, or passions of various kinds, yet in the end facing abjection – humiliation, degradation, social isolation, or even destruction. For informing all of Whitehead's writing is an ironic vision of the human condition – or, more accurately, middle-class and especially lower middle-class life – as inescapably abject. Abjection became an important theme in late twentieth-century literary, cultural and political theory, mainly drawing on psychoanalytic discourse and focusing on certain avant-garde writers such as Louis-Ferdinand Céline and Jean Genet. More recently, however, theorists have tried to merge psychoanalytic approaches to abjection in sociological ones, and an alternative approach is to understand abjection in terms of theories of social constructionism, or the assumption that individuals are formed in relation to society.[63] Whitehead's ironic vision of human life as inescapably abject may be fruitfully understood within such an approach.

The sources of the vision that informs *The Autobiography of Jack Ketch* and most of Whitehead's fiction were literary and ideological on one hand and social and personal on the other. Whitehead's ironic vision strongly resembles that in one of his – and the Newgate novel's – most important literary models, early Spanish picaresque fiction, which had been well known in Britain and Europe since its first publication. More broadly, Whitehead's ironic vision seems to draw on two important contemporary socio-cultural and literary sources. His writings and his comments on himself reveal no strong religious impulse but do suggest a secularized version of contemporary protestant Evangelicalism's insistence on sin – the inescapably flawed and fallen condition of humanity, redeemable not by any human effort but only by divine grace. Such religious views were widely and aggressively disseminated in Whitehead's early years and had a particular appeal among people of his own class. Whitehead, however, envisions no spiritual or social redemption for his fictional protagonists. A secular and more obvious source of Whitehead's ironic vision was the preceding generation of Romantic poets and novelists, and certain ones in particular. Poems such as George Crabbe's 'Peter Grimes', an account of a child-murderer eventually driven from society, to psychological abjection and suicide, powerfully represented individual crime and abjection without social or sacred redemption, just as Whitehead does repeatedly in his fiction. Lord Byron and Percy Bysshe Shelley, in their narrative and elegiac poems, formulated an ironic though more noble vision of humanity as heroically aspiring to something beyond themselves yet failing to achieve it because of cosmic circumstances, their own innate limitations, or the state of society. Mary Shelley's novels such as *Frankenstein* (1818) and *The Last Man* (1826) illustrated a form of Romantic irony of heroic but futile aspiration similar to that found in the poetry of Byron and Shelley. Gothic novels such as Charles Maturin's *Melmoth the Wanderer* (1820) and James Hogg's *Confessions of a Justified Sinner* (1824) offered disturbing representations of the psychology of criminality in transhistorical context. Though Whitehead drew on such writers' vision of the human condition, ultimately his fiction represents humanity not in terms of the Romantic irony of doomed yet somehow heroic aspiration, but in terms of abjection and even horror and it is more consonant with aspects of modern literature from Fyodor Dostoyevsky to Samuel Beckett and pulp crime fiction.

Whitehead's construction of a negative version of Romantic irony, as radical social alienation and abjection, was likely grounded less in certain aspects of Romantic literature than in his personal and his wider social experience. His personal experience taught him the crucial difference between the commercial middle class or petty bourgeoisie on the one hand and the gentrified professional middle class on the other, between the ungenteel and the genteel. His education taught him the elaboration of this difference through a system or discourse of interlocked cultural and social distinctions comprising family background, education, culture and cultural consumption, including literature.[64] The earlier account of Whitehead's life here showed how he was raised in comfortable and perhaps affluent circumstances in the commercial, and hence ungenteel, middle class, but was given a genteel education at a school for sons of middle-class business-people, professionals and landed gentlemen – a predecessor at the school was Percy Bysshe Shelley, son of a baronet and country squire. Whitehead was then set to work in an ungenteel commercial position which he seems to have disliked and probably disdained, and instead he aspired to the ostensibly 'higher' socio-cultural status of literary artist which his education and reading had pointed out to him. As a result, by the time he began publishing his work he seems to have developed a personal sense of Romantic irony – of his inherent subjective unsuitedness for what he saw as the crassly commercial world in which he lived – expressed in Romantic literary terms in his first substantial work, his poem *The Solitary*. This sense of himself seems to have darkened as he struggled to achieve his literary, cultural and social aims. The heroism of the Romantic ironic protagonist could become a form of abjection – rejection by and expulsion from society and indeed the cosmic order of meaning and value. By his own and others' testimony, Whitehead developed a sense of self-worth humbled and high ambition thwarted by his refined nature and the capitalist and industrial society of his time, including increasingly market-oriented conditions of authorship. This sense of personal abjection was expressed in his writing, elaborated through his literary art into an ironic vision of humanity, though represented most frequently and forcefully, as in *The Autobiography of Jack Ketch*, in terms of middle-class and lower middle-class life.

In ideological terms, or the open and developing structure of Whitehead's beliefs and values, this ironic vision can be seen as a version of contradictions in middle-class moral values, cultural practices, social relations and economic investments in his time and as experienced in his own life. Some historians have argued that during the first half of the nineteenth century there developed in all social classes, though for different reasons, an attitude of abasement, sinfulness, or abjection and a view of life as 'atonement'. For the lower and lower middle classes, the historian E. P. Thompson has seen this culture of abjection and atonement as a consequence of their disappointment at the failure to achieve revolutionary transformation in the established order of hierarchy and exploitation at the end of the eighteenth century and to their increasing immiseration in the early nineteenth century with the advance of a capitalist wage system and industrialization. For many such people, secular revolutionary hope was replaced by religious hope for a millenarian apocalypse – a 'chiliasm of despair'.[65] For the middle classes and many in the upper classes, the historian Boyd Hilton has found a sense of the contradictions in the capitalist and proto-industrial or industrialized system in which they were increasingly the investors and, all going well, the profit-takers. Such people had to know of the social misery, economic injustice and worse that could be caused by this developing capitalist system and of their complicity in it. The guilt and the philosophical, ethical and religious self-justification resulting from this knowledge constituted a powerful contradiction in middle-class social psychology, making Whitehead's day what this historian has called the 'age of atonement'.[66]

Whitehead's social experience and observation would have made him aware of the fundamental contradictions of contemporary middle-class life, especially among lower middle-class 'tradespeople' such as his own family. No doubt similar contradictions were experienced in all classes at this time, but it could be argued that these contradictions were more acute for those of the lower middle class, for their situation was particularly demanding yet unstable. Their family and business life were usually inextricable from each other and their economic credit depended on their social standing, and vice versa. This situation required personal and familial self-discipline for the maintenance of social respectability and avoidance of expensive personal, business, or social weaknesses, such as drink and gambling, financial speculation, or fashionable social emulation, such as Whitehead's father's 'expensive library' or his son's 'gentleman's' education. Moreover, most lower middle-class family businesses lacked stable income of the kind derived from landed property, were chronically under-capitalized, depended on marriage and family for capital and other forms of business support and were vulnerable to changes in fashion, to government policies they could hardly influence (trade, taxes, regulations, infrastructure development), to the vagaries of economic cycles they could neither understand nor control and of course to what could be counted mere misfortune.

Worse, the stakes of identity and status were higher for those of Whitehead's class. Whitehead would have known through his family and community of his class's conflicted condition, torn between ambition to achieve higher status and fear of falling lower, between desire to affect higher status through conspicuous cultural consumption and fear of dangerously over-extending themselves in just that way. He would have experienced directly the fine gradations of class status in his day, especially within the middle classes and between them and those nearest them 'above' and 'below' in the social scale. In Whitehead's early life, historic patterns of fairly easy movement back and forth between skilled working class and lower middle class were changing and social distinction was becoming more pronounced. For the lower middle-class family business, commercial success could be the basis for social ascent into the professional middle class or even higher but commercial failure could precipitate descent into the lower classes, the mere labourers, or even the criminal underworld. For many middle-class people, such a decline would seem an abjection and a horror; not just decline in social status but loss of social identity, disappearance into what would seem a social and cultural abyss, moral relativism and unmeaning. Finally, and perhaps most importantly, to one who had been educated and who aspired 'above' the condition of the lower middle class, that condition could seem to be already abject, fallen or excluded from the meaning and value of 'high' culture and from those whose cultural practice and property it was.

Whitehead's fiction represents such abjection or the possibility of it across all levels of society, in the past and present, but especially in the contemporary lower middle class. It does so with autobiographical intensity, giving the impression through particular detail and handling of material that the author has experienced the kinds and structures of feeling, if not the same actions or life events, that his fiction represents. In fact, Whitehead did experience such an aspiration and fall, not into the lower classes or criminal underworld but into the paradoxical world of literary bohemia or 'Grub Street', where high cultural ambition, activity and status were licensed by social and cultural convention to dwell among lower-class or lower middle-class material circumstances. But Whitehead's fiction should not be regarded as merely autobiographical. No doubt his representation of abjection had an autobiographical motivation, or confessional aspect, but even when writing for money he can be credited as a conscious literary artist aiming to generalize his subjective and social experience in a broader vision of the human condition.

Whitehead developed and elaborated his ironic vision in various ways across his career. In what he regarded as his legitimately literary work, he developed several forms created and established by his Romantic predecessors. In his early Shelleyan meditative poem *The Solitary* and his sonnets he uses Romantic irony more conventionally. In these texts, the figure of the poet sets forth in characteristically Romantic expressive lyric form his sense of subjective suffering and alienation from a predominantly middle-class social, economic and cultural order. In *Jack Ketch*, examined in more detail later, the principal and subsidiary narrators recount their careers of crime leading, in the principal character and narrator, to an ironic elevation as the agent of death and, in the secondary characters, to abjection and isolation or death. In Whitehead's historical novels, drama and narrative poems he retrojected his vision of the inevitability of social abjection into the past in different but parallel ways. In *Richard Savage*, set in the eighteenth century, the eponymous first-person narrator recounts his career of apparently inescapable and inexplicably repeated excess, error and failure, despite his manifest talents, high ambitions, good intentions and worthy friends. Though there are touches of self-reflective moralizing in the novel and a hint of spiritual transcendence through love at the end, Savage's life ultimately seems abject, meaningless, a kind of horror. The omniscient third-person narrator of *The Earl of Essex*, set in the early seventeenth century, recounts the protagonist's career of self-destruction, caused by his own intemperance, impulsiveness and meanness, cleverly exploited by his enemies, despite his nobility, innate gifts and ability to inspire loyalty and love. In the end, the lives and deeds of Essex and his followers, whether abject or noble, spectacular or obscure, seem futile, a dead end. *The Cavalier*, set in the late seventeenth century, dramatizes the inability of a noble man and his nobler wife to obtain justice; and despite their moral rectitude, high ideals and domestic heroism, the play shows their entrapment and near-destruction by typical schemers of a selfish and corrupt society. If the play's ending rewards the hero and heroine for their nobility and virtue, this was apparently not the closure Whitehead intended and the Hargraves were to die, abjectly and meaninglessly, the victims of others' ignoble passions and society's and government's inability to deliver justice. In the historical narrative poem 'The Story of Jasper Brooke', a despotic father schemes to advance his family against his daughter's love for an 'unsuitable' man, but only causes their and his death. In another historical narrative poem, 'Ippolito: A Chimera in Rhyme', the title character attempts to obtain his love through black arts, but only succeeds in killing her and then himself. Both poems could provide a moral, but do not, leaving the reader with a sense of the schemers' abjectness and a feeling of revulsion if not horror.

In Whitehead's shorter pieces for magazines and annuals, whether 'light' or 'tragic', he developed the same kind of irony, though usually in contemporary scenes and lower down the social scale, conventionally subject for humorous treatment and by far the more frequent mode in his short fiction. In this fiction, Whitehead adapts the episodic, anecdotal, humorous form of one of his most important literary models, early Spanish picaresque fiction. 'Five-and-Thirty or Thereabouts' recounts the schemes of Bob Nuneham, aged fifty-seven, who wears a wig, false teeth and rubber calves in order to pass for thirty-five so that he can inveigle an apparently younger woman into marriage; but he learns that she is already married and, with her husband, intends to dupe and defraud him. Made a laughing stock, but with a lucky escape, he decides henceforth to appear his own age. Such stories play humorously on the failure of schemes that middle-class or would-be middle-class people devise to pursue their own interests, however ignoble or lofty. Some stories reverse this plot, however, rewarding those whom others try to victimize or those whose schemes are well meaning but misguided. 'Drinkwater Cobb' tells how the eponymous hero, a tobacconist, is inveigled by Griskin the pork-butcher into marriage to his daughter, with no dowry and against his friends' advice; but Cobb finds that Betsy Griskin in fact makes an excellent wife and her stingy father soon goes bankrupt. The appeal of such stories is less in the plot than in the humorous treatment of the subject; but the humour cannot conceal the possibility of dire consequences in the plot and the feeling remains that something bad could happen and may have happened already. 'Miss Jifkins's Benefit' tells how the eponymous protagonist, a professional confidence trickster, assumes the identity of a respectable but distressed gentlewoman and organizes a fake charity benefit in a commercial pleasure garden, only to have bad weather drive away the prospective customers, leaving her empty-handed and in debt. The story is humorous and offers conventional poetic justice, but Miss Jifkins faces a desperate future at the end. Such grim possibilities are fully realized in Whitehead's longer works and in the small group of 'tragic' stories Whitehead published in *Bentley's Miscellany*, including 'Edward Saville: A Transcript', and 'The Narrative of John Ward Gibson'.

The Autobiography of Jack Ketch

The most complex representation of Whitehead's negative Romantic irony is, however, his novel *The Autobiography of Jack Ketch*. Though published early in Whitehead's literary career, it already contains, fully developed, the major features of the fiction, both verse and prose, that he would produce for the rest of his life. *Jack Ketch* is more richly ironic than any other single work of Whitehead's, however, and anticipates the work of later novelists, such as Dickens and Thackeray, who may have learned from him. *Jack Ketch* brings together the two main modes of his fiction, the 'tragic' and the 'light', juxtaposing humour and horror, the comic and the Gothic, in order to unfold Whitehead's distinctive and disturbing vision of the irony of lower middle-class life, the abjection or fall outside middle-class identity, social meaning and cultural value. The novel elaborates this irony through a set of related formal techniques. There is the referential nature of its narrator-protagonist's identity. This narrator's character and meaning are established through his humorous style and the play of language in his narrative and the novel's dialogues. But the humour is then juxtaposed with descriptions of horror and the grotesque, which are reinforced by the novel's illustrations. Finally, the novel's meaning is elaborated through a web of inset and subsidiary narratives, in relation to the governing narrative, that of Jack Ketch. This structure carries only part of the novel's meaning, however. *The Autobiography of Jack Ketch* develops this structure in relation and reference to a long history of the figure of 'Jack Ketch' and to a larger tradition of true and fictitious criminal biography and autobiography, in much of which 'Jack Ketch' is the symbol of executive state justice. It is through this complex fictional structure and inter-textual play that Whitehead participates in particular aspects of the tradition of 'Newgate narratives', or the debate and discourse around crime and punishment, in terms of his own ironic vision of human life.

As its title indicates, *The Autobiography of Jack Ketch* rests its representation of the irony of lower middle-class life upon the paradoxical social, moral and legal position of its narrator and protagonist: 'Jack Ketch' had long been the well known nickname of the official hangman,[67] conventionally treated as a social outsider, outcast and abjected. The irony was similarly indicated in the different title the novel carried after its first edition, *The Autobiography of a Notorious Legal Functionary*. For the public hangman was a commonplace yet striking paradox, officer of the law yet licensed committer of the worst of crimes, representative of the crown and state yet a murderer by profession. Further, most readers at this time would expect an 'autobiography' or 'life', especially from a personage of lower-class origins such as Jack Ketch must be, to recount difficulties overcome and eventual success—an expectation Jack refers to in his opening chapter. But most readers would regard accession to the office of public hangman as at best a paradoxical or ironic success and see a further fundamental irony in the official agent of death recounting such a 'life'.

In his fictitious 'autobiography' of the well known figure of the common hangman, then, Whitehead was developing a long line of similar or related representations of Jack Ketch in English culture. For example, the satirical *Letters from the Dead to the Living*, published in 1702, contains a letter 'To the most Illustrious and High-born Jack Ketch, Esq.' from Charon, in classical mythology the boatman who ferried the souls of the dead across the river Styx to the underworld for a small payment. Charon complains that his income has fallen off because of a lack of executions by Jack, despite the presence of a notorious 'hanging judge' on the bench. Five years later, a satirical publication entitled *Athenian Sport; or, Two Thousand Paradoxes Merrily Argued, to Amuse and Divert the Age* (1707) included 'Paradox XXIII: That a Hangman is the most Honourable Calling, in a Letter to the most redoubtable Executioner of High Justice, Jack Ketch Esq.' As readers would know, the appellation 'esquire' was reserved for those who could claim to be 'gentlemen', that is, members of the gentry and the learned professions but certainly not the common hangman. Yet the hangman practised what could be seen as a 'craft' or skill requiring specialized knowledge, for which he was remunerated as a public official carrying out an office that was constitutionally an extension of the powers of the crown.[68] This construction of 'Jack Ketch' as a paradoxical figure enabled satire on social difference and common human mortality and became commonplace through the eighteenth and early nineteenth century.

A few years after publication of *Athenian Sport* the paradox of 'Jack Ketch' was enacted in reality when John Price, who had held the office of common hangman and thus been 'Jack Ketch', was himself hanged in 1718 for causing the death of a woman he had attempted to rape. The case received wide circulation by its inclusion in various versions of the eighteenth- and early nineteenth-century popular compilation known as the 'Newgate Calendar'.[69] In later eighteenth-century editions the account was embellished and melodramatized by an engraving showing Price/Ketch being arrested while accompanying a condemned man to the gallows – in actuality a fictitious incident. Whitehead was widely and deeply read in eighteenth-century history and belles-lettres and he likely knew *Letters from the Dead to the Living, Athenian Sport* (its long poem punning on the word 'hang' would have particularly appealed to him) and numerous other humorous references to 'Jack Ketch' in literature of that time and he certainly knew the 'Newgate Calendar'.

In the late eighteenth and early nineteenth centuries the figure of 'Jack Ketch' became even more widely and diversely used in literature of all kinds. During the French Revolution and Napoleonic wars, British counter-revolutionaries compared French Revolutionaries and their English sympathizers to a Jack Ketch eager for executions. In the writings of early nineteenth-century reformists, Jack Ketch became a symbol for the ruling classes and their established order of church and state, which sustained its power by instilling fear of punishment for dissent or complaint and which exploited the many, thereby creating poverty and crime, which it then punished. For example, in defining 'tax-gatherer' John Wade's *Political Dictionary* (1821) related the office to the system of parliamentary corruption through the practice of buying and selling the right to represent a borough in parliament. The *Dictionary* declared, 'As the office of the Tax-gatherer is the *lowest*, and frequently the *last* performed on the unhappy victim to oppression, he may properly be denominated "Jack Ketch to the Borough-System."'[70] At the 1832 London Congress of the Co-operative Societies of Great Britain and Ireland, a Mr Wigg denounced the 'present system' of privilege and hierarchy for stimulating self-interest, competitiveness and exploitation: 'This system has given rise to circumstances which have made men thieves, rogues, knaves, highwaymen, and housebreakers; and these classes of culprits have given rise to lawyers, judges, commissioners, magistrates, thief-catchers, and jailers— and though last not least, to Jack Ketch himself, to put people to death for their crimes.'[71]

More pertinent and recent still was a book published less than two years before Whitehead's novel. This was the satirical pamphlet, *The Hangman and the Judge; or, A Letter from Jack Ketch to Mr. Justice Alderson* (1833) by the prominent advocate of legal and penal reform, Edward Gibbon Wakefield, author of *Facts Relating to the Punishment of Death in the Metropolis* (1831). *The Hangman and the Judge* was published by Effingham Wilson, who had published Whitehead's first book, the poem *The Solitary*, two years earlier. In Wakefield's pamphlet, Jack Ketch's argument to the judge is that hanging not only benefits hangmen and judges, who are partners in the 'business' and profit from carrying it out, but it creates crime by hardening the hearts of the people, thus making them more likely to commit crime themselves. Ketch gives the judge as an example a hanging he was called out of town to perform on a child:

Ten thousand people came to dabble in the young murderer's blood. That was the youngest fellow-creature I ever handled in the way of our business; and a beautiful child he was too, as you may have seen by the papers, with a straight nose, large blue eyes, and golden hair. I have no heart, no feelings; who has in our calling? but those who came to see me strangle that tender youngster have hearts and feelings, as we had once. Have—no—had; for what they saw was fit to make them as hard as your servant or his master. They saw the stripling lifted fainting on to the gallows, his smooth cheeks of the colour of wood-ashes, his limbs trembling, and his bosom heaving sigh after sigh, as if body and soul were parting without my help. It was not a downright murder; for there was scarce any life to take out of him. When I began to pull the cap (not yours but mine) over his baby face, he pressed his small hands together (his arms, you know, were corded fast to his body) and gave me a beseeching look; just as a calf will lick his butcher's hand. But cattle do not speak: this creature muttered,—'Pray, sir, don't hurt me.' 'My dear,' answered I, 'you should have spoken to my master: I'm only the journeyman and must do as I'm bid.' This made him cry, which seemed a relief to him; and I do think I should have cried, myself, if I had not heard shouts from the crowd: poor lamb! shame! murderer! Quick, said the sheriff; ready, said I; the reverend chaplain gave me a wink: the drop fell: one kick, and he swayed to and fro, dead as the feelings of an English judge.

The crowd dispersed; some weeping, with passionate exclamations; some swearing, as if hell had broke loose; and some laughing, while they cracked blackguard jokes on the judge and me, and the parson and the dangling corpse. They had come for the sight: they would have come to see an angel murdered. They had come to get drunk with strong excitement: they went back, reeling and filthy with the hot debauch. They had come to riot in the passions of fear and pity: they went back, some in a fever of rage, some burning with hate, some hardened in heart, like me or you; all sunk down in their own respect, ready to make light of pain and blood, corrupted by the indecent show, and more fit than ever to create work for us, the judge and the hangman. Oh, wise law-makers, who thought to soften the hearts of the people, to make them gentle and good, to give them a feeling of respect for themselves and others, by showing them sights like this!

Jack sums up his argument: 'In order to have plenty of criminals, the grand point is to brutalize the people.' Wakefield knew that such a viewpoint was associated with reformists and his Jack Ketch goes on, with obvious irony:

Sir Robert Peel and I have always said that reform would ruin the country; and our words are fast coming true. The first reformer was an Italian fellow named Beccaria. If he had been hanged, as he deserved, we might not have been troubled with your Benthams, Romillies, Montagues, Buxtons, Ewarts, and the like.[72]

Wakefield's Jack Ketch glories in his hard-heartedness even more than Whitehead's does, but the social psychology invoked by both texts is the same.

In this long line of representations of 'Jack Ketch', the eighteenth-century satires establish the humorous and satirical potential of the figure and construct it as a paradoxical or ironic one, exposing the contradiction between Christian values and judicial murder, between humanity and the justice system and between Jack Ketch's important or 'high' role in the state and his detestable and 'low' occupation or 'trade'. The account of the actual hangman John Price in the various versions of the 'Newgate Calendar' sets forth another paradoxical figure, appealing to a popular sense of natural justice – that of the hangman hanged – and there were other real cases where criminals agreed to turn hangmen in order to escape their own punishments. Whitehead's novel does seem to ignore the representations of Jack Ketch in the pro- and anti-Revolutionary literature of the 1790s and just after, for Whitehead's Jack makes no claim to be an important state personage, but rather holds himself up as a moral warning:

> Nobody can accuse me of being nobody. I think it will be agreed, on all hands, that Jack Ketch is a personage of no common importance, or insignificant consideration, when it is remembered that he is (if not unlikely to be called upon to give the coup de grace to the community at large) a portion, at least, of their daily thoughts, and a salutary check to their projected operations. (p. 6)

The relation of Whitehead's Jack Ketch to more recent representations in reform literature is, however, central, if undeclared. There are obvious differences between Whitehead's novel and such texts as the Co-operative Societies proceedings and Wakefield's polemical pamphlet, but all use 'Jack Ketch' to set forth what could be called an economy or dialectic of abjection, in which abjecting or attempting to abject others eventually abjects oneself. All call upon what could be described as a social psychology of heart-hardening and abjection; the disruption or disintegration of social relations by selfishness and self-interest, leading inevitably to social marginalization or exclusion, whether individual or collective, willful or involuntary. The difference is that Whitehead's novel attributes individual abjection not to systemic inequality, exploitation and injustice, but rather to individual willfulness or to particular circumstances that are beyond the individual's control.

Whitehead appropriates and adapts the historical figure of Jack Ketch for his own purpose through characterization and especially Jack's narrative voice. Though there are several 'voices' in Whitehead's novel, the dominant one is Jack's: it is his 'autobiography'. The improbability of the common hangman actually recounting his life was enhanced by the justifiable assumption that such a personage was typically one of little or no education or culture; an assumption encouraged by the novel's frontispiece, a medallion portrait of 'Jack Ketch' as a burly lantern-jawed figure wearing a 'belcher', or polka-dot neckerchief named after a famous boxer and favoured by lower-class men. Whitehead – or Jack – breezily dismisses the problem of Jack's style in the novel's 'Advertisement', which states that Jack 'called in the aid of an obscure man of letters' to improve his correctness and style by 'adjusting his somewhat capricious orthography'; by 'clipping his vernacular tongue, so that it may speak with fluency and correctness'; by correcting the grammar; by sticking 'a flower' or literary trope 'here and there'; and by throwing in 'the required amount of moral reflection'. The 'Advertisement' also promises that, should the public receive favourably Jack's account of how he came to be the common hangman, he will also publish 'his more mature experiences' – presumably in office – as '"The Ketch Papers"' (p. 2). After this obviously ironic statement Jack launches his text with a prefatory chapter in a manifestly literary style, citing the eighteenth-century moralist Samuel Johnson's view that every book has something to teach and continuing with a critique on literature of the day, the vanity of authors and Jack's own importance as the agent of death and the enforcer of legislated morality, ornamented with a few commonplace classical allusions and references to the French moralist La Rochefoucauld and the Roman moralist Cato and a reference to the fairy-tale character Mother Hubbard that undercuts the foregoing ones.

The style, tone and range of reference in this opening chapter set the prevailing mode of narration for the rest of Jack's narrative, in a compact with the reader, which suggests that this is a comic, or at least humorous novel, in which bad things and bad characters may loom, but will not happen, or will happen humorously. The narration is ironic, jocular and literary, though not learned, for the range of Jack's references, quotations, and allusions is within a common education, predominantly the Bible, Shakespeare, well known poets (Milton, Pope, Gray), commonplace classical allusions, and well known Latin and French phrases. Three references do stand out, however, partly revealing the author behind the narrator's mask: an allusion to William Godwin's dark reformist novel of 1794, *Things as They Are; or, The Adventures of Caleb Williams* (p. 52), an echo of Byron's dark social satire *Don Juan* (p. 158), and citations of the sardonic French aphorist La Rochefoucauld (pp. 6, 81, 97). Later in his autobiography, when recounting his descent into cruelty and crime, Jack's narration takes on at times a detached and sombre tone, but only briefly, and Jack soon returns to his characteristic vein of humorous narration.

The characteristic feature of this humour is play with language, including hyperbole, circumlocution and in particular punning. By no accident, this narrative style is also that found in early Spanish picaresque novellas, especially Quevedo's *El Buscòn* (*The Swindler*). Here, for example, is Jack's reflection on the suicide of his uncle and predecessor as hangman:

> I have heard of some approved instances of individuals who, having lost a leg, nevertheless feel acute physical pain in that particular portion of space which that useful member of the body corporate in fact no longer occupies. Is this a bonâ fide sensation? Undoubtedly. But does it not appear absurd, and in the highest degree ridiculous? No question about it. Now, it seems to me, that to grieve for individuals who no longer exist, though it may be natural in one sense, and proper to do so, is, philosophically to speak, a lamentable defection from reason and common sense. The will may and

can repress that grief; whereas, in the other case, no power can prevent that sensation. The senses are arbitrary, but the feeling is a slave. And as a man, by relinquishing his amputated limb to the earth, may thereby supply such nourishment to the ground as will stimulate the growth of some tree, from which in time he may recruit himself with a wooden substitute,—so, by dismissing our deceased friend from our minds, we thereby leave room for the growth of another friendship; and though he be a wooden-headed fellow—the only genuine lignum-vitæ[73]—what matter? (p. 183)

The burlesque of philosophical argument, the play on words and ideas, and the grim or even grotesque subject matter, especially for word-play, recall the narrative of Pablos in *The Swindler* and are characteristic of Jack's narration, as of the narration in Whitehead's later short fiction.

A typical passage occurs very early in Jack's narrative, as he tells of his father: 'Let me not mince the matter,—for mincing it will not make the matter less, although the several portions may be smaller,—my father was a thief' (p. 13). After his father is hung, Jack reflects, in an extended play on words, 'It behoved him to depart, since it was now evident that, had he been permitted to remain amongst us, he would have been much more likely to act as a clog upon, than to serve as a spoke in, the wheel of our domestic vehicle of existence, which was now threatening to break down at every jolt in the road, and at every rut in the highway of adversity' (p. 16). Much later, Jack reflects after his uncle's suicide: 'He was indeed no more,—and hereafter could be no less' (p. 180). This is the prevailing style of Jack's narrative to its end. These features are not limited to Jack alone but are extended into the novel's dialogues between Jack and various other characters, especially the deadbeats, rogues and criminals – all abject figures in various ways and most given to punning and wordplay. In fact, in this novel, playing on words is usually a sign of ethical doubtfulness or criminality, Jack being the most prominent and relentless of the punsters while the good characters' discourse is free of such tropes.

In the earlier part of the novel in particular there are the scenes of interactive punning and wordplay in the aptly named Magpie and Punchbowl public house – the magpie is proverbially a thieving bird, as Jack himself notes (p. 14), and one preferring glittery but usually worthless objects, the verbal equivalents of which would be the pun and its like. There was in fact a Magpie and Punch Bowl pub in Bishopsgate Street, London, at this time, and Jack gives the location as 'equidistant from, and contiguous to' Paul's chain and Knight Rider Street (p. 14), which would place the novel's Magpie and Punchbowl in Carter Lane. Considering the novel's clear association with the hangman and Newgate prison, however, Whitehead may have intended his readers to recall the well known Magpie and Stump pub just opposite the prison.[74] The novel's Magpie and Punchbowl is a dilapidated place, run by a slovenly woman and her daughters and frequented by a variety of abject characters who feature in various incidents and relationships through the rest of the novel and most of whom keep up a banter of punning and wordplay among themselves. But the punning and wordplay are kept up in dialogues throughout the novel, even in moments of serious import, such as Jack and Wisp's farewell before the latter's departure for Australia as a transported felon. The domination of the novel's discourse by such humour may seem incidental, or an expression of its author's own bent. Those who knew Whitehead himself testified that he was a master punster in congenial society, in particular the bohemian tavern society that he frequented. Nevertheless, there is an important artistic purpose to this feature of the novel, deeply rooted in the changing politics of language in the century or more before *Jack Ketch* was published.

The characteristic humour of Jack and his associates had long been regarded as a 'low' form of wit and puns and their supposed users were alike considered abject, one indicating the abjection of the other. In the eighteenth century, puns were associated with marginalized and despised people of various sorts. There was, for example, *The Irish Miscellany* (1746), which claimed to be a 'compleat collection of the most profound puns, learned bulls, elaborate quibbles, amorous letters, sublime poetry, and wise sayings of the natives of Teagueland'. Puns were associated with the lower classes by being a feature in the often reprinted jest-books of street literature, such as *Joe Miller's Jests* and its imitators and *The Wise Men of Gotham*, in which the silly Gothamites make unwitting puns. Patrons of popular literature were unabashed in their enjoyment of puns, however, and in fact associated them with gentlemanly and upper-class drollery: individual puns and jokes and whole collections could be associated with famous wits, as in *Derrick's Jests . . . Containing a Pleasing Variety of Repartees, Puns, Bon-mots, and Other Species of Humour* (1769), supposedly collected from a former master of ceremonies at the fashionable spa town of Bath, and *Rochester's Jests . . . Containing a New Collection of Merry Stories, Repartees, Jokes, Puns* (3rd edn, 1766), supposedly from the seventeenth-century rake and scurrilous poet, the earl of Rochester. Later in the century, such collections were associated with more contemporary and politically disruptive figures, such as the raffish parliamentary reformist John Wilkes and the French Revolutionary sympathizer and reform pamphleteer Tom Paine.

Condemnation of puns was, however, a recurring topic with eighteenth-century literary and moral critics, and was associated with often repeated comments attributed to Samuel Johnson and John Dennis. Johnson's contempt for most puns was attested several times by his biographer James Boswell, so that the definition of the pun as 'the lowest form of wit' was widely attributed to Johnson. Another remark circulated in various versions came from the critic John Dennis and originated in an anecdote in Benjamin Victor's *An Epistle to Sir Richard Steele, on his Play, call'd The Conscious Lovers*. According to the story, Dennis and the composer Henry Purcell were unable to get a 'drawer', or waiter, to serve them in a tavern, and Purcell remarked that the tavern was like the table they sat at, in having no 'drawer': 'Says *D----s*, (starting up) God's Death, Sir, the Man that will make such an execrable Pun as that in my Company, will pick my Pocket, and so left the Room.'[75] By Whitehead's day the association of puns and pickpockets, or thieves and lowlifes in general, was well established in literary discourse.

In the eighteenth century puns had also been a topic of learned treatment, either satirical or philosophical. Satirists ransacked ancient and modern literature for puns and affected to establish rules for punning, as in Jonathan Swift's *Ars Pun-ica, sive Flos Linguarum: The Art of Punning; or, The Flower of Languages; In Seventy-Nine Rules* (1719), and Philalethes' *Ars Punica: Pars Altera; or, Truth Vindicated . . . Being a Faithfull Collection of Ecclesiastical Puns, Quibbles, Græcisms, and Conundrums* (1721). Later, philosophers of language and rhetoric took up the topic in serious vein. In his treatise *Elements of Criticism* (1762), Henry Home, Lord Kames, described the pun as 'this species of bastard wit' (ch. 13) and though he acknowledged that 'playing with words is a mark of a mind at ease, and disposed for any sort of amusement' (ch. 13), he also dismissed it as 'the meanest of all conceits' (ch. 17). Another major Scottish Enlightenment philosopher, John Burnet, Lord Monboddo, declared in his treatise *Of the Origin and Progress of Language* (1776) that the play on words was 'not at all fit for grave composition' (part 2, book 2, ch. 18). Finally, the association of puns with poor taste, inferior social rank, or even foreignness was stated forcefully by the Earl of Chesterfield in his widely circulated *Letters* to his son (1774) on how to be a gentleman: 'The reign of King Charles II (meritorious in no other respect) banished false taste out of England, and proscribed puns, quibbles, acrostics, etc. Since that, false wit has renewed its attacks, and endeavored to recover its lost empire, both in England and France; but without success; though, I must say, with more success in France than in England' (letter 105).

Johnson, Kames, Monboddo, Chesterfield, and others spoke for a social formation invested in establishing a standardized and stable language and usage as major instruments of knowledge and power for a professional middle-class elite collaborating with an upper-class ruling order. In such a construction of language, 'lowness' was suspect, to be excluded, abject. In the early nineteenth century, however, the pun and its associated tropes began to be rehabilitated, along with many other 'low' values, practices, and literary genres, especially in the broad literary-cultural movement later known as Romanticism. In this respect, Romanticism was a movement for reform in the cultural sphere with political implications. The learned literary critic and poet Samuel Taylor Coleridge disparaged poor puns but recognized effective ones as an important instrument of intellectual analysis and understanding. Coleridge initiated a reconsideration of the pun as a multi-faceted verbal ambiguity of serious intellectual, moral and imaginative import, characteristic of the greatest literary works and to be uncovered by the literary critic – the forerunner of modern academic criticism based on the discipline of 'close reading' promoted by such works as William Empson's *Seven Types of Ambiguity* (1930). The critic and essayist William Hazlitt could denigrate puns, in his *Lectures on the English Poets* (1818) saying of Shakespeare, for example, as many had done before, 'He was fonder of puns than became so great a man' (lecture 3, 'On Shakespeare and Milton'). In his *Table-Talk: Essays on Men and Manners* (1821–2), Hazlitt associated punning with 'cleverness' rather than with 'force or perseverance' (essay 9, 'The Indian Jugglers'); but he also acknowledged that 'No one likes puns, alliterations, antitheses, argument, and analysis better than I do; but I sometimes had rather be without them' (essay 3, 'On Going a Journey'). Many literary men, such as Charles Lamb, the leading essayist, promoted punning. Lamb was known for his puns in company, and published an essay 'On Popular Fallacies' in which he defended puns under the heading, 'That the Worst Puns Are the Best'. One of the more widely read series of humorous-serious periodical pieces, involving much punning, was the 'Noctes Ambrosianae', appearing in the successful and influential *Blackwood's Magazine* from 1822, and dealing with current literary, intellectual, social, and political works, issues, and figures.

Meanwhile, if the earlier joke books such as *The Wise Men of Gotham* and *Joe Miller's Jests* came to seem old-fashioned around 1800, many of their jokes and puns transferred to a wider variety of fashionable new products, with titles such as *The New Wit's Magazine* (1805), *Odd Fellow's Jest Book* (1805), *Colman's Jests* (1810, named after a famous comic playwright), the *Encyclopedia of Wit* (1811), the *London Budget of Wit* (1817), *A Fardel of Fancies* (1824), *The Cabinet of Mirth* (1825) and others. In a higher sphere, aristocratic and well-to-do dandies of the 1810s and 1820s took up punning, often involving display of their expensive education and as a proof of cleverness and unseriousness, or freedom from the need to be serious. Cashing in on this trend, in 1826 the upmarket publisher Sherwood and Co. put out *The Punster's Pocket-Book; or, The Art of Punning Enlarged*, with illustrations by the fashionable artist Robert Cruikshank.

The writer who turned punning into 'high' – and both fashionable and popular – literary art, however, was Byron, in his verse novel *Don Juan* (1819–24). There was already a large body of Romantic humorous verse that played with conventional hierarchies and decorums of literary language, discourse, and form and used far-fetched, blatantly punning rhymes to challenge the social and cultural formations that had an investment in those hierarchies and decorums. *Don Juan* linked these techniques and purpose to a radical view of the human condition as ironic and abject, as negatively comic rather than transcendently tragic. In *Don Juan*, puns and punning rhymes serve several purposes – to expose moral hypocrisy, to deflect and deflate earnestness, to democratize by vernacularizing poetic language and discourse, to amuse in order to arouse moral or political indignation. Perhaps most importantly, *Don Juan* uses puns and especially punning rhymes in the trope of bathos, or rapid descent from the sublime to the ridiculous, or abject, in a general strategy to destabilize language and meaning and dislodge them from conventional moral, aesthetic, and politic canons, thereby opening them to reconsideration and reimagining. Byron's demonstration of the power of punning did not and has not entirely reclaimed the trope but, along with others such as Lamb, Hazlitt and the 'Noctes Ambrosianae' circle, Byron showed its literary and ideological – and commercial – possibilities. From at least the 1820s, punning was a feature of commercial literary discourse and culture, of the social interactions and literary productions of the kind of magazine-based literary society in which Whitehead participated. By the time he published *The Autobiography of Jack Ketch*, his predecessors in the Newgate novel such as Gaspey and Bulwer had already availed themselves of this form of humour in their characterizations of the abject and criminal.

Whitehead continues this development, clearly placing his puns and punsters under the shadow of Newgate and abjection, with aims similar to but going beyond those of his Romantic predecessors. In his appropriation of the poetics and politics of the pun and wordplay in *Jack Ketch*, Whitehead had several aims. He aimed to create a conventionally and plausibly appropriate 'low' cultural sociolect for his circle of 'low' characters and especially his narrator-protagonist. He aimed to reinforce his juxtaposition of humour and horror in the abject lives he depicts. Through the scenes at the Magpie and Punchbowl he implied the association of literary bohemia with the socially marginal and abjected as worlds of specialized knowledge and discourse and aimed to give a contemporary avant-garde literary colour to his portrayal of low life. More largely, he aimed in his own way to destabilize language as the foundation of meaning and value in line both with his Romantic models, especially Byron and Shelley, and with his own vision of the negative irony and abjection of middle-class life.

The punning humour of Jack and his associates also serves to heighten the scenes of horror and the 'tragic' narratives in the novel; this juxtaposition is reinforced by the novel's illustrations. The scenes of horror represented verbally are several, involving all characters and include Wilmot's desperation when his attorney Snavel fails to appear with the money awarded Wilmot by the court, Wilson's midnight murder of Beaumont, Wilmot's deliberate revenge killing of Snavel, Jack's uncle's suicide, and others. The 'tragic' narratives are principally those of Wilson and Misty. These scenes and narratives are framed by, though not rendered in, the humorous style. Rather, they are narrated in a straight-forward, almost stark manner. In this way the humour and horror play off one another, intensifying each other. The illustrations are adapted to such contrast and tension, and set up the tone and punctuate key points in the novel. Only three illustrations could be said to be humorous and the rest portray important moments in the novel simply and without melodrama or caricature. The frontispiece is a humorous medallion portrait, verging on but not reaching caricature, of Jack Ketch enclosed in a noose rope and signed in an unskilled hand, 'Yours in death, john [sic] Ketch'. The title page has an appropriately corresponding vignette of a prison-like arched alcove containing a skull in judge's cap and neckpiece above a pair of black shoes and perhaps the hood put over the head of the hanged at execution, with a rope and felon's chains intertwined. These images indicate the grim humour to follow. With one exception the illustrations to the story itself are not, however, in caricature style, being simple line drawings of a succession of scenes of dejection, disaster, or abjection, including Misty being tormented by his school pupils, a humorous medallion portrait of Jack's mother with a surround of felon's irons indicating her sentence of transportation for theft, the violence of Jack's aunt against his uncle the henpecked hangman, the distress of Jack's tormented wife Catharine, the wretched Haynes wresting from Wisp money stolen by them and Haynes from Haynes's employer, the death of Catharine's pet bird as an omen of her own death, the death of Wilson's father on learning his son is a murderer, the discovery of the murder weapon by Wilson's own children, Catharine's death from a broken heart, Wilmot's murder of Snavel and finally the eager Jack's interview with the London sheriff and Newgate chaplain for his late uncle's job as public hangman.

Humour and horror are juxtaposed structurally in a web of inset and subsidiary narratives that emerge from and merge with Jack's narrative. Jack's is the principal and framing narrative; there is the substantial inset narrative of James Wilson, a murderer hanged by Jack's uncle; there is the narrative of Misty, Jack's former schoolteacher and there are the more briefly sketched stories of various minor characters. Jack's 'autobiography' is in humorous-ironic mode, while the inset narratives are in Whitehead's 'tragic' mode, adapting features of Gothic fiction and anticipating certain of Whitehead's later magazine stories such as 'Edward Saville: A Transcript' and 'The Narrative of John Ward Gibson'. But Jack's narrative also contains prominent elements of the 'tragic', or Gothic. The 'tragic' and 'Gothic' inset narratives thus emphasize these elements in Jack's humorous narrative, while making the humour seem more grim and ghastly. The subsidiary narratives cycle into Jack's dominant narrative, recounting the same plot of abjection from different individual perspectives and in different discursive modes.

Misty's narrative takes up about a tenth of the novel as he recounts his life story to Jack late in the book (chs 20–1). Misty tells how his extremely sensitive nature exposed him to being easily wounded by others, and particularly his father, who harboured an inexplicable aversion to him – a situation similar to that of Richard Savage in Whitehead's later novel. Misty found a soul-mate, however, in Clara Marston and a timely legacy from an uncle enabled him to marry. But Clara's mother had higher ambitions for her and arranged her marriage to Mr Western, a successful London merchant. In despair, Misty ran through his money and experienced the degradation of poverty and a succession of humiliations. As he tells Jack, "'how dreadful a thing it is to be proud and poor. I felt it,—it was hell to me: not the physical want,—not starvation,—not tramping the streets all night without a shelter for the head, or a resting-place for the sole of the foot,—but the insult—the contumely—the scorn: I felt it until my nature was changed . . .'" (p. 195). Misty resolved to confront his father and demand his birthright but found his father had remarried and had a son and Misty was again rejected. Wandering the streets of London, he learned that Western was about to be hanged for forgery and witnessed the execution. Exulting, he sought Clara, but she had disappeared. He then learned his father had died, leaving his estate to the second son; viewing his father's coffin, Misty kissed the face of the corpse in forgiveness and as he tells Jack, "'. . . I have been a happier and a better man since that day. I hewed away, as it were, the morbid and decayed branches of my nature; and what remains is fresher, and of a greener leaf'" (p. 200). There was one emotional trial remaining for him, however. For some time he eked out a poor and toilsome life as a lowly clerk. Then one evening he was visited by Clara, asking forgiveness and seeking a reconciliation; Misty forgave her but resolved never to see her again. Soon after, he learned that his younger half-brother had died and his father's estate reverted to himself. So Misty's tale concludes; he has been avenged for others' mistreatment of him and he is well-to-do, relieved from further prospect of numbing toil or poverty, and, more important, enriched by the humanity acquired from suffering. Yet he seems a solitary and abject figure, with nothing and no-one to live for.

The tale of James Wilson, which takes up about a fifth of the novel, is grimmer still, reminiscent of earlier Gothic fiction and anticipating Whitehead's later magazine stories of futile vengeance, such as 'The Narrative of John Ward Gibson'. Wilson's narrative is set apart in the novel's text, and titled 'The Confession of James Wilson'. It is ostensibly a manuscript recovered by Jack's uncle the hangman from the effects of a man executed for murder – the convention of the 'found' manuscript was a familiar sign to readers at the time to expect something in the Gothic mode. This text takes up most of the long fourteenth chapter of Whitehead's novel, as Jack reads it aloud to his uncle. In this manuscript, Wilson recounts his life from childhood, as the son of a benevolent and mild-mannered village clergyman. Raised with his orphan cousin, Lucy Cowley, he fell in love with her and considered them as betrothed, but the arrival of the handsome, dashing and talented Francis Beaumont changed the situation and Wilson's temperament. Soon Lucy, Wilson's father, the servants, all were charmed by Beaumont. Despite himself, Wilson, too, loved Beaumont, but inevitably the youths quarreled, and Beaumont always established his superiority to his rival – as Wilson confessed to him, "'Oh! yes, I know my inferiority," said I, bitterly; "every one takes care to remind me of that'" (p. 120). As the years passed, Wilson realized that Beaumont had effectively marginalized him, without intending to. Cherishing his sense of abasement and abjection, Wilson conceived a plan to kill his rival and one night in a dark lane he did so. He was immediately horrified at the deed, but escaped detection and suspicion fell on a farm labourer, Williams, whom Wilson helped to abscond in order to divert suspicion from himself. Wilson's plan seemed to work: the household were grief-stricken at Beaumont's death and turned to him and eventually he and Lucy married and had children. Tortured by guilt and fear of exposure, however, Wilson found that his triumph had only made him more, if secretly, abject. Events conspired to reveal the truth. While visiting his sick father, Wilson's expression when Beaumont was mentioned disclosed the secret and the old man died of horror. Williams returned, having realized Wilson's guilt, and demanded blackmail. Then Wilson's children accidentally found the murder weapon while playing. Wilson cruelly revealed his secret to his wife, before poisoning her, and even his children now shrank from him in fear. All meaning and social relationship gone, he fled like an animal, was taken while hiding in a barn, tried and convicted. Before his execution, like many before him in real life, he composed his 'last dying words and confession', ending on the conventionally pious note:

> Of those who read my story, how few, perhaps, will pity, how many will condemn me. Alas! it is not given to man to see the heart of man. From God, at least, I tremblingly hope for mercy and forgiveness,—and I die at peace with all men.

The sentiment hardly seems to compensate for the horror of Wilson's account of descent, almost deliberate and purposeful, into the abyss of moral and social abjection, an account given additional force by the first-person narrative mode.

There are two similar descents, those of Haynes and Wilmot, represented in the novel, though indirectly through incident, dialogue and the accounts of others. Each story loops through the novel, as the characters appear, disappear and reappear. Jack first meets Tom Haynes, a well dressed young warehouse clerk, at the Magpie and Punchbowl. It becomes evident, however, that Haynes is deeply troubled and spending recklessly. One evening he reveals to Wisp and Jack that he has been surreptitiously 'borrowing' from his employer, Marley, against his salary, but has fallen irretrievably behind and left Marley a letter confessing his crime. Wisp sees an opportunity, takes Haynes in as a lodger and with Jack persuades him to help in robbing the warehouse office. They break through the roof and Haynes descends into the office, but they are interrupted by Marley and Wisp and Jack flee. The next day, Jack and Wisp are fighting for the small amount Haynes managed to hand up, when he appears, disconsolate: out of compassion,

Marley declined to arrest him, only deepening Haynes's guilt and abjection. He seizes the small plunder from Jack and Wisp and returns it to Marley and then sinks into a depression. Wisp and Jack learn that Haynes had a childhood sweetheart whom, along with his mother, he feels he has betrayed by his crime. Haynes asks Jack to tell Marley of his repentance, and then dies.

Wilmot's is also a story of descent into poverty, abjection and crime, but with a different twist. When Jack and Wisp first meet Wilmot, he is a client of their employer, the attorney Jabez Snavel, engaged in a typically long drawn-out lawsuit over property. Unexpectedly, the suit is resolved and a large sum is paid out to Snavel for his client. The lawyer absconds with the money ('snavel' was slang for 'steal, appropriate dishonestly') and, incidentally, with Jack's aunt Mrs Ketch, though not before Wisp extorts a small sum from Snavel for himself and Jack. Expectations dashed, the wretched Wilmot disappears, but some time later seeks out Jack and eagerly asks about Snavel, but Jack has no information. Jack learns from his old friend Gibbon, with whom Wilmot is lodging, that Wilmot has been living in poverty and, penniless, had to watch while his beloved daughter died of consumption. Then Jack accidentally meets a ragged and wary Snavel and when Snavel inquires after Wilmot, Jack lies and tells him that Wilmot is dead. Relieved, Snavel then tells Jack that he lost both the money and Mrs Ketch when shipwrecked *en route* to the United States. Jack decides to sell Wilmot the information of Snavel's whereabouts for twenty pounds and does so. He also agrees to inveigle Snavel to Wilmot's room, and leaves the two alone. There, to the horror of Jack and his friends, Wilmot cuts Snavel's throat with such ferocity he almost severs his head. His vengeance fulfilled, Wilmot is arrested and convicted of murder, though his case receives wide public sympathy. Jack's uncle also sympathizes with Wilmot, and expresses to Jack his reluctance to carry out his duty as hangman in this instance. Jack offers to fill in, to his uncle's relief. Ironically, however, uncle Ketch hangs himself that night, perhaps while trying out a new noose knot – he is proudly professional and studies his craft – perhaps despondent at having had to suppress personal feelings in the line of duty for so long, or at the social isolation attendant on the nature of his profession. Wilmot is spared on grounds of temporary insanity and Jack, having demonstrated his ability to yield personal friendship to professional duty in the case of Wilmot, is appointed hangman in his late uncle's place by the sheriff and the Newgate chaplain.

Jack is the centre for this web of narratives of abjection, and his own story is of similar kind, though as the ending of the novel shows, it is also significantly different. Broadly, Jack's autobiography recounts his progress from orphaned son of criminal parents (his father hanged and his mother transported to Australia), through petty clerk, an unemployed married man living on his wife's meagre earnings, a would-be burglar, a skilled pickpocket and an attempted extortionist, to inheritor of his uncle's job as the official hangman. The early part of the novel is more humorous in tone, both in treatment of Jack's own experience, rendered with wry comedy and energetic language, and in the episodes in the Magpie and Punchbowl tavern, with its assembly of caricature types, humorous dialogues involving much punning, and comic episodes and intrigues. Though narrated humorously, however, even this part of Jack's narrative has grim and Gothic elements, just beneath the surface, from his treatment by his parents, their grim fates, his prospect of eventually following them to the gallows or the penal colony, his enduring of his aunt's verbal and physical violence, his situation as the half-starved and ragged under-clerk of Snavel and his witnessing of the crimes of Snavel and his fellow clerk, Wisp, and the despair of Wilmot. Such episodes and their humorous manner of being told are highly reminiscent of much of the earlier tradition of fictitious criminal autobiography, especially the Spanish picaresque novels, and the early parts of such recent Newgate novels as Gaspey's *Richmond* and *George Godfrey*, and Bulwer's *Paul Clifford*. In some respects, this part of *Jack Ketch* also anticipates Dickens's *Oliver Twist*, which began appearing in *Bentley's Miscellany* two years after publication of Whitehead's novel.

Jack's narrative develops a more consistently Gothic tone – with Jack as the self-confessed Gothic villain of lower middle-class life – after he has married Wisp's sister, Catharine, whom he effectively kills through neglect and mistreatment. These are the crimes of private life and the domestic sphere that Whitehead would continue to depict in his writing, whether treated humorously or pathetically. As a character, Catharine is the model wife, moral, virtuous and loving, but this characterization goes beyond the sentimental or even the Gothic as a representation of female victimization. Not only does Jack neglect his wife, lie to her, threaten to beat her, live off her small earnings as a bonnet-maker, ignore their child and leave it with a baby-farmer who probably lets it die, but he ignores her pleas to stay on the right side of the law, rebukes and mocks her concern for him and, it is suggested, urges her to turn prostitute in order to support him. These acts of indifference and cruelty are echoed in Jack's dealings with others, such as Haynes, Wilmot, Snavel and Misty, whom he treats as objects, to be exploited for his own benefit if opportunity arises. Yet Catharine submits herself completely to her husband. She abjects herself to him, but her abjection contrasts with his and thus emphasizes and heightens it. Her abjection to him is motivated by love and spiritualizes or transcendentalizes her. His abjection is motivated by purposeful rejection of love and social relationship. With each successive act of cruelty and self-interest, Jack reflects on his wilful hardening of his heart as though it were an accomplishment. In this, Jack resembles other characters in the novel, such as his brother-in-law Wisp, who confesses to him, "'my heart's like this inkstand, hard, and full of black filth'" (p. 147). Jack himself confesses a few pages later, after Catharine has died,

> The ice becomes harder and more stubborn, as I have heard (but I leave that to the philosophers to determine), after a thaw; and no sooner was Catharine consigned to the earth than my heart closed up. My feelings were as the bitter waters of Marah, and the coffin of my wife was not of the tree that might make them sweet. I had now become hardened.

> (p. 153)

To become hardened as Jack describes it is, as with James Wilson, to lose the capacity for human relationship that is exemplified in Catharine and so to be abjected from sociality, and society. Jack's Biblical allusion here, to the bitter waters of Marah, widens the implications of this situation. Jack refers to a passage in the book of Exodus in which Moses, having led the Israelites into the wilderness where the only water they can find is brackish, is shown by God a tree that, thrown into the water, makes it drinkable. This Old Testament passage was long understood by commentators as a prefiguration of Christ's martyrdom for humanity on the 'tree', or cross, in the New Testament,[76] and hence Jack's reference suggests that he is abjected not only from society but from divine salvation. The implication that Jack is spiritually abjected, or damned, is strengthened by association of the long-suffering domestic martyr Jack's wife, Catharine, with the 'tree' and hence with Christ.

Ironically, however, it is just this hardness and abjection that obtain for Jack the stable social identity and meaning he has been pursuing through the novel. His hard-heartedness and abjection fit him to succeed his uncle as the common hangman, a job that gives Jack financial security, frees him from the necessity of crime, secures him a kind of middle-class standing, and places him, as he boasts, in an 'office in the executive government' (p. 9) – a characteristic pun referring at once to the branch of government that carries out or executes legislation and to the state's function in hanging those condemned by the judiciary in their execution of the will of the legislature. By a double irony, however, Jack's new profession is one abhorred by society, leaving its practitioner in a condition of continuing social abjection. For Jack's profession is to break, by appointment and for pay, the sixth commandment of God in the Bible – represented terrifyingly to the wretched James Wilson in letters of fire: 'Thou shalt do no murder' (p. 133). But Jack, far from regretting this condition, or like his uncle being driven by it to melancholy or suicide, embraces it gladly as the culmination and closure of his 'progress' in life. This ironic closure is also the beginning of Jack's 'life', in the sense of his autobiographical text, which, as the opening chapter of the novel makes clear, he has written retrospectively after achieving his institutionalized and remunerated abjection.

Such a closure, in ironizing crime, destabilizes established notions and fixed definitions of what crime is. English 'crime' comes through French from Latin *crimen*, 'judgment, accusation, offence' from the Latin verb *cernere*, 'to decide, give judgment'. In general usage, a 'crime' is an act judged to be such by someone or some group, officially appointed or not. Historically, 'crime' has been applied to a wide range of socially disapproved actions, some punishable by law, some that may on occasion be punished by social convention and communal action and some merely disapproved of. The novel sets forth a wide variety of 'crimes' in the broad sense of wrongs that are done by one person to another, from those of Jack's parents to Snavel's absconding with Wilmot's money and Wisp's extortion of a share, to Haynes's extortion from his employer, Jack's casual picking of pockets, his abuse of his wife, Wisp's attempt to keep Jack's share of the burgled money, the suspicious fate of Jack's child at the hands of the baby-farmer, Misty's rejection by his own father, and so on and on. Some of these are illegal, or punishable by law, and some are not, some are punished and some not, some are punished by the state and some punished by personal vengeance or community condemnation, some cause remorse or worse and some do not. These 'crimes' range from petty cruelties in everyday life and relations through petty deception and cheating to statutory misdemeanours and felonies such as pickpocketing, burglary, and extortion, and what has long been regarded by society as the worst of crimes – murder. It is in fact the murders, covering a wide range and culminating ironically in Jack's appointment as state murderer, that most forcefully dramatize the question of what crime in general means in this novel. Haynes in effect kills himself out of remorse for what others in the novel seem able to do with no conscience. Jack's uncle, the official hangman, hangs himself for doing what he was appointed and required to do – including hanging his own brother, Jack's father. Snavel indirectly causes the death of Wilmot's daughter and is in turn killed by Wilmot. Wilson is self-tortured by his crime, it is treated with abhorrence by others and he is eventually convicted and hanged for it. Wilmot is convicted of Snavel's murder but he receives widespread public sympathy and is reprieved. Jack in effect kills his wife out of hard-heartedness and his child out of neglect; his neighbours condemn his behaviour and even threaten reprisal; but instead of being punished he is rewarded for that very hard-heartedness by being made official state murderer, by yet another irony, thanks to the approval of a clergyman and a sheriff – representatives respectively of church and state.

The theme that links all of these 'crimes', be they crimes by law, social convention, or community standards, is betrayal, set against its opposites, love, faithfulness, loyalty and forgiveness. Most of the characters who appear in the novel betray or attempt to betray others in one way or another and the few who do not are repeatedly, cruelly, or even fatally betrayed, but yet maintain a self-sacrificing and almost superhuman loyalty and forgiveness, if not to their betrayers then to other cherished relationships. Again, there is a wide variety and a network of such relationships, including among others Snavel's betrayal of Wilmot and Wilmot's fidelity to his daughter; Wisp's betrayal of Snavel and

Wisp's wife's betrayal of Wisp by attempting to seduce Jack once Wisp has been condemned to transportation; Jack's betrayal of his wife and her loyalty to him; Misty's betrayal by his father and by Clara and his forgiveness of both; Haynes's betrayal of and forgiveness by Marley and what Haynes feels to be his betrayal of his mother and his sweetheart. Beneath this recurring pattern of betrayal on the one hand and self-sacrifice, loyalty, and forgiveness on the other may lie a Christian doctrine, but the novel, whether regarded as Jack's or Whitehead's text, stops short of making this teaching explicit, as the moral of a particular incident or the novel as a whole. Nor does the novel develop a secular version of the Christian doctrine by sentimentalizing self-sacrifice, loyalty and forgiveness, as many or most novels and dramas of the time did. Indeed, the characters who exemplify these traits in this novel – or in any of Whitehead's novels and much of his short fiction – hardly seem to benefit from, prosper by, or achieve happiness through them but rather end up as abject or almost as abject as any other character. Catharine dies broken-hearted; Misty and Wilmot are left solitary figures. In Whitehead's fictional world there seems to be no redemption, religious or secular, but only abjection, of one kind or another.

This ideological burden of Whitehead's novel is not developed solely through its techniques and plot, however. Whitehead enriches the meaning of his novel by playing it off an already well known and well established literary genre. In the *Autobiography of Jack Ketch* Whitehead was developing and adapting the European tradition of fictitious criminal biography and autobiography, including rogue or picaresque romance, going back to the sixteenth century and extending to Whitehead's own day. Works in this tradition were humorous and satirical, but also often grotesque and grim, and – by Whitehead's time – in many cases politically subversive, merging with elements of Gothic romance and in the 1820s assuming the fictional form called the 'Newgate novel'. Whitehead's novel addresses this long and diverse tradition.

The form of the rogue romance can be found in such ancient works as Apuleius's *The Golden Ass* (or *Metamorphosis*), which had several editions and translations in the 1820s, and Petronius's *Satyricon*, with many eighteenth- and early nineteenth-century editions. The genre emerged in modern form with sixteenth- and seventeenth-century picaresque or 'rogue' narratives, including the Spanish novels *Lazarillo de Tormes* (anonymous, 1554), *Guzman de Alfarache* (Mateo Alamén, 1599–1604) and *The Swindler* (*El Buscón*, Francisco de Quevedo, 1662; known in Whitehead's day as *The Sharper*); *The English Rogue* (Richard Head and Francis Kirkman, 1665–71); and the German novel *Simplicissimus* (Hans von Grimmelshausen, 1668). The form then incorporated techniques of middle-class realism and 'philosophical' social criticism, later appropriating Enlightenment themes of reform. In the earlier eighteenth century there was the French novel *Gil Blas* (Alain-René Lesage, 1715–35), translated and often reprinted in English, followed by Daniel Defoe's fictional criminal autobiographies *Colonel Jack* (1722), *Moll Flanders* (1722), and *Roxana* (1724). In the mid-eighteenth century there were Henry Fielding's satirical novel, *Jonathan Wild* (1743), which is the fictionalized biography of a real-life thief turned thief-taker (1683–1725), and Fielding's more literary novels, *Joseph Andrews* (1742) and *Tom Jones* (1749), followed by novels of Tobias Smollett such as *Ferdinand Count Fathom* (1753). In the age of Revolution the tradition was adapted again, with English 'Jacobin' (or pro-Revolutionary) fiction such as William Godwin's *Things as They Are; or, The Adventures of Caleb Williams* (1794), Mary Wollstonecraft's *The Wrongs of Woman* (1798) and Thomas Holcroft's *Bryan Perdue* (1805); and English 'anti-Jacobin' (or counter-Revolutionary) novels such George Walker's *The Vagabond* (1799). Late eighteenth- and early nineteenth-century Gothic romances often featured or included *banditti* and outlaws, vicious or virtuous; rogue and criminal fiction had been adapted for the theatre since the eighteenth century; Byron popularized the glamorous outlaw-outcast-rebel in narrative poems such as *The Giaour* (1813) and *The Corsair* (1814); and the figure was reworked in the Romantic 'anti-heroes' of novels such as C. R. Maturin's *Melmoth the Wanderer* (1820) and James Hogg's *Confessions of a Justified Sinner* (1824). The form was adapted to Newgate themes in fiction in the two decades preceding *The Autobiography of Jack Ketch* and there was the renewed popularity in the 1820s of long established true crime compilations led by *The Newgate Calendar*.

By this time, changes in moral and cultural values and the intense public debate on crime and punishment made this long tradition of fictitious and factual criminal biography and autobiography controversial. A public and literary debate on crime fiction in general and the 'Newgate novel' in particular was already underway when Whitehead published *Jack Ketch*. True and fictional crime stories in newspapers and chapbooks were becoming increasingly popular, raising concerns among the upper and middle classes about the dangerous example these set to their lower-class and lower middle-class readers. At the same time, social and cultural critics addressing the middle classes increasingly insisted on certain kinds of social respectability and literature with a moral influence, encouraging an opinion that much earlier literature, including picaresque fiction and novels by Defoe, Fielding and Smollett, was indecent and corrupting and ought to be censored or suppressed. On the other side, public interest in, and parliamentary debate on, penal and law reform encouraged novelists to take up the picaresque tradition and renew the politically provocative reform fiction of the 1790s. In the mid-1820s the journalist Thomas Gaspey, who wrote fiction as a sideline, published two novels depicting crime from the petty to the capital, and criminals from low life to high. More prominently, by the later 1820s, Bulwer's novels *Pelham* (1828), *The Disowned* (1828), and *Paul Clifford* (1830), in particular, followed on the controversial popularity of villain-heroes of Gothic romances and Byron's pirate and rebel anti-heroes. These works stirred a debate on the dangers of glamourizing crime, even or especially when linked to overtly stated reformist views. For the fiction of crime and punishment was by now, and had been since the Revolution controversy of the 1790s at least, clearly related to the public debate on these subjects in newspapers and magazines, reform and anti-reform pamphlets, studies of crime and prisons, moral and social polemics and parliamentary committees, reports and legislation. Furthermore, there was clearly emerging a debate, *within* the fiction of crime and punishment, between various authors, worked out through both form and theme, and in which formal choices indicated ideological and political differences and alignments.

Whitehead could rely on many or most of his readers knowing some or all of these works and much of the meaning of *The Autobiography of Jack Ketch* may come from the way it plays along, with, off and against this diverse body of literature. *Jack Ketch* most closely resembles the earlier picaresque and rogue autobiographies, particularly in its account of Jack's early life and his ironic transformation at the end of the novel into a 'solid' citizen. Jack's birth and upbringing in the lower and criminal classes, his observation of trickery and betrayal, his experience of being abused and exploited, his social marginalization, his turn to crime, his learning to disregard conventional morality and his lucky accession to the job of public hangman, all told with humour and verve, resemble *Lazarillo de Tormes*, Quevedo's *The Swindler* and Defoe's novels *Moll Flanders* and *Colonel Jack*. *The Swindler* and its protagonist Pablos seem especially close to the early chapters of *Jack Ketch*: for example, Pablos's father, like Jack's, is hanged by his uncle the public hangman and the mothers of Pablos and Jack are both thieves. More generally, like one or other or all of these works, Whitehead's novel provides a 'realistic' or plausible representation of contemporary life lower down the social scale than that likely known to his readers, it has a well realized and ironically self-deprecating first-person narrator, it includes inset narratives by other characters to vary the presentation of central themes, it has a view of life as survival of the cleverest and most unscrupulous, and it presents society as inherently unequal, unjust and hypocritical. Whitehead's novel is somewhat less tumultuously episodic and open-ended than these predecessors, however, concentrating on fewer incidents and characters, thereby achieving greater intensity in representing the central character's radical social alienation and abjection.

More pronounced are Whitehead's departures from the mid eighteenth-century picaresque and rogue novel and the late eighteenth-century reformist novel. Like Fielding's eponymous anti-hero in *The Life of Jonathan Wild* and Smollett's in *The Adventures of Ferdinand Count Fathom*, Whitehead's Jack Ketch is a low-life villain whose adventures are recounted humorously, though in the first person rather than third and with a fortunate outcome rather than punishment for his misdeeds. Further, unlike Fielding's more famous rogue and picaresque novels, *Joseph Andrews* and *Tom Jones*, Whitehead's novel uses first-person rather than authoritative third-person narration, avoids broad social satire, has few learned references and allusions and does not turn its protagonist from an apparent scapegrace and criminal into a virtuous gentleman at the end. Like many reformist 'Jacobin' novels of the 1790s, such as Godwin's *Things as They Are*, Holcroft's *Hugh Trevor*, Wollstonecraft's *The Wrongs of Woman*, and Hays's *The Victim of Prejudice*, *Jack Ketch* uses first-person narration to enhance reader sympathy with the protagonist, combines representation of everyday life with elements of the Gothic and depicts lower- and middle-class life. Unlike those novels, Whitehead's does not indict systemic inequality and injustice to account for the crime, horror, and abjection it depicts; and it combines the everyday and the Gothic in representing lower middle-class life in order to present Whitehead's vision of negative Romantic irony rather than as a form of political protest. In fact, Whitehead's novel is more like those of the so-called 'Anti-Jacobin', or anti-reformist and anti-Revolutionary, writers of the 1790s, especially a first-person villain narrative such as George Walker's *The Vagabond* (3 vols, 1799), which also incorporates elements of earlier rogue novels.[77]

The engagement of Whitehead's novel with the more recent 'Newgate novels' is just as complex. Like Whitehead's *Jack Ketch*, Thomas Gaspey's *Richmond; or, Memoirs of a Bow Street Runner* (1827) and *George Godfrey* (1828) are fictitious autobiographies, titled for their rogue-like protagonist-narrators, include characters and episodes of wrongdoing and crime, are set mainly in contemporary middle- and lower middle-class life, incorporate narratives of other characters, have an apparently episodic structure, and contain few learned and literary references and allusions. But Gaspey's novels are longer than Whitehead's *Jack Ketch*, are more packed with adventures, including some in exotic places, emphasize the comic and humorous, have few Gothic-like episodes or elements, are more satirical than ironic, have sentimentally happy endings and despite their protagonists' mishaps and misdeeds do not contemplate social exclusion, crime, and abjection as *Jack Ketch* does. Gaspey's Newgate novels were important forerunners and models for Whitehead's and Whitehead likely read them, but it was Bulwer's *Paul Clifford* (1830) that opened a major public and literary debate during the 1830s on the representation of crime in fiction, a debate in which Whitehead's *Jack Ketch* may be seen to participate.

Paul Clifford appeared after Bulwer had already published several widely read and controversial novels that combined Godwinian 'Jacobin' reformism and Byronic dark sensibility. In *Paul Clifford*, the title character of which is partly based on the real highwaymen Dick Turpin and Tom King, Bulwer seemed to many to make the Godwinian-Byronic novel more ideologically dangerous by glamourizing crime and criminals. The controversy increased with the publication of further novels based on the lives of actual criminals, found in the *Newgate Calendar*, including Bulwer's *Eugene Aram* (1832) and William Harrison Ainsworth's *Rookwood* (1834, representing the highwayman Dick Turpin), with cheap imitations of these in serial parts, and popular dramas based on them.[78] Read against these works, Whitehead's novel could seem a response to them, grouped with though preceding and different from Dickens's *Oliver Twist* (serialized in *Bentley's Miscellany* 1837–8), Thackeray's *Catherine* (serialized in *Fraser's Magazine* 1839–40) and Whitehead's own *Richard Savage* (serialized in *Bentley's Miscellany* 1841–42). Unlike the Newgate novels that preceded it and especially the most controversial, *Paul Clifford*, Whitehead's *Jack Ketch* retains first-person narration, does not represent upper-class life, does not glamorize criminals or romanticize crime, neither indicts nor satirizes systemic inequality and injustice for causing misery and crime, includes a number of episodes of horror, has few literary and learned references and allusions, cannot be said to have a 'happy' ending, and is relentless in its representation of the social isolation, exclusion, and abjection of its principal character, as well as others.

Of those novelists who engaged in the Newgate debate after the publication of *Jack Ketch*, or, more accurately, capitalized on public interest in the Newgate debate and Newgate novels, Dickens and Thackeray followed Gaspey and Bulwer in satirizing systemic injustice and personal self-interest and they emphatically followed Whitehead in refusing to glamorize crime and criminals and in showing the degradation and abjection of lower-class and criminal life, while Ainsworth followed the example of Bulwer to fortune and fame. Thackeray perhaps equaled Whitehead in scenes of horror, with the burning at the stake of the novel's eponymous protagonist at the end of his novel *Catherine*, based on the real life murderess of the 'Newgate Calendar', Catherine Hayes. But in *Oliver Twist* Dickens seems purposely to reject Whitehead's perspective, perhaps referring obliquely to Whitehead and *Jack Ketch* when he has the narrator of *Oliver Twist* observe:

> Men who look on nature, and their fellow-men, and cry that all is dark and gloomy, are in the right; but the sombre colours are reflections from their own jaundiced eyes and hearts. The real hues are delicate, and need a clearer vision.[79]

By the time Dickens published these sentences in the serialized version of his novel in *Bentley's Miscellany*, of which he was the editor, he had also published some of Whitehead's darker short fiction there, including 'Edward Saville: A Transcript' and most of 'The Narrative of John Ward Gibson'. Dickens's first social novel could be read, in its trenchant criticism of institutions, its sentimentalizing of human goodness, its transformation of its apparently abject protagonist into a gentleman, its happy ending, and its avoidance of irony, to be an implied rejection of Whitehead's negative Romantic irony and plot of abjection.

It was later novelists, all probably ignorant of Whitehead's *Jack Ketch*, who would develop other representations of abjection in different directions, often around issues of crime and punishment. Their works include T. P. Prest's *Newgate: A Romance* (1847, included in this series), Fyodor Dostoevsky's *Crime and Punishment* (1866), Franz Kafka's *In the Penal Colony* (1919), Louis-Ferdinand Céline's *Death on the Installment Plan* (*Mort à crédit*, 1936), Samuel Beckett's trilogy *Molloy, Malone Dies*, and *The Unnamable* (1951–3), Jean Genet's *The Thief's Journal* (*Journal du voleur*, 1949), and Jim Thompson's pulp crime fiction of the 1940s to 1960s. These later novels cast light on *Jack Ketch* in different ways, but Genet's *The Thief's Journal* and Thompson's pulp fiction may serve to show briefly how such modern works can illuminate Whitehead's novel as a distinctive and disturbing 'Newgate narrative'.

Like Whitehead's novel, Genet's purports to be an autobiography, recounts a succession of crimes of various kinds, contains subsidiary stories of criminals and crimes, reflects ironically and even humorously on its subject matter, recurs repeatedly to instances of sacrifice and betrayal and, most important, dwells on the theme of abjection as social fall and exclusion, yet as a kind of radical truth of the human condition accessible particularly to those who embrace abjection. Genet's narrator repeatedly announces his fascination with and admiration for treachery, theft and homosexuality, just as Whitehead's Jack flaunts his betrayals and thefts as practices that willfully transgress the values of respectable middle-class society. Genet's 'Jean', like Whitehead's Jack, pursues abjection as a triumph and success, but less as a rejection of the humane and social or transcendence of convention and more as a destabilization, disruption, and disintegration of 'non-criminal' values and the social practices and political institutions based on them. Like Whitehead's *Jack Ketch*, Thompson's *The Killer Inside Me* (1952) is a first-person, often humorous and verbally playful narrative of a man, in fact an officer of the law, engaging in crime and even murder as a willful rejection of love and sociality and embracing of his own abjection. In fact, a feature of much modern popular 'hard-boiled' crime fiction is the lawman of some kind, publicly or self- appointed, who is hardened, often criminal, and psychologically, spiritually and often materially abject – socially alienated, marginalized, isolated and deliberately so.

Genet's novel was taken up as an oppositional, counter-cultural, even revolutionary manifesto by such figures as the novelist and philosopher of existentialism, Jean-Paul Sartre. Thompson's fiction had a modest success in its time and has since become a literary cult. Whitehead's novel doesn't go as far as Genet's or Thompson's, and it retains only a small place in nineteenth-century literary culture. It, too, offers a viewpoint from outside conventional middle-class society, but it is a view from the developing cultural space of the literary and more particularly literary bohemia, rather than from a self-consciously vanguardist sexual, social and literary counter-culture, or a dissident, populist, alienated subculture. Nevertheless, *The Autobiography of Jack Ketch* remains not only a distinctive formulation of the 'Newgate narrative' and an important if long overlooked link between earlier and modernist representations of the abjection of criminality as a destabilizing and thereby potentially reformative kind of knowledge. Whitehead's novel is also a complexly ironic, richly allusive, and original if disturbing treatment of a theme that would become central in modern philosophy, literature, and human and social experience – abjection. Perhaps, as Jean Genet's thief-narrator suggests, in the epigraph to this introduction, the final irony of a work such as *The Autobiography of Jack Ketch* is this: its subject requires or inspires a literary achievement that compensates for, if it does not cancel, that subject.

Notes:

1.   J. Genet, *Journal du voleur* (Paris: Gallimard, 1949), pp. 219–20:
        For my abjection was my despair. And despair was strength itself—and at the same time the means to wipe it away. But if the work is most beautiful, demanding the the energy of the greatest despair, the poet had to love men to undertake such an effort. And he had to succeed. It is well for men to distance themselves from a profound work if it is the cry of a man monstrously sunk in himself.
2.   C. Whitehead, application to the Royal Literary Fund, December 1852; British Library, Royal Literary Fund records, case 856; subsequent references to Royal Literary Fund documents are to this case; the *New Dictionary of National Biography* states that Whitehead's father was 'possibly the Joseph Whitehead listed in contemporary trade directories as the proprietor of wine and brandy vaults in Tottenham Court Road'.
3.   In Whitehead's December 1852 application to the Royal Literary Fund for financial assistance he gives his birth date as 4 September but in his application of December 1854 he gives it as 8 September.
4.   Quoted in H. T. Mackenzie Bell, *Charles Whitehead: A Forgotten Genius*, new edn (London: Ward, Lock and Bowden, 1894), p. xvi.
5.   Supporting letter from Henry Grey, with Whitehead's application to the Royal Literary Fund, December 1852.
6.   Whitehead's application to the Royal Literary Fund, 31 October 1843.
7.   Supporting letter of Henry Grey, with Whitehead's application to the Royal Literary Fund, December 1852.
8.   One stanza, referring obliquely to a love interest, was dropped in the 1849 republication of *The Solitary*.
9.   Mackenzie Bell, *Charles Whitehead*, p. 33.
10.   *Friendship's Offering, and Winter's Wreath* (1833), pp. 241–48.
11.   *Friendship's Offering* (1834), pp. 325–45.
12.   In *The Solitary, and Other Poems* (1849), Whitehead altered the first line: 'As yonder lamp, in my vacated room,'.
13.   In 1849 Whitehead changed 'commence' to 'begin'.
14.   *Friendship's Offering* (1835), pp. 140–1.

15. *Friendship's Offering* (1835), pp. 140–3; 289–94.
16. The letterpress title page is dated 1834, though the engraved title page is dated 1933.
17. One of the Baggs was T. Bagg, engraver.
18. The *Court Magazine; or Belle Assemblée* had absorbed *La Belle Assemblée; or Bell's Court and Fashionable Magazine* (1806–32) and then turned into the *Court Magazine and Monthly Critic* (1836–7), after which it was absorbed into the *Lady's Magazine and Museum of the Belles Lettres* (1838). This history indicates the instability of fashionable literary periodical publishing at the time.
19. Signed 'Omega', *Court Magazine*, 1:4 (October 1832): 184–7; reprinted in *Smiles and Tears* 3 vols (London, 1847), III.303–14.
20. Signed 'Omega', *Court Magazine*, 1:5 (November 1832): 250–53; reprinted in *Smiles and Tears*, I.276–88.
21. Signed 'Omega', *Court Magazine*, 2:2 (February 1833): 85–90; reprinted in *Smiles and Tears*, I.123–44.
22. *Court Magazine*, 11:4 (October 1837): 168–73; reprinted in *Smiles and Tears*, III.124–43.
23. Literary references in this passage: Thomas Noon Talfourd, *Ion* (1836), a popular verse tragedy; Sir Edward Bulwer (1803–73), poet, prolific and popular novelist and author of several Newgate novels, and later a politician; Felicia Hemans (1793–1835), prolific and widely respected author of historical narrative poems, lyrics, memorial poetry and verse drama.
24. *Library of Fiction; or, Family Story-Teller, Consisting of Original Tales, Essays, and Sketches of Character*, 2 (April 1837) 257–76 (p. 274).
25. *Library of Fiction*, no. 2 (May 1836): 58–73.
26. G. Hodder, *Memories of My Time, Including Reminiscences of Eminent Men* (London: Tinsley Brothers, 1870), 355–6.
27. K. J. Fielding, 'Charles Whitehead and Charles Dickens', *Review of English Studies*, new series. 3 (1952): 141–54 (p. 142).
28. Whitehead's application to the Royal Literary Fund, 21 June 1836.
29. Letter from Charles Dickens to Richard Bentley, Dec. 1836, *Letters of Charles Dickens*, vol. 1, ed. M. House and G. Storey (Oxford: Clarendon Press, 1965), pp. 207–8.
30. *Bentley's Miscellany*, 1 (February 1837), pp. 155–65.
31. *Bentley's Miscellany*, 1 (May 1837), pp. 461–4, on p. 463.
32. *Bentley's Miscellany*, 2 (August 1837).
33. *Bentley's Miscellany*, 2 (September 1837), pp. 240–53; 3 (April 1838), pp. 355–66; 4 (October 1838): pp. 383–96.
34. *Bentley's Miscellany*, 4 (October 1838), p. 396.
35. Part 3, stanza 26, ll. 226–34.
36. Whitehead's application to the Royal Literary Fund, 24 November 1837.
37. Mackenzie Bell, *Charles Whitehead*, p. 30.
38. I have been unable to trace a publication by Whitehead with this title. Letter dated London, 4 February 1843; British Library, Add. MSS, 46650 f.265.
39. C. Turnbull, *Australian Lives: Charles Whitehead; James Stephens; Peter Lalor; George Francis Train; Francis Adams; Paddy Hannan* (Melbourne, Canberra, Sydney: F. W. Cheshire, 1965), p. 5.
40. *Ketch-penny*: or catchpenny; designed merely to sell.
41. Mackenzie Bell, *Charles Whitehead*, pp. 19–20, 31–2.
42. British Library Add. MSS 46613 f. 332.

43. Whitehead's application to the Royal Literary Fund, 31 October 1843.
44. Whitehead's application to the Royal Literary Fund, December 1852.
45. Quoted in Mackenzie Bell, *Charles Whitehead*, p. xiii.
46. John Leech (1817–64), humorous artist and illustrator, working for *Bentley's Miscellany* and *Punch*; he illustrated Whitehead's novel *Richard Savage*.
47. Quoted in Mackenzie Bell, *Charles Whitehead*, pp. xiii–xiv.
48. Mackenzie Bell, *Charles Whitehead*, p. 32.
49. Whitehead's application to the Royal Literary Fund, December 1852.
50. Letter dated 9 July 1845, *The Letters of Charles Dickens*, vol. 4, ed. Kathleen Tillotson (Oxford: Clarendon Press, 1977), p. 330.
51. British Library, Add. MSS, 42993 ff. 872–904.
52. For publication details of the essay mentioned here, see the Bibliography.
53. *Bentley's Miscellany*, 22 (Aug. 1847), pp. 119–25.
54. *The Letters of Charles Dickens*, vol. 5, ed. G. Storey and K. J. Fielding (Oxford: Clarendon Press, 1981), pp. 538-39.
55. Hodder, *Memories of My Time* (1870), pp. 356–58.
56. Whitehead's application to the Royal Literary Fund, December 1852.
57. C. Pearson to H. T. Mackenzie Bell, 25 Sept. [18]84; Mackenzie Bell Papers, University of California at Los Angles Library, Special Collections, box 9.
58. 'Off! Off!', *Household Words*, 8:198 (Jan. 1854), pp. 442–5; 'Nemesis', *Household Words*, 13:317–318 (19 and 26 April 1856), pp. 326–34, pp. 344–53; these attributions are made by K. J. Fielding who says they are 'presumably' by Whitehead; K. J. Fielding, 'Charles Whitehead and Charles Dickens', *Review of English Studies*, 3 (1952), 141–54, on p. 154.
59. Reference to the Melbourne writer Fergus Hume's best-selling novel, *The Mystery of a Hansom Cab* (London: 1886)
60. J. Smith, Appendix, in Mackenzie Bell, *Charles Whitehead*, pp. 295–6. Referred to here, besides figures already documented elsewhere in this introduction, are John Wilson (1785–1854), humorous writer under the name 'Christopher North', and novelist; and poet and artist Dante Gabriel Rossetti (1828–1882).
61. Turnbull, *Australian Lives,* p. 19.
62. Quoted in Turnbull, *Australian Lives*, p. 20.
63. On the social psychology of abjection see J. Kristeva, *Powers of Horror: An Essay on Abjection*, trans. L. S. Roudiez (New York, NY: Columbia University Press, 1982). Kristeva's highly suggestive approach is based on psychoanalytic theory, whereas the one taken here is informed by social constructionism, or the assumption that individuals are constructed as such in relation to the society in which they live. For an effort to converge psychoanalytic theory with social theory, and dealing with the topic of abjection, see K. Oliver, *Colonization of Psychic Space: A Psychoanalytic Social Theory of Oppression* (Minneapolis, MN: University of Minnesota Press, 2004).
64. See P. Bourdieu, *La Distinction: critique sociale du jugement* (Paris: Les Éditions de Minuit, 1979); *Distinction: A Social Critique of the Judgment of Taste*, trans. R. Nice (Cambridge, MA: Harvard University Press, 1984).
65. E. P. Thompson, *The Making of the English Working Class*, rev. edn (Harmondsworth: Penguin Books, 1968), pp. 411–40.
66. B. Hilton, *The Age of Atonement: The Influence of Evangelicalism on Social and Economic Thought, 1785–1865* (Oxford: Clarendon Press, 1988).

67. E. Chambers and A. Rees, *Cyclopædia; or, An Universal Dictionary of Arts and Sciences* 5 vols (1778–88): 'Jack-Ketch is a name given by the populace to the common hangman' ('Jack-Ketch', vol. 2, 1779); the phrase was in circulation since the 1670s, at least, perhaps from an actual executioner of the time, known for the brutal way in which he did his work.

68. See G. D. Robin, 'The Executioner: His Place in English Society', *The British Journal of Sociology*, 15:3 (Sept. 1964): 234–53.

69. See for example, A. Knapp and W. Baldwin, *The Newgate Calendar*, 4 vols (London: J. Robins, 1824–6), vol. 1, pp. 114–16.

70. J. Wade, *A Political Dictionary . . . Being an Illustration and Commentary on all Words, Phrases, and Proper Names in the Vocabulary of Corruption* (London: T. Dolby, 1821), entry 'Tax-gatherer', p. 112.

71. *Proceedings of the Third Co-operative Congress . . .*, ed. W. Carpenter (London: William Strange, 1832), p. 25.

72. *The Hangman and the Judge; or, A Letter from Jack Ketch to Mr. Justice Alderson; Revised by the Ordinary of Newgate, and Edited by Edward Gibbon Wakefield, Esq.* (London: Effingham Wilson [1833]), pp. 5–6; for Wakefield, Beccaria, Bentham, Romilly, and Buxton see the headnotes to selections from their reform writings in vol. 1 in this series; Basil Montagu (1770–1851) was a lawyer and reformer of the laws of bankruptcy and a staunch campaigner for reduction of capital crimes and prison reform; Sir Robert Peel (1788–1850) was a Tory (conservative) politician and prime minister who nevertheless introduced many reforms, including consolidation of laws relating to crime and a modern kind of police force; William Ewart (1767–1842) was a politician and campaigner for legal reform, especially reduction of the number of capital crimes.

73. *lignum vitæ*: a kind of tree used in medicines, from Latin meaning 'wood of life'.

74. 'The London 1839 Public House & Publican Directory as listed in London 1839 Pigots Directory', http://londonpublichouse.com/LondonPubs1839/index.shtml, accessed 5 August 2007.

75. B. Victor, *An Epistle to Sir Richard Steele, on his Play, call'd The Conscious Lovers*, 2nd edn (London: W. Chetwood, 1722), p. 28.

76. For example, J. Hall, *Contemplations on the Historical Passages of the Old and New Testaments*, originally published 1612-26 but reprinted in popular editions into the nineteenth century; Book 5, Contemplation 1.

77. See selections in volume one of this series.

78. Dick Turpin, Eugene Aram, and Jack Sheppard were included in the various editions of the *Newgate Calendar* and represented in chapbooks before publication of *Jack Ketch*; Tom King, the 'gentleman highwayman', was known through his association with Turpin; dramas based on *Paul Clifford* and *Eugene Aram* were staged in 1832.

79. C. Dickens, *Oliver Twist*, ch. 34; book 2, ch. 11 in the original serial publication.

SELECT BIBLIOGRAPHY

I. Books, Written or Edited

The Solitary: A Poem, in Three Parts (London: Effingham Wilson, 1831); republished with other poems in 1849.

Lives and Exploits of English Highwaymen, Pirates, and Robbers, 2 vols. (London: Bull and Churton, 1834). Paris (in French), 1835; Philadelphia, PA, 1835; Hartford, CT, 1836; Hartford, CT, 1838; Hartford, CT, 1840; London, 1842; Hartford, CT, 1847; Hartford, CT, 1849; Hartford, CT, 1854; New York, NY, 1860; London, 1883.

The Autobiography of Jack Ketch (London: Edward Churton, 1834). Dated 1835. Philadelphia, 1835; Paris (in French), 1839; as *The Autobiography of a Notorious Legal Functionary*; 2nd edn. (London: Edward Churton, 1836); 1838 (3rd edn); 1840 (4th edn); Philadelphia, PA 1835.

Victoria Victrix: Stanzas Addressed to Her Majesty the Queen (London: Edward Churton, 1838).

Richard Savage: A Romance of Real Life, first published in parts in 1841–2 in *Bentley's Miscellany*. 3 vols (London: Richard Bentley, 1842); 1844; 1845 (Bentley's Standard Novels); 1896; *c.* 1900; 1903.

The Earl of Essex: A Romance, 3 vols. (London: Richard Bentley, 1843).

Memoirs of Joseph Grimaldi. Edited by 'Boz'. With Illustrations by George Cruikshank. A New Edition, with Notes and Additions, Revised by Charles Whitehead (London: Richard Bentley, 1846.

Smiles and Tears; or, The Romance of Life, 3 vols (London: Richard Bentley, 1847).

Woman's Worth; or, The Three Trials: A Play in Four Acts. 1846. Not published.

The Poetical Works of William Cowper. With a Memoir by Charles Whitehead (London: W. H. Reid, 1847; republished, London: J. Kendrick, 1849, 1852, 1857).

The Cavalier: A Drama in Three Acts. Produced at Haymarket Theatre, London, 1836; published 1849 with *The Solitary, and Other Poems* (see below).

The Solitary, and Other Poems; With The Cavalier, a Play (London: Richard Bentley, 1849).

The Life and Times of Sir Walter Ralegh: With Copious Extracts from his 'History of the World' (London: N. Cooke, 1854).

II. Pieces in Periodicals and Books

Fiction

'The Malcontent', *Monthly Magazine*, 10 (November 1830), pp. 522–8.

'My Father's Legacy', by 'Omega', *Court Magazine*, 1:4 (October 1832), pp. 184–87; reprinted in *Smiles and Tears* 3 vols, (1847), vol. 3, pp. 303–314.

'History of the Decline and Fall of Little Felstead' by 'Gibbon Redivivus', signed 'Omega', *Court Magazine*, 1:5 (November 1832), pp. 250–3; reprinted in *Smiles and Tears*, vol. 1, pp. 276–88.

'The West Indian', by 'Omega', *Court Magazine*, 1:6 (December 1832), pp. 280–3; reprinted in *Smiles and Tears*, vol. 1, pp. 145–58.

'The Captain', by 'Omega', *Court Magazine*, 2:1 (January 1833), pp. 43–6; reprinted in *Smiles and Tears*, vol. 3, pp. 292–301.

'The Miniature', by 'Omega', fiction, *Court Magazine*, 2:2 (February 1833), pp. 85–90; reprinted in *Smiles and Tears*, vol. 1, pp. 123–44.

'Confessions of a Lazy Man', by 'Omega', *Court Magazine*, 2:4 (April 1833), pp. 185–8; reprinted in *Smiles and Tears*, vol. 1, pp. 232–41.

'The First Day of Term', by 'Omega', *Court Magazine*, 3:1 (July 1833), pp. 20–23; reprinted in *Smiles and Tears*, vol. 1, pp. 263–75.

'The Choice', by 'Omega', *Court Magazine*, 3:2 (August 1833), pp. 55–8; reprinted in *Smiles and Tears*, vol. 3, pp. 210–22.

'The Modest Man', by 'Omega', *Court Magazine*, 3:4 (October 1833), pp. 161–6; reprinted in *Smiles and Tears*, vol. 2, pp. 103–22.

'The Self-Tormentor', by 'Omega', *Court Magazine*, 3:5 (November 1833), pp. 210–15; reprinted in *Smiles and Tears*, vol. 1, pp. 159–75.

'Some Account of the Late Daniel Lambert, Esq. With Selections from His Papers', by 'Omega', *Court Magazine*, 4:4 (April 1834), pp. 137–43; reprinted in *Smiles and Tears*, vol. 2, pp. 245–65.

'The Rivals', *Court Magazine*, 5:1 (July 1834), pp. 28–34; reprinted in the *English Annual* (1836), pp. 156-72; reprinted in *Smiles and Tears*, vol. 1, pp. 176–95.

'The Whimsey Papers. No. I' (unsigned), *Court Magazine*, 5:3 (September 1834), pp. 115–18, with the subtitle 'No. I.—Introduction—Thoughts on Procrastination—Mope the Poet for Posterity, &c.'; reprinted in *Smiles and Tears*, vol. 2, pp. 219–29.

'The Whimsey Papers. No. II' (unsigned), *Court Magazine*, 6:4 (April 1835), pp. 166-70, with the subtitle 'Vague Conclusions Concerning Selfishness and Benevolence—Vivid the Casuist—Skinflint the Misanthrope—Green, the Good-Natured Man'; reprinted in *Smiles and Tears*, vol. 2, pp. 230–44.

'Mr. Firedrake Fidget', *Library of Fiction*, 1 (April 1836), pp. 26–33; reprinted in *Smiles and Tears*, vol. 2, pp. 204–18.

'Some Passages in the Life of Francis Loosefish, Esq.', *Library of Fiction*, 1 (May 1836), pp. 58–73; reprinted in *Smiles and Tears*, vol. 1, pp. 1–35.

'Sebella: A Tale of Venice', *Library of Fiction*, 1 (August 1836), pp. 278–80. Signed 'C. W.'

'The Man of Two Lives', *Monthly Magazine*, 22 (October 1836), pp. 331–46; reprinted in American periodical *The Albion*, 3 December 1836; reprinted in *Smiles and Tears*, vol. 1, pp. 196–231.

'Edward Saville: A Transcript', *Bentley's Miscellany*, 1 (February 1837), pp. 155–65; reprinted as 'The Elopement' in American periodicals *Every Body's Album* (March 1837), the *New-Yorker* (April 1837), and *Spirit of the Times* (April 1837).

'Who'd Have Thought It?', *Court Magazine*, 10:2 (February 1837), pp. 72–80.

'A Word or Two about Geoffrey Gooch', *Library of Fiction*, 2 (April 1837), pp. 257–76; reprinted in *Smiles and Tears*, vol. 3, pp. 223–49.

'The Youth's New Vade-Mecum', *Bentley's Miscellany*, 1 (May 1837), pp. 461–64.

'The Flamborough Election', *Court Magazine*, 11:2 (August 1837), pp. 55–61; reprinted in *Smiles and Tears*, vol. 3, pp. 167–85.

'The Narrative of John Ward Gibson', *Bentley's Miscellany*, 2 (September 1837), pp. 240–53, 3 (April 1838), pp. 355–66; 4 (Oct. 1838), pp. 383–96; reprinted in *Smiles and Tears*, vol. 2, pp. 289–322; vol. 3, pp. 1–60.

'A Memoir Found in a Gentleman's Pocket-Book', presented to the Court Magazine by Mr. Quizley, *Court Magazine*, 11:3 (September 1837), pp. 120–26; reprinted in *Smiles and Tears*, vol. 1, pp. 101–122.

'The False One: A Tale of Russell Square', *Court Magazine*, 11:4 (October 1837), pp. 168–73; reprinted in *Smiles and Tears*, vol. 3, pp. 124–43.

'The Clever Young Man', *Court Magazine*, 11:6 (December 1837), pp. 249–54; reprinted in *Smiles and Tears*, vol. 2, pp. 308-28.

'The Three Ravens', *Bentley's Miscellany*, 9 (February 1841) pp. 180–6; reprinted in *Smiles and Tears*, vol. 2, pp. 146–73.

'Wanted—A Widow', *Bentley's Miscellany*, 9 (March 1841), pp. 319-28; reprinted in American periodical the *Albion* (April 1841); reprinted in *Smiles and Tears*, vol. 2, pp. 144–66.

'Eleanor Bingley', *Bentley's Miscellany*, 10 (September 1841), pp. 261–70; reprinted in American periodical the *Spirit of the Times* (October 1841); reprinted in *Smiles and Tears*, vol. 2, pp. 123–45.

'Old Green, Offley's Regular Customer', by 'A Man About Town', *Bentley's Miscellany*, 11 (1842), pp. 329–33.

'Orlando Griffin', *Bentley's Miscellany*, 14 (September 1843), pp. 287–96; reprinted in *Smiles and Tears* as 'All's Well That Ends Well', vol. 3, pp. 287–96.

'Five-and-Thirty or Thereabouts', *Bentley's Miscellany*, 14 (December 1843), pp. 562–71; reprinted in *Smiles and Tears*, vol. 3, pp. 80–101.

'Miss Jifkins's Benefit', *Bentley's Miscellany*, 16 (October 1844), pp. 343–49; reprinted in *Smiles and Tears*, vol. 2, pp. 61–77.

'Confessions of De Loude Chisleham', *Bentley's Miscellany*, 17 (January 1845), pp. 70–82; reprinted in *Smiles and Tears*, vol. 1, pp. 70–100.

'Mr. Yellowly's Doings', *Bentley's Miscellany*, 17 (May 1845), pp. 490-504; reprinted in *Smiles and Tears*, vol. 1, pp. 36-67; reprinted in American periodical the *Anglo American* (June 1845).

'A Curvet or Two in the Career of Tom Wilkins', *Bentley's Miscellany*, 18 (September 1845), pp. 229–37; reprinted in *Smiles and Tears*, vol. 3, pp. 102–23.

'Dick Sparrow's Evening "Out"', *Bentley's Miscellany*, 18 (November 1845), pp. 498–508; reprinted in *Smiles and Tears*, vol. 3, pp. 55–79.

'The Suburban Retreat', *Bentley's Miscellany*, 22 (August 1847), pp. 119-25.

'The Two Painters', *Bentley's Miscellany*, 30 (August 1851), pp. 148–57.

'The Orphan', serial fiction in unknown weekly publication; not completed; summer–autumn 1852.

'Nemesis. In Four Chapters', *Household Words*, 13 (19 and 26 April 1856), pp. 326–34; 344–53.

'Emma Latham; or, Right at Last', *My Note Book* (Melbourne, Australia) from 13 February 1858.

Non-fiction

'Songs of England', by 'Omega', *Court Magazine*, 2:6 (June 1833), pp. 299–304.

'The Stock-Broker' and 'Tavern Heads', in *Heads of the People; or, Portraits of the English*, ed. Douglas Jerrold, illustrations by Kenny Meadows, 2 vols (London: Robert Tyas, 1840–41), vol. 1, pp. 17–24, 113–68.

'Flora Macdonald: The Heroine of the Rebellion of 1745', review, *Bentley's Miscellany*, 19 (April 1846), pp. 325–8; reprinted in American periodical the *Anglo American* (April 1846).

'Pizarro and His Followers', *Bentley's Miscellany*, 22 (September 1847), pp. 306–12.

'The Wooden Walls of Old England', review, *Bentley's Miscellany*, 22 (November 1847), pp. 513–19.

'The Insurrection in St. Petersburg in 1825; with some Account of the Conspirators', prose, *Bentley's Miscellany*, 22 (December 1847), pp. 615–24.

'Aliwal and Sir Harry Smith', *Bentley's Miscellany*, 23 (March 1848), pp. 317–21.

'Bohn's Standard Library', review, in 'Literary Notices'. *Bentley's Miscellany*, 23 (March 1848), pp. 323–4.

'Caricatures and Caricaturists', review, *Bentley's Miscellany*, 24 (October 1848), pp. 419–26.

'Memoir of Captain Marryat, R. N., C. B.', *Bentley's Miscellany*, 24 (November 1848), pp. 524–30; reprinted in American periodicals the *Albion* (November 1848) and the *Eclectic Magazine of Foreign Literature* (January 1849).

'Schiller and His Contemporaries', review, *Bentley's Miscellany*, 25 (February 1849), pp. 193–6.

'"Arthur Bouverie", and "Hylton House" (novels)', in 'Literature', reviews, *Bentley's Miscellany*, 28 (July 1850), pp. 109, 110.

'Banks and Bankers', review, *Bentley's Miscellany*, 28 (July 1850), pp. 84–5.

'Ebenezer Elliott, The Corn-Law Rhymer', review, *Bentley's Miscellany*, 28 (October 1850), pp. 416–18.

'Dr. Layard and Nineveh', review, *Bentley's Miscellany*, 29 (January 1851), pp. 102–6.

'The Railway Mania', review, *Bentley's Miscellany*, 29 (January 1851), pp. 111–12.

'The Literary Career of William Ellery Channing', review, *Bentley's Miscellany*, 25 (January 1849), pp. 88–90; reprinted in American periodical the *Eclectic Magazine of Foreign Literature* (March 1851).

'Swedish Novelists', review, *Bentley's Miscellany*, 30 (August 1851), pp. 212–14.

'Memoir of the Late Dr. Lingard', *Bentley's Miscellany*, 30 (September 1851), pp. 225–30.

'Off! Off!', *Household Words*, 8:198 (January 1854), pp. 442–45.

Poetry

'Viola', *Friendship's Offering*, (1833) pp. 241–8.

'Ippolito: A Chimera in Rhyme', *Friendship's Offering*, 1834, pp. 325–45; reprinted in *The Solitary, and Other Poems* (1849).

'Six Sonnets' and 'The Riddle of Life', *Friendship's Offering*, 1835 (i.e., late 1834), pp. 140–3; 289–94; reprinted in *The Solitary, and Other Poems* (1749); reprinted in American peridoical the *Museum of Foreign Literature, Science, and Art* (December 1834).

The Squib Annual of Poetry, Politics, and Personalities for 1836, edited by Charles Whitehead (London: n. p., 1836).

'Rather Hard to Take', *Bentley's Miscellany*, 2 (Aug. 1837), pp. 181–2.

'The Story of Jasper Brooke', *Illuminated Magazine*, 4 (January 1845), pp. 152–6; (April 1845), pp. 311–16); reprinted in *The Solitary, and Other Poems* (1849).

'The Spanish Marriage: A Dramatic Story, in Three Parts', *Victorian Monthly Magazine*, 1:2 (July 1859), pp. 167–78, signed 'C. W.'

Secondary Sources

Fielding, K. J., 'Charles Whitehead and Charles Dickens', *Review of English Studies*, N. S. 3 (1952), pp. 141–54.

Hodder, G., *Memories of My Time, Including Reminiscences of Eminent Men* (London: Tinsley Brothers, 1870).

Mackenzie Bell, H. T. E., *Charles Whitehead: A Forgotten Genius* (London: Ward, Lock, and Bowden, 1894). Augmented edition of Mackenzie Bell, *A Forgotten Genius: Charles Whitehead* (London: Elliot Stock, 1884).

The Nineteenth Century Index: http://c19index.chadwyck.com/marketing/index.jsp

Turnbull, C., *Australian Lives: Charles Whitehead; James Stephens; Peter Lalor; George Francis Train; Francis Adams; Paddy Hannan* (Melbourne, Canberra, and Sydney, F. W. Cheshire, 1965).

—'Charles Whitehead', *Australian Dictionary of Biography*, online edition, 2006. http://www.adb.online.anu.edu.au/biogs/A060422b.htm

A CHARLES WHITEHEAD CHRONOLOGY

1804	Born in London to wine merchant and his wife, eldest of four boys and three girls (4 September).
1820s	Working as a clerk in a commercial house.
1830s	Contributes to various periodicals and literary annuals, including the *Monthly Magazine* and *Court Magazine*.
1831	Publishes meditative poem, *The Solitary*.
1833	Marries Mary Ann Loomes (29 October).
1834	Publishes compilation *Lives and Exploits of English Highwaymen, Pirates and Robbers* which went through several editions. Publishes novel, *Autobiography of Jack Ketch* (dated 1835).
1835	Edits the *Squib Annual* (dated 1836) for Chapman and Hall.
1836	Second edition of *Jack Ketch* as *Autobiography of a Notorious Legal Functionary*. Asks the Royal Literary Fund for financial help and is granted twenty pounds (June). Play *The Cavalier* produced at the Haymarket Theatre (15 September). Edits publisher Chapman and Hall's *Library of Fiction* (discontinued 1837), with contributions of his own.
1837	Contributes short fictions and comic poems to new literature magazine, *Bentley's Miscellany*, edited by Charles Dickens. Again requests help from the Royal Literary Fund and is granted fifteen pounds (November).
1838	Third edition of *Jack Ketch*. Publishes poem *Victoria Victrix*, celebrating the queen's accession.
1839	Anonymous French novel, *Mémoires du bourreau de Londres*, published at Paris, absorbs some characters and incidents from *Autobiography of Jack Ketch*, but is otherwise largely a different work.
1840	Revival of play *The Cavalier*. Publishes 'The Stockbroker' and 'Tavern Heads' in *Heads of the People* (vol. 1, 1840), edited by Douglas Jerrold with illustrations by Kenny Meadows.
1841	Begins serializing novel *Richard Savage*, based on an eighteenth-century figure, in *Bentley's Miscellany*; completed 1842.
1843	Publishes historical novel *The Earl of Essex* (3 volumes). Publishes short fictions in *Bentley's Miscellany*. With supporting letter from Charles Dickens, requests

financial help from the Royal Literary Fund, stating that he and his wife are being supported by his sisters, and is granted twenty pounds (October).

1844–52 Works for publisher Bentley assessing manuscripts and revising and correcting works for publication.

1845 Publishes short fictions in *Bentley's Miscellany*. Publishes two pieces in the *Illustrated Magazine*, edited by Douglas Jerrold.

1846 Contributes material to new edition of Dickens's *Memoirs of Joseph Grimaldi*, based on life of a famous clown, it goes through several editions. Writes *Woman's Worth; or, The Three Trials: A Play in Four Acts* (not published) for Royal Surrey Theatre.

1847 Publishes *Smiles and Tears; or, The Romance of Life*, a compilation of his short fiction previously published in magazines. Contributes a memoir to edition of *Poetical Works* of William Cowper; it goes through several editions.

1849 Publishes *The Solitary and Other Poems*, by subscription, to pay for maintenance of his insane brother in an asylum.

1850 Revival of play *The Cavalier* at Sadler's Wells Theatre.

1852 Mother dies. Dismissed as publisher's reader by Bentley after eight years service; begins serialization of a fictional work apparently entitled 'The Orphan', in a new newspaper, but quarrels with the editor and it is dropped. With supporting letters from Dickens and Douglas Jerrold, requests financial help from the Royal Literary Fund, and is granted twenty pounds (1 December).

1852–4 Writes a tragedy, not produced. Contributes a tale to the *Illustrated London News*; contributes two articles to weekly fiction periodical, the *Home Companion* Re-engaged as a reader by Bentley.

1854 Contributes a piece to Dickens's periodical *Household Words*. Publishes *The Life and Times of Sir Walter Ralegh* in the 'Illustrated Library'. Requests financial help from the Royal Literary Fund, stating he is considering emigrating to New Zealand to set up as a schoolteacher at Otago and is granted twenty-five pounds (December).

1856 Revival of *The Cavalier* at the Lyceum Theatre. Publishes another piece in *Household Words*. Leaves with his wife for Australia on the *Diana*, probably under some kind of engagement with the Melbourne *Argus* newspaper (13 November).

1857 Arrives in Australia, settling in Melbourne (17 March).

1850s–60s Contributes to various Australian periodicals including *The Examiner* and Melbourne *Punch*.

1858 Beginning of a novel, *Emma Latham; or, Right at Last*, serialized in Melbourne magazine *My Note Book*.

1859 Publishes verse drama 'The Spanish Marriage' in the *Victorian Monthly Magazine* (July).

1860 Wife dies of pulmonary consumption in Yarra Bend Asylum (21 August).

1862 Applies unsuccessfully for admission to the Benevolent Asylum; admitted to the Immigrants' Home. Picked up from the street destitute and exhausted, and dies of liver disease and bronchitis in the Melbourne Hospital (5 July). Buried in a pauper's grave.

1868 Revival of play *The Cavalier.*

A NOTE ON THE TEXT

The text has been set from my copy of the first edition and compared with the second (1836) and third (1838) editions. The second edition has some minor changes; the third edition appears to have been set from the first, not the second. Second and third editions bear the title *The Autobiography of a Notorious Legal Functionary*. The first and second editions were published by Edward Churton, the third by J. Chidley. A few silent corrections have been made to punctuation. Whitehead's spelling and usage were consistent with those of his day and have been left unchanged. They include such things as 'in-' where now we would use 'en-', as in 'incumbrance' for 'encumbrance'; and single final consonants where now we would use double, as in 'recal' and 'befel'. A few of Whitehead's spellings could be typographical errors or simply unconventional. Churton's use of double quotation marks first, and single quotation marks for quotations within quotations, has been reversed here to conform to modern British usage.

Yours till death
John Ketch

THE

AUTOBIOGRAPHY

OF

JACK KETCH.

WITH FOURTEEN ILLUSTRATIONS, FROM DESIGNS
BY MEADOWS.[1]

J.Smith, Jᵗ.

LONDON:
EDWARD CHURTON, 26, HOLLES-STREET.
(LATE BULL AND CHURTON.)

MDCCCXXXV.

ADVERTISEMENT.

It may be deemed a pleasing evidence of candour to confess that, in accordance with a modern usage adopted by other great authors, our Autobiographer has called in the aid of an obscure man of letters, for the purpose of adjusting his somewhat capricious orthography, – of clipping his vernacular tongue, so that it may speak with fluency and correctness, – and of applying salutary bandages to Priscian's head.[2]

He has also employed him to stick a flower[3] here and there, throughout the volume; and to throw in the required amount of moral reflection.

He has been further advised to announce the publication of his more mature experience, under the unambitious title of 'The Ketch Papers,' should the public receive with due favour the performance which he now tremblingly commits to its merciful consideration.

LIST OF ILLUSTRATIONS,
ENGRAVED BY SMITH AND BRANSTON.[4]

THE
AUTOBIOGRAPHY OF JACK KETCH.

———

CHAPTER I.

'No book was ever written,' says our great moralist, 'but something, however small, may be learned from it.'[5] I quite coincide in the opinion of our great moralist, at the same time that I beg to qualify my acquiescence by remarking that, in these our later times, many books are written from which no information, even of the most trivial or minute kind, can by possibility be gathered, of a nature such as may fairly be supposed to be comprehended in the Doctor's aphorism.

We may, indeed, be further satisfied, by a perusal of many of these crude performances, of the extent of human folly and ignorance, and of the Protean shapes and infinite varieties of aspect they assume. We may learn that, of all the professions, businesses, or trades, which it is a man's genius or fortune to pursue, in none is the chance of deserved eminence so doubtful, so precarious, so uncertain, as in that of an author. Here, all that served him in good stead before is valueless, useless, unprofitable, unless he can vivify his material by that spark within, which is so often out – unless he possess that divine afflatus which we may puff all the breath out of our body ere we contrive to muster it. There must be some inward power, or there will be no outward manifestation.

The present is a literary generation; but it is an age of writers, not of readers. We learn to write before we have been taught to read. Every one of us is so much wiser than his neighbour that no wonder we are all fools alike. This was not wont to be the case. Formerly the author said what he thought, and printed; now we think what we shall say, and publish. Well, if a man has something to tell us of a flea which was not before known of that small specimen of volatility, let him incontinently skip into print and hop into immortality; if, however, he speak of conjectural antediluvian mammoths, and such 'small deer,'[6] let him treat with the trunk-maker, and open a negociation with the pastry-cook.[7]

As a general principle, I hold that the cobbler should by no means be permitted to step beyond his last, lest he should incite others to walk in his shoes, who, by madly persisting in so hazardous a course will never, in all probability, be enabled to pay for them. It is the province of the king to be kingly; to reign over his

subjects with exemplary clemency; to wield his sceptre with becoming moderation. But when he beckons a goose to the foot of the throne, that he may draw a
quill from that convenient biped, it usually happens that he becomes 'the great
sublime he draws.'[8] The peer, also, cannot reasonably claim, for his delinquencies as an author, the privilege of peerage; the bishop cannot expect the benefit
of clergy.[9] The literary physician usually presents us with a prescription worthy
of Hippocrates, rather than with a draught smacking of Hippocrene; the lawyer
commonly tenders a performance to which the perusal of a bill of costs were the
bliss of Elysium; the architect, who might perhaps be equal to the construction
of another tower of Babel, [10]discovers a strange confusion of languages when he
enters the vestibule of the temple of fame; and the merchant's bill of literary lad-
ing discloses a freight of such portentous tonnage as no one in his senses would
venture to ensure over the sea of oblivion.

Such being the almost invariable calamity that attends amateur, or occasional, authors, it might naturally be imagined that, in process of time, the almost
insurmountable difficulties of the profession would operate as barriers to the
exclusion of the misguided many, and serve as a protection to the privileged few.
But it is not so; for even as besotted individuals, when they have supped full of
pleasure, when they have partaken to satiety of the excitements of unprofitable
dissipation, return at length to their fire-sides, and have something still at home
to gratify that self-love which Rochefoucault says, and I believe, constitutes the
mainspring of all our actions, whether good or bad;[11] so, in like manner, our dis-
appointed author, shut out of the wide fields of speculation which philosophy,
science, art, and above all, nature, open to his inspection, has yet himself to fall
back upon. A literary cipher, he places himself before it, and becomes a good
round sum. He splits himself in half and goes to buffets with his moietied self.
He 'pours out all himself'[12] into a bottle of ink, shakes the two together, and his
book is made. He writes his autobiography.

This is the very thing I am about to do; but from a very different cause.
Nobody can accuse me of being nobody. I think it will be agreed, on all hands,
that Jack Ketch[13] is a personage of no common importance, or insignificant consideration, when it is remembered that he is (if not unlikely to be called upon to
give the coup de grace[14] to the community at large) a portion, at least, of their
daily thoughts, and a salutary check to their projected operations. It has, indeed,
been said that 'marriage, like hanging, goes by destiny;'[15] but the destiny, I conceive, is the only point of similitude between the two predicaments; for, whereas
the former creates a noose which is intended to last for life, so the latter contrives
one which will by no means permit it to last.

The one destiny, therefore, perforce kicks out the other; although it must be
confessed the subject of the hymeneal[16] fate not unfrequently hardly waits to be

kicked, but walks off to eternity well pleased at the opportunity of making so advantageous an exchange.

But although to be hanged may, as a mode of speech, be truly said to be a matter of destiny, yet it must on no account be understood to mean any thing else than that death is the common lot of all. For, let it be perpetually borne in mind, hanging is the only natural death. All other deaths are purely accidental. This truth is so obvious that it scarce requires to be dwelt upon. The fear of death is the strongest weakness (so to speak) of our human nature; the dread of hanging is equally strong: the repugnance to the manner of death evinces equal weakness and pusillanimity. This dread of death, and this fear of hanging, are so common that I hardly care to weary the reader (as yet unhanged) by examples. How does the father usually proceed in the bringing up of his children? He impresses upon them the conviction that they must at one period die; and he corrects their juvenile errors by the information that they will surely come to be hanged. And as the rook is hatched usually upon a tree, – when it is of sufficient strength of pinion takes its flight thence, – frequently returns thither to hop from spray to branch, and from branch to twig,   and is at last picked off by some relentless marksman – so the human creature may truly, although figuratively, be said to be born upon the gallows tree – to leave it for awhile – to return to it – to gambol round it – to view it in all its branches – to twig it – and at length to be brought down from it with a fatal drop. Again, for what are the laws made? For the protection of person and property? No. For the taking away of life? Yes. For, inasmuch as the punishment of our original sin[17] was death, and as none of us are exempt from sin, so our legislators have wisely and benevolently proposed to themselves to second the intentions of the Deity by making so many laws that terminate in death[18] as leave the chances of accidental expiration exceedingly small, and accordingly justify me in the assertion that hanging is the only natural, if not the most genteel, manner of departing life.

But accidents, after all, will happen. All men are not suspended. It is a common saying that 'he who is born to be drowned will never be hanged;'[19] meaning, in other words, that water is a dangerous element. Some, also, die in their own beds, some in the beds of strangers; others, again, in the bed of honour.[20] Some, however, achieve greatness, while many have greatness thrust upon them.[21] Some hang themselves, although many are hanged. How then are accidents to be prevented? Our judges, it is true, like physicians in a case where the preservation of life is concerned, do certainly, in matters relating to death, stimulate and excite nature, and hold out such inducements to the community as render it a matter of wonder that they resist them; yet still the number of untoward and calamitous instances of chamber practice[22] in the dying business is frightful. The truth is this, our natural death, from what cause I know not, assuredly is not popular. Certain it is that the prospect of another world, even to the most religious or exemplary of men, is no inviting one; certain that it is not 'pleasant through such loop-holes,' as the gallows affords, to 'peep at such a world.'[23] With all due respect, however, to the prejudices and weakness of mankind, I must still consider this repugnance to our truly national and natural mode of dying singular, if not absurd. For what possible difference can it make to any person, I should be glad to be resolved, whether he die in a perpendicular or a horizontal position? – whether he lie or hang? – whether he be suspended or extended? What possible choice can there be, in a wise man's estimation, between giving up the ghost, as is the chamber usage, or giving into the ghost, which is the custom of the forewarned. To pay the debt of nature[24] in one's bed is to do a thing lazily and reluctantly which must be done at last; to discharge the amount betimes of a morning, well dressed (I admire a neat and respectable apparel on such occasions), is not only to wipe off the score, but to satisfy it strictly according to law. You have witnesses to prove the payment. You carry away a receipt for all demands. You are out of her books, at all events, even though you 'stand aye accursed in the Calendar.'[25]

Besides, and in addition, the death itself is an honourable one. You meet and satisfy the justice of the case. No man has the slightest claim against you; – you are absolved from every thing. Who can say he is wronged who is not redressed? What personal wrong have you committed for which your death does not amply atone? Look, on the other hand, on those who are unhappily hurried away before their maturity of years, or wisdom, brought them to the gallows. How different is this picture.

Here we see long existing debts, outstanding feuds, unaccounted and unaccountable hostilities, hungry relatives, expecting legatees, joyful heirs; grief at three and sixpence a day, called mutes;[26] extract of onion, called tears; white handkerchief, otherwise mouth-stopper, or nose-propper, or both, called mourning.

Be assured, therefore, my dear reader, that 'the drop'[27] is the drop of all others best calculated to prove a cordial to your sinking spirits. Believe me, it is far better that your personal property should be taken possession of by the considerate executioner, than by the rapacious executor. Rest satisfied that it is more gratifying and honourable to be cut down, than to be cut off, in the prime of existence; be assured that the thread of life is more handsomely terminated by a few yards of rope than by the lengthiest yarn that was ever penned by the panegyrist, or paid for to the poet; and, finally, that they who boast of having been descended from a long line of ancestors, have not half the cause of triumph which you will possess, who may justly claim the merit of descending from a long line without any assistance from your ancestors whatever.

Need I say more, intelligent reader, to prove the surpassing superiority of this method of demise over all others? Nor let the vulgar prejudice of ignorance bias you against the truly noble and excellent contrivance which, let me trust, you are one day to test in your own person. You do not die and make no sign; on the contrary, although it is said that 'good wine needs no bush,'[28] yet, let me tell you without such intimation we should not know where good wine was to be had. You are an emphatic sign, therefore, hanging forth for the purpose of catching the eye of the passenger, that he may learn where better accommodation is to be found than this vile tavern called the Globe pleases to afford. Was not the coffin of Mahomet suspended between heaven and earth,[29] and does it not retain its impartial situation to this day? Does not the earth itself hang in the infinity of space? What does the moon? hang. What does the sun? hang. The stars? hang. They are all hanged. Hang it, then, why can't you hang likewise? Let it not be said that I do not 'do unto others as I would they should do unto me.'[30] My time is not yet come; besides, I can do it for myself. Look then upon the summons to hanging as the call of nature. The ties of nature are strong; she yearns for her children; she will have them come and see her; she invites them to an ordinary[31] at eight o'clock; she wishes them to take the air for an hour. At length she dismisses them to their beds, which, whatever way they had chanced to prefer, they must come to at last. I am the chamberlain; *I tuck them all up.*[32]

By this time our acute reader will understand the drift and tendency of my preceding observations. To sum up, however, in brief, all that I have before set down at large, it may come perhaps to this: – that of the books recently written, and now in course of publication, nine-tenths are, and will be, so utterly unworthy a grave and judicious person's perusal as to implicate the unwary reader in the stigma which must inevitably fix itself eventually upon the authors. Further, that a tribe of literary locusts, called autobiographers, is at this moment enveloping the atmosphere of letters in Egyptian darkness; a Cimmerian gloom, which neither the rod of Moses,[33] nor any other rod with which I am acquainted, is able to disperse. I have gone on to show that my elevated office in the executive government[34] has supplied me with opportunities, whether derived from the experience of what I saw, or from reflecting upon what I have seen, which do not fall to the lot of those who, reading nothing, knowing nothing, seeing nothing, being nothing, carelessly diffuse themselves into three volumes,[35] and thereafter change their 'fleshy nooks'[36] into spacious habitations; convert their wooden heads into handsome furniture; exchange their literary night-caps for fleecy hosiery,[37] and their barren wreaths of bay or laurel[38] for wholesome and sufficient vegetables.

Moreover, I have vindicated the importance of my office, and the high and ennobling objects which it was originally appointed to fulfil. I have shown that not only is hanging honourable, but that it should be sedulously sought after. I have proved that the laws were originally framed for the purpose of teaching us the way we should go; and that if, after all, we do not all of us encourage the growth of hemp,[39] so that it may spring up out of the ground even to a level with our necks, it is no fault of the legislature. They at least prepare the ground, till the soil, sow the seed, and reap the produce. It might indeed be desired that the fate of Phalaris[40] might be meted out to those who have been so apt, if not to invent, to apply the invention so largely; but I fear the credit of the application is hardly considered sufficient to justify the extension of it to those who, if they do not deserve this honour, can perhaps lay small claim to any other distinction from their countrymen. Let them, then, console themselves with the words of Cato –

> ''Tis not in mortals to command success;
> But we'll do more, Sempronius, we'll deserve it.'[41]

Let us, on the contrary, strive to reach that which they only deserve. Death is the great overtaker of all our schemes; these thwarted, he makes room for the undertaker. Let us not trouble either more than is absolutely necessary; let us not expect that the 'insatiate archer'[42] will set his broad arrow upon us. And, as for the undertaker – inky impertinence! sable superfluity! heavy lightness! serious vanity! black imposition! What maggot in the head of a clodpole ever begat the notion that it was good to be relinquished to the vagaries of worms? The very beasts make merry at the extravagant conceit: the notion causes a defunct dog to smile: *ex gratia*[43] the mastiff of Mother Hubbard –

> 'She went to the undertaker's to buy him a coffin,
> When she came back the dog was a laughing.'[44]

And well he might! Let then the undertaker, like Actæon,[45] when he beholds this naked truth bathing in the waters of philosophy, go to the dogs forthwith. Science hath nobler aims, or rather ends, for human and reasoning beings. Be loyal even in death; – be disposed of at his Majesty's pleasure![46]

I am about to write my autobiography; but let it not be supposed that I purpose to set down every event in my life that ever made me its subject or its victim. Such a thing were impracticable, even did my inclination incite me to the undertaking. Many occurrences in an eventful life like mine must necessarily be but imperfectly shadowed forth through the haze of memory; and a whole existence, seen through such spectacles, appears but a surface broken by a few remarkable convulsions of affairs. The fatal tree[47] indeed is a tree that, engrafted, bears much and various fruit; some plucked at maturity; some pecked by the birds of the air; much crushed, like mast, between the jaws of swinish sensuality; some, windfalls that the rude blast swept off into the bosom of vice, which might, with gentler airs, have been gathered into the lap of virtue. 'This was the tree at which Jack and I parted,' was the exclamation of a poor girl whose lover had taken leave of her at that particular spot. How many Jacks, equally promising and constant, have taken leave from this self-same place! How many have taken shelter under the leafless, but not barren, repose of this same tree! How many a gay young fellow, cruising on the ocean of dissipation, extravagance, and ruin –

'Youth at the prow and pleasure at the helm,'[48]

has been fain at length to put in at this port, and to go forth on his last long voyage at the rate of one knot an hour!

Of these it shall be my present hint to speak – and with them, and their eccentric and incalculable movements, will my own business be intimately involved; so that my proceedings may, not very elegantly, but appropriately enough, be likened to the contrivances of a cunning and skilful cur, who threads the mazy entanglements of a tabernacle of jumpers;[49] and participates in all the pleasure of the party without the unnecessary trouble of exercise; and without more excitement than suffices to give a proper zest and relish to the scene itself.

It is a common saying that 'you may bring a horse to the water, but you cannot make it drink.'[50] We ourselves, nevertheless, may drink our fill; but it will be enough for me that I bring the horse to the water. If I supply the stream, my readers may do as they please whether they choose to stoop their heads and partake of it, or no. And with respect to the moral which, rightly considered, is such a reflection of a man's own self as his exact notions of right and wrong enable him to discern, I cannot promise that the course of my existence has flowed in so unruffled a stream as will permit him to perceive it very distinctly. Enough to express my conviction that, as, according to the poet, there are 'books in the running brooks;'[51] so in every book – in every thing – good, bad, and indifferent, there is an emphatic moral, if but philosophy could find it out. With such philosophy I hope my reader may be endowed; and I have no fear that we shall go on to the end of the chapter with mutually profitable and advantageous results.

CHAPTER II.

I<small>T</small> is a condition entailed upon us by nature that we should be born in accordance with her dictates, and after a certain fashion prescribed by her. I myself have every reason to believe that there was no deviation from the usual course in my particular instance – and that I neither sprang out of the head of my father, as sin from the head of Satan;[52] nor started out of the ground like one of the Dragon's teeth, sown by that ancient woolgatherer, surnamed Jason.[53] Indeed, there is every reason to believe that the perpetual emptiness of my father's skull precluded any possibility of doubt about the matter, so far as he was concerned; – and my mother, – dragon enough, although she was, Heaven knows! had only lost, when I was born, one double pronged grinder, which, I am well certified, having reverently sprinkled with salt, she committed to the devouring flames.[54]

It is now about forty years ago since I first saw the light – if light it may be called that struggled painfully through the closely-jammed houses, which seemed, for common security, to have linked themselves arm in arm, as it were, and to have run for protection into the darksome secrecy of Rose and Crown Court.[55] If my reader wish to slake that thirst after knowledge which is so common a complaint now a days – and desire to be satisfied touching the particular locality of this interesting place, let him penetrate an alley nearly opposite the northern extremity of Newgate;[56] and, after descending a flight of stone steps, he will find himself in a narrow street, out of which, on one hand, the required Court may possibly be discovered.

It was here, then, that I first beheld the extremely inferior and adulterated light, for the niggard supply of which I have accounted; and it was here that those *prima stamina*[57] of ideas were kicked and cuffed into me which have mainly contributed to make me what I now am. And here, considering the peculiar profession of my parents, it might be a matter of natural wonder that they should have chosen to domiciliate themselves in a quarter so nearly contiguous to that great mansion, stronghold, or fortress,[58] into which they were, in all probability, destined, at no remote period, to introduce themselves, or rather to be introduced. But it will be easily accounted for when it is remembered that there are some peculiar, anomalous, and pervading instincts in nature that invite every thing and every body to be nearest to mischief wherever it is to be found. There never yet was a moth that did not love to play at hazard with a candle; there never was a burnt child that did not afterwards perpetually hover about the fire; the man never fell down a precipice that did not often project his chin over the edge, that he might see from what height he had fallen; there never was a Bankrupt that did not leap into the Gazette;[59] ruin never stared a man in the face who did not attempt to stare her out of countenance. In accordance, therefore, with this principle, law, or impulse, of nature, my parents took up their abode in the vicinity of Newgate.

Let me not mince the matter, – for mincing it will not make the matter less, although the several portions may be smaller, – my father was a thief. He was, I say, *de facto*, a thief, although *de jure*,[60] he was, or should have been, a waiter. The napkin he occasionally carried under his arm hung just low enough to cover and conceal his fingers, and the employments to which they were unceasingly devoted. And, as we are told by Plutarch, in his life of Pericles, that there was a sect of philosophers, at that period, whose doctrines were so unpopular that they were fain to inculcate them disguised as musical professors,[61] – so the philosophy of my father (which I imagine is adopted practically to a much greater extent than the insufficient exposition of its principles would seem to warrant) required that he should overlay it with some external covering of sufficient plausibility to conceal, but at the same time not so close or diurnally worn as to cramp or restrain, his motions in the pursuit of his more congenial profession. The title of waiter, accordingly, was a sort of pretext – a kind of conductor to glance off the lightning with which a censorious world, enveloped in the clouds of prejudice and ignorance, is always too ready to smite the endeavours of the philosophical explorer. It was the homage he chose to pay to the weakness of mankind – a generous apology, which, like that of Mr. Colley Cibber,[62] might appropriately be entitled 'an apology – *for his own life*.'

But, if my father sought, by means like these, to make up for the financial deficiencies of his conventional profession, or rather to substitute another mode of life, leaving the former as a quintain,[63] a mere lifeless block, at which hoodwinked credulity might tilt[64] at pleasure, the while he thus indifferently levied contributions upon the community at large; my mother, on her part, was in nowise backward to follow his commendable example; and, revolving in her own small sphere, to throw such light upon the domestic perplexities around her as her borrowed effulgence enabled her to emit. In accordance with this determination – (if, indeed, it were not a pre-conceit of her own) – she, also, erected a battery in the shape of a washing-tub; and, armed with a bar of yellow soap and sufficient ammunition of pearlash,[65] set suspicion at bay, and held the world at defiance. In other words, she became a washerwoman. Thus, then, were two masked batteries effected, from which these two defenders of our small garrison were enabled to make such reprisals on their common enemy – the world – as permitted them to display as respectable an appearance in the Court as any of the few other inhabitants of that colony could contrive to establish; and, when it is borne in mind that my father, in his vocation, or rather, *va*cation, as waiter, was sometimes called upon to attend public dinners, it must be confessed that a good opportunity not unfrequently presented itself of picking up a few trifling items of advantage not contemplated by his employer at the moment of his engagement. It must be acknowledged that nothing can be a more simple operation than, while apparently drawing a cork, to be actually drawing a handkerchief, or extracting a snuff-box; and handing the plate is quite as troublesome, and not half so agreeable, as handing off the plate[66] – which it was my father's expert custom to do. Whether the one suggested the other I cannot say; or whether, as is most likely, the very sight of it communicated an agreeable warmth to his animal system which tingled to his fingers' ends, I will not determine: certain, however, it is that, whether from an inherent passion for such valuables, or from a confirmed habit of abstracting them, they were frequently to be seen emerging from his pockets before he retired to rest for the night. My mother, too, while wringing her hands at the washing-tub, was painfully employed in devising schemes whereby she might lay them upon something with advantage and security; and although her success was hardly proportionate to the spoliating conquests of my father, yet the very frequent appearance of silver spoons, and such small luxuries, testified that she kept in advance of the dustman[67] with praiseworthy diligence. Indeed it must be confessed that, to all the pestilent loquacity, my mother added the furtive attainments, of the magpie;[68] and I will venture to say that, if the latter had carried on its depredations in a house at which she was permitted an ingress, not even the church steeple would have been a secure repository for the goods it might have, in the first instance, so ingeniously taken to itself.

But, though both had testified uncommon alacrity hitherto in appropriating to their own use such property, or portions of it; as the laws have decreed shall justly belong to those who possess it (and for my part, I cannot conceive why the last possessor should not be included in such protection);[69] yet it is only natural to suppose that immediately I made my appearance on the surface of society, and became a proper member of that family – it cannot be doubted, I say, that a much greater degree of vigilance should be shown, and a much more alert activity should be exhibited in scraping together such necessaries as the increased expenditure and the probable increase of family might seem to suggest the expediency of. And, indeed, a year or two after my birth, it became more imperatively necessary that my parents should devote themselves exclusively to the professions to which it had pleased themselves to call themselves; for my father had at length been unluckily detected, not so much in waiting upon, as in laying wait for,[70] gentlemen; and my mother, almost at the simultaneous moment, was discovered to have been busying herself, after she had cleaned the things, in walking clean off with them; so that the masked batteries, of which I have spoken, were demolished; and these two worthy creatures began to be alarmed lest the white napkin of the one should suddenly convert itself into a black cap,[71] – and the washing-stool of the other should transform itself into a gibbet.

In the meanwhile my education was not neglected. From the first moment of my life, my assiduous mother had tried strange conclusions with me. She had put in force various mystic manœuvres whereby my future destiny was, or was supposed to be, accurately ascertained. Every dream that took lodgings in her brain, when it abandoned the premises, left some token, in which the prominent feature of my life was to be distinctly perceived. The wish nearest to her heart, or rather most contiguous to her pocket, had ever been that I should, figuratively to speak, walk in my father's shoes; figuratively to speak, I repeat, for she well knew that in all probability that exemplary character was more than likely to render up the ghost with his shoes on, rather than relinquish them to me in the usual disgraceful manner. That her wish was to be gratified at some period – distant or near – she was well satisfied. Again, that there might not be the smallest doubt of the matter and manner of my death, nature had taken care to plant behind my left ear a symbolic mole, prophetic of the inevitable knot. So that, after all, if at this game of chance my mother did not come off clearly the winner, it might truly and appropriately be said to resolve itself into a tie.[72] From this well-defined mole, however, my mother contrived to bear up against a sea of troubles[73] which threatened to surround us, rightly judging that if a man is born to be hanged he at least does something to deserve his fate; and, as there's many a slip between the cup and the lip,[74] so, in like manner, there may be said to be many a goose between the neck and the noose;[75] of all which geese, if I was destined to pluck them, she promised herself to put in for the giblets.

And, as it so fell out, there was no small degree of philosophy on the part of my parent, in thus clinging to the skirts of futurity in preference to waiting upon the 'what comes next' of the present; for my father, in a very few years, so managed matters as to bring himself quietly to anchor in the secure harbour of the condemned cell. He had, it appears, many times previously to his last fatal mistake, been found walking with his hands, not in his own pockets, but in the pockets of others; and had been, for a long space of time, so intimate with magistrates and their myrmidons[76] as to have attained to the dignity of a suspicious character,[77] – a term applied, it seems, to those of whose characters there cannot be any reasonable cause of suspicion.

My mother had received no such notifications of the impending calamity as were usually vouchsafed to her. Her nose had not recently itched – a sign portending speedy vexation; neither had the fire burnt on one side of the grate, a mysterious announcement of sudden death in the family; so that when an officer waited upon her, and intimated that Mr. Snatchaway Ketch had actually been investing himself in the authority of a distraining broker,[78] without any legal warrant for such investment – in other words, that he had been entering a house and had been seized in the act of retiring with the portable property discovered there – the poor woman was at an exceeding non-plus, and concluded at once that he who, in the first instance, was not able to save his neck by the activity of his heels would be now very likely to be furnished with the opportunity of plying the latter nimbly enough, without much chance of saving the former more effectually than before. She felt, indeed, that his time was come, and that he must go – and calculated to a moment the duration of the connubial engagement between them; beyond which she was no longer to expect anything from his hands or from his dextrous employment of them. She, however, consoled herself partly by application to the gin-bottle, but chiefly with the practical enforcement of a system of ethics of her own; by which all such as were, whether by misfortune, or whatsoever other cause, excluded from the possibility of serving her for the future, were consigned to oblivion in a trice; and were well got rid of, so that she dismissed them without any cost or trouble to herself.

And it was now that she displayed a decision of character, and an extent of resources, which, under the circumstances, were not a little remarkable. She busied herself incessantly in levying contributions upon her neighbours, under the pretext of supplying her husband's wants during his sojourn[79] in prison; but as money purposed to be applied in a given manner seldom finds the destination to which it was originally intended, so the money thus procured never found its way to the hapless individual who had been set up as a sort of shrine, at whose feet such offerings should have been properly laid. For, my mother very naturally argued that to pamper the corporeal appetites of one who was soon to be converted into an ultra-ascetic in such worldly delights would be about as useless a proceeding as if she were to whistle jigs to a milestone – or to reprint the almanack of the year on the last day of the calendar.

As for my father, no part of his life became him so well as the leaving of it.[80] It behoved him to depart, since it was now evident that, had he been permitted to remain amongst us, he would have been much more likely to act as a clog upon, than to serve as a spoke in, the wheel of our domestic vehicle of existence, which was now threatening to break down at every jolt in the road, and at every rut in the highway of adversity.

'Jack,' said he to me, as he laid his hand, furnished with a set of exceeding long fingers, upon my head, 'to-morrow morning I shall be hanged by the neck.' My head fell upon my left shoulder at this announcement, and I would have wept, but could not. My heart was too full for appropriate words, and I scorned to utter the base coin of hypocrisy. 'Walk,' he continued, 'my dear Jacky, in the right path – keep within the law – and you're safe enough. And, as for the world, *that* for it;' – and he placed his thumb on his nose, and stretched his fingers forth, shaking them convulsively. But he now became moody and restless, and kicked me out of the cell, to make room for the ordinary,[81] who waited upon him for the purpose of dispensing a species of consolation to which he was far from being accustomed. The doctrine of the reverend gentleman, however, was not very agreeable, since it held out few inducements to him to make interest for a place in another world, where his peculiar skill would be in no requisition; and he took leave of society on the following morning with evident regret and reluctance.

But, with whatever regret and reluctance my father might have given up this terrestrial ball, I, to say the truth, was by no means sorry that he was gone. The man had been a plaguy source of vexation to me, having been accustomed from my earliest youth to make me the scapegoat for all his sins of omission in the predatory line, by laying upon my shoulders the burden of his insufficiencies in the shape of blows, and by driving me into the wilderness of streets to browse upon such pasture as my unskilful footsteps led me to discover. So that when my mother took me home again, after witnessing the ceremony of his leave-taking,[82] I was exceedingly glad, and made merry so far as my very juvenile capacity of pocket enabled me to give outward signs of a mirth that was striving within me with most agreeable alacrity.

CHAPTER III.

No sooner was my father committed to the tender mercies of Surgeons' Hall,[83] than a number of old women – neighbours and friends of the family – entered the apartments, and commenced a discourse touching the future prospects of my surviving parent and myself, most clamorously. Each had an unformed cub of a plan which she began to lick into shape[84] with a tongue of desperate persever-ance; until at length they all pitted their pet monsters one against the other, and made hideous discord, to which the howling of a millenary of wolves, whether baying the moon, or short of supper, might be considered soft music. From their incoherent ravings, however, nothing could be gathered so certain as the cir-cumstance that the gin, of which there was a plentiful supply, was finding its way into their ancient and ruined brain-pans, with no common alacrity; – and now the particular appositeness of what they uttered, to the matter in hand, became a secondary consideration, or, more truly to speak, became a question of no moment at all.

'I'll tell you what it is, Mother Nimblejaw,' cried my parent, at length, to a most evil-looking old harridan, who was wielding her tongue at the further end of the room with frightful vigour; and who now, upon being thus suddenly addressed, caused another glass of gin to leap, like another Curtius,[85] down the yawning gulf of her windpipe, which, however, did not close up suddenly. 'I'll tell you what it is – it's easy to talk about putting the boy out in the world; but who'll take the poor orphan, I should like to know, since Ketch's misfortune?' and the tender reminiscence drew tears of gin-and-water from her eyes – 'no, no, he shall stay with his mother; won't you, Jacky?' – and she offered me her glass to drain.

I was fain to grin an amiable consent to the proposal – holding forth 'a flag and sign of love, which was indeed but sign;'[86] for I question whether all the love that could be mustered between us on a case of emergency would have furnished forth a rat with a decent stock of family affection.

'Well, Mrs. Ketch,' croaked the other in a tone of deprecation, 'I know when boys *do* get out into the world, though they only have their food found them, there are so many little things to be picked up, – so many odds and ends: – now, my Jem – you remember Jemmy?'

'Him that was sent over the water?'[87] demanded a mnemonic nuisance, with a somewhat ill-timed abruptness.

'Yes, poor lamb;' returned Mrs. Nimblejaw, raising her apron, with a quite unneccessary[88] and uncalled-for solicitude, to anticipate a moisture that was in no danger of making its appearance. – 'Well, when Jem was at Slush, the apothecary's, you can't tell what a number of perquisites and vails[89] he used to bring home – the beautifullest things, sometimes – and you knows, at last, Slush wouldn't have prosecuted, only he was bound over – Jem was a dear good boy to me – and a sad loss I've found him since he left us.'

It was plain to behold that these words sank deep into the mind of my mother, – whose breast, ever most anxious for her own particular advantage, had taken the partial and temporary success of Jemmy Nimblejaw as a comfortable precedent, or a special example for my future imitation. The ultimate destination of that youth, however, tended in no wise to qualify the ardour with which he now began to instil notions into me subversive of those strictly ethical proprieties which, by some means or another, have obtained in civilised countries.

As yet I was of too tender an age to profit largely by these crooked counsels; for, although the policy of preying upon handkerchiefs may be insisted upon at a very early period, yet the practical carrying out of these principles, exemplified in the pulling out of these handkerchiefs, cannot well be begun before the juvenile fingers are enabled to reach the pockets into which they are intended to make so gingerly descent.

Still that which is accounted true of poets holds equally good of pickpockets – who are born, not made; – and nature will out – whether into the fields of Parnassus,[90] or into the streets of London – whether she stir to exertion the pupil of Apollo, or the disciple of Mercury.[91] – And, as nothing stimulates to larger or more hazardous undertakings so strongly as a full enjoyment of the benefits derivable from lesser speculations – so my earlier ventures, converted, as they were, to my sole pleasure, soon excited in me a rabid hunger and an unquenchable thirst after future benefits of a more enduring and exquisite nature. While yet a boy, I was the alternate torment and pride of applewomen, who, sometimes too truly, presaged that the plunder I had obtained would be its own exceeding punishment, and that an inward conscience would teach me that, if I had no bowels[92] for them, I at least should too surely feel that I had them for myself. Nor were those peripatetic anomalies, who minister to the cravings of individuals whose 'unhoused free condition'[93] compels them to breakfast *out*, less sensible of the skill with which I turned their agreeable goods into gifts; for, as I held constantly in mind the advice of Cornaro, or of some equally Hygeian[94] maximmonger, that you should 'after supper run a mile,' so I not unfrequently found it excellently expedient to do so after breakfast, merely tarrying by the way for a moment to lay hold upon those stale delicacies which pastry-cooks show to the morning air in the door-way, for the purpose of meeting the eyes and the pockets of the youthful, but not too fastidious, epicure. And, until I was well qualified to prey upon adults, I accustomed myself to pounce upon the unfledged, and, upon many occasions, urchins, who employed themselves during the oyster advent in levying contributions upon the congregated shells, were dismissed by me to their grottos with all the solemnity of visage and vacancy of scrip[95] peculiar to ascetic hermits. Nor was that multifarious brood of children whose particular custom or delight it is to flatten their noses against shop-windows, during a process of investigation of their contents, less subject to, or sensible of, my exactions; and the idle apprentice and the leisurely errand boy were too frequently fain to tax their ingenuity in the contrivance of a story in which the loss of goods intrusted to their care should be involved; which story, for the purpose, perhaps, of rendering it '*very* like a whale,'[96] was accompanied at the same time with a great deal of blubber.[97]

But it was now high time that the rudiments of my vernacular tongue should be made plain to me, and that (although I might never have occasion to

'Waft a sigh from Indus to the Pole,'[98]

or be required to calculate the distance between these two extreme localities) I should be instructed in the first principles of writing and arithmetic. For this purpose, such interest was agitated in my behalf as succeeded in obtaining admission for me into the parish school. Here, let me confess, neither the eleemosynary instruction afforded, the individual selected to dispense it, nor the objects imbibing it, were much to my mind. – I yearned for a more ample range – I desired a more extended field. I thought with the immortal Milton that

'That which before us lies in daily life
Is the prime wisdom;'[99]

and, for my part, I had no idea of a thing lying before me without stooping to pick it up. And, to say the truth, had I been ever so zealously disposed to cultivate learning at its root, Mr. Misty,[100] our tutor, was by no means alert at supplying us with implements, or furnishing our brains with intellectual preparatory manure.

Misty was a poor, tall, thin, placid creature, in whom the energies proper to man appeared never to have existed, or to have long ago expired. He looked like the reflection of some gentleman in black who had managed one day to leave his shadow behind him upon the pavement, which after having lain torpid for some time, and been trampled upon by every passenger, had, at length, got up and walked off to get a precarious living for itself. And, indeed, the living he contrived to acquire was such as might be supposed scarcely to keep a shadow warm at midsummer, the whole of his financial economy being comprehended in the pittance of thirty pounds per annum.

How, therefore, the mysterious Misty contrived to exist may be considered indeed a mystery; but certain it is that, at the appointed hours of the charity school, he was never known to absent himself, going through the routine of duties imposed upon him with praiseworthy gravity, if not with laudable success. But when the time appointed for the performance of these duties was at an end, Mr. Misty took his departure no one knew nor cared whither; although the shaking of his hand every morning, and a timid flush of pale pink sometimes trembling at the extremity of his nose, betokened an intimate connection with spirits[101] which, like their ghostly namesakes, are sometimes brought from their vaults for the purpose of summoning to the dwelling place of death the wretched creature invoking them.

It cannot be a matter of extraordinary wonder to those who are accustomed to judge of the tree by its fruit[102] – or rather, to calculate the produce by the seed sown – to be told that, under the hands of this melancholy person, very few of the parish plants were enabled to flourish; or that I, not intellectually stronger or more pliant than the rest, became mentally stunted and stultified: in truth, Misty, whether hitherto unaccustomed to, or as yet unskilful in, that art by which the young 'idea is taught to shoot,'[103] I know not; but he either taught us to shoot round corners, or to fire with blank cartridges, so that one half of us at least never saw what we were aiming at, and the remainder never contrived to bring down any kind of wisdom or discursive knowledge worth the trouble of digestion, or indeed that it would be expedient or necessary even to bag. The consequence of this failing or inherent incapacity on the part of our tutor was that, during our academical shooting season, or, to drop metaphor, our school hours, I was more prone to the study of the theory of picking pockets (in the pursuance of which art I sometimes compelled Misty to officiate as lay-figure[104]) than of ransacking the hidden treasures of learning; and I could not but feel a just contempt for those who, with myself, were accustomed, with faces of sour dissatisfaction, to stand ranged before our lugubrious preceptor – like vinegar cruets facing a bottle of hock – or small blocks of granite in front of a huge pillar of black marble – or grey geese before an ostrich in mourning for its sand-engulfed, egg-enveloped, offspring.

Let me, at the same time, take credit to myself for the inward stirrings of an ambition that prompted me to activity in less unworthy devotions. There was a mill-horse[105] uniformity in thus halting round a circle, to which I was not blind enough to submit myself. Having been for the space of four years at this hateful seminary, I was impatient to cast my slough, and to endue myself with the worldly wisdom of the serpent. During this period I had, in spite of myself, and

Misty in the Parish School

perhaps in spite of Misty, mastered the knowledge of reading; I now panted for the opportunity of perusing mankind. I had long ago gone beyond pothooks and hangers,[106] and desired to acquire a pot of my own to suspend upon the former, even though in the search of it I should become one of the latter. I had now attained a good running hand,[107] and mightily wished for the opportunity of running it into any particular place out of which coin, or its equivalent, might be forthcoming. Two years still lay before me, ere the expiration of my thraldom; the friends and advisers of my mother recommended, nay, insisted upon, the full and perfect period of my education. I would willingly have surrendered my own two ears, if time would have consented to swallow up the other two years in his capacious maw before they were yet done. Towards the consummation of an end whereby this eternity was to be cut off, I set my wits at work, and in a short time, partly by my own exertions, but chiefly by strange good luck, my best hopes were realised.

I was, as I before pretty plainly intimated, heartily sick of my diurnal exercitations; but most especially did the course of life prescribed for me on the Sunday affect and disgust me. My invariable situation in the organ-loft,[108] with that immense musical instrument thrilling and vibrating through every bone in my body, together with the enforced warbling of hymns, in which I was never an adept, and wherein my deficiencies were, as it were, *swopped*[109] or exchanged for punctual visitations on the cranium, dealt out by an observant and prompt functionary, were at the same time most offensive to my feelings and repulsive to my nature. The last physical nuisance I had hitherto partly assuaged by an immortal hatred of the wretch deputed to dispense it, and by those multifarious face-makings behind his back which soothe the spirit, while they indicate the excitement under which it labours. At length, one Sunday, when the oft-repeated magic touch of the creature's wand had transformed me into a malignant fiend, I contrived to set my newly-shod heel with such fearful emphasis on the monster's toe, and simultaneously to make so yielding a pincushion of his fatted calf, as caused the beast to yell most blatantly, to the infinite terror of the congregation, who verily believed that the organ was grinding to powder a hecatomb of vivacious hyænas, and to the mortal dismay and bewilderment of the clergyman himself, who departed rapidly from the pulpit without beat of cushion[110] or ceremony of benediction.

For this gross and (as it was falsely represented) unprovoked outrage, I was, to resort to vulgar phraseology, 'hauled over the coals,' or brought before the parish authorities deputed to take cognisance of these offences, whose eyes, indeed, glistened like the bituminous articles I have above referred to, upon an inflamed and partial statement of my case. But when, in addition to the present shameful transaction, a series of ancient accusations was brought against me, touching certain unconsidered trifles belonging to the school, which I unfortunately had not only touched but unceremoniously abduced,[111] a fiat of dismissal was suspended over my head, ready, on the slightest repetition of such acts, to pounce upon my cap and other insignia of parochial investiture, and to dismiss me into the wide streets an outcast and a wanderer.

For this result I was not only prepared but impatient; and now I was resolving to fulfil the condition upon which my expulsion from the doors of the parish school hinged, when an event occurred which just fell out in '*the nick of time*.'[112] I set down the expression advisedly, representing, as it does, accurately, the temporal accident to the two parties interested. To me, as one of these parties, it was so; to the other party it was literally the 'nick of time,' for she heartily wished the time at the devil in which so unexpected a calamity w as brought about.

My mother, my sainted mother – for so popular authors delight to express themselves – and not inappropriately might she be so termed, seeing that her destruction was consummated on a Saint Monday[113] – had laid herself open to a suspicion – nay, not so, rather had got herself shut up to a certainty – on a charge of not accurately distinguishing the rights of property. She was seized, and found to be possessed of various goods to which, when strictly questioned, she could make out no intelligible claim. She indeed pleaded her nine points,[114] but the law in this instance did not recognise them as potential;[115] and the worthy creature, after causing twelve grave gentlemen to lay their heads together, was by another grave gentleman commanded to expatriate herself for life.

Here, then, was an occasion upon which the parish might bestir itself in the person of its authorities, in a summary, and, at the same time, a legitimate, manner. I came of a bad stock – that was sure enough; equally certain was it that I myself was a black sheep,[116] from whom no wool worthy of manufacture into a cloak of sanctity was likely to be forthcoming. They argued, accordingly, that as 'what is bred in the bone will never come out of the flesh,'[117] I should be turned into the streets, to starve if I pleased, for the remote chance, perhaps, of getting out the peccant humours immediately my bones made their appearance through my skin.

But I felt that such a result was not likely to happen. Experience had been afforded me, and to be cautious I knew was to be safe. My father before me had 'made himself air and vanished;'[118] I was for other than for dancing measures of that description. My mother had betaken herself to water,[119] and vanished also; I, on the contrary, was determined upon sticking to the earth as long as it would bear me.

In consequence of this determination, or rather because my mother had paved the way for my reception at that place, I proceeded to my uncle's house. Here it was that, immediately I set my foot upon the premises, I felt myself emphatically at home. I had time and space not only to turn myself about, but to consider deeply about what I should turn myself.[120] I was now of an age to get

My Mother—my sainted Mother.

my own living with my own hands, and by the sweat of my brow; but I inwardly meditated that no perspiration should exude thence, unless it were compelled by the agony of thought into which I might occasionally be plunged by reflecting upon the best possible means of subsisting with the least possible labour or trouble to myself.

CHAPTER IV.

MR. JOHN KETCH,[121] under whose hospitable roof I was now fain to take shelter, had looked upon me his sole nephew, from my earliest infancy, with eyes of singular affection and regard; and had at all times, and upon every fitting occasion, presented me with such tokens of his esteem as were most gratifying to me. He had for many years past performed the onerous and important duties of hangman to the metropolis; and it was he indeed who had waited upon my father with fraternal tenderness, and when he fell upon his neck[122] at the last moment, committed something to his private ear that was instantaneously effective in absolving him from the further troubles and anxieties of this world. Let no one presume to imagine that there was the slightest lack of affection on the part of my uncle towards his relative; he would have done as much for his own father, had he been still extant, but (and it is a strange coincidence) some other functionary had performed that office for him many years before.

But however great his affection for my father undoubtedly was, my uncle was disposed to transfer it, with all its arrears of interest, to me. He saw in me, so he was pleased to say, faculties which, if propelled in the proper direction, might render me worthy, not of a better fate, for that he conceived be too presumptuous an ambition, but of a destiny of a more marked and distinguished character than my father had been happy enough to attain.

It will readily be conceived, perhaps, that Mr. John Ketch was an enthusiast in his own profession: he was so. He considered himself the great Katterfelto[123] of the state, and the community at large were his puppets; he looked upon our artificial state of society as a scheme whereby all the individuals composing it were naturally pre-disposed to fall into his hands. It was to him a sort of game, in which they who ultimately contrived to evade his fingers were either cheats, or so utterly unskilful as to be worthy of no account. Next to himself, therefore, he delighted in those who, having emptied the pockets of as many of the participants in the amusement as their abilities or chances afforded, were at length constrained to throw up the cards and to fall in, like long leases of tenements upon which he had always claimed an indefeasible ground-rent. I then, in my uncle's eyes, was a small but goodly fabric, capable of vast repairs and improvements, never likely to be unoccupied, and altogether a very advantageous property – to myself when any one would let, to society when any body could take, me.[124] But my uncle argued upon wrong premises; for, as it so fell out, my lease never fell in.[125]

Mr. John Ketch was an individual of a somewhat singular and remarkable exterior. His face was as nearly as possible a perfect square, and his extensive ears appeared like pinions which had originally wafted that unique physiognomy to the position it now occupied; or, perhaps, they might more truly be likened to convenient handles, which nature had somewhat unceremoniously made use of for the purpose of lifting his head upon his shoulders. His eyes perpetually wide open, as though under the influence of surprise; while the volatile pupils belonging to them danced about like bedlamites frisking at the windows of a private madhouse. Nor was his nose less astonishingly peculiar, resembling as it did the gnomon of a sun-dial; while his mouth most nearly approximated in size and shape to the orifice of a letter-box. When the reader has succeeded in harmoniously combining these several features into a perfect picture of the original, I shall call his attention to an enormous hump between the shoulders of my relative, and to a pair of bandy or bow legs, which, to himself unsightly and inelegant, were convenient thoroughfares for straight-forward dogs agog for pleasure or provender, who trotted through them with equal satisfaction and dexterity. It may not be amiss to add that, when he walked, he carried his head on one side as one who listens; it may have been that he had contracted the position from his habitual custom of seeing others who had a rope round their necks, or, perhaps, because he feared that he might some day find himself with one entwined about his own.

However this may be, it was his habit when he lived; and I choose to record these reminiscences respecting him, relating as they do to one of the very few for whom I ever entertained the slightest love or affection.

I have said that my uncle was an enthusiast. In his walk of life, which may properly be called a rope walk,[126] he met with nothing but, in some way, or by some process or another, it was made referable, or bore some analogy, or tended directly or indirectly, or partly belonged to, his peculiar vocation. His very books were selected with an eye to his pursuits. Thus, with an amiable simplicity, he had been induced to purchase 'Montague on Hanging,' 'Ure on Dyeing,' 'Strype's Memorials,' an old copy of the life of 'Apollonius Tyaneus,'[127] and many others which it would be needless and, perhaps, tedious to record. He had also amassed a splendid collection of ropes with which he had been at some pains to furnish his apartments; and the histories of those celebrated heroes who had been formerly appended to them constituted a fund of knowledge which, transferred unto me, became a kind of pre-experience of the world, and of the exceeding difficulties an independent man, or a man independent of the world's opinion (which is the same thing), has to encounter during his sojourn here. To these recitals (often enough repeated, I must confess) I at all times lent a willing and an attentive ear, to the infinite delight of the old gentleman, who prognosticated that I must at some future period inevitably become a great man, and one to whom the same praise might be given which was awarded by the poet to Roscommon; that is to say, I should, dying, leave no line which I could wish to be destroyed.[128]

With this near relative I had now lived for the space of three years, scarcely earning my salt by the services I was enabled to render at his household, which were for the most part of a menial and debasing nature; and ofttimes ill at ease and anxious concerning my future prospects, which a long and strict study of the Newgate Calendar[129] taught me that I ought long ago to have commenced to behold through a somewhat more lucid atmosphere. It is true that I partook of the pleasures of the town as they occasionally presented themselves, my uncle never failing to conduct me to witness the executions, and other exciting enjoyments; but I was now old enough to desire something more than mental profit from these examples, and panted for an opportunity of showing that I could see a noose without running my head into it; and that, however well the cap might fit, I was far too prudent to risk trying it on.

To say the truth, there was another and a strong reason why I wished to be forthwith emancipated from my state of ignominious dependence. My uncle was certainly an unobjectionable companion; and one with whom, had I a *carte-blanche*[130] to pursue my particular advocations without overlookance, – diminution of spoil under the pretext of interest in it, or interference in the arrangements necessary to the capture of it, – I say, these trifling objections put into the form of stipulations, and ratified by the other contracting party, I perhaps might have found it convenient, and even pleasing, to remain with the old gentleman till fairly turned from his doors. It may be, by the bye, that in the possible event of such a contract being entered into, I should have insisted upon the performance of a minor condition namely, that, in future, my uncle should restrict himself to an epitomised abstract of events, which he had been accustomed to narrate, I cannot but think unpleasantly, at large. As it was, however, and under the circumstances, he was a quiet and inoffensive creature, seldom bestirring himself with much alacrity, except during the Sessions,[131] when his entire human economy underwent a total change, – tying other people up[132] out of doors with enviable calmness, and at home tying himself down to the sedate enjoyment of his pipe and a pot of ale, with a portion of which he regaled me and such friends as occasionally dropped in to visit him.

But the man possessed one grievous fault in the person of a predominant wife, who ruled the house, and indeed the whole neighbourhood, with a tongue of iron. She was what is called a bustling woman, or a good housewife; that is to say, she pounced upon all the furniture at once, overturned the coal-scuttle, threw the kettle on the hob, scalded the cat, made a terrific lunge at the fire, scattered the bystanders, and, a moment after, was heard trampling in the room over-head, wrestling with a feather-bed, and grappling with the tortured bed-posts till they whined, or rather screamed with agony. Had this been all, we might have forgiven an infirmity which, perhaps, we had thought was constitutional, – an unpleasing, but unavoidable, exuberance of animal spirits: we might have sup-posed, had my uncle and I acquired a classical taste,[133] that the good woman was in the habit of offering up these noisy ceremonies as sacrifices to her Penates, or household gods; had we been superstitious, or delighting in fanciful mythology, we might have regretted that any lubber fiend who purposed to stretch himself on the hearth should fling himself out of the premises with a rheumatic affec-tion of the back; we might have feared lest the lares,[134] in consequence of such frequent levellings of the poker at the grate, should have had their skulls cracked, or have been fairly overturned into the flames. But Mrs. Margaret Ketch was a diurnal server-up of domestic broils. She never was so happy as when she made us wretched; and when we were down at zero, her quicksilver[135] mounted up to fever heat. She was a kind of female Talus,[136] who, without an iron flail (unless her alarming tongue might be so called), contrived to thrash and beat the chaff out of us in a very abominable and unchristian manner. As for my poor uncle, he was in no respect a match for her, either physically, intellectually, or oratori-cally. If he attempted to open his mouth in hostile expostulation, it was closed in a trice, with a crash that omened ill for the perpetuity of his jaws; if he sought to reason with her vagaries, she was *upsides* with[137] him, as she termed it, in a moment; if he betokened war, she sprang upon the inviting lappets of his skull, and, raising his writhing frame into the air, returned him to his seat, affrighted, spiritless, afflicted, fallen. Nor did I fare much more prosperously in my occa-sional revolts, or futile attempts to breast this outrageous torrent; but I was flung into cupboard or closet, there to pine till bitter constraint compelled me to assume compunction or remorse; or shot down into the sable secrecy of the cellar, minutely to inspect sea-coal,[138] or with listless eye to con the fortuitous arrangement of infinite lumber which preceding years had gathered to them-selves in that comfortless depository.

For these oft-recurring wrongs done to my person, I cherished an immitiga-ble antipathy to my kinswoman, – an antipathy which, on comparing notes with my uncle, I found could only be equalled by the cordial hatred which he had also long encouraged to her prejudice. But, great as my loathing to the individual might have been, I had every sufficient reason to believe that it was met more than half way by the extreme aversion she felt for me; so that, between us all, the amount of detestation on every side was monstrous and almost incredible. Perfectly cognisant of this unpleasing sentiment on her part, and fully aware of its existence in my own person, it was an unceasing source of wonder to me that

Mrs. Margaret Ketch had ever permitted me to make her house my domicile; a wonder only less than my surprise that I had suffered myself to be inmate of it for so long a space of time.

It is true that I contrived, during the latter period of my stay, to make such reprisals on my enemy as my ingenuity, whetted by revenge, instructed me in preparing; and I found that these practices were most pleasing to the old man, who, either for lack of skill, or from a deficiency of courage, had never done himself the pleasure of exchanging his injuries for smaller parcels of the same kind; or rather, of making her take out the wholesale stock of goods (for so she considered them) with which she supplied him, in retail assortments of the same articles. Old Ketch, I say, literally winked at my proceedings, and with 'nods, and becks, and wreathed smiles,'[139] egged me on to the mischief-working adulteration of her dram-bottle, the utter derangement and destruction of her domestic economy, and oftentimes the wretched ruin of her personal convenience. It may readily be supposed that these congenial conceits, put practically into force, when they excited no suspicion of their inventor, caused extreme private mirth to bestir itself in us; but, unfortunately, squint[140] suspicion not seldom turned its eye upon me, and I was fain to suffer such castigations as her inhuman rage deemed commensurate; thereby restricting the mirth to one who, perhaps, would willingly have purchased the pleasure with the amount of pain I was doomed to pay for it.

But my sojourn at this place was to have an end. One evening, my uncle and I had been discussing our pot of ale, which we were making away with something in the manner that Hamlet might be supposed to commence the drinking up of the Easel;[141] that is to say, we were swallowing it with no unnecessary delay; and now the emptiness of the pot demanded that it should be replenished a third time. On my arrival at the Red Lion for this purpose, whom should I behold at the bar, somewhat sophisticated,[142] but Mrs. Margaret Ketch? But why should I have put the predicament in the interrogative form? thereby insinuating to my reader a possible surprise, which, indeed, did not exist in the case at all, that worthy lady being frequently to be found at the same resort in the same condition.

'Hilloah! young devil-skin,' cried she, as I was slinking from the premises, hoping to have been unobserved; but that husky voice, imparted by incessant gin, again recalled me: 'Hilloah, young devil-skin,' for that was the quaint name which she familiarly applied to me, 'tell your uncle I shall be home directly;' and she dismissed me with a curse which she was frequently pleased to invoke upon my person. Having possessed myself of my ale, I returned home, and communicated the unwelcome intelligence as I was bidden, not forgetting the supplementary anathema with which she had presented me.

This naturally fired a train of reflection which it was by no means uncommon to us to kindle. 'I'll tell you what, Jack,' said my uncle, at length, taking his pipe from his mouth, and erecting himself in his chair, 'that 'ere woman, Jack, is the very devil.' 'Or one of his young ones,' cried I; the identical remark and the same answer having been made a thousand times before. 'One of his young ones, boy,' retorted he, 'the old one himself disguised in a worse shape; I'll be blowed if I know what it is to have a moment's peace; I leads a dromedary[143] life altogether.' 'A dromedary[144] life,' I repeated: 'a thousand times worse; the humps of all the dromedaries in Egypt, and your own into the bargain, wouldn't enable you to bear your existence with that old cat.' 'Come, no nonsense, Jack,' cried my companion, who, like many other people, did not much like derogatory remarks made upon anything behind his back, '*you* let my hump alone, will you? I tell you that 'ere woman, getting queer[145] at the gin-shop, is a fulsome varmint; – I say, Jack,' and the old man closed one of his eyes, and smiled his mouth into a semi-circle while he accomplished the appropriate action, 'it's too good for her a precious sight, but I should like to have the tucking on her up,[146] that's all.'

'You should, should you, you villain?' resounded a voice too intimately known, and its owner burst headlong into the room, making her way in the direction of my uncle, who, with his mouth transfixed with the grin it had assumed previous to her entrance, sat paralysed in his chair; 'I'll teach you to tuck me up, you rascal;' and the nose of the culprit was snatched with a gripe to which that of a vice were mere amiable dalliance. What followed I know not in detail, for I waited not minutely to inspect these operations; but, betaking myself to the other end of the room, was insanely endeavouring to push myself through the wall. I, however, by a kind of mad instinct, had seized upon the poker, well knowing that, although at that particular moment the pervading fury might knock me down with a feather, it was the very last thing she would prefer to choose for that purpose.

'And you, you ragamuffin!' she roared most odiously, as, relinquishing my uncle's nose, which now looked like a pasteboard profile, she was about to seize upon that of her nephew; but a plaguy dig in the ribs, communicated by my weapon, unconsciously to myself, somewhat disconcerted her; which dig being immediately followed by a vexatious knock on the head, resembling any thing but an encouraging tap, laid her senseless at my feet.

'I say, Jack, you've done it now, hav'n't you?' said my uncle, smiling faintly through his tears which torture, not grief, had called forth; but at this moment several neighbours forced themselves into the apartment, and took such a view of the matter as the peculiar bias or leaning of each prompted him to prefer; all, however, troubling their heads painfully about a business which only properly concerned one head not belonging to either.

When these were gone, and Mrs. Ketch duly carried to bed, the result was discovered to be not so bad as had been feared by her temporary attendants; and my uncle and I were about to reseat ourselves, – he to adjust his disorganised

Mrs. Margaret Ketch wreaking her Vengeance upon her Husband.

features, and I to ponder on the event which had just occurred, fraught as it must be with a change, whether for good or for ill, to myself – when the door opened, and un elderly gentleman made his appearance, of whom more in the next chapter.

CHAPTER V.

MR. JABEZ SNAVEL,[147] who now seated himself by the fire, after carefully dusting the chair with his handkerchief, and taking in each hand a skirt of his coat, lest the weight of his person should disagree with its texture, was what used to be termed an attorney, but is now known by the more ambitious title of a solicitor.[148] His practice, however, such as it was, lay more in criminal than in civil cases. Mr. Jabez Snavel was perfectly well aware that, as self-preservation is the first law of nature, so the practice of a written law that was brought in aid of that object, or was supposed to assist to that end, would, in all probability, be as well remunerated as the pursuance of any other branch of law with which he was acquainted. He knew very well that, when the law is broken, to the law you must apply for means to make it appear that it is not so. At all events, the compensation must be of the same material as the outrage. In like manner, one poison is prescribed to expel another; and it is popularly believed that the best way to catch a thief is to set another after him. This was Mr. Jabez Snavel's view of the question.

But this gentleman, I fear, in spite of his excellent and irrefragable arguments, very seldom contrived to bring his clients off, when their causes were brought on; his peculiar system being, when a hole had been effected in the great mesh or net of law – not to show the victim another small hole by which he might, perchance, escape, but to take him boldly up to the very fissure he had made, that he might there contend that there was no hole at all. No wonder then, that, while cases of this description were suffered to stand on their own merits, the platform[149] occasionally gave way, and his unhappy clients found that though, indeed, they had good legs to stand upon, there was nothing beneath their feet upon which they could by any means be permitted to stand.

Let us, therefore, at once, look upon Mr. Jabez Snavel as one whose ostensible profession was to save other people's lives, but whose real object and extreme desire had ever been to get his own living – and, I believe, after a little reflection, we shall all agree that this latter aim most commonly supersedes any consideration for others – even with the best of us; and, amongst the worst, I incline to think that others are seldom considered at all, except as exceedingly useful agents or tools, which may occasionally be handled with profit and advantage.

In furtherance of such views as the demand for daily existence brought before his eyes, Mr. Jabez Snavel was accustomed to call upon my uncle, whose interest, it may readily be imagined, was sometimes not to be despised, in the introduction of him to those who had cause to fear that they had given the law a pretext for hanging them out of the way at once. This will promptly account for the appearance of Snavel upon the present occasion – and intimate to the reader the probability that such good offices on the part of old Ketch were mutually advantageous, – the lawyer, perhaps, encouraging too much gratitude to baulk his friend of his accustomed perquisites upon the occasion of such windfalls; and the other possessing too lively a sense of his own interest to patronise any one who was likely to do so.

But as Mr. Jabez Snavel is destined to make a slight figure in my history, I cannot do less than introduce him in a more bodily shape than I have hitherto done, – at the same time that I communicate such a general idea of the man, in his moral capacity, as will be not inconsistent with a principle I have laid down for my own guidance; namely, to set down nought in malice, – but, on the contrary, to speak as I have found, and to draw conclusions from sufficient data; a safe principle, by the bye, so far as I am concerned, – seeing that very few of my friends would much care for the estimation in which the world might hold them; and the small minority of those who did would be quite indifferent as to the estimation in which they were held by me.

Mr. Jabez Snavel was in height not more than five feet from the level of the floor, – slender as the expectations[150] of a sixth brother, and mild and affable as a moonbeam at the assignation of lovers in a romantic poem. His invariable black clothes were brushed with a perseverance worthy of a better suit, and his shirt-frill and small white cravat were plaited with a care that reflected the highest honour upon the laundress employed in getting them up. If there was any one thing that might be supposed to detract from the prepossessing *tout ensemble*[151] of Mr. Jabez Snavel, it was his voice, which, perhaps, resembled that of the prodigal son, after a banquet upon pea-shells, in that it was somewhat husky.

But the moral conformation of the man was not a little singular. He had absolutely not the most remote notion that there was the slightest distinction between right and wrong; or indeed that such words symbolically represented two moral extremes. He might, perhaps, like the younger Brutus,[152] doubt the reality or existence of virtue, if the question had ever been mooted in his presence; but, in truth, he had never thought about the matter at all; and knew no more of her dictates than the French citizen of prose;[153] unlike that simple-minded individual, however, in this respect, that he had never unconsciously practised that of which he ingenuously confessed his ignorance. Mr. Jabez Snavel, accordingly, looked upon Fortune[154] as the great arbitress of the affairs of this world; and the conduct of men, under given circumstances, was applauded as prudent, or stigmatised as rash, even as his own opinion decided upon the financial result of such policy. For he knew that the best-laid schemes often failed from some unknown cause; and was therefore fain to set up a goddess whom he called Fortune, to supervise and to consummate all human proceedings.

The reader will not be in a situation to wonder, bearing these peculiarities of Snavel in mind, when he is informed that that person was totally free from some debasing passions which afflict and degrade greater men. He knew not envy, hatred, or malice; but was principally solicitous to improve his own worldly estate, without grudging the gifts of fortune bestowed upon others. He as little cared for the means whereby others became possessed of their property as he stickled at safe contrivances to make that property his own. He was himself – they were themselves: – they got all they could from whom they could – he took all he could from them. Such was the little man who seated himself at my uncle's fire-side in the beginning of this chapter.

'Well, my good friend, and how does the world use you?' said he, taking a pinch of snuff from a vast Scotch mull,[155] which he drew from his pocket; – 'trade stirring, eh? – I fear not – very little business doing just now – very light cases these sessions – mere petty larceny doings, I see; – but how is this? – you look bewildered – down upon your luck? as the vulgar say – fie, fie – ' and the professional man winked his eye at me, as a notification that he was to be understood as facetious; whereupon I assumed an applauding grin.

'Why, Mr. Snavel,' responded my uncle, with a sigh, 'I can't say but I am rather so – my old woman has been at it again – ' and he directed his thumb to the ceiling, by way of hint that she was above, 'but this once she has *napt* it;[156] ha'n't she, Jack?' and the old gentleman appealed to me by an expressive nudge with his shoulder.

'Why, how is this, Master Johnny?' cried Snavel, turning to me affectionately (he had ever shown a seeming love for me, and I believe would have caressed a succabus,[157] had it stood in the same relative position to my uncle); 'how is this, my man, your good uncle talks in riddles; come tell me all about it, my lad,' and he led me before him.

Thus encouraged, I gave a succinct account[158] of the whole transaction, with a praiseworthy delicacy towards one of the company present, softening down the provocation given by him; and with a natural disregard of the absent party, inflaming the assault committed by her as much as possible.

'Let me go to your good lady,' said Snavel, after a pause, suddenly starting up, 'I'll soon set this small matter to rights' – and he undoubtedly possessed great influence with my aunt – 'it's an absurd quarrel altogether;' and, mounting the stairs, he was soon heard, in soothing tones, expostulating, convincing, entreating, and advising, the too intolerable invalid.

'He's a rare clever dog, that Snavel,' whispered my uncle in a hoarse undertone; 'by goles,[159] he's the only man to manage Peg Ketch, after all – I wish he had her with all my heart.'

A further expenditure of kind wishes towards Snavel was at this moment rendered ill-timed by the appearance of that gentleman, who advanced towards the speaker, shaking him cordially by the hand, saying, 'It's all right, my friend; Mrs. Ketch is now perfectly aware that you spoke in jest; and that Johnny meant nothing by what he did – it was all a mistake; but, you know, my good sir, women will be capricious. Do you know, she won't permit our Jack here to stay in the house after to-night – no – she certainly expresses herself idiomatically, I might even say oddly, when she says, 'out he must bundle' to-morrow morning.'

My uncle looked amazingly chap-fallen at this intelligence, and I am inclined to believe that my own physiognomy was at that moment rather calculated to inspire pity for its longitude than to excite interest by its placidity of expression. To be cut by my own relations; this was the unkindest cut of all; and besides, at this very time, I knew no place in the world in which I could put my head, except my hat, which was at the present juncture sorely deficient in crown, and withal much damaged by inclement weather and other casualties.

Mr. Jabez Snavel was the first to break this ugly silence, into which we had been so suddenly plunged. 'I'll tell you what I'll do,' cried he, 'I'll take John into my office, if you have no objection, and make a man of him; he shall have his food and clothing found[160] him, and he can sleep on a mattress under the desk; and in time, perhaps, his services may entitle him to a liberal salary.'

'No, will you, though?' said my uncle with emotion; 'you're a good fellow, Snavel, and I'll do as much for you another time; you'll find Jack a sharp lad – knows every thing; and if he is rather wild it's no fault of his'n; it's his natur – he can't help it; and, besides, he does it all on the sly – sly young cove, a'n't you, Jack?' and the reference was accompanied by a well-meant cuff on the ear.

'Well, well, sir,' said Snavel, with the important air of one who has the obligation for once on his own side; 'we shall see what can be done with the youth. What say you, Mr. John, are you willing to become one of the honourable profession of the law?'

I expressed my gratitude as well as a rather vague sense of what was due to that sentiment impelled me, and accepted the proposal with avidity, – not so much from any knowledge on my part of the advantages of the situation itself, as from that undefined feeling which prompts youths of a similar age to lay hold of the first opportunity of escape from domestic thraldom that presents itself, whether it assume the shape of a stool in a counting house, or a cabin in an East Indiaman.[161]

This affair being for the present arranged, our visitor insisted upon standing a sufficient quantity of gin and water – a beverage of which he himself partook largely, and with great seeming comfort to himself; and, after much conversation, chiefly carried on between the two elderly gentlemen in a whisper, Mr. Jabez Snavel took his leave and commended us to our beds, to which we both retired considerably fuddled; this being the first night of my public initiation[162] into the mysteries of the bowl; and the eve of the day that was to present me to the world, another candidate for its smiles, and a new votary at the shrine of Mammon.[163]

As I lay asleep, a thousand incongruous images presented themselves before me in succession. My father was again active in his vocation, and anon again dangled in the air. My mother was busy once more calculating my destiny in a tea-cup;[164] my companions in the parish school came out of the darkness and stood before me, and Misty was amongst them. The organ pealed in my ears; the verger shrieked, and the parish authorities made way for my uncle and his helpmate, her unsightly skull clotted with gore.

I awoke, but the morning was yet only half awake, and the old familiar furniture of the room indistinctly revealed itself to me. Every thing around, that I had so often seen, appeared, now that I saw it for the last time, as though it knew and regretted my departure. Unmoved as ever, it still looked with a graver and a sadder stillness, and seemed as though it were conscious that after I was gone it should be degraded into unserviceable lumber. The old chair, one of whose legs had been broken and never amputated, leaned towards me with affectionate attachment. The portrait of Jonathan Wild[165] gazed upon me with less malignity than usual – nay, wore almost a benignant expression. The patched and broken casement wished itself whole again for my sake; and the small truckle bed, as I arose from its sacking, creaked out an affectionate farewell.

I descended the stairs, and entered the room below. The shutters were yet closed, and I heard nothing but the ticking of the venerable clock. I sat down, and could almost have wept to leave my misery behind; it had almost become dear to me. But, with more wisdom and less sentiment, I arose and proceeded to black my shoes, and to make such other arrangements as my fitting appearance in a professional office required from me.

CHAPTER VI.

HAVING taken an affectionate leave of my uncle and bestowed a mute malediction on his good lady, who lay blaspheming in her chamber, I made the best of my way to Stork Court, a snug locality situated in one of those narrow streets that appear like winding cracks or fissures made by the sun in the great mass of buildings that constitute the right hand portion of Cheapside.[166] On my entrance into the dim and silent office of Mr. Jabez Snavel, which looked like a small nook into which a portion of the past had hidden itself, a young man, seated at an elevated desk by the side of a dingy window, demanded my pleasure. It were, methought, presumptuous to explain at once that I had come hither for the purpose of dividing the sway of this small monarchy; I contented myself, therefore, by stating that I wished to see Mr. Snavel; whereupon, being informed that he had not yet made his appearance, I was requested to sit down. While I thus waited with my hat between my knees – a custom sanctioned by immemorial usage, but which I preferred as a temporary means of concealing its numberless failings on the respectable score – I had full leisure to examine the future sanctum, or congenial studio, in which my ulterior designs were, as I believed, to be prepared for the London market. Upon looking around me I saw, and as my eyes accustomed themselves to this new light, which was as darkness, I saw distinctly that I was sitting in a room about nine feet by seven, furnished with a double desk, two stools, the chair I occupied, and a number of square boxes piled one upon the other. Over the fire-place hung a law almanack, marked with long stripes of ink in several places to denote the periods of term;[167] and by its side depended a small paper on which were notified the several sittings. A door led out of this melancholy dungeon into a lesser cell, which having for its bowels a square table and an arm-chair, was accustomed to receive and digest, as I rightly surmised, the daily person of Mr. Jabez Snavel himself. Having completed my survey of these surrounding circumstances, the monotonous scratching of a pen directed my attention to the young man engaged in wielding it, in whom I began to feel that natural interest excited and claimed by those with whom we feel that we are about to be indirectly or otherwise, slightly or intimately, associated. He was of a spare form, or, as it is called, habit of body; tall, but with a stoop in the shoulders and a contraction of the chest. Through his lantern jaws a light beamed, as of consumption; and the eager expression of his eyes might have been mistaken for acute intelligence, if it did not too plainly indicate acute hunger. His head was surmounted by a plentiful quantity of dusty hair, apparently seldom teased by the comb or confined by a night-cap; for it stuck out in all the fanciful directions which the quaint vagaries of slumber pleased to point out for it. This capillary coronal, being of a hue resembling mud or brick dust, or rather a mixture of the two, was not ill-matched by his brown coat, which, buttoned close up to his chin, came only half as far down as a metal-buttoned waistcoat of evanescent yellow, and possessed sleeves which were far too aristocratic to descend low enough to cover his wrist bones. There was an anxious folding of the dirty check neck-cloth, also, which disclosed too plainly that in whatever sum he might be indebted to his washerwoman, the debt had not been contracted recently. This scrutiny being completed, I was becoming impatient for the appearance of my new master, and had begun to play with my heels in the manner usual upon such occasions, when the young man descended from his desk, and placed himself by the fire-place.

'Is your business with Mr. Snavel very important?' he inquired, as he raised a small rusty poker, and inserted it gently into the grate towards a spark, which, thus appealed to, moved itself lazily on towards another coal, and, after a moment, burst into a passing flicker of derision. 'Perhaps,' he added, as he replaced the fire-iron, 'I should be able to give you an answer?'

'No, sir,' said I; 'I am the young man come to be his clerk. I was to be here the first thing this morning.'

'Oh! you're young Ketch, are you?' cried he. 'I've heard Snavel speak of engaging you. How is your uncle?'

Having answered these interrogatories, we slid into easy conversation, touching principally on general topics; at length he demanded, a little abruptly, 'Do you know old Snavel?'

'Only slightly, sir; I've seen him at my uncle's occasionally.'

'Don't call me 'sir,' good Ketch,' cried my companion, 'call me Wisp – Will Wisp.[168] But, old Snavel, – you'll find him a sad old rip;[169] upon my honour he is. Now, what the deuce[170] can he want with you here? there's nothing to do – the devil a scratch – you'll be compelled to eke out your work as the boy did his manners, ha! ha! Have you any money about you?'

I confessed to the proprietorship of eighteen-pence, which, by-the-bye, my uncle had given me as a farewell largess.

'Well, well,' said he, 'I don't want it: just stand a pot of half-and-half before Snavel comes. I've a small loaf in my pocket, and you get a little bit of cheese for a relish; let's enjoy ourselves.'

I was too happy to acquire a new and, as I hoped, a valuable, friend at so inconsiderable an outlay, and departed on my mission, presently returning with the required liquid.

'Aye, that'll do, my good fellow, set it down,' cried Wisp, as I brought in the pot, and he produced a twopenny loaf. 'Snavel won't be here for an hour. Come, let us sit down and keep the fire warm; stop, let's put on another coal – the bushel's almost out, by jingo! and not a farthing of petty cash to pay for another, and old Nubbley never gives tick.'

I could not but draw inferences from this heedless gossip, of the limited extent of Snavel's finances, and began to harbour strange apprehensions of a defalcation in my year's salary; or, more properly to speak, of the unenviable possession of a somewhat Horatian[171] revenue – namely, the bare enjoyment of my good spirits to feed and clothe me; a property by the way belonging, and it were to be wished, exclusively so, to prismatic cameleons.[172]

'There never was such a miserable curmudgeon as Snavel,' continued my companion, after a pause, filled up on his part by nearly emptying the contents of the pot, 'and then the fellow's as poor and as sanctified[173] as a church mouse; here, I've been with him these four years, and the deuce a skurrick[174] do I get more than fifteen shillings a week, – the wages of sin, I call it, for it's death[175] to me. I wish I had concluded an engagement with old Racoon, of Quality Court, – there was a pound a week and the chance of increase; but why do I wish it? Racoon mizzled[176] about a month afterwards,' – and he pointed significantly to the floor with his fore-finger. 'Well, well, all's for the best; I shall get on, I suppose, by degrees, as lawyers go to heaven – ha, ha!'

Finding my friend thus communicative, I discovered it in my nature to acquaint him with the circumstances under which I had been induced to close with Mr. Jabez Snavel's proposal, and took the liberty of hinting my suspicions of the regularity of current specie in return for my services. 'Ho! ho! and so the old boy made the offer to you?' cried Wisp. 'Well, I say nothing; only, don't you wish, eh? – do you see the joke?' – and he winked his eye, and buried his nose in the pewter vessel for a length of time; 'and you're to sleep under the desk, are you?' he continued; 'come, that *is* a good one, however; why, there was young Meagrejoint presented up the spectre in that very hole just before I knew Snavel. Mother Wizen[177] said that, when she came one Saturday night to do out[178] the office, there he was, stiff as a glass of three-quarter grog;[179] – hang me, if she didn't say he looked, when they took him up for all the world like a long rush-light[180] – one to the pound, only half dipped – there's a chance!'[181]

This recital touching Meagrejoint detracted greatly, I must confess, from the half share of mirth which, under other circumstances, I might have been induced to contribute to Wisp's merriment, particularly when I reflected that the fate of that unfortunate youth might stand a chance of being repeated in my person;

but I strove manfully to conquer my mental dismay, and succeeded in fetching a wretched smile that struggled painfully with my jaws, like a bereaved Merry-Andrew[182] striving to break open a sepulchre.

'Well, well,' rejoined Wisp, who evidently saw and pitied my painful feelings, 'it's not so bad, neither; what's the use of sighing, while time is on the wing – or while he's on his perch either, if that's all: you must make shift for a time; Snavel won't be able to hold out much longer, I'm thinking, and so it's all one: you'll not find the mattress one of the largest, by the bye – short and sweet, like the old woman's pie-crust,[183] as the saying is; – but, hilloa! here he comes;' and, with a dexterous jerk, my fellow clerk hurried the empty pot into his desk, and sprang on to his stool with a celerity evidently attained by frequent practice.

'Well, my boy, John, and how are you this morning?' exclaimed Snavel, with affable demeanour, as, accompanied by a tall and elderly gentleman, he entered the office. 'I say, Mr. Wisp,' and he turned towards my friend, who appeared deeply occupied in transcription, 'can't you find something for this young gentleman to do? – he's a nephew of my friend, Mr. John Ketch; pray set him about something instantly, we are to make a lawyer of him.' 'Indeed, Sir,' answered Wisp, respectfully, 'I was not aware; I'll find him employment directly;' and as the two gentlemen retired into the back office, the facetious young man bestowed a grimace upon his master.

'Here, Ketch, take and copy that,' cried he, 'it will do as well as any thing else; come, spring into Meagrejoint's seat; here are pens, ink, and paper.'

With a nervous trembling of the fingers, and my tongue servilely following the direction of every letter I formed, I proceeded to copy an indenture which Wisp laid before me, and was soon immersed in the study of that extraordinary language which, for purposes best known to themselves, has been so long common to the lawyers.

'I say, Ketch,' cried Wisp, at length, 'did you see that gentleman who went into the back office with Snavel? – he's our only respectable client; how the old rascal obtained the carrying on of his cause I don't know; it's a chancery suit,[184] and expected soon to be decided. Poor Wilmot! I'm sorry for the old buck;[185] he's an honest fellow, and tipped me a guinea[186] once: we get Sly and Sharp to carry on the cause for us. Wilmot will get a good round sum when the thing is finally settled.'

Wisp's further statement was cut short by the opening of the door, and Mr. Snavel and his respectable client came forth; the former saying, as he passed through the office, 'Mr. Wisp, I am going with Mr. Wilmot, and shall probably not return again to-day. Will you see that John is properly informed of the arrangements for his lodging? John, Mr. Wisp will see that your comforts are attended to:' and he departed with his friend.

'You be d—,' cried Wisp, emphatically, as the door closed after them. 'Yes, John, I'll see your comforts attended to; did you hear the precious old scamp? Come, let's knock off for to-day; it's three o'clock – dinner time; I'll be back again in two hours.' 'And I'll go,' said I, 'to my uncle's; I want to say a word to him;' and, raising my hat, I made the best of my way to Rose and Crown court, for my mind misgave me mightily as to the carrying on of my fleshly establishment under this unforeseen arrangement.

The old gentleman made many wry faces at my proposal to take a portion of my salary in advance though his pockets; but at last consented to furnish me with a trifle towards the attainment of an object which he rightly considered of immense importance; that is to say, the study of the law, with a view to learn how, safely, to escape its provisions; an aim which I believe is pretty generally pursued, although, I fear, not always successfully carried out in the end. Having succeeded in my paramount object, I returned to my professional duties, and was soon after joined by Wisp, with whom I lingered out the time till eight o'clock, much to my worldly[187] furtherance and profit; and, indeed, I now began to feel that there was something worth the exercise of such gifts as I possessed, whose attainment I was led to hope would be found not beyond the reach of my capacity.

'Come, Jack,' cried my friend, as the clock struck, 'I'll show you where I spend my evenings, and introduce you to a few good fellows; I intend that you shall be one of us. The Magpie and Punchbowl is not far off; two nice girls in the bar – there's a chance for you, you young dog;' and he led me away, not unwilling, to the public house bearing the only half appropriate sign of the Magpie and Punchbowl, – the former, indeed, serving as an exceedingly fit symbol of the chattering landlady, but the latter by no means accurately shadowing forth the quality of drink usually in course of imbibition at that convenient hostelry.

CHAPTER VII.

I CHOOSE to conceal the name of the street in which the Magpie and Punchbowl was situated, for very obvious reasons; but it may not be improper to hint that the house to which that not unfrequent but, I cannot help thinking, remarkable, sign belonged, was so located that a stone's throw, in the right direction, whether from Paul's chain or Knight Rider street, must inevitably have broken the Punchbowl, or knocked the Magpie on the head; or, in plain language, the house was equi-distant from, and contiguous to, these two points. A very feeble glimmer made itself visible at the bar window, and the half obliterated chequers[188] on the door-posts emphatically announced that the jovial crew which had been once accustomed to lend original brilliance to the parlour had departed – some perhaps to a more congenial Hole in the Wall, others probably to a less congenial hole in the earth; all, however, from the Magpie and Punchbowl.

And yet Mrs. Malkin[189] and her two daughters lingered in the premises; whether from affection to the spot itself, from long habit, or from that cause which compels us all to move in the precise sphere we occupy – namely, an inability to retire into, or to create another – I know not; and hither a few miserable individuals, whom the tyrant's plea, necessity, constrained to much loathed temperance, – together with one or two, whom want of a better taste, or desire of such company, attracted, accustomed themselves to resort.

'Well, and how are you to night, Mrs. Malkin?' cried Wisp, as we turned into this desolate place of entertainment, and halted at the bar.

'Still very ill, lad, with the rhumatis,'[190] answered a fat but ghastly woman, whose round face of suet appeared to be tied up with a pudding cloth; the features of which face had motion given to them by bread and cheese and onions, which her dirty fingers were raising to her mouth – 'can't do nothing for it but eat and drink;' and she captured another onion with the point of her knife.

'But Miss Susan is quite well, I hope,' said Wisp, directing his attention to a rather pretty girl, who sat opposite her mother similarly employed, and who, thus accosted, smiled complacently. 'Well, Grimes, there you are,' again exclaimed the urbane Wisp, nodding to a warlike person about thirty years of age, who smoked his pipe by the fire, and sipped at intervals from a glass of gin and water. 'Yes here I am, as usual,' answered Grimes, with a hoarse voice, as though all the colds in the kingdom had been left in his keeping sine die;[191] 'confoundedly out of temper too; that scoundrel Grogit was to have called and paid me the money he borrowed of me, but the devil a bit has he been here;' and he made a significant[192] inclination of the head towards Mrs. Malkin, who was looking in another direction, and winked knowingly to Wisp: 'but who have you got with you?'

'A young friend of mine,' answered Wisp, 'a small limb of the law.'[193] 'A limb of the law!' retorted the other, 'a funny-bone, I should imagine, for he sticks close to your elbow; come, that's a good one, d— me!' and he burst into ferocious cachinations. 'You'll find Westminster Abbey and Uncle in the parlour,' cried the landlady, interrupting this sally of merriment. 'I call little[194] Gibbon, Westminster Abbey'[195], she continued, addressing herself to me, probably perceiving my surprise at this novel announcement; 'he's such a solemn-looking subject, a'n't he, Wisp? – and as for Uncle, every body knows Uncle.'

'Well, I'll join them,' returned Wisp; 'send us in two pints of porter and two empty pipes: oh! *you* can bring them, Betsey;' and he chucked under the chin a little red-haired girl, who at this moment found her way to the bottom of the stairs, with a pail of dirty water in one hand, and a miscellaneous collection of short and long brooms, dust shovel and candle, in the other. 'Don't be in a hurry, that's a *good* man,' exclaimed Miss Betsey, speaking through a profusion of locks which carelessly fell over her face; and she wriggled along the passage, her very legs bending elastically under their burden, and at length deposited herself in the back kitchen.

The parlour into which we now introduced ourselves bore, it must be confessed, a most repulsive aspect. About half a dozen tables, wearing on their surface a variety of glutinous rings, mementos of former pots, were shone upon by a solitary candle placed upon one of them; while more than double the number of chairs leaned carelessly against the wall with their arms a kimbo, like a parcel of idle footmen whom nobody was willing to employ. An old engraving of a Durham prize ox stood mournfully in his black frame against the wall, and an eviscerated magpie in a broken glass-case protruded its post-mortem intestines, which had been furnished for it by the original preserver in the form of a wisp of hay. The window was hung with faded red curtains, in and about which the busy spider had woven his wily web; and the sash retained its accumulated dust of years; a matter, by the bye, of no great importance, since nothing could be seen through it but a dead wall, surmounted by fragments of glass bottles, whose efficacy was chiefly ascertained by the unanimous testimony of tender-footed grimalkins.

Seated, or rather, hanging over the fire, as though they feared lest it should suddenly dart up the chimney, and so leave them to perish, were two persons, – the one a rather elderly gentleman in black smoking his pipe; the other a young man of apparently short stature with his feet on the fender, his elbows on his knees, and his head clasped between his hands. Could my eyes deceive me? No. The elderly gentleman was, indeed, Misty, my tutor at the parish school. A change had fallen upon Misty since my last perusal of his physical economy; his hair was silvered, his features more marked, and the expression of his face was that of a pervading melancholy. It is true, I had heretofore seen him employed in a very different occupation; but it might naturally be imagined that his present pursuit would rather tend to relax and chasten the severe solemnity which he was wont to wear during the hours devoted to scholastic exercises.

While I thus sat persuing[196] my ancient acquaintance, and applying from time to time to the pint of porter which Miss Betsey had placed before me, Wisp was engaged in conversation with Westminster Abbey. Directing my attention to that individual, I discovered a very short and apparently robust person about four and twenty years of age, of a remarkably steadfast and fixed countenance, whose broken nose stood in the centre of a face fearfully marked by the small pox, like a rude mark set up in a desert to warn the traveller of frequent pitfalls. His shoulders aspired to his ears, the extremities of the latter resting not ungracefully on the peaks of the former, and his hair stood up on his scalp like the bristly crown on the apex of the Monument.[197]

'Come and sit with us, young fellow,' cried Gibbon, who had observed me gazing at him with profound attention; 'Wisp has told me who you are; where's your uncle? we never see him here now; he's too proud to visit us, I fancy, – got up in the world, I suppose; – a kind of mushroom *Ketch-up*,[198] eh?'

'None of your vile puns,' interrupted Wisp, addressing the other, whose gravity of visage forbade the imputation of quips or verbal eccentricities of that nature.

'I will whisper my witticisms, good brother-*in-law*,' retorted Gibbon, as gravely as before, 'to whom I please; torturing syllables is not half so bad as torturing silly fools, as you do: don't you think me a rum[199] fellow, Ketch?'

I protested that I did think him a very rum fellow.

'You'll think so, indeed, when you know me better,' he continued; 'my name is Edward Gibbon – christened after the great historian:[200] fine fellow, that Gibbon; but not half so fine as this Gibbon. I call myself the handsomest rascal in London – a killing dog.'[201]

'Killing, indeed,' cried Wisp, with a sneer, 'calculated to kill any one who looks at you.'

'Come, come, that's too bad,' said Gibbon, evidently well pleased, for he looked graver than usual; 'now, point me out where I am deficient in attractions, and I'll explain. You think me too short? Well, I shall never go to my *long* home,[202] that's certain. My shoulders are too high? Perpetual shrugging them at the vileness of human nature. My hair straight and bristly? It has stood on end so long at the wickedness of mankind. My face marked with the small pox? Well, how can you call it a plain[203] face? And as for my nose,' and the panegyrist placed his finger upon it – 'that nose was once a Roman – not a rum one, mind, a Roman[204] – I thanked Scroggins for breaking it; it made way for a joke I had long been labouring with: I now call it 'Gibbon's Decline and Fall of the Roman Empire.'"

These conceits, though they tickled me mightily, were received with strange coldness by Wisp, and with utter listlessness and inattention by Misty; and I now began to discover that little Mr. Edward Gibbon was one of those studious wags who painfully employ themselves in the elaboration of puns, and whose reasoning faculties are entirely absorbed, if not destroyed, in the operation. It was evident, also, that the present sally was a mere cold repetition of the same eternal jokes which he was accustomed to let off upon every new acquaintance.

At this moment a very smart young gentleman made his appearance in the room, and was hailed by Wisp and Gibbon with evident marks of satisfaction, by the familiar title of Tom Haynes. There was nothing in the appearance or manners of this young gentleman that might not with equal applicability be predicated of a thousand others constantly to be seen in this vast metropolis.

'Haynes, my boy,' cried Gibbon, 'what are you going to stand? – we're all waiting to whet our whistles – the pots are empty – I'm confoundedly dry.'

'Oh! you're like the old woman's dishclout,' said Wisp, 'you look best when you're dry. – Don't you think he does, Haynes?'

'Well I don't know but he does;' answered the new-comer, who was clearly[205] one of those soft easy cushions who, or to sustain the metaphor, which, contribute to the comfort of rogues while they sit at ease in their seats. 'However,' continued Haynes, 'I'll stand two pots of ale with great pleasure; and Uncle and your young friend shall join us.'

'I had rather be excused, Mr. Haynes,' said Misty, now opening his mouth for vocal purposes for the first time, 'I shall soon be going, and – '

'Oh! but you must,' interposed Haynes, ringing the bell, as he sat on one of the tables.

'What do you please to want, gentlemen?' said Grimes, mimicking a waiter, as he thrust his head into the door, 'two pots of ale – oh! your most obedient; I'll be after them like shot through a holly-bush:' and away he went, presently returning with the prescribed quantity.

'I'll just take one glass and run,' cried Grimes; as he set down the pots, 'I'm talking over the old girl about my score.[206] I say, Wisp, it was all a hum[207] about Grogit; mum's the word.'

'When do you mean to get rid of that voice, Grimes?' demanded Gibbon, who was evidently trolling for a pun; 'it's rather a rough customer – one would swear you had swallowed a bear, and yet it's quite unbearable.'

'Swallowed a bear!' retorted Grimes, swallowing down his ale 'and one would swear you had been brought up by a bear, you ugly cub – that's a good one, d—n me;' and he roared with huge bursts of laughter: 'when do I mean to get rid of my voice?' he continued, 'never; it's more than I can do; I got cold when I was wrecked coming home from New York: you'd have set up your shoulders, d—n me, if you had been tossed about three days and nights on a tar barrel, as I was; yes, by the Lord, you'd have wished your nutmeg-grater chaps to be grinding grins[208] in the Magpie and Punchbowl, I'm thinking;' and away hurried the polite Grimes, leaving his adversary not a little discomfited at these personal allusions.

'There he goes,' cried Westminster Abbey, 'to pay off with his mouth that which mother Malkin will never see at the end of her fingers; the only tip she'll get will be promises from the tip of his tongue; and her attic rooms,[209] like her *rheumatics*, will never do her any good, depend on't.'

'Do not speak thus,' said Misty, solemnly: 'private character ought not surely to be trifled with; and the infirmities of a woman should at least be exempt from ridicule.'

'Well done, my old preacher,' returned Gibbon; 'I can't help thinking Uncle's rather sweet upon the widow,' and he tipped us the wink: 'why, I only said, Mr. Misty, that the old girl's rheumatism was not likely to be of much service to her; now, I think, it will carry her off one of these odd days; yes, as the poet says, she'll

"Die like a rose of a rheumatic pain."[210]

'As the poet does not say, you mean,' cried Misty calmly: 'I wonder, Mr. Gibbon, that a young man of your abilities should descend so low as to such villanous[211] puns – or, grant the pun, where is the sense of your misquotation – do roses die of rheumatic pains – ridiculous! Now, gentlemen, I appeal to you whether such mangling of fine poetry be not only absurd, but I had almost said, impious. The poet – the immortal Pope – in his Essay on Man, is endeavouring to reconcile us to the physical functions wherewith we have been endowed, and proceeds to contend that were our senses, for instance, finer organized than they are, we should be subject to many miseries from which we are at present exempt. Our too nice sense of smell, he says, would cause us to

'Die of a rose in aromatic pain;'

now, I think, you cannot but see the extreme absurdity of the quotation selected by our friend for the peculiar sustenance of his verbal diet. Good night.' Saying which, Mr. Misty drew his hat from its accustomed peg, and retired for the evening.

I could not but feel surprisd at this discourse from the mouth of Misty, bearing in mind the peculiar indifference with which he was formerly accustomed to superintend the studies committed to his guidance. I had yet to learn that, with the best opportunities of observation, and the closest scrutiny of motives, habits, and opinions of the heart and mind, there is still in many men much that can never be understood by others, much that can never be explained by themselves. And, whether it be that I have read mankind to less purpose than others, or that such specimens of the species as I have attempted to peruse have been more apt to cloak and to disguise their real natures than the great mass of their fellow-creatures, I still maintain that men are better and worse than they appear to the common eye – better in purpose – worse in thought – with more fair and legitimate excuse for their actions than they can properly lay claim to in justification of their natural tendencies. The truth is we are all creatures of one common nature, and to follow her is sometimes to follow that which were better left without pursuit.

I do not see or say that these reflections are obviously consequent upon the new aspect in which Misty had presented himself to me at that moment; I was unconsciously led into a train of thought of this tendency, and, as, perhaps, it may cast its shadow before the coming events, which will be disclosed to the reader in due time, I choose to let it remain as it now stands.

By this time the pots were empty, and with the ale vanished the conversation, which, indeed, that beverage had stimulated. Gibbon sat hopeless of further puns, smoking a small pipe in the chimney corner. Haynes left us, on the plea of making another call at the west end of the town, and Wisp, shaking himself from his chair, proposed that we should depart for the night. As we passed the bar, I discerned that Mrs. Malkin was asleep in her chair, with a huge slate before her on the table, and a piece of chalk lying in her lap; her two daughters were curling their hair with an old newspaper; and astounding snortings, gruntings, and incoherent oaths, proclaimed that Grimes had taken his wearied limbs to a bench in the tap-room where he enjoyed but moderately refreshing repose.

As we walked together towards Stork Court (for Wisp kindly offered to escort me to that obscure spot), he was exceedingly anxious to ascertain how I relished the company of the new acquaintance to whom he had presented me. 'You will find them all good fellows,' said he, 'when you come to know them, although Gibbon is a bit of a bore with his wretched puns, and Misty proses afflictingly sometimes. Haynes is a nice lad – plenty of money and always stands treat when he comes; and as for Grimes, he's always the same. Know him once and he's the same for ever.'

Upon further inquiries concerning these delectable companions, it appeared that Mr. Haynes occupied a respectable situation as clerk to a Manchester warehouseman in the immediate neighbourhood; that Gibbon performed the various duties, with equal ability, of assistant, scrub, shoe-black, and representative of a proctor in Doctor's Commons;[212] that Misty had thrown up his professional duties as tutor at the charity-school; and that Grimes occupied a back attic in the Magpie and Punchbowl; running a reckless score; making alternate love to the widow and Miss Caroline; officiating as occasional waiter and constant customer, and, in short, lending such a willing hand to the house, and such a ready stomach to its contents, as made it impossible for the inmates to live with or without him. Wisp also communicated in confidence a tender *penchant*[213] which he had been led to conceive for Miss Susan, and hinted that in all probability some money would be forthcoming in case of a marriage being contracted between them, sagely remarking that, where there was so much dirt, there would, in all probability, be found under it a respectable share of mopusses.[214]

With all these details yet in my mind, and a newborn desire to see more of a society so congenial to my inclination, I retired to the couch once occupied by the ill-fated Meagrejoint, and in a short time was lost to the consciousness of all the fretful and vexatious concerns of existence in the enjoyment of a placid and prolonged slumber; for I was yet of an age when the animal spirits rise triumphant over the petty weaknesses and humours of the more sophisticated flesh; and the straw bed and plain worsted rug yield to the pressure of the body, and cling to the flexible and vivacious limbs with all the soft elasticity of down, and more than the warmth which the ermine's gorgeous skin can invest a monarch withal.

CHAPTER VIII.

MONTHS rolled on, – to adopt the approved language of the popular Novelist, – and I still discovered myself duly rising every morning out of my miserable lair to *desk*ant,[215] as Gibbon was wont to say, on my own deformity of secular position;[216] and every night I was regularly to be found in the back parlour of the Magpie and Punchbowl, extracting thence such wild honey as flowed from the lips of its nocturnal visitants. I know not, for my own part, whether the desire of novelty or the force of habit be the stronger, but I am disposed to believe that the latter exercised its functions with more complete sway over my temperament, so that I have been at all times attached to 'things as they are,'[217] so long as they have been endurable, rather than to fanciful and speculative changes,[218] whether in the politic or the corporeal body. Misty, it is true, shortly after my introduction to this retreat, had abandoned his old haunt, and no intimation of his prolonged existence in the flesh had been accorded to us, save the testimony of Haynes, who had beheld him one evening going into the Italian Opera,[219] habited in a manner quite above the available strength of his accustomed wardrobe, and altogether a different man from the 'Uncle' who was wont to ruminate over his pipe in the chimney-corner of the Magpie and Punchbowl. And, indeed, were I not hastening to affairs of some special moment, it might not be uninteresting to speculate on the extraordinary change which wealth, or presumed wealth, works on those who are supposed to be basking in its beneficial beams; a metamorphosis only to be equalled by the influence it appears to excercise[220] on others who may happen to be spectators of such prosperous reverse of fortune.

It is no less surprising than true that, when a man has converted his rags into bank notes,[221] and has partaken of that outward alteration which such conversion commonly brings with it, he is looked upon as a very different individual, even by those who can have no conceivable interest in his prosperity, from the miserable object he was before accustomed to present; he exacts respect and he receives it; and familiar Tom and Dick becomes an obsolete appellation. How the double change is brought about, it is not my happiness to know, neither is it my pleasure to inquire; it may be sufficient to record that the fact is so. Hence it is, perhaps, that men, unwilling, I suppose, to descend so low as to worship

Mammon for his own sake, and, as it were, in the very person of his representative, consent to set up a kind of scape-sheep,[222] on which to lay the burden of
their votive offerings; and, as was wittily observed by a contemporary writer, we,
accordingly, pay a homage to good coats which it is by no means to be understood that we direct to the individual encased therein; – good coats, he says,
are invited to good dinners; good coats furnish an *entrée* to Almack's;[223] and
the superfine takes precedence of plain broad cloth.[224] My friend is inclined to
think that to this ceremonial of worship we are indebted for the word *coterie*,[225]
expressive, he supposes, of a select meeting of unexceptionable raiment. But I
have wandered from my subject.

I have said that Misty had departed this life of unquiet repose, and had risen
to a higher sphere. Haynes, on the contrary, was become a more frequent attendant at our orgies. Yet it was plain to behold that this young gentleman was, from
some cause or other, ill at ease; with a wayward and reckless joyousness that
augured suspiciously for the healthiness and stability of his mental conformation,
his expenditure became profuse and unaccountable, and he appeared to wish to
drown some carking and irremediable care in drafts of spirituous potency. And,
as certain persons are invited to a funeral, either to eke out the mourning, or to
seem to contribute a due share of consolation by appearing likewise to mourn, so
were we called in to aid in the consumption of that which Haynes was too happy
to dispense; for he appeared to imagine that, by enjoying ourselves at the expense
of his imprudence, we made ourselves parties to the same; whereas, whether we
did so or no was not a matter of the slightest conceivable importance to us. Little
Westminster Abbey, in truth (I say it, *ex-cathedrâ*[226]), was by no means willing
that any thing coming into his net in this manner should not be considered as
fish; and whether it were a spirit of health, or otherwise, to him it came in no
questionable shape. As for Grimes, everything that was laid before him, whether
edible or of potable properties, might be thenceforth viewed as something that
was presently to be as nothing; the passing memory of a meal, or the transient
recollection of a draught. Had he been invited to dinner in the old Egyptian style,
he would have attacked with speculative voracity the '*memento mori*'[227] usually
placed upon the table in the form of a skull; and I really incline to think that at a
pseudo-fashionable party, he would have been Gothic[228] enough (in spite of the
prohibition of a modern aristocratic novelist[229]) to swallow as much port as the
unsophisticated *parvenus*[230] might unwittingly set upon the board.[231]

But, to leave these my excellent companions for a while, let me return to
my equally exemplary master, Mr. Jabez Snavel. That worthy individual had, for
some time past, bestowed his individual attention upon, and directed his whole
energies to, the consummation of a wish devoutly prayed for[232] by his one client,
Mr. Wilmot, and whether it was owing to the voluntary activity of the Chancel-
lor, the laborious activity of Messrs. Sly and Sharp, or the prevailing perseverance

of Mr. Jabez Snavel, I am at a loss to affirm; but certain it is that judgment was given in favour of our client, and a sum of money amounting to 2286*l.* 16*s.*[233] was ordered to be paid out of Court forthwith, for the particular use and benefit of Mr. Henry Wilmot.

During the agitating period between the day fixed for the coming on of the case and its final decision, up to the hour in which the money was to be placed into the very hands of my master, Mr. Jabez Snavel had evinced a nervous impatience, somewhat inconsistent with his character as a mere middle-man, authorised to receive funds for the peculiar use of another party[234] and had attempted to propitiate us, his convenient drudges, to wit, Wisp and myself, by an expenditure of such words as are said to butter no parsnips,[235] and I believe would be equally inefficient towards the oleaginous mollification of any other vegetable. With such 'soft nothings,'[236] I say, did Mr. Jabez Snavel contrive to delay with decency the payment of certain hard somethings in the shape of wages which both to Wisp and myself had been long due.

I believe, if there be one thing in the world that will contribute towards causing a lawyer to look amiable, it may be the payment of his bill of costs. It was not an unreasonable inference, accordingly, that the expectation, or rather the certainty, of such an event, cast a kind of unusual halo around the physiognomy of Mr. Jabez Snavel, and contribute to the vast outlay of gracious promises and soothings, in which, by the bye, it was the common practice of that gentleman to indulge to a nauseous extent. To this cause, and to this alone, did I refer those plastic and voluntary offerings. But Wisp, more conversant with the world, and cognisant of the various sinks and sewers of iniquity in which it abounds, had begun, as he informed me, 'to smell a rat;' and was active in enunciating phrases and broken sentences, in which 'more is meant than meets the ear.'[237] He had begun to build fanciful castles in the air, and was 'sagacious of his quarry from afar,'[238] whence he might draw material wherewith to convert them into substantial and habitable tenements. What could possibly be meant by these vague hints? It is true, that, independent of a satisfactory settlement with Snavel, we had well-grounded hopes of receiving a donation from Wilmot, of an amount more accordant with the nature of the poor man under these exciting circumstances than commensurate with our merits as individuals, or due to our deserts as active functionaries at the disposal of Mr. Jabez Snavel? but these several expectancies, resolved into one grand total, were surely hardly sufficient to justify the extent of atmospheric architecture in which my friend was indulging; being, in fact, quite too small in amount to pay for the erection of a pig-sty on the earth – not to mention the animal to whom, and for whose convenience, it might, if raised, be supposed to be dedicated.

Mr. Jabez Snavel had only once exhibited himself to us on the auspicious day which was to bring a long expected fortune to Wilmot, the payment of a long bill of costs to Snavel, and long-wished for wages and gratuities to Wisp and myself. He had proceeded from his office early in the morning for the purpose of securing the money, which, like Alcestis from the grave,[239] was never supposed to be seen again on this earth; and had left us with an intimation to that effect. Mr. Wilmot, however, had lingered out the entire day in dreadful hope of his momentary return; and (for nature will find way either in present instalments or in the future aggregate) was under the influence of some extraordinary emotion which he found it impossible to control. He had been calm till now; and the unvarying placidity of his countenance, and the uniform mildness and softened grace of his manners, had won even upon Wisp and myself – both, to say the truth, not unwilling to find occasion for laughter in any specimen of the human species which might by chance evince any thing that might be construed into softness or weakness of heart. I said he had been calm till now; but now the means of future happiness almost within his grasp, he was unmanned, and the perspiration gathered on his brow in heavy drops which, as they rose, he wiped languidly away. 'Will Mr. Snavel *never* return?' said he, at length, as the evening was drawing in, and no Snavel appeared for the purpose of drawing out;[240] 'he certainly must have concluded the business long ago; surely, nothing can have occurred to delay the payment of the money.'

Wisp, with an agitation scarcely less than that apparent in Wilmot, expressed his hopes that no such calamity had occurred.

'I do not scruple to confess, gentlemen,' continued Wilmot, addressing us, 'now that this matter is brought to a close, that to this money have I looked for my extrication from the most horrible state of misery, wretchedness, starvation, that man was ever placed in by the baseness of friends; or rather, let me say, the world.'

'Indeed, sir,' cried Wisp, listlessly, 'I am sorry to hear – '

'It is very, very strange,' cried Wilmot, interrupting him impatiently, 'that Mr. Snavel should not have returned ere this; bless me, it's eight o'clock;' and the poor man played the devil's tattoo[241] on the floor with a skill which must have drawn an applauding sentiment from the personage whose name that composition so appropriately bears.

'I hardly think, sir,' said Wisp, 'that you need expect Mr. Snavel this evening; you may be certain either that some very particular business[242] has detained him, or that he has not succeeded in his object to-day: you had better call the first thing to-morrow morning.'

'No, no; I'll wait till midnight but I'll see him,' exclaimed Wilmot, violently: but a moment after, with a caprice peculiar to that state of feeling, starting up, 'but no, no,' he mused audibly, 'if it were so, I might wait long enough; and if not, why, to morrow is full soon – 'twill be but another to the calendar of misery. Tell Mr. Snavel,' he cried, turning to Wisp, 'if he *should* come after I am gone, to call upon me directly: I ask it as a particular favour.' And with a heavy sigh our only respectable client left us to ourselves.

For some time after the departure of Wilmot, my friend Wisp was sunk in gloomy meditation, his head having fallen into his open hands, and his elbows resting upon the desk. 'D— the old rascal,' at length he blasphemed, shaking himself with a chilly shudder, and tossing the law-list[243] into the partition of the letter-box set apart for general delivery.

'Why so, Wisp?' I inquired, innocently.

'Not Wilmot, Jack, but old Beelzebub – Snavel;' and he snappishly decapitated the miserable candles, whose heads during the last half hour had swelled vastly in the flame, like patients afflicted with the St. Anthony's fire;[244] 'the scamp has fairly tipped us the double – hush.'

At this moment a step was heard in the passage. 'Hush, hush,' whispered my companion, 'it's Snavel, by jingo!' And now the head of that person was cautiously intruded into the gently-opened door. 'Is Wilmot here, boys?' demanded the mouth appertaining to that slightly flushed physiognomy; and, as Mr. Jabez Snavel became by degrees more distinctly revealed to us, it was apparent that he had not been applying to the street-pump for the invigoration of his frame.

'Mr. Wilmot is gone, sir,' said Wisp, 'but left word that you were to call upon him the instant you returned.'

'Um – ah! call upon him!' muttered Snavel, as though such a request were about the last thing in the world to be attended to.

'Will you be so kind, Mr. Wisp, as to carry candles into my office? I shall be busy for half an hour. John and you needn't wait, – I'll lock up the office myself.'

'You forget, sir, that we are busy,' cried Wisp, as he prepared the candles.

'Busy! about what?' inquired Snavel, with unwonted testiness.

'Hockley's case must be prepared for counsel by to-morrow; his trial takes place on Friday,' said the other; and, having set the lights on Snavel's table, he resumed his situation at the desk.

'Well, well, proceed by all means,' exclaimed Snavel, with unusual vivacity; 'let us get the poor rogue out of his scrape, or he'll be Hockley in the hole,[245] Mr. Wisp – eh?' and he laughed like a bevy of ducks just come off a water party; and with this novel specimen of pleasantry retired into his room.

'Now, Jack – now, Jack, I'm going to try it on,' exclaimed Wisp, across the desk in a low tone; 'that half-and-half, though, we had at Mother Malkin's has made me deucedly nervous; just feel my hand – cold, isn't it?' and his teeth chattered audibly. 'Keep your courage up, Jack – don't be down in the mouth, you dog:' a piece of advice, by the way, which might have been better reserved for himself; for, in spite of a fearful rattling in the throat, which my friend intended to stand, by way of proxy, for a chuckle, it was evident that Wisp was not at this precise moment likely to be mistaken for a modern Hercules, or a laughing philosopher.[246] 'I say, Ketch,' he resumed, after a pause, 'creep on tiptoe to the key-hole of Snavel's door, and tell me what he's about.'

I did so; and presently discovered Mr. Jabez Snavel in the act of leaning over his desk, a pen in his mouth, his spectacles on his nose – through the glasses of which his eyes appeared to be verily about to start – his fore-finger and thumb actively employed in plucking up the corners of what I discovered to be bank notes, while a slight motion of his lips indicated that he was occupied in the agreeable practice of addition. All these several particulars did I succinctly and silently impart to Wisp, who thereupon descended from his stool and proceeded to the office door.

'Ketch,' said he, in an attenuated whisper, as he fumbled with the lock, 'go back to the key-hole and mark, if you can, where he conceals the flimsies; that's a good fellow.'

I obeyed instinctively – for the object of this scrutiny I never once attempted to divine – and, stooping down, with somewhat less caution than before, my nose gently dropt upon the brass handle of the door, which thus slightly assaulted, nevertheless uttered a kind of complaint to the lock to which it was so service-able an appendage. My eye, however, was level with the key-hole precisely in time to behold the rising figure of Mr. Jabez Snavel, who, startled by the noise, began to scramble about with his hands in a wonderful manner; while I with two superhuman strides regained my stool and alarmed Wisp, who went and did likewise pretty much in a similar fashion.

All was hushed for a few minutes, and then the closing of the snuffers and its restoration to the stand proclaimed that Snavel had extinguished one of the can-dles, and presently afterwards that gentleman himself opened the door. With his hat on, and his coat closely buttoned, did Mr. Jabez Snavel walk into the office, saying, 'Come, gentleman, we must all go together to-night, for I shall probably be here very early to-morrow morning, and shall therefore require the key of the office; but how is this, Mr. Wisp?' turning to that trembling culprit – 'the door is locked.'

'The door is locked,' repeated Wisp, like an echo with the ague.

'Why is it locked, sir?' said the other in a loud voice, advancing to the desk, and leaning on my shoulder.

'Why, sir,' answered Wisp, with something like calmness, 'our wages have been long due – and we are greatly in want – and – '

'*Our* wages – *we* want!' cried Snavel, surprised, appealing to me; 'and are you, John, a party to this?'

I hung down my head, but ventured to mumble an unintelligible history of the lankness of my pockets.

'Ho! ho! I see how it is,' tauntingly resumed Mr. Jabez Snavel, with a sneering laugh; 'a conspiracy, eh? But I'll pack you both off to-morrow you impudent scoundrels – tomorrow, sir,' addressing Wisp sternly, 'you shall be paid, when you must prepare to leave my office.'

'To-night, Mr. Snavel – to-night if you please, sir,' answered Wisp, boldly; 'I can't wait till tomorrow, – it must be to-night.'

'*Must* be! *must* be!' echoed Snavel; 'well, upon my soul – '

'Must be,' – exclaimed the other promptly, and he advanced towards his master; 'and a word in your ear. You have got Wilmot's money in your pocket.'

'Well,' faltered Snavel, 'what if I have? But I have not.'

'Come, Snavel, no nonsense,' interrupted Wisp; 'you can't gammon[247] me. I have seen it; I saw through the key-hole.'

'This is very extraordinary conduct, Mr. Wisp,' faltered the other; 'what do you mean? If I have got it, I am going to take it to Mr. Wilmot.'

'Over the bender,'[248] said Wisp, with a laugh, tossing his thumb over his left shoulder as he spoke.

'Come, come, let us understand each other, Wisp:' soothingly expostulated the delinquent; 'you want your salary – you shall have it; and you John, shall receive your's;[249] and now we are friends again;' and Snavel produced from his pocket a purse containing an enviable weight of coin.

'It won't do,' said Wisp, coolly, taking his heel from the fender, for he had been standing authoritatively with his back to the fire: 'I shall have more.'

'More!' roared Snavel, with a circular mouth, and eyes of the same orbicular shape, 'more!' and he huddled his purse again into his pocket in a trice, as though the very demand would twitch the strings asunder, and cause the money to be forthcoming of its own accord.

'Yes, more,' roared Wisp, imitating his master: 'I'll tell you what it is, Snavel,' and he approached his victim – 'you have got Wilmot's money,' and placing his face on a direct level with that of Snavel he uttered in a never-to-be-forgotten distinct and emphatic tone, 'and *you are going to mizzle*[250] *with it* – that's the long and the short of the story. Now, come, what do you say to that?'

It occurs to me that had any one of my readers beheld Mr. Jabez Snavel at this precise moment, he would have frankly confessed that the inimitable statue of Laocoon[251] is but a paltry counterfeit of agony compared with the rueful reality of that being's visage, when the unexpected truth announced by the prophetic Wisp entered his aural appendages, and thence descended into the very part of his body where the heart is supposed to reside, but where in Snavel's breast that piece of human furniture was not to be found. Indeed, Mr. Jabez Snavel, like other lovers, had given away his heart long ago to a mistress, which perhaps was neither Honour nor Virtue; and had never sought to reclaim it, rightly judging that it could be of no value even to the owner, and that, in fact, it was not worth its keep, even taken at its full valuation.

'My good friend, Wisp,' cried Snavel, after a pause, having seated himself in a chair, where he sought to allay his agitation by mopping the perspiration[252] from his brow, 'what *is* the meaning of all his? You alarm me, you do indeed, by these vague hints. I have no such intention; and if I had, how can it concern you? Let us meet to-morrow morning, and make an amicable settlement.'

'Carry me out and bury me decent, after that,' retorted Wisp: 'and you think I'll let you escape us so easily, do you my old buck? no, no. Here, Jack,' and he beckoned to me – 'just step to Mr. Wilmot's lodging, and tell him to come here instantly.'

'Now, Wisp, my good fellow, Wisp – can't you be quiet and reasonable,' interposed Snavel, in a servile tone of expostulation; 'can't we arrange this matter? hush it up, eh? what do you say?'

'Two hundred pounds,' said Wisp, resolutely.

'Two hundred pounds!' shrieked Snavel, with a voice resembling something between a whistle and a whirlwind.

'Come, come,' said Wisp, 'I can't be kept till the devil's dancing hour[253] for you; either say you will, or you will not. I'll have you taken up, I will by G—, if you don't come to terms presently.'

'It can't be done,' cried the lawyer, 'I have yet committed no offence.'

'Well, as you please,' carelessly responded the other, 'you know your own business best; either give me two hundred pounds, or relinquish the whole.'

'You shall have it,' cried Snavel, in a decisive tone, drawing out his pocket-book; and with a heavy heart he selected bank-notes to the amount required – 'but upon one condition – I'll have an acknowledgment.'

My mind misgave me when this article of the treaty was put forth, and I twitched Wisp by the coat-skirt. 'An acknowledgment! well' – and Wisp released himself from my grasp – 'you shall have it. You will not be likely to exhibit it, I imagine; come Jack, if your father was a glazier, he didn't make you of glass – stand out of the light,' and pushing me aside, the excited contracting party seized a pen and drew out a formal acknowledgment of the sum received, specifying the right owner of the property from whence it was drawn.

'Here it is,' exclaimed Wisp, and he handed it to the lawyer.

'Then here is the money;' – and Snavel, with a heart-rending sigh, presented the notes to his inexorable clerk.

'The devil speed you!' cried Wisp, as he opened the door.

'And you,' retorted Snavel, as he darted from it, and was out of sight in a moment.

'Well, Mister Jacky, and what do you think of all this?' cried Wisp, snapping his fingers; 'won't this do, my boy? This is winding up the concern properly, I'm thinking; you shall have fifty pounds of it, you rascal, and we'll commence the world in style. Not a word at Mother Malkin's, or it's all up with us.'

Overjoyed at this splendid offer, I accorded the most unqualified praise to the manoeuvre, and to the manner in which it had been executed, and promised moreover to be as mum as an Egyptian mummy upon the occasion, stating at the same time the fact, that I was almost as dry as one of those curious specimens of modern manufacture.

'Then let us leave this paradise,' said my friend, slapping me on the shoulder, 'and bottle up our tears till a more convenient opportunity presents itself of getting rid of them:' and we took our departure from Stork Court, although perhaps with the consciousness of having performed a very honourable or exemplary action, yet, I will venture to say with quite as much mental enjoyment as the performance of these moral exploits usually confers on those who are prone to speculate in such extravagant and scarce luxuries.

CHAPTER IX.

ON our arrival at the Magpie and Punchbowl, we found the ferocious Grimes seated alone in the parlour, with an empty pot in his fist, and a short pipe in his mouth, warbling an uncouth melody. 'Hilloah! my boys, I'm glad you're come,' quoth he; 'I was just going to turn into my truckle-bed; the old girl hasn't left the bar this blessed day; the devil a pull at the tap have I had,' and he made a significant motion with his horny hand expressive of the act of drawing beer; 'and no more chalk on the slate for Jack Grimes, d— me.' Wisp speedily soothed his querulous feelings by offering to stand treat for a sufficiency of ale, and proposed an adjournment into the bar, where previously he had engaged a bed for me. 'I have managed it all with Betsy,' said Grimes, in one of those confidential whispers which serve to reach the most inattentive bystander; 'we're to cut our stick[254] in a few days; I've got her thumb to it;[255] an elopement, d— me; what a sentimental turn out! ha, ha!' and he burst into a vociferous laugh: 'well, it's a d— sight better than tossing three days and nights on a tar-barrel, eh!' an event, by the bye, which served as a constant reference to Grimes, when he would fain spin out his discourse. 'Here we are, mother,'[256] cried he, addressing the landlady familiarly; 'and *that* for your threats,' snapping his fingers; 'here's a gentleman offers to tip up for the guzzle – don't you, Wisp? Come, let us have some ale, for I am as dry as an alligator when the Nile is backward in coming forward; not a drop has passed my lips this day;' and this eccentric individual confirmed the assertion with his accustomed oath.

'La! how *can* you say so? Grimes,' retorted Mrs. Malkin; 'didn't I see you, when you thought my back was turned, through the window of the inner room, wrench a pint out of the tap like lightning? Now, you know you did, Jack – '

'Oh! by the Lord!' cried Jack, with a confused laugh, nudging us with his elbow, 'a rum old devil, isn't she?' and he made a peculiar grimace, which tickled the daughters amazingly, who giggled with much satisfaction.

'Now, Betsy, stir your stumps, my girl,' continued Grimes, clasping the waist of that delicate dust-heap; 'let us have an empty pipe and a screw, in a brace of shakes.[257] I say, Jack, do you twig[258] Wisp doing the amiable with Susan; fine girl, isn't she, – bust like a mermaid; like *the* mermaid, I may say, which I saw when I was three days and nights tossing about on the tar-barrel; but I'll tell you what,' in a whisper, 'she doesn't seem to use a comb[259] quite so often, d— me. Ha! ha! ha!'

With small talk of this agreeable description, relieved at intervals by supplementary grog, and long memories of by-gone events, contributed by Mrs. Malkin, we contrived to wear out the night till a late hour; when Miss Betsy, yawning and scratching her head, attended Grimes and myself to our several dormitories.

Wisp called upon me early on the following morning, agreeably to appointment; but I had risen, and had been waiting for him several hours before his arrival. Unable to sleep, I had amused myself during the night, with the strange vagaries of Grimes, who, in an adjoining apartment, tumbled about his bed, growling, singing and swearing in a fearful manner, – anon applying to the water-jug, and then dancing, or, more truly to speak, beating the floor with his heels in a distracted fashion, – a common custom, as Miss Susan informed me next morning, religiously and nightly observed by that person. Towards daybreak, however, he fell into slumber, and paid his welcome debt to the god of sleep 'through the nose;'[260] that is to say, by incessant and inhuman snorings.

In pursuance of a plan adopted and approved on the previous day, Wisp conducted me to a convenient house in the vicinity of the Seven Dials,[261] where we both underwent a change of apparel no less novel than agreeable, each tendering his tattered chrysalis in part – but very small part-payment for the gorgeous investment to which each now, without delay, transferred himself. This necessary ceremony performed, my friend escorted me to various places of noontide entertainment, and generously placed at my disposal the sum he had designed for me the night before, – a retaining fee, not unlike that usually tendered to lawyers, being bestowed for the purpose of concealing a rather inconvenient fact, but imposing a directly contrary duty, viz. that of keeping my mouth shut, instead of causing it to open.

'I would advise, Jack,' said Wisp, as we retraced our steps in the afternoon towards the Magpie and Punchbowl,' that we keep ourselves out of the way for a while. Wilmot may, perhaps, take out a warrant against Snavel, to whom the law is better known than trusted, and who, accordingly, has found out the use of his heels ere this; not, by the bye, that the magistrate could detain us, either,' he continued, musing; 'however, you had better go home with me of nights; I'll introduce you to my sister; she's a skull-thatcher.'

'A what?' cried I, with great simplicity.

'She throws the steel bar about,' said Wisp, laughing; 'a straw bonnet-maker, you goose; we shall be snug enough there; and Kate will be company for you; you're pretty much of an age.'

I had seen too much of womankind during my short sojourn in this vale of tears, to build up many anticipations of comfort in an establishment of which a female was one of the members; but, true to my nature, I held my peace for the present, inwardly resolving that, were the domestic comforts not altogether unexceptionable, I would forthwith take myself off to a more congenial habitation.

Our appearance at the Magpie and Punchbowl created an extraordinary sensation amongst its inmates, a sensation for which we were fully prepared being aware that the splendour of our external decorations was not likely to pass without remark, or to be viewed without suspicion.

'Hilloah! here's a pretty go, d— me!' exclaimed Grimes, as we entered; 'here's a turn out! I've read of a certain Jew going out to seek his father's asses;[262] but here are a couple of asses have gone forth in search of a certain Jew:[263] come, that's a good one, d— me. I say, my boys, you cut a rather different figure from me when I was tossing about three days – '

'Yes, they've been *wool-gathering*,'[264] interrupted Westminster Abbey –

'*Fleecing*[265] somebody, eh?' said Grimes; 'there's my pun to yours, my lad, that'll do for a grain of wit.'

'The fact is,' cried Wisp, coolly, 'Snavel paid up our arrears of salary, and I've a shrewd suspicion he's bolted; he gave us the sack[266] last night.'

'Gave you the sack,' remarked Gibbon, speculatively, for he proposed to hang a pun upon it, if possible, 'gave you the sack? – why, then, you're out of situation, I suppose; ah, then, you're worse than Falstaff's bill – you'll soon not have a ha'porth[267] of bread to your intolerable quantity of sack.'[268]

At this moment my uncle entered the room, and was hailed with gratulations denoting unusual satisfaction. 'Ah! old eyes-in-glass,'[269] cried Gibbon, shaking him by the hand, 'you're as good as physic to one; the very sight of you does good to one's inside, I protest.'

'I'm not likely to do much good to your inside, Master Gibbon,' said my uncle, drily; 'for I don't mean to stand Sam[270] for you to-night. – I say, nephy, – ' and the old gentleman came and sat down by my side, 'what d'ye think?'

I confessed that my thoughts were, at that moment, ranging along the vast high-road of infinity.

'Blow me, Jack,' continued he, filling his pipe leisurely, 'if Master Snavel ha'n't toddled with the old woman. Here, Mr. Wisp, I want a word with you. What d'ye think? blow me if Master Snavel ha'n't toddled with the old woman.'

'Ah! now I see,' cried I, 'why he took me into his office – to get me out of the way, uncle.'

'Why, to be sure it was,' cried the old man, making a circular drive with his fist, 'don't you see? the colloguing varmint[271] was always a comin', arter you toddled,[272] and I began to think, dang it, he's a bad lot, and so I told Peg. What odds? she's made her egxit with the feller.'

'But how do you know,' said Wisp, 'that they have gone off together?'

'Why, Lord bless your soul,' answered my uncle, 'didn't Mother Nimblejaw see 'em on the tramp at the peep of day while I was a snoozing; gone off – ay, I warrant.'

I presumed to hope that nothing was missing save the good lady herself, in which case I hinted that the single loss would not be too acutely taken to heart.

'Every thing of vally[273] as she could lay her daddles[274] on,' replied he; 'but she didn't know where the stuff was, Jack; I always kept a pretty sharp look out arter[275] that. But as for herself, you know, that's another matter; that's neither here nor there, as the hog said of the acorn. She was a cantankerous cretur, warn't she now, Jack?' but as the old man spoke; a tear stood in his eye, which however was brushed off hastily.

Wisp now related to the old gentleman every particular relative to Snavel, involving a shrewd suspicion of his departure with Wilmot's money, reserving to himself a knowledge of the *coup de main*[276] by which he had succeeded in causing a small portion of the plunder to flow into his own pockets; and accounting for the magnificence of our apparel by stating that our arrears of salary had furnished us with sufficient funds to justify so otherwise extravagant an outlay of capital.

'Ho! ho!' cried my uncle, taking the pipe from his mouth, and scratching his ear with the end of it, 'that's how he does it, eh? That's wot I calls doing the thing bang up to the mark, by goles.[277] Oh! He's a cunning chap – deep as Garrick,[278] blow me! That accounts for my seeing the gemman[279] in the passage, when I called at Stork Court this morning; my eye! how he was a letting fly at his knowledge box[280] with his fists, right and left, ding dong, so precious hard!'

Wisp heaved an involuntary sigh at this recital, and, to confess the truth, a pang of no agreeable nature shot across my left side when this picture of Wilmot's despair was brought before my mind. 'I'll tell you what I'll do,' said my companion in a whisper; 'I'll despatch a five pound note to Wilmot in a blank cover; he'll never know who sent it – eh? it will be something for the poor devil.' I applauded the resolution warmly, but with more particular ardour that no proposition was broached to make up the sum between us; my own share, now that I more maturely considered the matter, being in all conscience small enough – a feeling I incline to think very common with mankind, to whom individually the lion's share of the spoil is precisely the proportion that each would willingly be permitted to enjoy.

'I say, Mr. Haynes,' cried my uncle across the room to that forlorn person, who was sitting disconsolately in one corner, 'don't be down upon your luck, man; you look, for all the world, like a swell going to be hanged.'

'Hanged!' cried Haynes, starting, with a stare that caused a burst of merriment in the company.

'Yes,' roared Grimes, vociferously, 'he looks something like me when I was three days – '

'Come,' interrupted Wisp, 'we have had that story so often. Well, he does remind me of Haman[281] – '

'Of *a man*, certainly,' interrupted Gibbon, 'just about to be turned off.'[282]

Haynes smiled a ghastly grin, and complained of sudden indisposition. 'After all,' said he, evidently with a wish to goad his spirits into a pace accordant with the speed of the company, 'after all, I'd lay a trifle I don't cut so miserable a figure as Westminster Abbey.'

'Who shall be umpire?' inquired Grimes, with an oath.

'Oh, uncle Ketch there will be the best *hump higher*,'[283] cried Gibbon, with an extraordinary proportion of gravity, an infallible criterion, as I have before said of the degree of pleasure he experienced in his own puns.

'I was a going to observe,' interrupted my uncle, whose mal-treatment of words was perfectly undesigned, and who had not the slightest notion that such infant children of the tongue were ever cut asunder with malice prepense by the would-be Solomons[284] of the world of wit, 'I was a going to observe that Mister Haynes brought to my mind a young swell who was hanged for forgery; I did the job for him. Oh! He'd been a rig'lar blood[285] in his time – rum-ti-tum with the chill off. Well, I'll tell you: when he was a going to be turned off, what does he do but he comes up to me, 'Ketch,' says he, and he looked white about the gills – says he, 'how does it feel when the drop falls?' 'Lord bless *your* soul, my jolly master,' says I, 'how do I know? I never tried it of a summer's morning by way o' divarsion.' There was a speech of the silly cretur; warn't it now? a man of edication too, as ought to ha' known better.'

'Come, Jack, come,' exclaimed Wisp, hurriedly, 'let us be jogging; we shall be too late for tea:' and, in spite of the remonstrances of the company, he seized his hat and prepared to depart.

'What! are you for toddling?' said my uncle, addressing me; 'well, give us your fist, Jack. I say, boy, what do you mean to do now? Come to my crib[286] one of these odd days, and I'll take you to the great house,[287] and show you some queer culls;[288] they'll teach you a trick or two worth knowing. You must take a turn at your old trade – eh? Nobody's never the wiser; you've as clean a hand[289] as ever I heard on,[290] seeing as how you were never brought up to the salt-box[291] move.'

I was fain to satisfy my relative with vague generalities, purporting that such a recurrence to the old system would be, under present circumstances, impolitic; satisfying him that if things did not turn out quite so prosperously as I had reason, or rather desire, to expect, I would certainly avail myself of his hint and return to my old profession.

'Well, every horse to his own manger, that's all I says,' remarked the old gentleman, with a face of serious importance, his original visage indeed assuming the appearance of that of a philosophic owl that had discovered the scientific mystery of squaring the circle,[292] and carried the demonstration of the problem in its own physiognomy; 'all I says is, be fly to[293] everything – no gammon[294] – uncommon fly, Jack,' and winking his eye with extraordinary sagacity of expression, he suffered me to retire.

As we proceeded across Smithfield towards the lodging of Wisp, which he informed me was not a hundred miles distant from[295] St. John's Gate, he threw out dark hints of a communication which Haynes had promised to make to him on the following evening, and sounded me touching my probable concurrence in any plan which might possibly be formed to make our fortunes at once. 'For,' said he, 'I know Haynes has something to lay before us, and if it should turn out practicable, why, don't let us be like the mastiff who would'nt eat the cold pudding for the fear the pug-dog might want it. But not a word,' he added, as we mounted the door-steps of the house in which he resided, where a miscellany of children had congregated for the purpose of reclining, 'not a word to my sister of our proceedings; she's a poor sensitive creature, and would rather drown than hang any day in the week.'

'Well, Kate, my girl,' said he, with gaiety, as we entered the room, to a young creature who came forward and received him with a kiss, 'I've brought our new lodger, Mr. Ketch, an interesting, but I grieve to add, a too diffident youth,' – and with much solemnity he introduced us, – 'the exalted and to be exalted[296] Mr. John Ketch – the elegant, accomplished, and lovely Miss Catharine Wisp.'

Wisp for once in his life had spoken truth, so far as the last adjective descriptive of his sister was concerned; for certainly my eyes had never before beheld so beautiful a creature as stood before me at that moment. Could I ever so well describe beauty, I should forbear to do so, conscious that the nearest approximation to fidelity is, after all, but an ungracious catalogue, of which the separate features are but idea-less items. Let me then say that this young creature awoke in my breast that feeling which, I believe, is common to human nature, and which, although perhaps it is most often created by beauty, not unfrequently excited by causes, whether of association, sympathy, or fate, into which I am not philosophically curious enough to inquire.

'I have almost finished tea,' said she, in the softest voice that was ever heard, 'but I can make you some instantly; you so seldom come home before night, William, that I did'nt expect you.'

'Oh! Don't make fresh tea for us,' cried Wisp, carelessly, 'put some more water in the pot, and give it a mantua-maker's twist;[297] that'll do. Ketch is not solicitous about souchong.'[298]

While Miss Kate was busy about these operations I had already decided in my own mind that I was desperately in love, a conclusion to which most people arrive precisely a moment after that sentiment has taken possession of the heart, in spite of a vast deal of nonsense uttered by crazy sentimentalists, who perhaps are anxious to believe that others are desperately in love with them, notwithstanding every reasonable evidence to the contrary. Conceive an alderman unconscious of his passion for turtle,[299] or a young wife married to an old husband unconscious of her desire for a jointure;[300] or, indeed, anything else that is most inconceivable. And yet, to state both sides of the question, we see matches take place every day in which the love of either party would seem to be perfectly unconscious; but perhaps such contracts may be entered into upon a blind faith in the dicta of the aforesaid crazy sentimentalists, who have made the contracting parties believe that they are desperately in love with each other, *because* they are entirely unaware of the smallest atom of love existing between them.

'I'd have you to know,' said Wisp, glancing towards his sister, who, having filled out tea-cups, had return to her needle-work, 'that Kate has got a new sweetheart. There's young Chisel, the carpenter over the way, perpetually casting his bright coffin-nails of eyes out of the window for the purpose of engaging her attention. Is Chisel to be the happy man, Kate? I fear you'll go round the wood and take the crooked stick at last.'

I mumbled something which I conceived might be applicable to the subject, heartily wishing the susceptible Chisel in a coffin of his own manufacture, or that, if I were to be the crooked stick, I might be laid over the shoulders of that obnoxious rival, – when Miss Kate applied herself to the insinuations of her brother.

'Don't believe him, Mr. Ketch,' said she blushing, 'Mr. Chisel is no sweetheart of mine; and if he were – '

'It's no business of mine,' interrupted Wisp; 'however, you might make a worse choice; mind you don't stoop and pick up nothing after all.'

'No fear of that,' said I, with a prospective eye to my own claims; and methought a smile of reciprocal love stole over the countenance of the sister.

'I do wish, Mr. Ketch,' cried Miss Kate, when her brother had retired for the purpose of procuring some beer for supper, suddenly dropping her work, and raising to mine the softest eyes I ever beheld, 'that you would exert your influence with William. I know you have some power over him, he has spoken of you so often. I'm sure that horrid Magpie and Punchbowl does him no good, and he won't be ruled by me. Do advise him to keep away from such places, and come home earlier of an evening.'

I promised to exercise all the interest I possessed, or was supposed to possess, with my friend; and was rewarded in return with one of those sweet smiles which at that moment I deemed the most ample remuneration for services not already performed that human being could desire to receive; and before we separated for the night I was already so captivated as to retrace the whole of my past life with a feeling something allied to disgust, and to marvel how I had so long consented to endure an existence that, under this new predicament of feeling, appeared to me but a cheerless void, for which the whole of my future life must be actively employed in felicitous events adequately to compensate.

CHAPTER X.

SEVERAL months elapsed, and during that period nothing had been heard of Snavel or his whereabout, nor had Wisp or myself once chanced to encounter the unfortunate Wilmot, who, for aught we knew, or indeed cared, had long since gone to that bourne whence no traveller returns,[301] by a conveyance of his own making. Several changes had however occurred in the internal arrangements of the Magpie and Punchbowl. The inexplicable Grimes, whose fortuitous existence at that establishment might to some, at least, have been supposed to be voluntarily prolonged for a certain purpose, took the opportunity one morning of making plain to the meanest capacity his particular object in thus sojourning at a place where, as was grievously apparent on the wainscot in the bar,[302] an inordinate quantity of chalk had been wasted in the registration of refreshment, which, as it so turned out, had only served to pamper his vital energies towards the feat he now took upon himself to accomplish. To speak plainly, Jack Grimes eloped with Miss Betsy Malkin one day, most unceremoniously taking leave, – and everything else that he could either by himself or by his conjugal proxy contrive to bear away from the premises.

This was rather a miserable circumstance for the widow, inasmuch as she had not only not contemplated the marriage of her younger daughter with Jack Grimes, but had actually designed that that interesting being should be devoted to Westminster Abbey. Little Mr. Gibbon, however, possessed as much greatness within him as was ever interred in his namesake; for he made light of the matter, and now laid more diligent siege to a worthy gentlewoman residing in the house at which his vocation compelled him to resort, who, as we understood, had held out such temptations as he could by no means bring himself to resist. Her graces of person, he told us, were what are usually termed retiring, or rather they had retired long ago without having done much execution; but she had substituted charms of a pecuniary nature, which our friend yearned most anxiously to possess: and at length his absence from the consumptive Magpie and the exhausted Punchbowl as plainly and intelligibly related his present destiny as though we had seen it communicated through the medium of a newspaper, wherein such events are philosophically disposed between the entrance and exit of human beings in this transitory sphere.[303]

Haynes had up to this moment abstained from adverting to the communication which, in a moment of extreme dejection, he had wished to impart to Wisp; and during the intervening period, much to the mortification of the latter and myself, although from time to time yielding to despondency, appeared to have lost sight of the particular subject which in the first instance promised so speedily to be brought upon the carpet, or rather the sanded[304] floor of the parlour in which we were sitting. Under these circumstances, more especially as no other alternative presented itself, my friend Wisp was fain – his finances being low, and having scarcely anything else to pop[305] – to pop the question to Miss Susan, and to receive with that invaluable helpmate a dower of some fifty pounds, fringed with reversionary expectations of a portion of the proceeds consequent upon the sale of the lease and goodwill of the premises, of which Mrs. Malkin was now minded to dispose.

It may appear strange to those who, not 'much pondering on these matters,'[306] are inclined at least to hope that the sudden influx of money imposes the duty of taking care of it, that my friend Wisp should in so short a space of time have ridded himself of the cash he had extracted from the custody of Snavel; but as we all live to verify some particular adage, so in like manner did Wisp confirm the truth of the laconic axiom, 'Lightly come, lightly go,' having become one of those persons whose enlarged notions are in an inverse ratio to their means of satisfying them. And, to say the truth, I myself had contrived to place myself in a false position of the like nature; and as matrimony appeared in our small circle to be the best and only means of present, although temporary, existence, I was tempted to give in to the prevailing rage, and to enter myself of the temple of Hymen[307] forthwith.

There were obvious objections to this measure which occurred to myself; although, to be sincere, I did not hold them of much account. I was yet very young, and had no settled means of subsistence. There were strong inducements, on the other hand, which far outweighed such considerations as may, perhaps, be of sufficient weight with some, although they never exercised much influence over me. In the first place, – I loved the girl; yes, let me not belie my own nature, – I *did* love Catharine. In the second, I had reason to believe that I was not indifferent to her; two reasons that gave additional weight, importance, and recommendation to the last, – she had a means of subsistence for herself in her own business which might, should other exertions fail, be strained into an available means of subsistence for two. I was a man of straw,[308] – she a maker of straw-bonnets; but it was strange, indeed, if she obtained from me the material for her manufacture. And, then, Wisp had never communicated to his sister the fact of Snavel's delinquency and flight, and of our consequent absence from his office, and to this moment the simple-hearted girl believed that we were still actively and regularly employed in our legal vocation.

But, had I been ever so scrupulously conscientious in the narration of my particular circumstances at that time, I believe that the poor creature herself would have overruled the objections that might have arisen out of it; for, by some means or other, I had created an interest in her heart which was surely not the less strong because undeserved; and when she married me I am assured she thought that any vices I might possess it would be her pleasing duty to eradicate; and that she herself should be sufficiently happy in the consciousness of making me so.

I know not whether this be the nature of woman, but I do know that this was her nature; and, although, all things considered, perhaps a more imprudent match could hardly have been made than between two people of our respective ages, – myself in an ostensible situation barely sufficient to support my own physical wants; yet she was so young, active, and ardent, that she seemed to require no stimulus, but her own unassisted will, to labour almost incessantly for our support, even after she had been gradually informed of the real position in which I stood with respect to money matters; although ignorant of the cause of my separation from Snavel, and of the length of time since that event had occurred.

Could my own motives be strictly analysed, I think they would be found to consist of blind waywardness and real affection, made to follow a certain law, which is called the first law of nature. I am not certain that any predetermination to compromise another's happiness can justly be laid to my charge at that period; and if there were, I can promise the reader that, while I am about the matter, I would make a 'clean breast' of it at once; although, I fear, the cleansing of the Augean stable[309] were an easier and a more agreeable employment.

'Take care of that precious creature, Jack,' said Wisp to me, with unusual outlay of emotion, on the day of our marriage, – '*there*, at least, I have not cause of self-reproach; my own imprudence has been its own punishment, nor have I ever trenched on her poor earnings a single farthing,' – and a tear stood in his eye, and seemed to stand there, surprised at its situation: – 'No, no,' he continued, 'I have loved her too well for that – poor thing!' and he turned upon me with earnestness and grasped my arms with his two hands, – 'Oh, Jack, for her sake keep a safe look out; were any thing to happen, you'd break her heart; I know you would – and mine, too, by Heaven!'

'Let each take care of himself,' I replied carelessly, 'as the donkey said when he danced among the chickens. I shall keep my weather eye up,[310] depend on't.'

'Pshaw!' said Wisp, sternly, 'I spoke seriously – I've a heart, Ketch, that can feel for another.'

I made a movement of my thumb over my left shoulder,[311] – 'and a hand, too, Wisp,' I added. 'Come, come, no nonsense;' and the conversation dropped.

But in calculating the sum of happiness I expected to become possessed of in the married state, I had made a capital error: – I had left the influence which I myself, an important figure in the result, must necessarily possess, out of the question altogether. I had by no means satisfied myself of the expediency of being restricted to that domestic routine usually acceded to by the husband; and reserved the full right of going hither and thither as I pleased, without question or expostulation. It is true, there were no words; not a single complaint on the part of Catharine, touching my habits, which, to say truth, were not a little irregular and incalculable; and the most angelic sweetness of her smile, and the soft glance of her eyes, which I never could bear to behold without emotion, were ever ready to bless me when at length I returned to my own house.

This was the misery: – I had married a young creature, not only ignorant of my nature, – if so I may call it, – but absolutely unable to comprehend the existence of such principles, or inverted principles as I possessed; herself as gentle and placid a being as ever brought virtue and innocence to the threshold of a villain. Relying on God, and her own honest exertions, she knew not the passions instigated by brutish instinct which I had inherited, or which had been planted within me.

'My dear fellow,' she would say to me, when she saw me brooding, as she mistakenly thought, over my hard fate in being thrown upon the world without any present means of getting my living, – 'do not despond; you see I can earn almost enough to support us for the present, and, by the blessing of God, you will soon, perhaps, hear of something that may suit you; we are yet very young, you know.' And with such consolations as her simple and generous heart instructed her in offering, would she vainly attempt to propitiate my rancour and daily increasing brutality.

For this it was that almost made me mad. Had she complained, I had had a hold upon her; I could have made reprisals, and justified myself by believing that she deserved them. But this sweetness awed, without disarming me. I dared not to look into my own heart. I could not cast off the old associations of mind and body that constantly beset, surrounded, and held me fast. I could not commit sin, – for she had taught me 'how awful goodness is,'[312] – without hating myself. I could not whisper to her former life, and my present designs – for I loved her. Let not the reader presume to scoff; yes, I *did* love her, and I feared lest I should break her heart.

In the meantime, Mrs. Malkin had succeeded in disposing of her public house to one of that great class of persons, who, whether under the influence of a sanguine temperament or an unlucky star, I know not, appear wilfully to rush into ruin, which to other eyes is as plain and evident as a simple sum of subtraction. Wisp, actuated by reasons of prudence, had, since his marriage, chosen to reside upon the premises, probably with a view to secure as much of the amount realised for the furniture, good-will, and lease, as the old lady could be brought to yield up; a sum not very great, it might naturally be supposed; being the mere garnish of a dish which had been appropriated to himself by the more sagacious Grimes. Haynes and myself dropt in during the evening, and proceeded to the now utterly dismantled parlour, for the purpose of taking a farewell of that solitary resort.

'Ketch,' cried Haynes, earnestly, turning to me, – and now I perceived the ghastly paleness of his face, – 'where are they going when they leave this place? – where is Wisp to be seen? – where are both to be found? Do you know,' he continued, smiling faintly, 'that I feel quite superstitious about this removal; I had become so used to the place. Where is Wisp? Oh! I can bear this no longer – something has happened to-day. Will you be my friend?' – and he looked at me with a fixed attention, and leaned his hand, which shook violently, upon my shoulder.

I went out in search of my friend, and proceeded to the bar. Mrs. Malkin was alone – asleep – and in that state in which ladies wish to be who love their glass. Calling Wisp from the bottom of the stairs, that busy person made his appearance with a pen behind his ear, for he had been taking a private inventory of the goods above stairs.

'Where is your wife?'

'Gone to look out for a lodging,' said he, 'and won't be back for an hour or two.'

'Haynes is in the parlour,' said I, in a whisper, 'we shall hear something at last.' He winked his eye, and followed me.

'Why, what's the matter, my good fellow?' cried he, as he entered, approaching the other, who was leaning disconsolately against the mantel-piece.

'Nothing, nothing,' faltered Haynes; 'I shall be better directly; leave me for a moment.'

'Leave you!' said Wisp, gaily, 'indeed I shall do no such thing. Come, let us have three chairs out of the bar, and I'll stand something short,'[313] saying which, he presently returned with half a pint of brandy, while I followed with the chairs.

'Now, don't be a d—d fool, Haynes,' said Wisp, pouring out the brandy, as we seated ourselves; 'here have you been for months shilly-shallying about some stupid matter that, I dare say, is not worth a curse; we're all friends here; now, what *is* the matter – take a glass.'

'Oh, God!' exclaimed Haynes, swallowing the brandy, and dashing the glass under the grate, – 'I can't tell you; don't harass me with questions; I'm quite unnerved to-night; let me go – somewhere' – and he rose.

'Tut, tut, tut, this is childish,' said Wisp, gently taking up the fragments of glass; 'we break what we can't make; you didn't use to be so; it's infernally foolish, Haynes; it is, upon my soul;' and he slapped him on the shoulder.

'I wish I had never been born!' sighed Haynes, and he sank back in his chair, clasping his forehead tightly with his hands.

'Wish you had never been born! Ha! ha! that's a good one, by jingo!' laughed Wisp; 'if a wish were a horse, beggars would ride, – and you know where they ride when they do get into the saddle.'

'Where I am going fast enough,' groaned the other. 'Oh, Wisp, – Oh, Ketch, it's all up with me; it is indeed.'

'Come, come, come,' said Wisp, with hasty impatience, 'out with it at once; don't spin a long yarn; short and sweet,' – and we drew our chairs nearer.

Haynes brooded sullenly for awhile; his head between his knees, and the palms of his hands pressed closely against his ears. At length, starting suddenly, he sat upright in his chair: 'Give me a glass of brandy,' said he, – and he drank it off hastily, – 'I will tell you all.'

'When I first came to London, I arrived as many others are in the daily habit of doing, that is, with scarcely a shilling in my pocket, hardly a shoe to my foot, and barely a shirt to my back. Mr. Marley[314] took me into his warehouse; gave me ample wages and light work, and treated me in every respect as though the circumstance of my being his servant, imposed on him the obligation of treating me like a human being and a fellow-creature; which is more, let me tell you, than falls to the lot of many; and more, perhaps, as the world goes, than a young boy, without recommendation, has any just reason to expect. Nay, he did more than this; – he solicited himself anxiously about my improvement; took pains to keep me out of bad or suspicious company, by restricting me to early hours, and, in course of time, admitted me into the counting-house. In a word, he was my only friend.

'My story is an every day one, and I shall, therefore, make it as brief as possible. Finding myself master of a more liberal salary than I had before enjoyed, with more time at my own disposal, and just of an age to be captivated by the pleasures and allurements of the town, I soon found that I saved nothing at the end of the year, as I had heretofore done; and, on the close of the following year, discovered that I was in debt. Well, there was nothing so bad in this; it was the imprudence of youth; ignorance of the value of money; old heads do not grow on young shoulders. I had a thousand excuses to make, and I did make them, – to myself. I dared not lay before Mr. Marley the real state of my affairs.

'In the meantime, one or two of my creditors became importunate. Christmas had passed away – my salary had been swallowed up, and there was nothing for them. What was I to do? They threatened to state their complaints to Mr. Marley; should I anticipate them? – throw myself at once upon his mercy, make a bold resolution of reforming for the future, and keep it? Had I done this, all had been well. I know he would still have stood my friend. I know he would have saved me. I had not the resolution to do so. Oh, Wisp! oh! my dear Jack! never, never, while you live, get into debt; if I *could* but tell you the misery, the horrible misery, to which it leads. But I will proceed.

'This is what I did, – and the devil prompted me. I enjoyed the full confidence of my master; and was his only clerk. It was my business to receive all the money, and to pay it regularly into the banker's. A sum became due, – or, rather, it was barely due, and the person by whom it was owing was in good credit with the house. He paid the money, and ordered another parcel of goods. My quarter's salary was also due in a few days. I appropriated to my own use the money paid by our customer, and discharged my more pressing debts with it, intending to replace the sum with my salary. From that moment until now I have never enjoyed a moment's peace. It was a simple operation, and fatally secure, as it so turned out. I did replace that sum with my salary.

'But, oh! that intervening period of a few days! Every step in the warehouse, – every approach to the counting house, – every look of my master, struck me with dismay, and filled me with horrible, horrible terror. I went not about my business, as I was wont to do; I spoke not to Mr. Marley as I had been accustomed to speak; I dared not look upon his face; – my self-esteem was gone.

'Can you not see the rest at once? No. How can you be supposed to see at a glance what I was too blind to behold? Do you suppose, that once mixed up with loose company, – once habituated to such habits as they exact from you, and at once made familiar with the means of putting off the evil day, with the assured consciousness, that, in all probability, you will never be discovered; do you suppose that it was possible to resist? You smile; but it is so. The weakness that, in the first instance, urged you to the commission, abides by you constantly. Again, again, and again did I adopt the same means of temporary extrication, with the same success, with the same reparation, and at the same miserable expense. At length, my immediately pressing debts became larger in amount than my salary in anticipation; so that, sometimes, when I had thus discharged them, a balance of this surreptitiously-obtained money remained in my hands, not only till my salary became again payable, but until some smaller sum fell due which would enable me, by retaining that, to discharge the larger and previous amount. Do you understand me? In plain words, I was getting into debt with my master to an extent which no portion of my salary, – let me say for a year, – for I must live in the meantime, and determined to live with the most exact frugality, – would enable me to repay. If, you see, it had been of the nature of a simple debt, fairly contracted, and I had had the opportunity, and had been permitted to discharge it by degrees, as my salary was drawn, I think I could have done it, – I think I could; – but, oh! how many a sum must be clandestinely held back, – what a dreadful interest of wretchedness must I pay before I could hope to make all straight again, even if my resolution of amending my life remained firm for the whole period.

'So help me God! – do me this justice, I beseech you, – a thought never entered my mind of robbing Mr. Marley. The books will show that; nor would I, for the world, wrong him of a single farthing. Oh! what narrow escapes have I had from discovery. What hair-breadth, – what providential chances that have turned my very soul within me. Oh! my friends, were a sum suddenly to be dropt out of heaven into these hands sufficient to discharge what I now owe, – for I *will* call it a debt, – I would fly to conclude this hell of slavery; I would pay it off at once, – at once, – and perhaps I might go mad; but I should never be happy again – never, never, never.' Here the unfortunate man covered his is with his hands, and wept long and audibly.

'I am easier now,' he resumed, after a pause, 'now that I have told you all. But let me ask, or rather, let me say, – how am I now situated? I am deficient nearly four hundred pounds; one of those miraculous escapes has occurred to-day – but I could bear it no longer. In a week or two all *must* have been discovered. I have been entangled in a labyrinth out of which I could not release myself. Besides, the credit of others might have suffered by my villany. But if it were not so, I can endure this life no longer – I cannot, by heaven! I have often thought of absconding with just as much as would pay my passage to New York – God forgive me! but I abandoned that plan. What *am* I to do? Oh! advise me for the best – advise me – counsel me – what *am* I to do?'

'Come, come, you're a cup too low, Haynes,' said Wisp, offering another glass of brandy, 'all may yet be well.'

'Impossible!' cried the other, mournfully.

'Impossible; why so? Let us see – what can be done? You say you have the control of the cash; well then, when you go to-morrow – '

'Go to-morrow!' exclaimed Haynes, 'to-morrow! I can never go there again. I have left a letter, stating everything in full, on Mr. Marley's desk, and am now cast upon the world a beggar, without a farthing, without prospects, without character – a common, paltry thief.'

'Fool! fool! infernal fool!' shouted Wisp, violently; 'what! leave yourself without a farthing in the world, or, in other words, without means of getting wherewithal to replace the money you have borrowed. Do you know the value of money, sir?' and Wisp turned ferociously to his companion, as though the cash had been abstracted from his own pockets; 'do you know that without money you *cannot* be honest, and that with it you can, and are – oh! you're an ass, a wretched ass. Why, if you had occasion to pawn your great coat, you'd wrap it up in your own skin. Can't you recal the letter?'

'He has read it long ere this,' said Haynes, 'and I am glad of it; my mind is now somewhat at rest. But, tell me, what I am to do? Where can I conceal myself? Will he prosecute, d'ye think?'

'And you have left your situation without a shilling to bless yourself with,' cried Wisp, not heeding the question, surveying him with extreme contempt. 'Oh lord! prosecute you? you ought to be prosecuted for a fool, and hanged before a lunatic asylum as a warning to idiots. You know where the cash is kept of a night.'

'I do, I do,' cried Haynes, listlessly.

'And know the premises well, of course; every hole and corner, I warrant. Well, well,' he muttered, 'it's not so very bad, after all. Come, Haynes, my boy, don't be downhearted; what's past recal is past sighing for: what can't be cured must be endured, as the saying is. We'll make you up a bed here to-night, and to-morrow we can talk over the affair more coolly.'

'Something can be made of this fellow yet, Jack,' said Wisp, as I took my leave for the night; 'he's precious soft just here,' and he tapped his forehead with his forefinger. 'Keep yourself ready for action; we're in over shoes, and must over boots. It's no use to do things by halves; there's a good chance for us, depend on't.'

With these hints, and a promise to communicate to me the earliest favourable intelligence, I left him with renewed spirits, and proceeded to my own home.

CHAPTER XI.

Wisp called upon me on the afternoon of the following day, in great apparent dejection of spirits. 'Here's a precious dance I've had,' said he, wiping his brow, 'removing to our new lodgings, and seeing the old woman as far as Chelsea, who has gone to live by the side of the river for the benefit of her rheumatism. Where's Kate? at home?'

I answered that she had gone out on business of importance; and so, indeed, she had, having stept as far as her employer's for her last week's earnings, without which our animal functions must cease to proceed.

'I can't get that fool, Haynes, into a proper train yet,' added Wisp, snappishly; 'the fellow has no pluck. I've taken him to live with us for the present; I mean to get rent out of him, though, one of these days. This is what I want to do, Jack,' and he took me by the waistcoat button, which he seemed to examine scrupulously as he proceeded; 'I want to do with him as they stuff turkeys – keep him fast, cram him well, and kill him afterwards.'

'Kill him, Wisp! hush, my dear fellow,' said I, 'what do you mean?'

'Tut, tut, I speak figuratively,' cried Wisp; 'this is what I mean: to get him into a line, don't you see? to make him place his hand, *thus*, on some of old Marley's stumpy;[315] to hand it over to us, and we'll bolt with it – eh, my Jacky?' and he rubbed his hands together with exceeding satisfaction.

Sundry considerations of moment appeared to arise instantaneously out of this proposal. 'It is easy,' I remarked, 'to talk about placing your hand, thus, on old Marley's money, but how should you like to place your hand *thus*' – and I held up my hand significantly – 'at the bar of the Old Bailey?'[316]

'Gammon!' cried Wisp, with a snap of the fingers; 'I don't care *that* for the Recorder, or the *corder*[317] either, as Gibbon would say. I tell you, Haynes is fly to the right move; he knows how to walk his body into the counting-house without danger; I got as much from him last night after you were gone. Besides, the watchman in Friday Street is always asleep in his box;[318] damme, he's like Oliver Cromwell's watch in the British Museum,[319] with his hands perpetually on his face, – but doesn't go his rounds every hour. Ha! ha! ha!'

This statement partly reconciled me to the proposition of joining in the expedition; and with assurances of the earliest notice of any yielding on the part of our indispensable accomplice, Wisp left me, probably to endeavour to expedite that communication as speedily as possible.

And to confess the truth, there were strong inducements that had no inconsiderable weight in moving me to take any part, whether active or otherwise, in this projected operation. My money was all gone; my wife's pittance scarcely sufficed to keep the wolf from the door; and my habits imperatively demanded a more liberal supply of cash than I was now enabled to devote to them.

It was the painful knowledge of these facts that prompted me to go forth on this evening, – whither I knew not nor cared, – with that listless feeling of pervading disquietude, which, by the higher classes termed ennui, and by the middle orders the dumps is most expressively styled by the class to which I belong, being 'down upon your luck.'[320] The Magpie and Punchbowl was at an end; that 'beautiful had vanished and returned not,'[321] – and in other haunts to which I had recently become habituated, I knew full well that without money I should be received like a dishonoured bill by the drawer, a first husband at his wife's second wedding, or the corpse of a man of genius at Westminster Abbey.[322] Besides, I had begun to hate the society of Catharine; I could not bear to see her so mild, and gentle, and patient, toiling for my subsistence, reserving of the small proceeds of her hard earnings, scarcely sufficient to provide for her own; and all this while as patient and contented as though it were the natural and proper course of things that it should be so. By heaven! I could not endure to sit opposite that affectionate creature, fed with her food, warmed by her fire, sheltered by her lodging, and blasted by the gaze of those eyes, which ever and anon were raised timidly from her work to speak hope and comfort to me.

I wandered forth into the streets, and as I paced hurriedly along, the devil began to stir within me. For what had I been brought into the world? to starve? No. Who were my parents? common thieves? Yes. Had they brought me up to a trade, or a profession, as other children were? They had done their best to do so. Why not follow it then like a man, for I was now of man's estate. Before me was a multitude, doubtless proceeding on some business, or at some period of the day or night occupied in employment. Behind me was a crowd pressing forward on similar errands. Hither and thither they came and went, and their indifference seemed to mock and to insult me. Beside me, as I hurried on, were shops gorgeously dressed and laid out with a variety of articles, whether of daily use or of fastidious luxury. 'Hanmer, jeweller,' I muttered to myself, as I stopped and lingered at a shop, gazing on valuables which one dash of my hand would transfer to me, – 'a dealer in precious stones, eh? a dealer in precious roguery, rather. If that diamond on the breast of your shirt, friend Hanmer, could speak of the villany that lies so safely and snugly beneath, what a tale would it tell; it would be 'diamond cut diamond,'[323] you rascal. If that ring on your little finger possessed the gift of speech, would it not relate how often it had been tossed up towards that rubicund nose;[324] if every jewel in your shop-window were suddenly summoned to its right owner, what a strange rustling in the cotton, what a marvellous commotion in the glass cases, what a strange vanishing of your stock in trade. Oh! rogues all, – alike villains, rascals, slaves, drunkards, thieves, – poverty is the devil, wealth the brightest angel of the million; – store of wealth, plenty of stealth; no mammon, no gammon.'

This ebullition of bile was interrupted by the egress of a stranger from the shop, who buttoning his coat closely, and pondering for a moment, apparently with a view to decide in which direction he should proceed, suddenly turned the corner of the street, and walked leisurely away.

I followed, but urged by what immediate impulse I know not. This was the very man upon whom, of all others, I felt an irresistible desire to renew my once familiar skill. Was it fate? I know not. Was there something in the appearance of the man that vibrated on the mysterious chain of association? It could not be, or I had hardly chosen him for my victim. Dropping, or rather lagging behind him till I came within hand-shot of the stranger, I cast one furtive glance behind me, and slid my fingers into his coat-pocket. My right hand had lost its cunning,[325] or was not 'in,' such is the technical phrase; and yet that could not be, for it was in; but just as I had abstracted a pocket-book, the firm grasp of the stranger detained me, and he turned.

'You have dropped your pocket-book, sir,' I stammered, and I picked it up.

'I certainly dropped it in my own pocket a few minutes ago,' answered the stranger, 'and you, it seems, have picked it up from thence. But heavens! can it be? Mr. Ketch?'

I started and looked up; it was Misty. Again I started and looked down. 'How is this, young man?' said Misty, calmly, 'that I detect you at this miserable occupation. But come with me; you are safe, I will not betray you;' and he led me with him to an adjoining tavern, where he called for candles and a private room.

'Bring this young man and myself some brandy and water,' said he to the waiter, who entered with lights. The man bowed respectfully, as though he knew my companion, and departed.

As Misty paced up and down the apartment, which he did for some minutes without uttering a word, I could not but perceive the almost miraculous change that had taken place in his person, and in those outward shows[326] which go so far towards converting beggars into gentlemen, and ordinary coarseness into extraordinary gentility. Misty, the poor, pale, miserable being of former days, was now transformed into an elderly gentleman in professional sable; and the pinched, hungry, and penurious visage of the former man had been exchanged for a fashionable face, wearing an air of aristocratic dignity and pride.

'Come, Mr. Ketch, take some brandy and water; it will calm your spirits,' he said, still continuing to pace the room. 'How is this?' he resumed, after a pause, standing before me and gazing at me earnestly; 'what! turned pickpocket! Mr. Ketch, I expected better things of you. Come, tell me, tell me at once, is this your first offence?'

I was fain, under the circumstances, to state that it was.

'I am glad of it,' he answered, emphatically; 'I am truly glad of it. But what has driven you to this step? What horrible necessity has compelled you to such an act? for nothing less, surely' – and he looked at me inquiringly.

I gave a condensed account of my history since last I had the pleasure of seeing him, repressing every thing that could vitiate my claims to respect from so nice and scrupulous a moralist; and made my marriage and domestic distress the channels through which his sympathy might freely, and without interruption, find an easy and legitimate channel.

'And you have married Wisp's sister?' answered Misty; 'I remember her. I saw her once; – poor thing!' and he mused for a moment or two. 'Do you know what you have done, or rather what you were about to do?'

I was silent.

'Do you know what you have done?' he repeated violently, striking the table with his hand.

Again I answered not.

'Do you know that you were about to commit an act, than which I consider the crime of murder itself less heinous. For murder has its passions, its despair, its revenge, its madness. But pick a pocket! skulk like a miserable wretch at the heels of a stranger! take that which is not your own, like a coward too, from one who has perhaps earned it by the honest sweat of his brow for his virtuous wife and innocent children. Oh! tell me not, tell me not,' he continued hastily, raising his hands, for I was about speak, 'tell me not of your motives, your necessities, your starvations; have you not hands, youth, strength, health? do you not acknowledge a duty to society, to yourself, to your family, to your God? And for this too?' and he threw the pocket-book on the table. 'I declare to heaven' – he raised his hands as he spoke – 'I do not think that all the wealth that was ever delved from the mine is a fair price in purchase of a mean action.'

Rochefoucault says, and some have declared the maxim a fine one, that 'hypocrisy is the homage that vice herself pays to virtue.'[327] I paid homage to these sentiments of Misty, but it was not the homage of hypocrisy. I felt for the moment humbled and abased, and would have retired.

'Do not believe, my boy,' cried Misty, more calmly, 'that I spoke in the heat of passion; you are mistaken if you think so: it was the warmth of friendship. Oh! do not run this course; do not play this game, in which they who win most, most fatally lose, and *are* lost. Let me impress this upon you, that there is no situation in life, however poor, low, – despicable some may call it, – out of which you may not extort respect and acquire honour. Be honest, be industrious, be patient, and the world is your slave; be otherwise – but I will not proceed. We shall meet again, probably, hereafter. Good night!'

He arose and opened the door. 'Give me your hand,' said he, with a melancholy smile, 'for old acquaintance sake;' he pressed it kindly – 'good night! good night!' and he closed the door. He had left a ten-pound note in my hand.

I ran out of the tavern like a maniac, knowing not whither I went, until I found myself in Covent Garden market. I wandered up and down the piazza bewildered, smiting my hands together, and to calm my inward perturbation, but in vain. At length I proceeded to an adjoining public-house, where I recruited my sinking spirits by copious draughts of brandy; and with something like calmness I contrived to find my way home.

When I entered the room, Catharine had prepared our simple supper, and had been waiting for me. 'Are you not well, John,' she said, taking my hat, 'you look pale; what is the matter?'

I motioned her to be silent, and sat down in my accustomed chair. The words of Misty had sunk deep in my heart, but remained there not to heal but to rankle. Why should I be subject to these homilies? What had I done to render them applicable to me? Alas! I knew too well that I deserved the damning reproach implied in every word of my former companion. But how could I now evade that reproach? – by avoiding him? No. I could not escape from myself. For the first time in my life, I began to examine my own heart. Never before had I even contemplated that the very freedom of absolute right involved and was restrained by duty. My morals were not lost, for I never had any, as somebody has said before me; how was I to procure a set? how cause them to act efficiently upon a mind so warped and degraded as mine? Time pressed; hunger, thirst, and beggary were at the door clamorous for admittance: action was the word. I had done before without morality by instinct; my reason instructed me that I must contrive to dispense with it for the time to come. Again, what was right? what was duty? It was my duty to provide for myself and my family; that was right, at all events. I clung to the letter, accordingly, and bade the spirit[328] go to the devil, and much good may it do him; he has need of it. I was resolved to put it aside and take my chance.

But though I had worked out this strange solution of a problem; though I had cast safe to shore this miserable wreck of comfort, my mind refused to subside into calmness, and my heart came not forth to calm or to gild the surging passions that seethed direfully within me.

While I thus sat, Catharine came towards me, and sitting down before me on the floor, as she was sometimes accustomed to do, placed her hands upon my knees, and looked up in my face.

'I know you *are* ill, John,' she said affectionately; 'come, tell me what ails you?'

'Nothing, nothing,' I replied hastily, turning away my head; 'leave me to myself – go to your supper.'

'No, no, I declare I won't touch a morsel unless you promise to partake of it. I know something wrong has happened, and you won't tell me of it; you're a very naughty fellow.'

'Will you have done!' I shouted. 'Take your hands away from my knees; you're a fool, and know nothing of the matter.'

She shrunk away for a moment, and looked wistfully at me. I had never been so harsh before.

'I didn't mean to offend you, John,' she said; 'I only thought – ' again she approached. I was silent.

'Now, my dear fellow,' she continued, creeping between my knees, and looking into my face, 'you know I can't be happy unless you are so. Do tell me what has occurred. I fear something at that horrid place you go to with William; if it's anything very bad, tell me at once. Oh! I am sure the company you keep will be our ruin – I know it will.'

I was mad. I knew not what I did. I struck her on the face with the back of my hand, – struck her while she was gazing at me, like an angel of pity and love. I saw a sudden twitch of the mouth; it could not be of pain; I had not struck her hard enough for that; and a flush came over her cheeks and temples, – but not of anger. I had wounded the poor creature's pride.

'Oh, John!' she cried, with a low but choking voice, 'you should not serve me so,' and she raised her apron to her face, and turned away her head.

I arose and walked, or rather strode, about the room two or three times, and then halting at the table, took up the plates, one by one, and dashed them on the floor. It was not passion, but the paltry pretext, or apology, for a former outrage, intended to indicate by subsequent violence, the previous excitement that had led to it. Having done this, I cast one glance at my poor wife, who was trembling before me, and hastened to the adjoining room, where I threw myself upon the bed, and burst into an agony of tears.

Catharine heard me through the thin partition that divided the two rooms, and came timidly to the bedside. 'Go away, and leave me,' I said sullenly; 'I shall be better soon.'

She took my hand as it was about to fall by my side, between her own, and kneeling down, kissed it silently.

What had I done? I had spurned, like a dog, the only being that loved me in the world; the only one to whom my life, my happiness, my common comfort was a moment's thought; one, also, to whom I had been indebted for all these. What reparation could I make – what vile palliation could I devise to my own heart? – and, then, her gentleness, her meekness, her generosity; no rebuke offered; no momentary passion displayed: my heart swelled within me as the consciousness of my own unworthiness struggled against my brutish and violent nature; and, for once, I wept like a child, – and was human.

We spoke not for some minutes.

'Oh! my dear, dear fellow,' said Catharine, at length, 'what dreadful misfortune has befallen us? Be calm, I implore you. Come, let me lead you into the other room.'

'Will you forgive me?' I uttered in broken accents. 'Will you forgive me, Kate?'

'For what, child?'[329] she inquired, mildly.

'For what I did just now. Oh, Kate! is it come to this? Am I a beast, – altogether a beast – ' and the words of her brother, on the day of my marriage, were brought to mind.

'No, dear, no; say not another word about it,' she exclaimed; 'you will never do so any more, – I know you won't,' and she rose and smoothed my hair from my forehead, which she kissed fervently. 'Come, you will be better now,' and she led me into the room.

I averted my head as we entered the room; I dared not look upon my wife; I was ashamed to meet those eyes, which, even now, were gazing at me with undiminished affection.

'Has anything really occurred?' she inquired, with more tranquillity.

'No, nothing,' said I, interrupting her. 'I was out of temper and spirits, – and a fool. See, here is something to go on with; take it, and keep it safely,' and I handed the bank-note to her.

She took it, and looked at it attentively, and then glanced at me. 'Why, John, – John Ketch. Oh! my God,' she shrieked, 'you surely have not – ' and she fell upon her knees before me, – 'Do not say it – if it is so.'

'Why, what do you mean, Kate?' said I, anticipating her thoughts. 'Come, come, it was got honestly;' and I related that I had met Misty, who had given me that sum out of pure friendship and affection for me.

'God be praised!' cried Kate, clasping her hands and bursting into tears. 'Oh! dear John, – John, – forgive me. I thought – '

'That I had stolen it,' said I, finishing the sentence.

'No, no, no, you are not so bad as that; I know you're not. Oh! my dear boy, do promise me this – that you will never, never take to thieving. Do forgive me; it would break my heart, – indeed it would.' The poor girl threw herself into my arms at these words, and wept for some minutes.

'But, no,' she added, wiping away her tears, and forcing a smile, 'I'm a poor silly thing; no, you *never* could be guilty of such dreadful acts. I would work day and night, John, before you should be compelled to take what is not your own.'

Every word the girl uttered stuck like a dagger into my soul. It was plain that she suspected me; it was clear, that when she came to know me better, she would hate and despise me, – and I felt that I deserved to be hated and despised.

'No, Kate,' said I, with a calmness that was far from real; 'this money was given to me by Mr. Misty, upon my honour; – not another word;' and I raised her up.

She smiled, and was happy, and took the note carefully away, locking it in her trunk. 'I will keep it for you,' said she, 'and pray that it may be a blessing to us.'

When I saw that innocent creature praying by her bedside, – which she did nightly, – I asked my own heart, will this woman, with all her virtue, goodness, and purity, be happy? Can it be so? No, no; it was impossible. And wherefore? My heart sank within me; – it could not reply.

CHAPTER XII.

IT is a common saying, that a certain place is paved with good intentions;[330] if this be true, I assuredly accomplished a small square of mosaic work on the night which I have just concluded in the former chapter. But when I arose on the following morning, a new and more comfortable course of reflection presented itself to me. And now I began, for the first time, to ask myself, Who is Misty? – what is he? – employed in what avocation? – engaged in what pursuit? Was it likely, I began to think, that he could hand me over a ten pound note, unless there were some extraordinary motive to suggest that proceeding? It was clear that he was a successful sharper, eager for a monopoly, and consequently jealous of an incipient rival. He had attempted to 'buy me off,' but it wouldn't do.

In this manner did I contrive to stifle any feeling that might possibly have arisen of gratitude towards my benefactor. Nor with less ease did I dismiss a compunctious visiting that still lingered about me with respect to my wife. What right had she to interfere between me and my private arrangements? Why should I suffer myself to be harassed by her canting importunities to reform my life? And it now occurred to me that she was in my power. I was safe in that quarter, – I knew that; – secure of her silence, whatever guilt or danger I brought home with me; certain of her passive acquiescence, and assured of my own authority. What, but a few hours ago, I had looked upon as a violent and an unjustifiable outrage, now appeared a salutary and a legitimate check. It would teach her better for the time to come, and establish my domestic power without question, cavil, or mistake.

This sudden revulsion of feeling into the old channel, may, to some, appear unnatural, but I am pretty confident that it is not so; – being, as I am, quite at issue with those moral philosophers who incline to augur prosperously of such deviations into comparative goodness as I displayed upon that occasion. These indications are, in fact, merely as the blaze of the candle ere it sinks into the socket; or, as it were, galvanic eruptions,[331] stimulating a lifeless body into momentary action, in which no human power can ever again cause, even for an instant, renewed existence. I was, at this period, morally a worse man than I had been before; for I became reckless, reserving of what may properly be called nature, only that particular cunning and foresight, which, I believe, are very generally planted in mankind, but which had been dealt out to me in no ordinary proportion.

Some days elapsed, and still Haynes 'hung fire,'[332] and was becoming moody and taciturn; Wisp was growing impatient and peremptory; and I had squandered away the chief portion of the cash presented to me by Misty, which I was compelled to wrest by little and little, amid tears and entreaties, from my wife. These, however, had ceased to touch my heart, although they irritated my feelings; and the consequences may be easily surmised. I repaid them by harshness, and sometimes even spurned my wife from me with curses and reproach. I felt that she was a hinderance to me; that she at length knew me; and I saw that she, at times, feared every glance of my eye, and every motion of my hand. She obeyed me as heretofore, but never without a sigh or a deprecating look that distracted me. When I went forth on my nightly carouse, I sometimes listened at the door, and heard her sink heavily into her chair to weep; and when I returned, I often surprised her in tears, which aggravated my dogged and intractable spirit into brutal and ferocious violence.

Pending the negociations between Wisp, Haynes, and myself, an idea presented itself to me, which was too agreeable a guest to be suffered to depart without entertainment. Should I betray Wisp and Haynes? Let me not be misunderstood. I bore them no ill will; there was no malice in the matter at all. There were the two principles: – 'Honour among thieves;'[333] – and 'Take care of yourself.' By an adhesion to the first, what should I acquire? – by a preference of the latter, what should I get? It was a choice, not of evils, but of possible good. Hesitating and pondering upon the matter, I found myself in Friday-street. Within ten paces of me was Marley's warehouse. I passed on the opposite side and discerned, seated in the counting-house, an elderly person engaged in writing. I had decided; my foot was on the threshold; – but, stop! – Was I certain that the old fellow would reward my extraordinary honesty? – might I not be caught in my own trap? I was in no condition to make terms, or to strike in support of them; and I felt, moreover, that I might very possibly find my own spoon in their dish, when I had not the least desire to partake of the repast I had prepared for them. Accordingly, applying my mind to a review of the other side of the alternative, I decided to be in the same boat with my companions, were it to conduct me to the land of Van Diemen,[334] or even, with the annexed discipline of a rope's end, to the other side of the Styx.[335] Fraught with these second thoughts, which mankind have consented to call the best, because they usually prompt a directly contrary course of proceeding to that pointed out by their earlier meditations, (a result highly favourable and agreeable to our vanity as reasoning beings,) I returned home.

Wisp had been awaiting my arrival with much impatience, and beckoned me to the window, that we might converse with greater secrecy. 'Well, Jack,' said he, 'it's all right; I've got our man into right trim[336] at last. – But come, come, Mistress Kate,' and he turned towards his sister, shaking his head, – 'that's not fair, – no listening, – it's a secret between Jack and me.' I also turned towards my wife, and the faint and sickly smile with which she had met the charge of her brother, departed from her countenance, and, with a heavy sigh, she proceeded with her work.

'You havn't whispered a word to Kate?' said I, in alarm.

'Pshaw! – take snuff out of a donkey's ear;[337] let me alone for that. Well, there's Haynes at home, more dead than alive; poor devil! He eats nothing, but takes out the difference in brandy. He has consented.'

'But how have you contrived to work such a change in the man?' I demanded, with a natural curiosity,

'How? Why, so,' – cried Wisp, complacently, – 'I've persuaded him that Marley intends to prosecute, and has set the thief-takers after him. I've roused the lion; don't you see? Lord bless us! there are more ways of killing a dog than hanging him.'

'Your language,' said I, 'is figurative, but alarmingly familiar. Who is to be the captain of this expedition? Suppose we should fail – '

'Now, don't let us count our ravens before they are hatched,[338] that's a *good* fellow,' cried Wisp softly; '*we* are all right; we are to be on the look out, outside the premises; Haynes is to collar the swag inside; we are to be the prevailing monkeys; he is to be the convenient cat's-paw; Marley's cash is to be the desirable chestnut. Now, don't fail – eight o'clock – my lodgings – ' and, with a significant nod of the head, enjoining secrecy, and a soft pinch of his sister's cheek, as he passed her, Wisp hastily left me.

'Is it not very extraordinary, Catharine,' said I, suddenly addressing my wife, 'that you will attempt to pry into my affairs? Have I not told you I will not allow it?'

'I did not wish to pry into your affairs,' she said, humbly, shrinking from my gaze; 'I was only anxious – '

'To hear everything that passed,' said I, interrupting, her tauntingly. 'Come, come, my girl, it won't do. I will be obeyed. If I ever find you again at this, you shall repent it; by Heaven, you shall.'

She arose, and turned to the window, agitated by some powerful feeling; for I could see her tremble violently, and her hands were pressed against her temples.

'What's the matter now? What tantrums are you in now?' said I, laughing scornfully.

'My head is bad; leave me, John; I shall be better soon,' said she, in a low voice; 'but, no, no; it is better now,' and she came towards me suddenly, her lips quivering and her eyes dilated into a fixed stare.

'John, I will speak – I must speak – if you kill me, I must. I *know* you are going to commit a theft. I have heard you speak of it in your sleep. Oh! God have mercy upon me, for I am a poor distressed woman,' – and she wiped her brow with her hands, which she now laid upon my shoulders. 'Promise me, promise me, – you shall, you shall, you shall, – not to go out with William to-night; – say you won't – swear you won't. Nay, you may beat me, if you please – trample upon me, but, don't, pray don't, do it. Oh! what will become of me!' and she screamed, and wrung her hands. 'Oh! John, you will break my heart – '

'Hold your confounded tongue, will you? you'll alarm the house;' and I seized both her hands in mine, and thrust her into a chair. 'I'll pay you off for this.'

She heeded me not; but, with a vacant stare waved her hands to and fro, and shook her head listlessly.

'Come, come, Kate, my girl,' said I, alarmed, 'compose yourself.'

She turned her eyes upon me wildly for a moment, and then, as if some sudden recollection darted through her brain, uttered a piercing shriek, and, rising from her seat, her arms extended in the air over her head, fell forward upon her face.

'D—n! here's a precious scene!' I exclaimed; as I bent over her. 'Mrs. Chadwick!' and I called the woman of the house, who was already on the stairs.

'Hoity, toity! what's the matter?' cried the alarmed woman, as she bustled into the room, – 'What have you been about, Mr. Ketch?' and she hurried on her spectacles.

'A fit, a fit; nothing more, mother,' I mumbled, for I had always been afraid of the old woman.

'A fit, a fit, you fool, then why don't you stir your stumps. Take one of her hands. Poor dear!' she continued, rubbing her temples, 'she didn't use to be troubled with fits; pretty creter![339] Why, darling, did they serve you so? My poor girl!' and the old woman with these fond but useless apostrophes, proceeded to apply such restoratives as we were enabled to muster.

'I'll tell you what, young fellow,' exclaimed the woman, looking into my face with an eye portending an evil speech, 'you don't treat this poor thing as you ought to do; you know you don't. I've heard you striking and beating her – I have. I wish I had you; wouldn't I tear your eyes out!'

'Peace, you old cat,' said I, muttering between my teeth.

'I won't, John Ketch,' she retorted, sharply; 'if any harm comes to her, I'll make the neighbourhood too hot to hold you. What! serve a delicate young creter in her situation as you do – ugh, you villain: striving and toiling and harassing herself as she does to keep you, you great, hulking, idle, good-for-nothing fellow!

Catherine, Mrs. Chadwick, and Myself.

Shame upon you! And you, poor lamb!' she continued, addressing her senseless charge, 'who might have had so many an honest, hard-working, respectable man to take care of you, and to be fond of you, and to cherish you – well! well!'

I know not what might have been the consequence of this sally to the old woman, whose unwelcome voice had thus announced a few unpleasant truths to me, of which I could have well spared the repetition, had not my wife revived at this moment.

'Hush! hush!' said I, 'she stirs.'

'Then take her feet gently, will you?' cried Mrs. Chadwick, 'and let us lay her on the bed.'

'Where am I? what's the matter?' said Catharine, faintly; 'where's John?'

'Oh! John's here,' said the old woman, testily, 'when nobody wants him. Compose yourself, my girl; are you in pain?'

'Dreadful, mother, dreadful. Let me see John.' I came to the foot of the bed. 'I must go, Catharine,' said I, hastily, 'but I'll be back soon,' and I took my hat. 'Mrs. Chadwick will stay with you.'

'Oh, John! you promised me that you would *not* go, didn't you? before I was taken ill. Well, well,' and she sighed heavily, 'I have done my duty; God preserve you and me, for oh! mother, I am very, very ill.'

'I dare say you are, child,' cried the old woman, mixing something in a wine-glass, 'you've enough to make you, heaven knows!'

'Don't heed what mother says,' said Catharine, softly; 'did I speak angrily to you? pray forgive me, and give me one kiss.'

As I stooped my head towards her, she shed tears, and whispered, 'Oh, John! do not, do not kill me; be a good fellow – pray do – Go to William, and put off your engagement; say you will?'

'I will,' said I, and kissed her, glad to escape upon such terms.

'Ah! go your ways,' cried the old woman, in a disgusting voice, 'you're no good wherever you go. Oh! let him go, girl,' she continued, seeing my wife attempting to rise, 'he'll find out the difference one of these days, I warrant me.'

With a curse both loud and deep, I slammed the door after me, and hurried to the lodgings of Wisp, solacing myself on the road with reflections on the weakness and folly of women, and fortifying my resolution against subsequent scenes of a like nature by pondering upon many of those maxims which have been designed to enforce decision of character, equally applicable and important in the pursuit of vice as in the more difficult attainment of ends that have, or profess to have, virtue for their object.

'Here you are, at last,' exclaimed Wisp, as I entered; 'now, Susan, call Haynes. That blockhead,' continued he, addressing me, 'has taken to whimpering; he'll make a precious mull[340] of it, I'm thinking. I tell him the more he cries – you know the rest,' and he winked as his wife retired from the room. 'I say, Jack, how are we to manage this affair?'

Before I had time to answer this interrogatory Susan returned.

'Lord bless you, Wisp, do go to that fool of a man,' cried she; 'I can't prevail upon him to get off the bed; the fellow's crazy, I think.'

'I'll do that,' said Wisp, as he slipped from the room, presently leading back our accomplice by the arm. 'Now, Haynes, my boy, cheer up – be a man; it's a sorrowful heart that never rejoices:' and with sundry consolatory and encouraging slaps on the shoulder, he seated Haynes in a chair.

There was a marked alteration in that individual since I had seen him a few days previously. He had grown miserably thin, and had sunk apparently into the last feebleness of age; his hair was sown with grey and his eyes, which seemed purposely averted from any human being, had retired into the socket as though they dreaded to behold the light of day. Unshaved and squalid, he sat shaking in his chair, and, in a word, was about as wretched an object as ever surrendered his capital of flesh to the Jewish exactions[341] of insatiate conscience.

'Susan, my girl, walk your limbs to the cupboard,' said Wisp, 'and fetch me the brandy bottle. Here you are, Haynes, – some of old mother's stock; come, take a cock's eye,[342] it will put a little life into you; come – sup, lad, sup.'

'What would you have me do?' said Haynes, listlessly, fumbling with his waistcoat.

'Now, lay hold; down with it. Here, Jack's come; you don't see Jack.'

'Ketch, how are you?' cried Haynes, extending a hand as dry as a mummy's glove, if such an article be worn by such contrivances, 'it's bitter cold, isn't it?'

'No, no,' said I, 'you're unwell; Wisp, another glass?'

Wisp was prompt with the necessary cordial, and our friend gradually revived under its influence.

'Now to business,' said Wisp; 'Susan, leave the room?'

'Indeed I shan't,' answered his wife, 'I like to hear all; hang them as are not worth trusting, I say.'

'You say,' retorted Wisp, 'you say anything but your prayers, and them you whistle; but sit down, girl, you may stay if you please.'

'What's the odds so long as you're happy,' cried Susan, and she opened her ears, and laid her hands on her lap; 'oh! eh, Wisp, you're a rare 'cute[343] one, and you know it.'

'I believe you, Sue,' cried Wisp, tickled at the compliment; 'now, my good fellows, to the point at once. You see,' he continued, seriously, 'nothing is easier than this matter. We in all probability get a good sum at a very little risk; we divide equally, or, perhaps, Haynes,' – and he turned to me, 'is entitled to a rather larger share than ourselves; what think you, Ketch?'

I nodded assent.

'Well, then, this is our plan: Haynes gets into the counting-house; we keep watch above; he collars the money, we receive it, and all jog home comfortably together, and nobody the wiser till to-morrow morning, when Marley will be let into the secret.' Here Haynes groaned and shook his head. 'Now, no nonsense, Haynes,' resumed Wisp, 'you know this will set us all up; to you in particular it will be a grand *coup*.[344] You can leave the country snug, and perhaps make a large fortune on the other side of the water, when you may return and spend it if you like, or stay and enjoy it there if you please. And now, Susan, lend a hand to this gentleman's great coat – on with it; have you put those remarkably useful implements into the pocket of mine?'

'Have I not?' cried Susan, briskly, producing a small iron bar in testimony of her forethought.

'And now a glass round for luck,' cried Wisp, as we all stood up. 'Hark'ee, Sue: don't throw out the furniture, my girl, when you see us return.'

'Throw out the furniture, Will!' exclaimed she, in surprise, 'what should I do that for?'

'Why, I'll tell you,' answered Wisp, setting down his glass. 'There was an old Jew who had bought a ticket in the lottery, and it occurred to him very forcibly that it must turn up a prize. He, accordingly, left special directions that if the family saw him return in a coach, they were forthwith to begin flinging the furniture out of the windows, being articles by no means suited to his sudden accession of fortune. Well, the lottery was drawn, and Moses found himself proprietor of a blank; the poor devil sickened at this, as well he might, and fainted at the wheel, like a criminal on the rack. A coach was called, Moses was huddled in; coach drove home – up went the windows – down came the furniture – ha! ha! ha! Come, Haynes, don't let us whistle[345] before we're out of the wood.'

'No, no, that wouldn't do – that wouldn't do,' said Haynes; 'we may be caught.'

'Pooh! pooh! that was not what I meant,' cried the other, taking his arm, 'let's be jogging; come, Ketch, don't lag behind:' and we proceeded on our expedition, the careful and superstitious Susan flinging an old shoe after us, for luck.

When we arrived at the scene of action, some caution was necessary in ascertaining whether the somnolent guardian of the night was not (for such things do happen) upon this occasion keeping himself awake for an hour, by way of alterative; but we presently discovered our fears to be perfectly groundless, that torpid person having coiled himself at the bottom of his watch-box, where he gave himself up to the pleasing illusion of dreams with the most enviable unconcern. We accordingly slid up the gateway by the side of Marley's warehouse without much fear of a surprise, and scaled the back wall with an energy that bade defiance to discovery.

'Now Haynes, my lad, be firm,' cried Wisp, when we had all mounted the parapet, 'it's too late to recede – we've passed the Rubicon.[346] Which of these is the skylight to Marley's counting-house?'

'It is here.' Haines pointed to a small dome, a little distance from the spot we at that moment occupied.

'Then wait here for a few minutes till I prepare it for your comfortable reception;' and Wisp crept carefully forward, sliding out of his pocket certain tools, with which he began to make a safe and convenient aperture.

'Oh! Jack,' said Haynes, as he stood trembling by my side, 'did I ever think it would come to this? A common housebreaker! a wretched thief, crawling into my benefactor's house at dead of night! Do you see that window?' – he pointed to the casement of a sky-parlour – 'that is where I used to sleep when Marley first took me into his office. Oh! what a wretch am I.'

'Hold your fool's tongue,' cried Wisp, in an angry whisper, proceeding with his labours, 'you'll alarm the people of the house.'

'The very moon seems to be gazing at us,' continued Haynes, not heeding our companion; 'oh! Ketch, you're the youngest of the three; do let this be the last crime we commit; for all the wealth of the world I would not hazard the perpetration of another. But I am in for this – I must go through with it; some fate urges me on – some uncommon impulse that I could not put off, if I would.'

'That's just as it should be,' said Wisp, softly, coming forward; 'now's your time to encourage that impulse; come along;' and he almost dragged the bewildered man to the dismantled skylight. 'Now, my lad, you do your part of the job cleverly, and it will be over in five minutes; drop yourself neatly on the desk, which is only six feet down; you know where the key of the safe is hidden – out with the cash-box; Ketch and I will draw you up again, and this mighty business is settled. Come, Jack, lend a hand; let us take care of his China[347] limbs: that's right – gently, gently,' and we deposited our automaton accomplice safely on the desk. 'Now, Jack, sharp's the word; shove the lantern into the staring blockhead's fist. Now, Haynes, stir about; hand us over something in the twinkling of a bed-post;' and Wisp exhibited extraordinary impatience to commence an acquaintance with the property now in imminent peril. Haynes did mechanically as he was bidden, and making himself master of the key of the safe, proceeded to unlock and to pry into its contents.

'Don't fall asleep, that's a good fellow!' cried Wisp, in a tone of remonstrance; 'what have you laid your fingers upon there? Hand it up; come, come, don't fumble with it – it won't bite.' Haynes, after looking about in every direction, as though the very furniture of the counting-house were a witness of his operations, handed a small bag to Wisp, who instantly jerked it into a yawning breast-pocket, which appeared to have been gaping for the very thing that now found its way to the depths of that convenience.

At this instant a light shot across the staircase window. 'Did you see that?' said I, tugging at Wisp's coat; 'we shall be nabbed, sure enough!' and again the same light illumined a lower window.

'Shove that cash-box up here, and be d—d to you!' cried Wisp, in an agony; and we both leaned over the skylight. 'Look at that fool, Jack, dancing about the floor instead of securing the ready;' and, to be sure, the wretched man below was hurrying hither and thither, taking up this thing and flinging down that, and, in a word, exhibiting a woful spectacle of perfect panic.

'What's the matter? I'm sure I heard a voice!' exclaimed Haynes, with a kind of whining shriek that terrified us not a little: 'who's coming?'

'Nobody,' said Wisp; 'now the cash-box – in your hand there; give it me, give it me.' Haines had just raised his hand for the purpose of obeying this command, when the door of the counting-house opened, and old Marley entered in shirt and slippers, with a pistol in one hand and a candle in the other.

'Christ Jesus!' exclaimed Haynes, as he dropped the box and fell upon his knees. Wisp and I tumbled backwards simultaneously, and crawling swiftly but silently along the leads, made for the parapet with a wise instinct.

'Did the old buck twig us, d'ye think?' inquired Wisp, as we dropped from the wall.

'Will Haynes split[348] upon us? that's the point,' said I, and we hurried through the gateway, and halted at the corner of the street.

'Let's wait and see the upshot,' cried Wisp, anxiously; 'we shall see that stupid ass brought out directly and given in charge.'

We accordingly lingered about for more than an hour in no desirable state of feeling, exchanging at intervals curses on our own folly for not having, in the first instance, managed the affair without the assistance of Haynes, whose pusillanimous conduct during the enterprise had certainly been the main cause of its failure.

'If the fellow,' said Wisp, gloomily, as we loitered about the post at the end of Friday-street, 'if the fellow had been in time with the cash-box, I would willingly have risked my neck not to have left him in the lurch; but this paltry sum in my pocket – it was not worth while: it's a dead take in,[349] that's what I think of it.'

'Aye, touching that bag, Wisp,' cried I; 'let us see what it contains; we had better be off. My lodging is not known – we shall be safe there; come home with me for to-night.'

'Well, I don't care if I do; and yet' – he paused, as if suddenly recollecting himself, and, methought, he clasped the bag closer with his hand, 'and yet Sue may be alarmed – I don't think there's much danger. Yes, I'll go home, at all hazards. Come early to-morrow morning, Jack; we can talk better about it after we have heard of Haynes.'

'No, no – not so fast, Master Wisp,' said I; 'do you think I don't see which way the wind blows? Come, come, none of that.'

'What do you mean?' cried Wisp, with apparent surprise.

'That I am not such a soft one as you take me for.'

'Oh! if you doubt my honour,' said Wisp, buttoning his coat, 'I can have nothing further to say to you. Good night.'

'No, come,' said I, coaxingly, 'don't be a fool, Wisp, I didn't mean to offend you; but there's nothing like a short reckoning, you know.'

'I tell you,' said Wisp, sharply, 'that you must wait till to-morrow. Indeed I don't know what I shall do now; you have suspected me, and for my part' – here he muttered some unintelligible threat, the purport of which, however mysterious the words, was perfectly well known to me.

I was fain to make a virtue of necessity, hardly deeming it prudent to court a quarrel at this present time, and contented myself by very strongly announcing my intention of calling upon him on the earliest hour of the morrow, when I took it for granted that my share of the spoil would be forthcoming. With this I left him, and betook myself to my own home in very considerable dejection of spirits, superinduced by the luckless issue of our adventure, and its probable consequences. The anxiety attendant on the evening's occupation and its result had, indeed, altogether banished any recollection of the state in which I had left my wife; so that when I opened my door, and discovered two candles burning, with a variety of articles upon the table indicating recent bustle, my mind was thrown back to a consideration of the earlier proceedings of the day, and leapt at once to a conclusion that made my heart, callous as it was, turn faint and sick.

Before, however, I had time to entertain the thought that intruded itself upon me, Mrs. Chadwick made her appearance out of the other room, her sour aspect assuaged into important placidity, bearing in her arms, as it seemed, a small assortment of fine linen.

'Here, John Ketch,' she said, in a mild but grave tone, 'if anything will make you a kind husband, this blessed angel will do so;' and she placed in my arms a new-born infant. I had become a father!

CHAPTER XIII.

THE softer affections are altogether controlled and guided by the precious metals. This may appear a startling assertion to those who, wallowing in wealth (as the bullionless express themselves) or established in a snug competence, are apt to consider that the love they bear (I speak hypothetically) to their wives and children, is a spontaneous or natural growth, with which the state of their exchequer has nothing whatever to do; and that without these agreeable stimulants the course of true love would run as smooth as though Plutus, the Neptune of Fortune,[350] were there, with his trident of gold, silver, and copper, to direct the stream into its proper channel.

Now, let no would-be philosopher, with head on one side, like one of his own guineas, attempt by argument to prove this, that, or the other, in opposition to what I advance, lest I should go further, and hazard an assertion, that there is *no* affection in the world independent of circumstances, and that in all cases where that apparently amiable sentiment is found, it is a certain *quid* in the mouth of a hypocrite, which, were it not there, might be *smoked*, and that some expected gain or advantage is the *pro-quo*[351] whereto his endeavours are tending.

Let me for one moment 'unsphere the spirit'[352] of Rochefoucault.[353] Does the reader imagine that the snug family man, with his complacent wife and six children, really feels any affection for those domestic implements? for so they are; – does the reader suppose that, were his sentiments towards them strictly analysed, it would be found that he cared a fig for the former, or for the latter six small raisins?[354] Oh, no, it is all selfishness. He looks upon them as upon fender and fire-irons, poker, shovel, and tongs; so many ornaments to his fire-side: they add to his respectability – they contribute to his comfort. Were the snug family man suddenly converted into an unsnug man with a family – let us suppose his three per cent. Consols[355] *reduced* to nothing – is it to be believed that the aforesaid fig and raisins would be a cheap purchase of the love of his wife and children towards him? No.

Perhaps the proposition involved in this hypothesis is hardly maintainable; but certain it is, that no money, no love, – else, why marriage settlements?[356] I may be disposed to concede the possibility that money may conjure up a small shadow – a ghostling of affection; but poverty lays[357] it with extraordinary expedition. The pauper with his arms full of children, shaking his head over an empty grate; do you think that

'With arms encumbered thus, and this head-shake,'[358]

he has any time, or inclination, or heart, for the softer affections? Believe, therefore, that as the prolonged circulation of the blood depends upon the continued circulation of capital, so, in like manner, and as certainly, does the current of affection, such as it is, wait upon the flow of currency.

I have said thus much with a view to make it more immediately evident, that my proper course of proceeding, under the then present circumstances, to rise very early on the following morning, and make the best of my way to Wisp's lodgings without the unnecessary formality of presenting myself to my wife, or of seeing my child; which I accordingly did, being, at that moment, most particularly of opinion, that to have risked my life like a madman for something which I might lose like a fool, was to do that which heroes alone are chartered to do, – whose example, indeed, I was never over anxious to imitate or applaud.

When I arrived at my place of destination, I found that Wisp was about to give me the slip, being in the act of swallowing a huge basin of tea, and a round of toast, as he stood at the table, fully equipped in hat and great coat. He seemed perfectly unconcerned at my presence; and when I informed him, which I did in very intelligible terms, of the purpose for which I had come thither, and my expectations that the compact between us would be carried out honourably and fairly, he smiled coolly, and went on with his breakfast. Setting down the basin, however, he suddenly delivered himself of these words: 'I'll tell you what, Jack, your talking is of no use; you shan't have a farthing of this money; it's little enough for one, and won't bear dividing.'

I was prepared for something of a similar nature, and was therefore not much surprised at this new scheme of equity; but proceeded to set forth the 'rights of the thing'[359] at some length; insisting upon the important but obvious point, that whether the amount of booty were small or large, Wisp was equally bound to divide it into moieties. I hinted also at the infinite divisibility of matter; and in conclusion proposed that we should at least toss up for the ownership of the small sum in question. To all these propositions Wisp turned a deaf ear; and I could plainly perceive that he had made up his mind to retain the whole of the money; a resolution which, much more than any other that can be adopted in this world, is likely religiously to be kept; since it cannot but occur to the experience of every man, that, although the promise of money is by no means to be looked upon as a certainty, yet that in the denial of it the party invariably keeps his word; the irrevocable laws of the Medes and Persians[360] are written upon the sand compared with the steadfast, enduring, and rock-like stability of a sentence involving a denial of money.

Sensitively alive to this fact, nothing appeared at the moment to present itself to me so expedient as bringing it to a wrangle, in which I hoped to succeed in acting upon Wisp's fears so powerfully as to induce him to come to terms; but in this design I was unsuccessful. Wisp, indeed, was no hero in point of courage, but I also had few claims to that distinction; and, if the truth must be told, perhaps my friend and I were about as perfect a brace of cowards as were ever called upon to settle a dispute, or to adjust a difference. 'When Greek meets Greek, then comes the tug of war;'[361] but when coward meets coward, I believe the tug is equally obstinate, although the war may not be carried on quite so furiously. The awkward part of this dispute was, that whether to retain any given or taken thing be an easier matter than to obtain it, as the defenders of a fortress are at an advantage over the besiegers; or whether Wisp was not *quite* so great a coward as myself, I knew not; but I was losing ground in this quarrel: and although we both flourished our jawbones menacingly enough to uninitiated Philistines,[362] yet we knew each other too well to anticipate much danger from the use, or rather abuse of them.

Wisp, I incline to imagine, saw his advantage over me in this business, and now not only would not bate a jot of his former resolution, but actually went so far as to threaten me with chastisement for my insolence and ingratitude, – as he was pleased to call it, – a piece of thrasonical[363] impertinence which improved my determination to prevent his escape from the room, at all events, even though in the struggle we should be both captured. Fraught with this intent, I placed my back to the door, and prepared to contest the pass with my opponent.

Wisp, thus set at defiance, became furious, and cast his baleful eyes around the room, in quest of some auxiliary weapon, which he soon lighted upon in the shape of a stout cudgel.

'Now, Jack, come out of that, will you?' said he, turning up his cuff, and spitting upon his hand for the purpose of obtaining a firmer grasp of the oak plant, which he proceeded to brandish. I stoutly refused to budge an inch.

'Brag is a good dog, but Holdfast is a better,'[364] said I; and I gave every conceivable evidence that I was bent upon emulating the latter quadruped. 'No, no,' I continued, 'I shall not let you off quite so easily, Master Wisp, depend upon it: honour among thieves, at any rate – let us understand each other – what do you mean?'

'Construe *that*, if you can,' he replied, and plied his cudgel upon my shoulders, while he spurned me like a dog with his feet; 'will you come out, you hound?'

No, I would not come out. I dared not at the moment close with my adversary, for two reasons; first, because I should thereby leave the door without a defender, and, secondly, because I believed him to be somewhat stronger than myself. I contented myself, therefore, with parrying his blows as I best might, and by keeping him at bay by the projection of my leg in all directions – a mode of warfare that annoyed his shins not a little. But it now became high time to adopt other measures against my enemy; for Wisp was raining blows upon me in prodigal profusion, and had nearly succeeded in dislodging me from my position. Slow to encourage resentment, I was yet slower to resent; but human nature is not altogether without its weaknesses and failings; and I began to feel, that to put up with this kind of entertainment was encouraging a bad precedent. I turned round, therefore, and faced my antagonist, and, watching the descending cudgel, caught it on my arm as it fell, and grasped it firmly between my hands; and with a sudden kick in the stomach, more remarkable to the receiver for its novelty than agreeable for its own sake, I caused Wisp to recoil to the other end of the room, utterly incapable of demanding a truce, or of offering any conditions of peace whatever.

But while I was debating within my own mind whether I should rush upon him, and, making the most of my temporary advantage, lay him senseless at my feet with my newly acquired munition of war, the door was thrust open, and Haynes entered the room slowly, and with a moody and wild aspect flung himself into one of the chairs.

'What wind blew *you* hither?' demanded Wisp, as soon as he recovered breath; 'how did you escape?'

'No matter; no matter,' answered the other; 'and yet I will tell you. Wisp, you are a scoundrel. When I told you my story I threw myself into your power; you might have saved me – a word would have done it – a word of friendly advice. What did you do? You inflamed and unsettled my mind; you rendered a desperate man more desperate; you converted vice and thoughtlessness into crime and ruin. You may say, and say truly, that I was a fool to be biassed by you,' he continued, passionately, 'who have no feeling – no pride – no honour. In a word, Marley has released me – has damned me by his forgiveness; and here I am, left to myself, – a precious legacy!'

'Why, what a puling blockhead are you?' retorted Wisp, scornfully; 'brush up your spirits, man, if you intend to rub on in this life; you'll want them, I'm thinking; and as for your cant, and conscience, and all that – come, it won't do – it's out of character entirely, – it's all flam, Master Haynes.'

'Mr. Wisp,' said Haynes, after a pause, during which he did not appear to have paid much attention to this speech, 'there was some money in a bag which I handed over to you; it was robbed from Mr. Marley – where is it?' 'Robbed from Mr. Marley, was it?' replied Wisp. 'Yes, it was robbed from Mr. Marley;' and he mimicked the querist happily: 'and it's a d— strange thing that we didn't rob Mr. Marley of a precious sight more. Where is it? What's that to you? – it's here;' and Wisp struck his breast pocket in triumph: 'd'ye hear it chink, eh? you sanctified humbug: you've seen the last of it, and so make your mind easy upon that score. Jack and I are not going to risk our necks for you, are we, Jack?' and he levelled a wink at me, intended to propitiate and to gain me once more to his interest. But it would not do. 'Ha!' cried Haynes, starting up, and approaching Wisp, whom he seized by the collar, 'is that your intention? Hear me, Wisp. By the God that made us, if you do not instantly produce that money – for I will have it – I'll dash your brains out against that wall;' and as he shook the other violently, his eyes flashed in a manner not to be mistaken for any thing but a determination to fulfil his threat to the very letter. 'What do you mean, Haynes?' exclaimed Wisp, evidently flustered, for now he found that he was no match for the powerful north-countryman, who held his metropolitan person in strict durance. 'I say, Jack,' and he appealed to me, 'will you see your friend ill treated in this manner?'

'You had better not move,' said Haynes, addressing me; 'I should be sorry to hurt you, Ketch; I pity you, upon my soul I do; you, also, I fear, have been misled by this villain; but, come,' and he turned to the bewildered Wisp, whom he forced into a chair, 'I've been trifled with by you too long;' and he dashed his left hand into Wisp's breast pocket, while he held him by the throat with the other.

It may be easily surmised, that during this scene I observed a harmless neutrality, quite assured that I should occupy a better position in respect of my claims, should Haynes succeed in wresting the spoil from my treacherous colleague. I was perfectly willing that the latter should be made to feel the iron scourge of tyrannous power, which he had sought to exercise against me. In vain did Wisp appeal to me, as he clung to the arm of his conqueror for the purpose of detaining him in the room; – in vain did he require the sanction of my concurrence in the sentiments he expressed, of wonder at the baseness of Haynes in thus declining to fulfil an original agreement; – in vain did he employ the identical arguments which I had fruitlessly urged half an hour before, the cogency of which he had himself refused to acknowledge; and when Haynes broke away from his hands, and was descending the stairs, I very coolly proceeded to follow him, hoping to make equitable terms for myself, without the slightest reference to, or regard for, the forlorn rascal above, who, with disarranged neckcloth and disordered spirits, was pacing the room distractedly.

But this, he of the money-bag would by no means permit. 'Do not attempt to follow me,' said he, turning an ugly eye upon me, 'it may be dangerous; I have a destination for this,' showing the money – 'a sacred destination, which you little dream of; you will probably see me again presently.' Much marvelling at the particular channel designed for this sum, and still hoping that part of it would terminate its course in my pocket, I retreated up stairs again, proposing to myself to wait for an hour or two in case Haynes should return, and, at all events, to ascertain to a certainty the issue of this adventure.

Haynes wresting the Money from Wisp.

'Give me your hand, Jack,' cried Wisp disconsolately, as I entered the room, 'I am sorry that that little dispute should have occurred.'

When a man has nothing else to do, and no particular motive for declining the courtesy, I hold that he may as well shake hands with another, as leave it alone; it exercises the muscles of the shoulder, at all events, and saves words. I gave Wisp my hand.

'I know why you left the room, Jack,' said he, slily, 'but it was no go.' I looked at Wisp also with equal cunning, and, as our eyes met, we distinctly read in each other's faces that we *knew* each other; and from that time forth, were duly qualified to become the best friends in the world.

While we sat discoursing upon the untoward issue preceding of our night's exploit, Mrs. Susan Wisp made her appearance, having waited at her mother's for a considerable time in momentary expectation of her husband's arrival. From thence, as I gathered out of their discourse, they had proposed to emigrate to some unknown region in the suburbs, where they might lie perdue,[365] until the impertinent curiosity of certain persons employed for the purpose of looking up free-thinkers in morals, and self-constituted trustees of property, should be in some measure abated.

Great was the chagrin of Mrs. Wisp, loud, likewise, her lamentation, when she learned the fact, that Wisp was no longer under the necessity of resorting to concealment, either of his own person or of other people's money; and might I be permitted to judge by the uncomfortable acidity of her visage, when she became acquainted with the manner in which the spoil had been wrested from her partner, I should conclude that, the money having once taken wings, if the devil had flown away with her husband, it would have been a circumstance of the merest triviality and lightness to her.

It was now not only curious, but instructive, to observe the light in which this worthy couple viewed the conduct of Haynes, – the motes in whose eye were flagrantly perceptible through the beams[366] that, could they themselves have seen them, must have assumed the shape of a gallows in their own; and, in short, there was no word bad enough for that individual who had done the very thing they themselves had decided upon doing. Whether, however, that very circumstance enabled them to designate the act by its appropriate and deserved epithets, I cannot take it upon myself to say; being, as I am, decidedly of opinion, that men generally are much more prone to discover blemishes in others than to detect faults in themselves; or, in other words, that, alert as lynxes to other people's defects, we are near-sighted as moles[367] to our own.

I readily grant that the above is not a very original, or a very profound, or an exceedingly novel reflection; but it will pass the more currently and handsomely when it is compared with some of the original ideas which our modern philosophers are in the habit of evolving; – ideas that contain within themselves a conservative property, which absolves them from the chance of ever becoming trite or common-place.

While Wisp and his wife thus discoursed in a manner so agreeable to themselves, a footstep was heard upon the stairs by the latter, who, with a nicety of ear peculiar to women, instantly recognised it as the step of Haynes.

'Oh! you're come back at last, are you?' said Wisp, as the other looked in through the half-opened door.

'Hold your fool's tongue, Wisp, can't you?' interrupted Susan, inviting Haynes to enter by several backward jerks of her head; 'come in, and sit down, that's a good man; – here, Haynes, I want to speak with you; – now, don't be a fool, standing there in the cold;' and several other bland and tempting invitations, which argued the foregone conclusion she had come to, of wheedling the party addressed out of something, which at that moment he had, as she supposed, the option of yielding up.

'I know ye both now,' answered Haynes, in a hollow voice; 'ye selfish and degraded wretches, – but you get no more from me.'

'Good luck to your ways,' said Susan; 'what have you done with the money you took from my husband this morning?'

'It's gone, – gone to its right owner: I have returned it whence we stole it last night, – that reparation, at least – '

'Returned it!' cried Wisp.

'Returned it!' screamed his wife.

'Returned it!' echoed I; and, certainly, of the almost infinite conjectures we had severally formed respecting its appropriation, this had never entered our brains, nor by any possible combination of ideas could have done so.

'Here,' continued Haynes, breaking the spell by which we had been so suddenly dumb-foundered, 'here is my last shilling; take it – 'twill buy a rope, at least, and save the hangman his trouble;' and he was about to close the door.

'And where are you going now, Haynes?' demanded Susan mildly.

'To my own room.'

'And so you think,' said she, starting up and exercising her tongue with extraordinary rapidity, 'that we are to keep lodgings for such dead-and-alive, die-away gentry as you, do you? Not we, indeed;' – and the young fury advanced towards Haynes with her arms a-kimbo, and her face disfigured by grimaces, as she shook her head mockingly at him; 'get down stairs, you mean, paltry rascal – ugh – you – '

Here, probably, for lack of a word sufficiently expressive, or, perhaps, deeming it better to finish, or rather to execute her sentence upon his countenance, she attempted to pounce upon her prey with her bird-like talons; but Haynes suddenly catching both her hands within his, swung her so smartly round, that she spun from the door to the other end of the room, with all the revolving rapidity of the Pythoness in a fit of prophetic inspiration.[368]

And, in fact, this is by no means to be considered a merely motional resemblance; for immediately the door was closed, and she heard the footsteps of Haynes in the upper room, Mrs. Wisp began to promulge her awful vaticinations respecting him in language more to be admired for its plainness than commended for its elegance, – and added the weight of certain blasphemous denunciations to give effect to her prophetic ravings.

While these anglings and twitches at futurity, as it were, occupied us below, heavy and deep groans from the room above alarmed us.

'He's at it again,' said Wisp; '"his custom always in the afternoon," as the man in the play says.'

'Let him lie, and howl till he's tired,' observed Susan; 'he'll let us know when he has done, I dare say.'

But, however familiar these sounds might be to Wisp and his wife, they were exceedingly obnoxious to me; and I took my hat with an intention to depart, but was prevailed upon by Wisp to remain a little longer.

'Let us all go up stairs, and see what the chap's about,' said he; and we crept softly thither.

The door was ajar, and I entered silently, motioning to my companions to remain in the passage. Haynes was undressed, and in bed, heaving to and fro and snatching at the pillows and counterpane with his teeth and hands. He saw me as I stood at the foot of the bed.

'Ha! Ketch, is that you, come to see me? – thank you, sit down.' I took a seat beside him, and watched him. He had become more calm, and lay upon his back; his eyes were open, and were wild and bloodshot, and his breast laboured with sighs that burst from him at intervals, as though they would force his soul out of his body.

'I say, Jack,' cried Wisp, softly, 'what's the order of the day? – what's he about?'

Haynes heard the affectionate inquiry, and sprung up in the bed. 'Where is that wretch?' he howled, and clenched his hands furiously together; 'tell him to keep away from me, or I shall tear him in pieces: let him not come near me, or he'll rue it – he'll rue it – he'll rue it;' – and he fell back again with a groan.

I went to the door, and entreated Wisp and his wife to depart. 'Leave him to me,' said I; 'he'll be better by and bye.'

I approached the bed, and took one of his hands; it was very hot, and his lips were dry as ashes. 'How is it, old fellow?' said I; 'come, cheer up – don't be cast down.'

He smiled faintly. 'Better – better – oh! much better; is Ellen Sewell come?'

'Ellen Sewell! who is she?'

'Aye, true, I am foolish; my brain was wandering: she's far away, – at Appleby – dear Appleby – oh! my poor mother.' Here he raved incoherently for some minutes, – of scenes in his early life, as I conjectured, and persons with whom he had been formerly connected, – but turning suddenly towards me, he said more collectedly: –

'My watch I gave to Wisp to pawn for me; we have been living upon it since I came here: my mother gave it me, Jack, when I left the north, – it was my father's; but there was a small locket that went with it – a common thing, not worth five shillings to any body but me. Oh! would I could see it now: could it be got, d'ye think? – but, no – no, it's all over;' and he threw himself despairingly on his side, and presently fell into a lethargy.

The day was closing in, and it was an unmercifully rainy afternoon. The waterspout was overflowed, and splashed its superfluous tribute upon the window panes; and the heterogenous[369] huddle of house-tops in the distance was enveloped in a misty and sullen gloom. My spirits became insensibly affected; and as it grew darker, and the heavy breathing of Haynes broke upon my ear, a kind of superstitious dread began to crawl over me; I was fain, therefore, to call up Wisp and his wife, who came at my bidding, like unseemly and obscene birds of prey, lured by a sagacious scent to a congenial carcass.

Wisp having looked about him for a moment, stept on tiptoe to a chair on which the clothes of the invalid were lying, and took them up, with a view of ascertaining the contents of the pockets.

'Halves,' cried I, in a whisper, laying my hand upon his arm.

'Here's my thumb,'[370] said he; and proceeded with his search. In the meanwhile, Mrs. Susan had drawn near the bed, and was gazing at her lodger with a face in which curiosity and compassion appeared mingled in equal proportion.

'Poor man!' she cried, 'he has been grizzling[371] a long while, but I never knew him like this before; what can be the matter with him?'

'Nothing but an old seal and two letters,' exclaimed Wisp, in a tone of disappointment; 'here's a pretty go: well, never mind, let us leave him alone for awhile – he'll come round in time.'

We, accordingly, descended into the lower room, Wisp, having lighted a candle, proceeded to peruse the two letters aloud. The first was from his mother, and contained such affectionate and endearing expressions, as in such documents from such relations, as I have been informed, are usually to be found. The second was signed 'Ellen Sewell,' and was written by a young woman to whom, as it would seem, he had been betrothed while yet a boy, and who reminded him of that circumstance, and, indeed, of many other tender things, chiefly interesting to the sentimentalist who may have exhausted the ready-made raptures of the Polite Letter Writer.[372]

'And this is all we have got for our pains!' cried Wisp, turning about the epistles between his fingers, and we both looked blank.

'All, indeed,' repeated Susan, sobbing and wiping her eyes – (these women are such soft fools), – 'poor wretch! he has somebody to care about him, if any thing should happen; do go, Ketch, and see what he's about – he's such a Peter Grievous,[373] he frightens me.'

Haynes heard me as I entered the room. 'Is that you, Ketch? – come nearer, that's a good fellow.'

I approached him. He laid hold of my arm, and raised himself from the pillow.

'Ketch, boy,' he said, – and his breath came thick and hard; 'I am dying, – nothing can save me; nay, don't shrink away from me, – I have poisoned myself.'

I uttered an involuntary cry of horror.

'Oh, Jack,' and he held me yet more closely – 'don't interrupt me, for my breath is passing away. Promise me to go to Mr. Marley to-night; he don't know you – you were not seen; tell him all – my death – my repentance: implore him to keep my disgrace from my poor mother, and that dear – dear girl; will you?'

I hesitated – I was at a nonplus[374] – I knew not what to say.

'Will you?' he repeated, anxiously.

'Yes, Haynes, I will.'

'God bless you!' – he fell from my arms like a stone.

I rushed down stairs and informed Wisp and Susan of this untoward circumstance, and the latter hurried out in quest of an apothecary, while Wisp and I, in much perplexity, traversed the room, talking such incoherent nonsense as people usually do upon such occasions.

But the doctor, when he did arrive, had come too late. Haynes was no more!

CHAPTER XIV.

IT would be found productive of very little interest to the reader were I to recount the several chances that befel me for a year after the demise of Haynes. I believe, however, that it is by this time universally known, that when individuals refuse to walk in those straight paths which industry commonly points out for them, there are certain convenient bye-paths by which the eccentric[375] may arrive at the same point by a short cut.

Indeed, if a man has once accustomed himself to live without the sweat of his brow, it will be a difficult matter to recal him to laborious occupation; necessity may do much, to be sure; but necessity has no law; and where there is no law there is no honesty.

I had traced out Misty during this period; and by dint of pulling a long face, and drawing a long bow,[376] and magnifying the wolf at the door[377] (which the reader need scarcely be informed, is by no means so prodigal of nutrition as the foster-mother of the Roman twins[378]), I had from time to time suffered him to become my banker for certain sums upon occasions of emergency.

And now more than ever did I curse the blind fate which had hurried me to the altar of Hymen, – an altar upon which it will be difficult enough, unless Fortune have a brisk hand in the operation, to lay a plain beef-steak, or even a common rasher of bacon.

Let no poverty-stricken proser presume to preach the joys of wedlock. What is love? A mere vapour – nothing more: an ignis fatuus[379] – a light-headed flame, running the devil knows how, – the devil knows where, – the devil knows for what purpose. The most popular loves with the poets, it is worthy of remembrance, were not accompanied by marriage. Antony and Cleopatra, – there was a gipsy![380] Helen and Paris, – there was a fool and a half, (good Troy) weight.[381] Diana and Endymion, – but the love of the former was all moonshine;[382] and 'that Latmos boy,' as some snivelling verse-monger calls him, was a mere lunatic.[383] There are many others worthy of mention, who, fools in other respects, were wise, in that they eschewed matrimony.

The pleasures of the married man, if any come home to his door, assume another shape; they may be the same, but, oh! how different. We discover them, if we find them at all – as sometimes we may detect our faithful Pincher in a mutton pie, or in a beef sausage recognise our defunct Dobbin[384] – with this difference to the poor man, that his accustomed pleasures seldom visit him in the shape of food.

But the length of this digression reminds me that I had intended to signify the fact, that my wife was now a source of peculiar trouble to me. Her health continued to decline so rapidly that she was not only unable to proceed with her work to any extent, but had been compelled to put out our child to nurse with a woman residing at Walworth,[385] to whom the small proceeds of her earnings were regularly transmitted – except, indeed, when I contrived to attack them by the way, which was not unfrequently the case.

I had long ago thrown off the mask; and as I kicked it from me, the cloven hoof[386] was discernible. Catharine was a dead weight, – one of the unproductive classes, as the economists say; and refused to get her own living by means which I once hinted at,[387] but never again dared to refer to. This contumacy on her part was the cause of much virulent abuse on mine; and – for why should I conceal it? – I began to hate her as an intolerable incumbrance, and to look forward to the probable termination of her illness as a happy release, both for herself and for me.

There are few men so callous, and at the same time so careless of the world's opinion, but they make some pretext for their baseness, in order to relieve their own conscience, and to satisfy the world at the same time. I started a pretext, therefore, that served the purpose, so far as I was concerned, exceedingly well. I affected a jealousy of Chisel, the carpenter, who lived over the way, and had, as I had been informed, paid Catharine very assiduous attentions previous to my introduction to her; and as nothing is so easy of growth as faith, at length I almost believed the truth of my own device. Certain it is, that the susceptible Chisel had at one time cast a sheep's eye[388] in that quarter; but I had been well advised, that had he borrowed all the sheepish glances of Banstead Downs,[389] he would never have succeeded in attracting the attention of Catharine Wisp.

But the assiduous Mrs. Chadwick, who to me had long become a kind of patent[390] disguster, was a tongue-wielder of no ordinary reach of octave, or vocal compass, and had bruited abroad my treatment of my wife with every exaggeration which malignity or warmth of feeling could suggest; insomuch that my character in the neighbourhood became notorious, and my going to and fro subjected me to insolent remark, and sometimes to violent menace.[391]

Amongst many others, Chisel was the particular individual from whom I chose to feel these insults most acutely. One day, as I was about to leave the door, I was greeted, as usual, by this person, who threw out a side-speech that bore reference to me, in a manner not to be mistaken. I smothered my anger as well as I was able, and merely said, 'What do you mean, Chisel, by insulting me whenever I have occasion to go abroad?'

'Why, this here is what I mean to say,' answered Chisel, 'that a man who will treat a woman as you do, is no man;' and he proceeded with his work, which at this moment, I remember, consisted of the manufacture of a coffin. 'It's a mortal shame,' he continued, 'that a sharp, clever man, like you, shouldn't be taught better; if you don't know how to treat your wife, you ought to be made.'

'And will your interference,' I retorted, 'have that effect?'

'I don't know that it will; but I think it's a burning shame, and so I *up* and told you my mind; you're breaking the girl's heart, I believe.'

'The speedier job for you, Chip,' said I, laughing scornfully; 'I see you're a hand at a black box.'[392]

Whether the cool indifference of this speech enraged the carpenter, or whether, which is more likely, the man had a certain treasured hostility in his breast, which he only wanted an opportunity of paying off upon my person, I know not; but it is certain that he visited my jaws with a blow which caused them to rattle after a strange fashion. I know not, also, how it was that, coward as I have confessed myself to be, I ventured a blow in exchange for his duly delivered present; and levelling a terrific return, it reached him just in the back settlements of the left ear, and enforced him to measure his length on the ground, without allowing him very sufficient time to decide upon the most graceful or becoming posture in which it might beseem him to extend himself.

This feat, upon which I prided myself not a little, established me in the vicinity as a dangerous person, and caused me to be regarded as one whose motions were to be attended by a halo of reverential silence; it moreover had a tendency to exasperate my already inflamed feelings against Catharine; so that by this time, I believe, if a mutually unhappy couple were to be found in London (hardly a supposition, by-the-bye), it would be discovered under our roof.

Yet, I could not but remark, from day to day, the change that was taking place in her appearance; or rather, not so much the alteration of her outward form and aspect, as those nameless variations of manner which indicate a heart ill at ease with itself and every thing that surrounds it. I had not as yet taught myself to *dwell* upon the inevitable and speedy termination of this state of mind working upon a delicate and exhausted frame, although I must have been, and therefore was, fully aware of it. I knew that the absence of her infant preyed upon her mind, and that, were the child recalled, it might wean her from the contemplation of other anxieties. I knew this, and yet I strenuously objected to its return; and she was compelled to console herself with that species of hope which is said to make the heart sick.

One day, when I returned from a successful attempt upon the sympathies of Misty, I surprised her in tears, bending over a cage, in which she kept a favourite Canary bird.

Upon looking into the cage, I perceived that the bird was dead; and there it lay upon its sanded floor – cold, light, and stiff.

I rebuked her for lamenting the poor little devil, which death had thus suddenly disposed of, – but not in my usual manner. I was elated by my good success, and spoke in a milder tone than I was accustomed to adopt.

'I should not so much have minded,' she said, weeping, 'but the poor creature died through my neglect; – but I never think of anything now;' and as she opened the door of the cage, and took out the bird, which she held sorrowfully in her hand and gazed upon, she added, in a low tone, 'well, well, it will be my turn soon.'

I was touched, I know not why – perhaps by the tone of voice, and I approached her. 'Why, what ails you, girl,' said I, 'that you talk thus?' She was silent for a moment, and then timidly raising her eyes, answered, –

'Oh! John, I am so wretched; I do wish so to see our little boy: pray let me go to-day to Walworth. I have not seen him for nearly six weeks, and Mrs. Adams has not called as she used to do. I fear something has happened.'

'No, no,' I replied, 'I'll go myself, and bring the child to see you this very night.'

Her eyes sparkled at this unexpected kindness, and she could not speak; – but she pressed my arm softly, and looked more gratitude than I ever deserved at her hands.

I went my way, however, and made the best of it to Walworth. To my repeated knocking at the door of the house in which Mrs. Adams had taken up her residence, I received no reply, and was at length informed by the next door neighbour, that the nurse had departed no one knew whither; and in short, had accomplished an exploit which is commonly designated 'shooting the moon;' in other words, had made herself invisible to the landlord, by walking off one night with all her 'bits of sticks;' and, indeed – or my informant belied her most wickedly – with all the (miscalled) fixtures also.

As I passed through the Borough, on my return home, much musing, and marvelling whither the inexplicable Mrs. Adams was gone, and wherefore she had not called upon us for so long a period, and how this circumstance would probably act upon my wife, whom should I behold alighting with much praiseworthy caution from a stage coach, but my respected uncle.

'Ah! uncle,' I exclaimed, slapping him on the shoulder as he turned for the purpose of departing from the vehicle, 'how are you, my old boy?'

The dead Bird.

'What! nephy,' cried he; 'Why I'm as hearty as a buck, only can't leap quite so high. I say, Jack, I'm gallows stiff a-riding on that 'ere coach, – let me lean on your arm.'

As we walked along, the old gentleman informed me that he had been upon a country excursion on professional business. 'Sich a queer cove, – sich an ugly varmint, Jack,' said he; 'hanged for the murder of his old woman. My eye! what a guy[393] he was. I've got a paper in my pocket: he comes up to me when he was a-going to be turned off,[394] and he says, 'Sir,' says he, with a bow, as I may do now, 'here's an important paper,' says he, 'which I've delayed to give to the proper person; will you take charge of it? it's important,' says he again; 'pray see that the clergyman of E. has it.'

'I will, says I, and makes *my* bow; and presently I turns my gentleman off. I say, Jack, I wish you'd come home and read it to me; you've more book learning nor[395] I; come along.'

No sooner were we seated in the accustomed room, sacred to so many recollections, with the customary pot of ale, than my uncle urged the reading of the paper he had brought with him. I accordingly snuffed the candle,[396] and opening the manuscript, which although small and neat, was not particularly legible, I read as follows: –

THE CONFESSION OF JAMES WILSON.

Let me pause awhile – what am I about to do? I am about to commit to paper a brief abstract of my wretched history. I am about to retrace the furrowed brow of memory, and to kindle again her stony eyes. I will leave the world this narrative of my crime, for which, if the hell of torture I have already endured will not amply expiate, to-morrow will make sufficient atonement.

It is Sunday morning; the bell is ringing to service. I see, even as though I were there, the parishioners of my native village, walking sedately in their Sabbath clothes, with happy faces of serene content, to the village church; I hear the hushed stir with which they reverently take their accustomed seats; I hear the soft sweet voices of the children, as they sing the morning hymn. My own children – innocent creatures! are they not there also? ignorant of their father's disgrace. I hear them breathe their inarticulate praises to the Almighty, while the organ swells and vibrates through that time-honoured building. Will not my darlings pray for their poor father? Will not the lips of my dear ones be moved in prayer for their absent father? Will not little hands be raised unconsciously in his behalf? They will; I know they will. And are there none beside to pray for me? Will not the name of James Wilson be breathed by many voices to-day? Yes, yes. Oh God! I thank thee for these tears.

The turnkey enters my cell. Is it a fine morning? It is a cloudless summer day. Within that ancient pile all is piety and peace; calmness and silence reign without and around. Green is the grass over the heads of the forefathers of the hamlet, and the sunshine is glowing upon their graves as though they were not cold in dissolution, but still slept warm with the consciousness of present existence. How different is this cell, where sunshine never entered, and happiness was never known to set her foot; this tomb of the living, which precedes death that it may rob the grave of its repose. But the term of my stay is short, and much yet remains to be done.

My father had been, since his first taking orders until the day of his death, pastor of the little village of E—, my native place. Mild and gentle in his manners, he was beloved by his parishioners, and perhaps exercised as much influence over them as any person may be supposed to do, whose pretensions are not backed by wealth, and whose kindness does not assume the air of patronage.

Our establishment at the time I speak of – my earliest recollection of its existence – consisted of three persons: my father, a kind of housekeeper, elevated by his humane consideration into an equal, and myself. My mother had been dead long since.

I was, I think, about ten years of age, when a very important change in our domestic arrangements took place. A sister of my mother died at this period, leaving a daughter nearly of my own age; this girl was consigned to the care of my father.

She was the daughter of a respectable medical man, who had entered into business in a large country town, where he bade fair to improve a daily increasing connexion; but dying a few years after his marriage, he had left my aunt with but a slender maintenance for herself and daughter, which however the careful woman contrived, during the short time she survived him, rather to increase than to impair.

Mrs. Cowley, then, commended her only child to the protection of my father, not only with sufficient to defray the necessary expenses of her board and education, but mistress of a small actual sum, which with care and prudent appropriation might, on her attaining the age of twenty-one, be deemed a desirable little fortune to such as make the possession of money on the woman's side a *sine quâ non*[397] of their affections, or a condition of their hymeneal negociations.

The addition of Lucy Cowley to our small circle was an event that I soon taught myself to believe was most auspicious. An unruly, obstinate, and wayward boy, in the society of my young companion I became humanised, and in some degree gentle and submissive; and my little cousin was in no wise backward to exert her artless ingenuity in contriving rewards and encouragement, whenever I exhibited evidences of a desire to conform myself to the reasonable and anxious wishes of my father towards my improvement and future well-doing in the world. In a word, long before I had acquired experience or derived informations as to the nature of love – indeed, even previous to my knowledge of its name,

I had become passionately attached to Lucy; and I will say, for I still believe it, that she herself at that time entertained feelings of a similar nature, no less strong than my own, for me.

Four years passed away, and during that time these feelings appeared to have strengthened and matured; insomuch that it was tacitly understood by my father, and openly hinted at by the officious kindness of Mrs. Goodman, the house-keeper, that in due time the happy conformity that existed between my cousin and myself, of tastes, habits, and opinions, would be cemented by marriage.

At this time my father was called to town by one of those periodical fits of ambition which afflict most men utterly beyond the sphere of fortune's regards, or the world's notice. He visited the metropolis to seek after preferment.

It appears that during his stay in London, he encountered an old college friend, upon whom fortune had looked favourably since their last meeting, and who expressed an anxious wish that his eldest son should be placed under my father's care and tuition for two or three years, in order to qualify him for an introduction to college. My father was of course glad to close with this proposal, and accordingly returned to E— with young Beaumont, a lad about a year older than myself, whose fine, frank, expressive countenance, lively and agreeable manners, and apparently open nature, recommended him instantly to the esteem of the inmates of the parsonage.

There was, I must confess, about the lad (I speak from too faithful a memory) that something which, not occasioned by beauty or handsomeness of person, or graceful and easy deportment, succeeds in making some people beloved at first sight by all who may become acquainted with them; in a word, Beaumont was a universal favourite.

I too loved him. We soon became constant associates, and our friendship promised a longer duration than is commonly ordained for such attachments; being founded not upon a sympathy of feeling, or a similarity of mental structure, which some foolishly conceive to be the only lasting basis of that sentiment, but growing out of the very antipathies of our natures.

Francis Beaumont was all spirit, gaiety, and alertness; I was moody, obstinate, and slow. He was passionate and forgiving; I was cold, and apt to brood over real or supposed grievances. I was what parents and relations, with more candour than kindness, sometimes term a slow, dull boy; Beaumont was quick, intelligent, apprehensive.[398] In a word, there was in each sufficient distinctness of character to flatter the self-love of both.

But there was one whose warm encomiums and admiration of Beaumont, whenever he chanced to be the subject of our conversation, I felt uneasy at hearing so often repeated. For a time I had encouraged and taken a pride in the praises accorded to him from all quarters, conceiving them to be, as it were, echoes of my own sentiments in his favour, and evidences of my sagacity and good taste in the choice of a friend; but at length these praises appeared to assume an invidious character, and to be rather awkward comparisons, out of which I was left to extract such fuel for my vanity as their extremely disparaging conclusions enabled me to seek – but to seek in vain.

I could have borne to hear the merits of my friend descanted upon – nay, I could have rejoiced in joining my tribute to his worth; but I could not bear that Lucy should tell me so plainly as she sometimes did, that she considered Beaumont in any respect superior to myself. She might, indeed, feel that it was so, but wherefore wound my feelings by so open an avowal of her opinion. Was this unkind? I think it was. And then the ground of her preference – for prefer him she did – was perhaps ridiculous, but it was a mint on which boys are most sensitive.

'You know, James,' she would sometimes laughingly say to me, 'that you are not so handsome as Francis, but I dare say you are as clever, after all; Frank often declares that you'll be a bright man one of these days.'

Yes – it was this that stung me to the quick; I was not so handsome as Francis Beaumont. I knew that full well. Nay, more – it was an insult, a flagrant insult. Handsome! ha! ha! ha! and I would laugh in the bitterness of my soul. I was about as ugly a brute as was ever selected to bear the brunt of boarding-school criticism; I was a contrast, not a comparison.

Whether it were chance, or the design of a mischievous fatality, I know not, but from henceforth these annoyances became incessant, and at last unbearable. Our old housekeeper, Mrs. Goodman, of whom I had been from my birth an especial favourite, had encouraged strange suspicions of the continuance of Lucy's affection for me.

'My dear child,' she observed to me one day, 'you must keep a wary eye on Frank Beaumont, or you'll get no Lucy, after all. To be sure he's a fine young lad as ever was seen; but what of that? For my part, I've no notion of your young gentry coming down to these parts to inveigle away our country maidens, or to fill their foolish heads with London stuff and nonsense. As I tell Lucy, though you're not so fine and genteel, you're a mortal[399] deal better: and if you're not sprightly and witty like, you've good common sense, I dare say. Still waters run deepest; a silent hog eats the most grains.'

At this compliment the old lady laughed as jocosely as an asthmatic wheeze permitted her to indulge in that recreation; and for once in my life I cursed her officious kindness, and betook myself to my room, where I pondered on my own deficiencies, and on the fatal mischance which had directed Frank Beaumont to our house, with whom I was, it seemed, doomed to be brought into perpetual and disadvantageous collision.

For, my father had also caught the infection. He has said to me more than once, when he approved of the progress I made in my studies, 'Come, James, this will do very well, my boy; considering all things, you're not so far behind your friend Frank as might be expected. The Almighty does not bestow on every one such gifts as he has lavished upon young Beaumont; but whatever your talents are, boy, cultivate them to his glory and your own mental profit and advantage.'

Was this to be borne? no; it made me mad. I studied almost incessantly, early and late; devoted myself heart and soul to the attainment of knowledge, and hoped to earn such praise for my exertions as it is cruelty to withhold, and worse than injustice to qualify. And here was another, who never studied at all, – who read, as it were, for the amusement of an hour, or to reconcile himself to a belief that he *did* make some progress, – who walked leisurely to the goal, not only to win the cup, but to fill mine with bitterness and mortification.

Good heavens! how could it be? Was there some spell upon me, – or were others infatuated; or was Beaumont supernaturally endowed? No, no; the Dispenser of events[400] had ordered that in every respect – physical, intellectual, and moral – I should fall short of my rival. What I strove to attain, he acquired without exertion; the applause I sued for, he obtained without seeking; and Nature had, it seems, made his face a letter of recommendation, whilst mine was a kind of threatening letter, unpleasant to peruse, and not worth attending to.

And yet I loved Beaumont. His noble and generous disposition, and the entire absence of triumph at my expense whenever I was eclipsed by the brightness of his more auspicious star, or his happier genius, assuaged as much as possible the rankling of the sting, that, nevertheless, festered within me at intervals with sufficient poignancy.

All this might have been cured – eradicated – forgotten. I had calculated the probable duration of Beaumont's stay with us; it might possibly not exceed another year: and although I saw that Lucy preferred him infinitely to me, and that he either affected or really felt an attachment towards her, I hoped that his absence, with a little reflection on the part of Lucy, in which the impossibility of their union would be naturally taken into account, – I trusted that, everything considered, I should in all probability succeed in making her my own, in accordance with the wishes of my father and the first impressions of Lucy herself.

Perhaps the aspect in which matters stood at this moment would have suggested to another the relinquishment of his claims; but with me the effect was contrary. I was determined to possess Lucy Cowley; in this one point I was resolved to be the victor. An event fell out just at this time that improved my resolution.

I overheard a conversation between these two; I listened at the keyhole, drawn by that irresistible presentiment which sometimes impels us to verify what our fears have shadowed forth. Hitherto I had never committed a mean action; but my pride been broken by the treatment I had met with from those around me, and to humiliate is to debase the spirit.

Without any uneasy feeling of shame, therefore, I listened at the keyhole, and was confirmed in all that my suspicions had long ago converted into certainty: that is to say, that Beaumont and Lucy loved each other. But this was not all; they spoke of the implied contract between Lucy and myself, and of the means whereby it might be rendered void; and concerted means of carrying on a correspondence when the term of Beaumont's sojourn with my father should expire, and he should be removed to college.

These measures duly arranged, Lucy in the exuberance of her spirits indulged herself by ridiculing the preposterous union which had been originally intended between us, and made herself somewhat merry by reviewing my manifold deficiencies of person, a topic not displeasing to many young ladies, and to her, apparently, a congenial and common subject of reference.

What effect this talk had upon the person addressed I know not, for he answered not a word. I had enough to do afterwards in arranging in my own mind the expression of conscious and triumphant superiority with which Beaumont must, without doubt, have taken the implied compliment to himself.

I slunk down stairs. My blood burned, not boiled, with a dull red heat. I was struck to the heart with shame, and mortified vanity, and wounded pride. No – these were not the feelings; it was horror. Horror at what? at whom? I know not. The feeling *was* horror, nevertheless.

I took two or three turns in the garden, and endeavoured to control the excitement under which I laboured, and succeeded at least in delaying its intended vengeance. I nursed it to keep it warm. What should I do? in what manner satisfy my rage? When I found myself in a situation to analyse my own feelings, I found that they partook not of resentment to Lucy Cowley, but were exclusively directed to Beaumont. What right had he to presume to listen to such detestable strictures? Was it not enough that he was my superior in such external advantages, but he must needs pamper his own vanity by permitting himself to dwell upon my defects? Envy, which is love turned sour, worked within me. I could no longer endure to be thrown into the shade by this boy; I *would* not bear it. But how was I to shift this load of vexation and misery? I should at least make myself ridiculous, and offer, perhaps, an additional point for amusement or contemptuous criticism. In one resolve, however, I was definitively confirmed – I *would* have Lucy Cowley. I swore it in the darkness of my soul, in spite of hell or heaven I would obtain her.

Beaumont approached me. 'Will you step into the orchard,' said I, 'I have a few words to say of some importance to myself.' I opened the small gate, he passed through, and I followed him. We walked some distance without speaking; my heart beat quickly, and my knees smote together and ached with the violence of my emotion. I broke the silence abruptly.

'Is it not too bad, Beaumont,' said I; 'that you should pay any attention to what that girl pleases to tell you concerning me?'

'What do you mean, my dear fellow?' he replied, smiling, with an air of surprise at my agitation.

'Oh! You know what I mean,' I retorted sullenly; 'Lucy and you have made up matters between you, I dare say; I heard you just now, too, amusing yourselves at my expense.'

'Heard us just now! impossible! how?'

'As I passed the door, my name was mentioned; I stopped and –'

'Listened, eh?' interrupted Beaumont, evidently glad of an opportunity of evading the charge; 'I didn't think, James, that you were guilty of eavesdropping.'

'Say that again,' cried I, fiercely, and I advanced towards him, 'and I'll strike you to the earth – I will, by heaven;' and I shook my fist violently in his face. He stepped back a pace. Beaumont was no coward, – older, and as strong as myself; but at this moment he was daunted, or perhaps confounded with surprise at my extravagant violence of passion.

'Come, Wilson, this is not the way in which *we* should settle our differences, at all events,' said he, after a pause; 'blows are bad arguments.'

'Well, what if I confess,' I exclaimed, with more calmness, 'that eavesdropping was the proper word: it was. I *did* listen; I have overheard all your conversation. What have you now to say?'

'Nothing,' said he, with an air of perfect indifference.

'Nothing!' echoed I; 'why, you cur—' His blood mounted at this word, and his brows were knitted suddenly, and he clenched his teeth and hands firmly together. 'Nay, I will be heard,' I resumed. 'Look you, Beaumont; Lucy Cowley and I have been contracted and devoted to each other almost since our infancy. I have always loved, and do still love her; till you came, she loved me. Promise me – and keep that promise I'll make you – that you never hold the slightest correspondence with her when you leave our house; that you resign all claim to her while you remain here, and, in a word, that you relinquish and utterly renounce her. She is mine, and mine she shall be; be assured of that.'

'Ridiculous!' cried Beaumont, scornfully; 'why, my good fellow, you're beside yourself. What claim have you to Lucy? Contracted! by whom? By your father, perhaps. What authority has he to influence her choice? You love her; well, so do I; and more, she loves me.'

'No matter; the promise you shall make and adhere to.'

'Shall?' cried Beaumont, in a tone of defiance, which he presently converted into a contemptuous laugh; 'you're jocular, my friend James. I am not used to be driven, and shall assuredly not submit to be bullied by one whom I consider in all respects inferior to myself.'

'Oh! yes, I know my inferiority,' said I, bitterly; 'every one takes care to remind me of that.'

'And what every one says must be true,' interrupted he, quietly. 'Know your place, then, and be silent, or I'll make you.'

'Make me! did I hear the words aright? make me!'

'Yes, make you. You talk of exacting promises from me, and a great deal more; I should be glad to see you attempting to exact them. No, no, my lad, I am not to be intimidated. Besides, you have applied a term to me which I am not disposed to bear or to submit to.'

'And will again if you provoke me to it.'

'Nay, you had better not;' and he came towards me with his fists clenched. 'Now, if you're not a coward' – I raised my hand; I would have struck him. I *could* have struck him to the ground at that moment; I feel that he never could have resisted the blow I should have levelled at him. But a something flashed across me – I dropped my arm; a change had come upon me in one instant. From a hostile antagonist I looked upon my rival as a helpless creature given up into my hands. I took in at one view the whole dimensions of the being before me, and, methought, my glance wound around him like the web of the spider. I reserved him for another occasion. 'It is very well,' I muttered; 'you have your way this once.'

'It is very well,' retorted Beaumont, tauntingly, 'when fellows like you have the worse part of cowardice to insult, and the better part of valour to escape with impunity.'

These words were soothing to me; and the scornful and spurning expletive with which Beaumont greeted me as I departed, sank like a congenial cordial into my soul.

I mounted up stairs into an old garret, unoccupied except by ill-assorted and useless furniture, and took a hasty and feverish review of the scene that had just taken place. Tears, scalding and bitter tears, rolled down my cheek; but they were tears of rage, not of weakness or contrition: and as I passed before my mind every word of insult that Beaumont had cast at me, I felt that no reparation which he could make should satisfy me.

'Yes, yes, it is all very well,' I exclaimed, in a frenzy, as I paced up and down the room, and brushed the tears from my eyes with my coat-sleeve; 'it is the fortune of some to command, and of others to be ground like the nether millstone; but I am not one of these. I will not succumb to this conventional exclusiveness. How is Beaumont my superior? His birth, perhaps, is in his favour; his person – let him boast of so miserable an advantage. Am I not a human being, with the faculties, passions, and feelings of humanity? Why is this handsome fellow to be perpetually thrust between me and my self-love?'

I proceeded to the window; it looked upon the garden. There was Beaumont, walking calmly and with an unruffled aspect, in apparently casual conversation with my father.

'Aye, such smooth-tongued hypocrites as this make the world their foot-ball,' said I, with mournful asperity. 'These *things*, with their varnish of virtue about them – soft and amiable hypocrites – monopolise the esteem and respect of the world; while I, and such rough diamonds – for so they insolently call us – have our faces ground by the insolent upstarts of society. Our faces ground – ha! ha! ha!' and I dashed my fists against my forehead – 'what grinding would make this visage endurable?'

It was a strange something that entered my brain when I was about to strike Beaumont to the earth; it came again with more distinctness and development of outline. I leaned against the wall, and wooed it to my bosom. The sunshine that entered the window at this moment, and hung about the room, turning the dust into splendour, typified the warm light which this recurring thought communicated to my feelings.

Beaumont was about to proceed immediately after dinner to the market town, three miles distant, for the purpose of meeting some relations who had been drawn to that place by the ensuing assizes, and it was arranged that he was to attend a ball at the principal inn; and as it would be in all probability rather late before he returned, he was to be furnished with the key of the door, that he might not keep any of the family sitting up for him, my father being a man of very early habits, and accordingly decidedly objecting to late hours. My intention – for it now became an intention – hinged upon this short journey of Beaumont's; and I had just completed the rough heads of my projected adventure, when the bell summoned us to dinner.

During that meal I attempted to appear composed, and even cheerful, and succeeded in concealing from the rest of the family (a desire which appeared to be seconded by Beaumont) that any misunderstanding had occurred between us. I, however, cast an inquiring glance occasionally towards my enemy, and sometimes our eyes met, but we averted them instantly; and, methought, there was a gravity, and even a melancholy expression about the face of Beaumont which I had seldom or never before observed.

Immediately after the cloth was drawn, under pretext of wishing to solve a knotty problem, I arose and retired to my own room. I had not been long seated, when the door opened, and Beaumont entered.

'Come, James,' said he, advancing towards me, 'do give me your hand; I can't bear that we should be unfriendly. I am sorry, very sorry, for what I said this morning. You know how passionate I am. Come, we were both in the wrong, let us shake hands.'

'You may think, Mr. Beaumont,' I replied, coolly, 'that we were both in the wrong; but I have no such impression, and I beg leave to decline your hand.' I looked up in his face, and perceived that tears were in his eyes.

'Nay, James, this is unkind,' said Beaumont, reproachfully; 'why cavil at a word? I know that I was very wrong, and that I insulted you grossly; forgive me, I beg you: and if you said anything to me that you may be hereafter sorry for, be assured that I forget it. Come.'

Beaumont again offered to me his hand.

'No,' I answered, doggedly, 'I will not accept your hand; I am not so easily satisfied in matters of this kind, and I not only reject your friendship now, but beg that it may be considered at an end for ever.'

Beaumont stood before me in silence for a minute, and the colour mounted into his face. 'Well,' he murmured, as he turned upon his heel, 'I am very sorry for your decision, and hope that you will think better of it.'

There was a melancholy in Beaumont's tone as he quitted the room, that struck upon some mysterious chord of my nature, for I wept long and silently, and would have prayed (not to speak irreverently) that the bitter cup might pass away from me; but the devil had laid hold upon me, and I felt as one ordained to do something which I had no power to evade or to decline.

Had this apology been offered before – had it been tendered at the moment of provocation, all might have been well; but it came too late. I had already made up my mind, and some unearthly power forbade me to bate a jot of my purpose.

The family, in due time, retired to rest. I also proceeded to my sleeping-room, but not, as yet, to bed. My father and Lucy had not, I believe, remarked anything extraordinary in my manners or conduct during the evening, for no observation to that effect occurred: perhaps, my moodiness and taciturnity had been of late too common to excite surprise, and our habitual associates are too accustomed to the face they know, to apprehend the meaning of any particular expression that passion may give to it. A stranger would have read horror and madness in my countenance on that evening.

It was a beautiful, moonlight, midsummer night. I raised the window cautiously, and looked out. All was silent. The roof of a wash-house rose within a foot of my window, grown over with stone-crop and aged moss: it was a safe venture for the feet. I got out, and thence descended into the garden by a ladder, which I had placed against the tiles during the afternoon. But I had forgotten to close my window, and climbed up again for that purpose. Within my chamber all was stillness and peace: it was full of the moonlight, and every object around was distinctly visible. There was my bible lying upon the drawers by my bedside – oh! should I return? should I delay my purpose? should I cast it from me for ever, and step once more into the pale of heavenly forgiveness? My head swam round, and my eyes were dizzy and full of a watery humour; – they were not tears. Eternity hung upon that moment. I closed the window, and descended into the garden. A few minutes' hasty walk, and I had crossed the orchard, and getting over a ditch, and proceeding along a field-path, I found myself in the high road.

What had I come forth at this hour of the night to do? What was I about to become? Who was I? These questions whirled through my brain as I reeled along like a drunken man; but I dare not, or could not, answer them to myself. And now my mind misgave me, and my knees smote together with dreadful violence. When I think upon that hour I almost pity myself, for then indeed I was a wretched creature. I had left my father's house at dead of night, liable to be discovered, and yet afraid to return; something commanded me to proceed, and I wrung my hands together, and moaned in the direful agony of my spirit. At this moment the sound of coach wheels arrested my attention. I had just time to conceal myself behind a hedge, when the London Mail drove rapidly past, and the sound of the horn announced its approach to our village. A thought struck me – should I hasten to London? – fly at once and for ever from a place where nothing but mortification and misery awaited me; and seeking for employment in some obscure corner of the metropolis, endeavour to procure a living for myself, and become a respectable and a happy man. Alas! I had but a few shillings about me; and utterly without recommendations or knowledge of mankind, how should I fare in a place like London? Besides, should I leave the field to Beaumont? Should I relinquish Lucy, whom I had sworn to obtain? – abandon my father, whose declining years I had promised myself to watch over and protect? 'No, no,' I muttered, and my self-possession returned; 'I will not verify their opinion of me at home – I will not turn out the fool they think me. Beaumont shall not live to exult over my downfall; and my father shall, perhaps, live long enough to know that he has been the unconscious instrument of embittering the youth, and blighting the aspirations of his son. I can forgive him and Lucy; but Beaumont – '

I started, for a well-known whistle reached my ear. Beaumont was returning, evidently in high spirits, whistling a tune which I knew to be a favourite. He had not yet turned the corner of the road, and I stooped and picked up a large chalky flint, and hid myself behind the hedge which had sheltered me from the sight of the mail-coach passengers. As he approached nearer, – and now his projected shadow was level with my eye, – my soul was filled with black and fearful horror, and my bosom boiled with malignant revenge. I gnashed my teeth, and clench firmly the stone in my right hand. He was before me – within five yards – now – now – or it will be too late. I raised my hand, and discharged with all my strength the broken and jagged flint. It struck him violently on the temple, and he fell on the path. I sprang over the hedge by the force of a wild instinct, and ran towards him. A thick black blood was gushing from a deep wound, and a groan, that vibrated through every vein in my body, burst from his mouth. 'Frank, my dear fellow, it is I; speak to me – James Wilson – I know not what I have done;' and I hung over the poor boy conscience-stricken: but conscience had come too late.

With a violent effort he raised himself upon his hands, and looked reproachfully, but sorrowfully at me. 'James – a murderer!' and he gasped for breath; 'but no, you shall not escape me; your father shall know this. Oh! James, this was a coward's action;' and he wound his hand in my neckcloth, and struggled to rise.

What was to be done? – my father to know of this: it would bring his grey hairs to the grave! But I thought not of this at the moment. A vague knowledge of my danger impelled me. There was no time to make terms. I drew out a knife, which I had found in the lumber-room during the afternoon, and made a thrust towards him. He parried it with his arm, and leapt to his feet, as though some supernatural strength had been suddenly infused into him. He ran from me a few paces – 'James Wilson – not for my sake, but your own – spare me!' he exclaimed; 'Oh, I have no strength left to defend myself.' Again we closed, and again I made a stab at his bosom, but in vain; for he fought with his open hands with the desperate strength of one who struggles for life. And now he had almost wrenched the knife from my grasp, when he fell forward on my shoulder, his face close to mine, and his eyes fixed upon me with an intolerable expression of mingled pity and contempt. I could not bear that look; but, collecting all my force, thrust my antagonist from me, and dashed the knife into his throat – once – twice, and again a third time.

With a loud cry I flung the knife from me, and my victim fell heavily to the earth, the blood gushing and rolling around him in frothy and bubbling profusion. I looked up, and the very heavens seemed to be, nay, *were* rent asunder, and mingled blood and fire streamed with a hissing sound in the firmament! I was distracted, and ran round and round the lifeless body, casting up my hands to heaven, not knowing whither I should turn or fly, – amazed and confounded at what I had done.

But the devil whispered to me – 'This thing must be hidden. No mortal in this world must ever know of this deed. It must be kept close – close; and the horrible secret must fester in your sole breast and brain for ever!' I went and knelt down by the body of Beaumont, and placed my ear to his mouth. Not a breath! I laid my hand upon his bosom, under the waistcoat. The heart had ceased to throb – yes, he was dead! But there was a warmth, too, that seemed to proceed from the body. Oh God! it was the blood crawling, and spreading, and clotting over the bosom! I thrust my dabbled fingers in the pockets of the murdered boy, for a cunning contrivance to evade suspicion presented itself to me; and drawing out his purse, containing I know not what – but it was heavy

– probably his friends had presented him with money on that very evening – I went and threw it into an adjoining pond, with a bead-purse which I also found about him, and which had been destined by him for Lucy Cowley; for I had heard them speaking of the present in the morning. This would indicate that the murder had been effected previous to a robbery, and glance off any suspicion that my own guilty conscience alone caused me to suspect might possibly attach to me. With like caution I cleared my hands and person of the blood that stained them, and returned home the same way I came, creeping stealthily into my room window, and retiring forthwith to bed.

The horror of that night can never be put into words. My vengeance being now completed, my better feelings returned. I would have given worlds – (oh! 'tis but a poor and mean phrase!) – I would have surrendered my soul's salvation, that this deed might be recalled. The kind – the generous boy, the friend of my youth, the companion of my studies; one whom I had loved as a brother, stretched by my hand on the common road, a ghastly, hideous corpse! But these thoughts gave way to others of more pressing import. How should I meet my father? How could I bear the glance of Lucy? How go through the dreadful scene of grief, consternation, and, above all, inquiry, that this event would occasion. Oh! I had not thought of this! The very name of murderer would be stamped upon my forehead. I should be detected by the most casual observer: – I should, perhaps, commit myself! Once I leaped from my bed, and resolved to fly. I could not endure the unconscious scrutiny to which I should be subjected. But this would be tantamount to a confession; and my father would live to see his son brought to an ignominious end, – and no longer. No, the trial – the dreadful ordeal must be gone through! – at all hazards I must await the issue of this terrible adventure.

In agony of mind and body not to be expressed, I lay upon my bed, filled with the most horrible apprehension and dismay; and saw the grey night wear away, and heard the cock count its night-watches till the first streak of morning showed in the sky, giving promise of a glorious day. The birds began to twitter in the boughs, and the light unfolded itself in radiant beauty, as though, since last the sun had gone down, all the earth had been sacred to peace, and had left the world for that short space to Nature. Oh! how I wished this day were well over, and yet dreaded its beginning! About four o'clock I heard our man arise and go out of his sleeping-room, which was over an adjoining out-house, into the orchard. In all human probability, the murder would now be discovered, and my term of wretched duplicity and anxious concealment must commence. Nor was I deceived: a hurrying of footsteps, a noise of voices in loud and hurried talk, and the huddling speed with which men usually bring unwelcome or alarming tidings, proclaimed that they had found the body, and were bearing it to our house. I shrunk beneath the bedclothes, which I drew closely around and over me; and, pressing my hands upon my ears, endeavoured to shut out the fearful news which was, alas! no tidings to me! A few minutes of mortal suspense elapsed. I ventured to listen; – there was a foot upon the stairs, and my door was burst open.

'James, James, for mercy's sake arise!' – it was my father's voice that spoke. 'Beaumont is murdered!' – and he shook me violently by the shoulder. 'The poor dear boy is killed! Merciful heaven! how shall I explain this to Beaumont?' and the old man wrung his hands, and wept like a child.

I affected to be in a deep sleep, but roused by this outcry I sprang up in bed. 'What say you, father? Beaumont killed; – who can have done it?' But I checked myself: my own anxiety so early expressed might have created suspicion. I held down my head, therefore, and pretended to weep – oh! that I could have wept; but my father heeded me not, and when he turned to implore me to come down stairs, my face, I doubt not, expressed a horror that to him was sufficient evidence of the concern I felt at my friend's fate.

It were needless to describe the consternation which this calamitous event produced in the village, or the means that were resorted to for the purpose of discovering the perpetrator: these inquiries, not directed for a moment towards our family or domestics, by whom the deceased boy was known to have been universally beloved, made me feel secure against detection, and comparatively easy on that score. Not so, however, in my immediate circle. When, at length, on the morning of the discovery of the murder I crept down stairs, I betook myself to a back parlour, and there sat alone, trembling and confounded; nor could my father or the housekeeper draw me thence, until after many entreaties had been resorted to. My father and Lucy, I might have seen, were too much occupied with their own feelings of grief, to be particularly interested by the manner in which my supposed concern manifested itself; and when I was brought before the body of my victim, they referred to a very different cause the horror which smote me to the ground, and left me struggling on the floor in all the torture of despairing contrition and remorse.

They had washed the body and laid it out in white linen on a bed, and Lucy had strewn flowers on the corpse. The face was placid, for mortality had not yet begun to settle there; and the deep wound on the temple had been concealed by his hair, and the gash in the throat was covered by the white garment in which he had been placed.

I drew nearer: there was a quiet, a repose about that beautiful face, that irresistibly attracted me towards it. I drew nearer, and sank upon my knees by the side of the corpse. My father and Lucy had retired. I took the cold and clammy hand of my injured friend. Oh, heaven! from the temple and the throat a black flood of clotted blood effused, and, with a piercing shriek, I fell senseless to the ground.

When I recovered my senses, my father and Mrs. Goodman were bending over me, bathing my temples with vinegar.

'Compose yourself, James,' said my father; 'this affliction has been too much for your spirits.'

'No wonder,' remarked the old lady; 'the boys were such friends. I'm sure they were more like brothers than anything else. The lad can't help grieving, Mr. Wilson, although it is sinful, as you were saying.'

My father sighed heavily. 'Will you see, Mrs. Goodman,' he said, 'that fresh linen be prepared for that poor dear creature there,' and he pointed towards the body. 'I expect his father here very shortly, and the inquest will meet at four o'clock.'

Could that sudden gushing of blood be an accident – could it be accounted for by natural causes, or was it a direct manifestation intended by heaven to point out the murderer, and to bring him to condign punishment? Whatever it were, it filled me with fear, and astonishment, and superstitious dread. Afraid to leave the body for an instant, lest it should speak with such miraculous organs the fearful secret, I was compelled, nevertheless, to retire to the adjoining chamber, and, during the protracted inquest, underwent such misery of apprehension as may, perhaps, plead for a limitation of my punishment in the other world – if, indeed, any future punishment can equal the hell of torment that I have endured since that day! At lenth[401] the verdict of the inquest was pronounced – 'Wilful Murder against some person or persons unknown.' And when they departed, I fell down upon my knees, and prayed to God in the bitter terror of my soul, that he would grant me time to make my peace with Him who seeth all things, and saw the anguish of my spirit. For I swore to devote the remainder of my life to repentance, and, by the grace of God, to order my life in such a manner as would entitle me, if not to find favour, at least to plead for forgiveness and mercy, from His goodness.

From that time forth, until the funeral took place, I scarcely left the body for a moment, except during meals; but watched constantly by the side of the coffin, waiting impatiently for the moment that was to consign it to the earth, and remove it for ever from the sight of men. That ceremony performed, the murder and its details would gradually slip from the tongues of the village gossips who delight in such stimulating narratives, or probably give place to some more exciting, if not more appalling, novelty.

The father of the unfortunate boy had been staying with us until the funeral was concluded; and during that time had conceived an attachment for me, founded, perhaps, on my supposed friendship for his son. When he took leave, on the evening of the day of the funeral, he led me aside, and with a broken voice and streaming eyes, said to me, while he wrung my hand affectionately, 'I have watched, my dear boy, the respect you have paid to the memory of that – ' here his voice failed him, and he sobbed aloud. 'This is foolish,' he continued, after a pause; 'my poor boy often spoke of you, in his letters to me, as his only friend; and I have seen enough of you to be satisfied that you deserved his praise. This is not the time to talk of such matters; but you must write to me, and inform me how I can be of service to you in your future life; in the mean while, accept this trifle as a mark of my friendship.' He placed a £20 note in my hand, and left the room, and, a minute after, I saw him through the window step into his carriage, and return to London.

With a bursting heart I retired to my own room, and thrust the note into my desk, and, for the first time since the murder, tears came into my eyes – blessed tears! for they relieved me – but not caused by any enviable state of feeling that had arisen out of the previous scene. On the contrary, a softened recollection of Beaumont's kindness and friendship, with the knowledge that never in this world could I make reparation to his family for the misery I had occasioned, wrought within me tenderly, but strongly; and, if it might have been, I prayed that I might be taken hence to a blind and deaf eternity, and resolved again into incommunicable dust. A tap at the door aroused me. – 'Come in.'

Lucy entered the room, and sat down beside me in silence. Her eyes were red with incessant weeping, and this was the first occasion since the death of Beaumont that we had been alone together. 'Uncle sent me out of the parlour,' she said; 'a stranger has called upon him on particular business. Will you permit me to sit with you? I cannot bear to be alone now!' and she wept silently.

We talked long and earnestly together, recalling the virtues and estimable qualities of the ill-fated boy; and I, who by this time had learnt my lesson of duplicity, bore my part in the conversation so adroitly as to strengthen the more favourable opinion that Lucy had recently adopted concerning me, in consequence of my constant attendance beside my departed friend.

When we at length descended to the parlour, we found my father musing in a melancholy posture beside the fire. 'My children,' he said, 'the ways of the Almighty are inscrutable, and seldom, indeed, does He permit murder to go unpunished in this world.' – What could he mean? I started, and turned deadly pale. – 'A person has been with me,' he continued, 'who informs me that an individual has been taken up on suspicion of having committed the murder.'

With a loud cry I fell upon my knees. Gracious God! I had never anticipated such a possibility as this. I had been too anxious to screen myself from suspicion to leave room in my mind for a supposition of this nature to enter there, even for a moment. They lifted me into a chair, and my father rebuked me for giving way to useless and irreligious grief, to an excess of which he ascribed the state of nervous excitement and weakness under which I was suffering; and I was presently carried to bed, with a strong tendency to fever, which I knew, if it mounted into delirium, would inevitably cause me to commit myself irrecoverably. But I subdued this by a strong effort of nature – which, upon great occasions, she is permitted to make – and strove desperately to conquer the thick-coming fancies[402] that ever and anon threatened to drive me into madness.

I felt that I had borne enough, and that it was high time to make to myself such consolation and comfort as my presence of mind and studious devices might contrive for me. It was by no means sure that this poor fellow, thus taken up on suspicion, would be committed. There *could* be no positive evidence against him, – I knew *that* well; and what if he were condemned? – it was no concern of mine. Oh, no! I could not bring myself to that. But I hoped the best.

I was right: the man was discharged in default of sufficient evidence; but, unfortunately, with that stigma attached to him, which mankind has mercifully consented to fix upon those who disappoint them by being acquitted or discharged just at the time when they are eager for justice in the form of an exhibition.

I opened my desk, and took out the £20 note. 'This is the price of blood,' said I, bitterly, 'and can never be of service to me in this world.' I walked over to B—, and with some difficulty traced Williams, who had just been discharged, to a small public house in one of the bye-streets of the town. I found him sitting alone in an obscure taproom, smoking a dry pipe, and apparently much depressed in spirits. Such men as Williams well know the consequences of acquittals like these; and being an idle and dissolute fellow, was aware that his character would go against him in the minds of those who take upon themselves the trouble of judging their fellow-creatures out of evidence supplied by their own assiduous conjectures.

'Well, Williams,' said I, addressing myself kindly to the man, whom I shook by the hand, 'I am very glad to hear you are cleared of the charge against you.'

'Ah! master James, is it you?' cried the poor fellow, brushing a tear from his eye; 'wasn't it too bad, now, to take me up on suspicion of murdering master Frank. God bless him, I wouldn't have touched a hair of his head for worlds!' And here the man spoke the truth; for of whatever other faults he might be guilty, he was not cruel or vindictive, but was known to be one of the most harmless and good-natured creatures breathing. I comforted the man, therefore, by expressing my entire conviction of his innocence; and, in conclusion, pressed the £20 note upon him, as some slight recompense for the inevitable loss of character under which he must suffer for the future.

Williams was much affected by my seeming generosity, and wrung both my hands with his hard fists with grateful vehemence. 'Well but, my young master,' he said after a pause, 'this large sum of money – ' he appeared to imply a doubt of the policy of accepting it. I accordingly told him the manner in which I had come by it, and assured him that I thought the most legitimate use of the money was to recompense an innocent man who had been in danger of suffering wrongfully. I made him believe, likewise, that I should inform the father of Beaumont of what I had done, but begged him particularly to keep the whole matter a profound secret.

'And where do you mean to go, Williams?' I asked, when I had finished this arrangement, and the man at length accepted the money; 'you will leave this neighbourhood of course?'

'Yes, master James, I shall go up to London, and see what can be done there. One of these days I shall return, when the murder is discovered, – as it will be, no fear of that. I saw the fellow.'

'Saw the fellow!' I gasped, 'what do you mean?' And now Williams related the substance of the evidence he had given on his examination by the magistrate, which I had not before heard. It appeared that he had been sleeping under a hedge on the other side of the field which I had been compelled to cross before I could get into the high road; and being awaked by a noise, he raised his head, and saw some person returning across the field, who, having cleared the ditch, was lost from view in our orchard, where, as Williams conjectured, he must have hidden himself till morning, there being no practicable egress from thence at any other point.

I appeared to listen attentively to this recital. 'What kind of man was this?' I ventured to ask.

'A short thin man,' answered Williams; 'let me see, about your height and build. Why, Lord bless me! – but no, that can't be, neither. You were not out that night, were you, master James?'

'No, no! – out? – how could I be out?' cried I, hurriedly; for had I not spoken thus I should have fallen to the ground: but I turned away my head, under pretence of ordering something to drink, and with a superhuman effort enforced apparent calmness upon myself.

When I looked again at Williams, his eyes were turned upon the ground, as though in thought; and when he lifted them, methought there was an expression I had never seen before.

'Come, drink,' said I, handing him some ale, 'and I wish you a prosperous career in London.' He shook himself out of his reverie, and took the pot in his hand. 'Well, well, when I *do* return to the village;' – he sighed, and drank a long draught of ale.

'When you *do* return, Williams, you must call upon me first. You shall never want while I can do anything for you.'

'Thank you, thank you, my young master,' answered Williams; but again he mused. 'Master James,' said he, scratching his head, 'depend on't the villain will be discovered at last.' He fixed his eyes casually upon me. I could not bear that gaze, but coloured violently, and my hand shook as I grasped him by the arm – 'Talk of it no more,' said I; 'it agitates me to hear it referred to.'

Williams was no expert reader of the human mind, as indicated in the countenance; or he appeared not to notice my confusion; but, starting up, protested
that he would proceed to London forthwith, where he had no doubt of being
able to obtain work, long before his present supply was exhausted. I warmly
encouraged this notion, and stuck close to him till I saw him fairly planted on
the outside of a London coach.[403]

Once more, then, I was comparatively safe and secure from all punishment,
except that of my own conscience. It was not likely that Williams would ever
return from a place like London, where he would find not only more incitement
to industry, were he so disposed, but likewise more impunity or toleration for
idleness, to which he was more particularly devoted. I returned home, therefore,
and endeavoured to make my mind easy, and to renew my old pursuits, – in
vain. I was perpetually haunted by the remembrance of a crime which, far from
serving the purpose for which I had committed it, embittered every moment
of my existence. There was Lucy, it was true, her at least I could secure; and, as
time passed away, I improved every opportunity of re-establishing myself in her
affection. But oh! in all other respects, what a wretched barter I had made of
comparative happiness for misery that no time, no repentance, could mitigate
or assuage! From a moody but high-spirited boy, I changed into a poor weak
pigeon-livered[404] man, not susceptible of insult or offence. I never slept an hour's
refreshing or undisturbed repose afterwards; and when I awoke in the morning,
the light was hateful to my eyes. I became weary of the world, and combated
strongly every proposal of my father to send me to college, in order to qualify
me for the Church; – a destination for which he had, since my infancy, designed
me.

Four years had elapsed, and it now became indispensably necessary that I
should decide upon my future trade or profession. It was placed before me in
such a light that I could no longer refuse to make my choice. And now this difficulty presented itself to me. I hated the neighbourhood; everything around me
too forcibly reminded me of that one action in my life which required no outward aid to be constantly present within my soul; – and yet I dared not to leave
the place. Something whispered to me, – it might be conscience, or, perhaps, it
was weakness, – that while I tarried in the vicinity of the spot I should remain
undiscovered; but that if I ventured to abandon it, I should be certainly and
instantly identified as the murderer of Beaumont. I must, therefore, constantly
reside in the neighbourhood, in order that I might be warned in time, by the
coming to light of any unforeseen circumstance, of my danger.

After many consultations with my father, it was at length agreed that I
should relinquish those professional pursuits for which my education had more
especially fitted me; and take a small farm contiguous to the parsonage, which
was now to be had on very advantageous terms; and that I should settle down

into a plain country farmer on a small scale. This was the more readily met by my father, that the medical man of the place was of opinion that my health would not permit the confinement of a sedentary and studious profession; and that nothing but active exercise and occupation would conquer an infirmity which he conceived, – and rightly, – could only have been caused by some inward anxiety operating and weighing heavily on the mind.

I entered, accordingly, upon my business as a farmer, and shortly obtained the consent of Lucy to our marriage; an event of all others most consonant with my father's wishes, and a cause of no ordinary comfort to myself. I hoped, if never again to be happy, at least to lead a peaceful and tranquil life, and inwardly resolved that the future course of my existence should, if possible, make some amends for my crime.

On the night preceding my marriage I had a dream – a dream that had visited me many, oh! how many times before, in which every horrible circumstance of the murder was acted over again. I awoke feverish and unrefreshed, and with that nervous sinking of the heart, which sometimes stayed with me for months, and then partially left me till some cause – or no cause – recalled it to its victim. At these periods my existence became intolerable to me; every thing around me assumed a new aspect of horror – every step alarmed me – every glance covered me with confusion. Was there the slightest household duty to be performed, it became burdensome and oppressive to me: the diurnal customs of courtesy were converted into serious ordeals which must be gone through; and I was utterly unable to sustain a conversation with even the most intimate relation or friend. This weakness at times so entirely overcame me, that I dreaded the sight of all acquaintance. If it were indispensable that I should meet them on business, I studiously compressed beforehand the speech that I should be compelled to utter, lest their eyes should have time to rest upon me. In a word, I dreaded the eyes of men, and was weary, – sick to death, – of the world and of myself.

On this particular and eventful morning, I found that my old infirmity had returned, and that now, when it was of such vital importance that I should put a good face upon the matter, I was suddenly deprived of all moral energy and strength. I was unable to descend into the breakfast parlour to encounter the gaze of my friends, and to meet with corresponding gaiety their innocent and good-natured raillery, or to respond to their affectionate congratulations. The perspiration stood upon my brow. I decided to feign myself sick, in order that my agitation and distress might be referred to that, and be supposed to *precede* my appearance before my friends; in other words, that it might not be imagined that *they* were the cause of my indisposition. I did so; and in a short time had so regained my composure, as to wonder at my absurd dread of encountering the company that was met upon this occasion to do honour to my approaching nuptials, and to sympathise in my prospective happiness. Lucy was, as usual, calm and apparently happy. I know not whether the occasion had called forth a more vivid remembrance of that one whom she had formerly loved; but if so, she did not exhibit any uncommon depression of spirits; and I am well contented to believe, that when she consented to take me for a husband, she had either out-grown her love for Beaumont, or looked upon it as a girlish liking, which, had he lived, she would have been constrained to stifle and to overcome; or, perhaps, I had succeeded in reviving the sentiment – of affection let me call it – which she had in the first instance encouraged for me.

We proceeded to the church, the avenues to which were crowded by the vil-lagers, anxious to testify their joy at an union between two persons who had become the general favourites of the place: and as my father led the way, – for he was to perform the ceremony, – many a blessing and good wish reached my ear, that fell like a curse upon my soul. At this particular juncture, the main cause of my hatred of Beaumont, and of my accomplished vengeance, came before my mind, which, since that fatal night, had never till now presented itself to me, namely, the fear lest he, and not I, should one day lead Lucy Cowley to the altar. Oh! what a triumph was mine! I had won the day, it is true, but what had I lost?

Where were we now standing? within a few paces of the altar; and the ques-tion I had proposed to myself was answered from below. Beaumont lay beneath that stone, and the echoes of my footstep were even now vibrating through the ashes of the murdered boy. Oh heaven! as we knelt before the altar, my feet were resting on that gravestone; and as my father proceeded with the service, and I looked up to make the responses, my eyes fell upon the Ten Commandments, – nor had I power to avert them. As I gazed, were my eyes dazzled? Was it strong imagination? No, no, there was the terrible sixth commandment, 'Thou shalt do no murder.'[405] A vivid and close fire burnt along each letter of each word, and gradually brought the divine prohibition before me, so that I might have touched it with my hand. It was no human power that supported me till the conclusion of the ceremony, when with a heavy groan I fell back senseless.

They restored me, at length, and I found myself surrounded by solicitous friends concerned for my sudden indisposition. Oh! they knew not my inward suffering – they guessed not the dreadful secret that I had kept so well. So well? – bitter, bitter mockery! I attempted to rise, but something held me back: I looked down; I had been lying on the grave of Beaumont. Was it an angel of heaven that whispered to me at that moment in mercy to my wretchedness? I bowed my head, and breathed a prayer – a short prayer to my poor friend; and I knew that from that hour forgiveness would be extended to me, and that he would inter-cede for me, and that I should at length find pardon from above.

I arose calmer, and with a lighter spirit than I had known for years, and vowed that for his sake I would cherish the young creature by my side, and make her as happy as a sinful wretch like myself could presume to be enabled to do; and I kept my vow: did I not? thou knowest, who art now in heaven.

How should my friends divine the cause of my illness? It was impossible that they should do so; – or Lucy, or my father, – and yet they must have thought it strange. Mysterious Providence! how long didst thou preserve me from infamy – how long didst thou permit me to carry this dead secret putrefying in my bosom. But true it is, no momentary suspicion entered their minds that could, although followed up with the most untiring perseverance, have led them to the horrible conclusion that *I* had murdered Beaumont!

'Poor Beaumont!' sighed my father, as we prepared to leave the church. He had been musing over the short and simple inscription. Lucy sighed also, and her hand was pressed against my arm involuntarily. Poor Beaumont! I repeated to myself; happy – happy – thrice happy – lamented with sincerity – mourned by the wise and good, and dying ere sin or sorrow could mar or obscure that noble heart! Could I have exchanged my fate with his; but no, I wished not that; had I but died, and were he living to enjoy the happiness which he might have deserved, and which I could never hope to attain in this world! But let me draw my narrative to a close; for the night wears apace, and my strength is almost spent.

For seven years all went prosperously with me that Fortune had power to direct: my Lucy brought me three children, and my father still lived to renew his youth in their innocent smiles. During this period my mind had gradually worked itself into something like comparative tranquillity; and although I cannot say that I ever enjoyed a moment of positive happiness, yet peace was not denied me, and hours of unembittered repose sometimes visited my pillow, and permitted me to make my peace with God, and to hope for mercy in the last dreadful hour.

At times, however – but more particularly in the season of the year when my crime was committed – on the anniversary of the bitter day – and on evenings, which by some strange association of the mind, worked through the senses into the heart of memory, and recalled the place, the hour, the atmosphere, the heavens, on that fatal night, – upon these occasions, I was again the victim of remorse, and my conscience arose before me in all its original terrors, and wreaked itself upon me with undiminished fury.

An event was now about to happen that threatened to renew my term of misery – my father was dying. As I knelt by his bedside, and received his blessing, I would have wept, but could not; these griefs – these common afflictions to which all men are called upon to submit themselves; these natural bereavements had no power to excite grief within me, – my heart was dead to these minor exactions of sorrow.

'My dear son,' said my father, with difficulty, 'I am about to die, and it is my great consolation to know, that I leave one behind who through life has shown himself so worthy of my affection.' He pressed my hand fervently. 'You have never, James, caused me a moment's unhappiness, and the Almighty will reward you for it. We shall meet, my son, in another world.'

I started and dropped his hand. A dreadful thought darted through my brain; yes, he must at length know my crime, and look down upon me from the other world with awful pity, or with sorrowful reproach. My head sank upon the pillow, and I groaned in agony of spirit.

'Calm this agitation, my boy,' exclaimed my father, moved by my situation; 'it is sinful – let us submit to the decrees of the Almighty.'

'Oh! I have a weight upon my mind which has tortured me for years,' I cried passionately. 'I can bear it no longer. Oh! my father, forgive me, – for I am a wretched man.' I paused, for my father had half raised himself in his bed, and bent towards me eagerly.

But no: should I embitter his last moments? Could I endure his curse? Could I meet his eye in heaven on the day of judgment? No, no, no. I struggled with my feelings, and conquered them; and as I raised my head from the pillow, I said with something like calmness, 'I am better now – I was foolish, and knew not what I said.'

My father sank back exhausted. 'Oh, James!' he cried, 'tell me what preys upon you; let me offer my prayers for your peace of mind when I am gone; surely, the foolish quarrel you had with poor Beaumont, on the day preceding his mysterious murder, – this cannot have – '

He stopped; for I had grasped his shoulder with the violence of a madman. 'Who told you,' I cried with a shriek, 'that I had quarrelled with Beaumont on that day?' and my eyes were fixed wildly upon him.

'Mrs. Goodman overheard you, and informed me many years ago of it, but I never mentioned it to you, lest I should hurt your feelings; such things should be forgotten.'

There must have been some horrible meaning in my face at that moment, for my father, when he opened his eyes, – for he had closed them as though in the act of recalling some indistinct memory to his mind, – started convulsively.

'Almighty God!' he cried, and clasped his hands, 'Sure nothing worse – James – James, in mercy tell me; you did not – murder – . Ha! – '

With a loud cry that would never depart from my brain were I to live an eternity, the old man sprang with a galvanic motion from the bed, and seized me by the wrists with his long and withered fingers. His lips moved, but he spoke not – he could not speak; and his white hairs seemed to stir with life upon his head. Oh! those eyes that were fixed upon me as he held me; but his grasp relaxed; he fell upon his knees and face with a broken groan. What a groan was that! I raised

The Death of Wilson's Father.

him – no, not *him* – I raised the body – for my father was no more; and lifting it into bed, rang the bell with violence for the nurse.

Mrs. Goodman rushed into the room. 'Oh! what a sight is here,' she exclaimed, wringing her hands. 'Oh! James, how did my poor dear master die?'

I muttered a hasty explanation and approached. The eyes were still open, and the face was convulsed into hideous deformity. Yes, he had died in a fit; it was a probable explanation; but it passed for want of a better. From that hour I knew my fate was at hand.

For a week after the funeral of my father, I locked myself in my own room, and brooded on the several occurrences of my life both before and subsequent to that one act which had destroyed my peace for ever. What steps should I now take? I could endure this life no longer. Shame, infamy, an ignominious death on the one hand; on the other, intolerable torture, worse than death. But what was to become of my family? These were the ties that withheld me from myself. I could not commit suicide – I could not expiate my offence by a public confession; and yet I knew not how I could drag on an existence that my strength would no longer support without, perhaps, the destruction of my reason.

While I pondered darkly upon these matters, it was intimated to me one morning, that a stranger wished particularly to see me, and had positively refused to depart without having first been permitted an interview. When I entered the room, the face of this person was averted from me, – he was looking out of the window. He turned suddenly upon hearing my footstep: it was Williams. I knew him instantly. I had been thinking of him five minutes before. It was strange – no – it was fate.

I motioned to him to take a seat, which he did, remaining silent for a few moments, and pressing the brim of his hat, as he turned it between his hands, with the perplexed look of a man who has something of moment to speak, and yet hardly knows how to put it into fitting words.

'You hardly remember me, Mr. Wilson?' at length he inquired.

'I do – you are Williams.'

'Well, sir,' he said, 'I am come to see you again;' he paused, and appeared confused, 'shall I make a short story of it – I want fifty pounds.'

My heart sank within me; yes, he suspected me; he had me in his power – he would give me up to justice. Oh! had I decided at that moment, – but I could not; had I confessed at once, – but it would have been extorted; and the only consolation which I had proposed to myself, would have been denied me – the sympathy, perhaps, that might be excited by my voluntary confession, in the hearts of those who knew me.

In a word, – for I dare not recount this degrading scene, – I made terms with Williams, who had been instigated to this experiment by some acute friend, to whom he had told the circumstance of my having sought him out and relieved him; and binding him by a solemn oath never to mention a syllable of what had passed between us, I gave him the sum he required, and suffered him to depart.

When he was well gone, I bethought me of my rashness in acceding to this request. What evidence had Williams to offer that could convict me? Could the evidence of a man after a lapse of so many years be entertained for a moment; of a man, too, who had not brought forward a syllable of a like import on his first examination? Would it not be viewed as a conspiracy to extort money? Undoubtedly. Ah! no, I felt that I could never have sustained myself during the investigation – that I must inevitably have committed myself; and I knew not till now how fatally strong the love of life works in us to the last; even to the very last on this side madness.

Let me well remember and recal my feelings on that day; a presentiment – a conscience informed me as I descended the stairs, that the stranger waiting to see me was Williams. I knew it: when he was gone, a dark cloud still lingered loweringly over my head; it was something in which Williams was to have no part.

That evening was a fine midsummer evening, and my children had been playing in the fields. They returned, as usual, to their supper. The little creatures were congregated in a corner, talking earnestly of something which they had found in a field on their return home. I chanced to look up, and not curious to know about what they were engaged, but to divert my thoughts, I requested to see their prize.

The eldest boy came forward. 'Father,' said he, 'we found this strange knife in the hedge of the orchard field; only look how rusty the blade is – it seems like blood.'

Merciful God! I knew it before I saw it: it was *the* knife – the very knife with which – My mass of blood was turned as I gazed upon it. 'Go, go,' said I, faintly, to the terrified children, – for they saw my frightful change; 'go to your mother in the kitchen.' They obeyed, and left me.

Yes, it was the very knife. I took it into my hand; that hand had grown since then, – but it fitted my grasp well. I remembered how it felt when I made the fatal plunge. Again I wielded it, and stabbed the air: oh yes! there it was, and then – My brain whirled round, and I clasped my head with my hands. I was going mad – no, not yet. My wife entered the room at this instant.

'My dear James, what is the matter?' she inquired; 'surely I heard you talking to yourself; what have you got in your hand?'

'Nothing, nothing,' I answered listlessly. 'Lucy, send the children to bed. No, take them yourself. I wish it, – instantly.'

'What, before they have had their supper?'

I waved my hand – 'Now, – now; I wish it, I wish it.'

She answered nothing; but retired, and left me once more to myself.

Wilson s Children finding the Knife.

'God of Justice!' I exclaimed, 'how long wilt thou persecute me? Have I not borne enough? Lord! look down upon me, for I am a miserable, miserable wretch, and cannot –' My brain began to wander. I heard my wife's step upon the stairs, and my children, as they went to bed. 'Hush! hush!' I heard her whisper, 'tread softly; your poor father is very ill.' My heart was melted, but I did not weep. How came that thought into my brain? – I know not, but I encouraged it. 'Yes, she is the wife of my bosom, and shall know all. I can bear this hideous secret no longer. She shall pray for me, and from her at least I shall receive consolation.'

'How do you feel yourself now?' said Lucy, as she entered the room; 'you have kept yourself too close since your father's death. Such immoderate grief is wicked.'

'No, it is not that – not *that*,' said I, shaking my head. 'Lucy, get me a bottle of wine; a glass or two will revive me.'

I swallowed two tumblers of wine – for my throat was parched, – while my wife sat in silence, gazing at me. She saw, doubtless, that something extraordinary had occurred to agitate me, and held her peace, awaiting an opportunity, when I should be more calm, to reason with my weakness.

'Take your eyes from off me,' I murmured, with a motion of my hand; 'I cannot bear them!' But my mind was now made up. At all hazards I would impart this thing to her: it would take an intolerable weight from my mind. Alas! I thought not at the time that I might transfer it to her's.[406]

I arose and approached her, and took a seat by her side on the same chair. 'Lucy,' I said, dejectedly, and my arm enfolded her waist, 'what is to become of me? – advise me, I implore you: oh! do not hate me – do not despise me: you know not what I have suffered – you never can know; but this I entreat – do not abandon me!' and my head sank upon her shoulder.

'Why should I hate or abandon you?' she answered quietly. 'Sure, never woman had a better or a kinder husband than I have been blessed with. Do not talk so; you are ill, and nervous, and excited; you have harassed yourself too much of late, but a little time will restore you.'

'Never, never, Lucy. Oh! I have something to tell you; promise me that you will not go mad when I whisper it; promise me – : but first, fall upon your knees and pray for me – for *my* prayers are no longer heard.'

She turned pale and trembled, and clasped her hands. 'Oh, James! what have you done? Tell me all.' Again she gazed upon me. I averted my head, and motioned to her with my hand. She obeyed me and fell upon her knees. 'What am I to do?' she cried, clasping my arm.

'Pray for me – one short prayer of yours will draw my soul out of hell, where it has lain these ten years.' I walked to the table and swallowed another tumbler of wine. The knife was lying there. I took it and brought it to her. 'Do you see this knife?' I inquired. 'Look at it, – look at it well.' She did so.

'I see nothing remarkable in the knife – the children found it – the blade is rusty. Oh, mercy! it is blood.'

'Yes, it *is* blood,' I answered, and dropped upon my knees beside her. 'With that knife I – '

'Gracious God! – James Wilson!' She gasped with horror, but had not guessed my victim.

It must be told. My mouth was at her ear, and I whispered distinctly, – 'With that knife I murdered Francis Beaumont!'

For three hours I hung over my senseless wife, chafing her temples, and attempting to restore her, but in vain. The church clock struck twelve; – could it be so late? – and I took her gently in my arms and carried her to bed. What now should I do? Yes, I would make a fire in the room and prepare something for her. I was proceeding to the door to descend for fuel when a loud shriek alarmed me. My wife was coming to herself. I flew towards her, and raised her head slightly. She knew me not for some time, but moaned piteously, and swayed her head to and fro, as though in delirium; but presently her eyes opened; she saw me – she knew me. Then, indeed, I felt that she *did* know me; for what an expression was there! Was it hate, or fear, or loathing? It was not pity or forgiveness. She pushed me away from her and turned away from me with a shudder that convulsed her frame. I dared not approach her again, but slunk down stairs guilty and confounded.

How I passed that night I know not; for my mind was vacant, and was discharged of all memory or feeling. It was morning when I awoke – if asleep I had been – and again I visited my chamber. I would have got into bed, for I was cold and benumbed, but Lucy shrank from me loathingly.

'Oh! for mercy's sake, do not forsake me!' I exclaimed, and clasped my hands in anguish. 'Do not *you*, of all the world, reject me; think of my wretchedness, – my torture, – and pity me, for I have need of pity. Speak to me, one word will comfort me, and save me from myself.'

She spoke not to me. Again and again I implored her; and for three days I knelt at her bedside and would have tended her like a slave, but she would take nothing from my hand. She had abandoned me, and now I had not a friend in the world. She might, perhaps, betray me – there was the wild fear that lost me!

I went down stairs at night, and the old power revisited me, which once before had prevailed over my soul. I knew that power again and encouraged it. What! had I not expiated my crime by years of horrible anguish, and fear, and despair? but must I commence anew another lease of torture, – of worse torture, – for my wife had deserted me, and the grave would refuse to receive me? My brain swam in wine, and my blood bounded madly through my veins; and once more the devil had me in his hand, and did with me as he pleased.

I was stirring early and made some strong tea. From my pocket I drew a small phial, which I had borne about me for years, lest it should be required in a case of sudden emergency, – and I poured the contents into one of the cups, which I took up stairs where my wife lay.

She would have rejected it as usual; but I was not so to be put off. 'In the name of heaven I command you to take this from my hand; it is something that will do you good; nay, you may hate and despise – but you shall this once obey me.'

She quailed beneath my glance, and took the cup; I stood before her and saw her drink the contents, – calmly I saw it, nor felt a wish to stay her hand.

'How do you feel? – speak to me – it may be the last time you will ever speak to me.'

'I feel better, I think,' she said languidly.

'Yes, yes, it will do you good, much good – ha! ha! ha!' and I laughed loud and long. That unwonted voice recalled me for a moment to myself; it seemed an echo of the past, for I had not laughed for years; and I rushed from the room, I knew not whither.

When I came to my senses, I found myself sitting on the floor of an upper room, with the knife in my hand, – that knife which heaven had returned to me by the hands of my own children! – I thanked not heaven for that; but muttered something, I know not what, as I turned it over, and examined it again and again.

A noise at the door startled me, and I looked in that direction. My youngest child – my Lucy, was standing just within the room, with her clear blue eyes fixed upon me, and her little hands at her mouth, as though she hesitated to approach me.

I beckoned to her with my finger, and nodded my head; 'Come here,' said I, 'I will not hurt you,' and I threw the knife from me.

The little thing moved a few short steps towards me, and said, in the earnest tone of a child, 'Oh, father, poor mother is so ill; do come to her,' and she approached and pulled me by the sleeve; for I had sunk into a dreadful stupor.

I looked up, and met the eyes of my poor child. 'Oh! thou little wretch!' I cried, with fond bitterness, folding her in my arms, and pressing her to my heart, 'what is to become of you?' The child screamed; she was frightened by my ghastly face, and pressed her hand against my forehead to loosen herself from my arms. I let her go, and she ran away to her brothers.

I followed down stairs, and entered the room where my wife was dying. As I approached the bed she saw me, and, I think, extended her hand towards me. With earnest eyes I perused those features which now wore death upon them with a hue not to be mistaken. Could I discern pity or forgiveness in that face? Yes; and she spoke to me of pardon and mercy both for herself and me. Oh! had these words come earlier; had she taken my bruised heart and bound up the wounds, which had been open so long, it might have been otherwise; but no, 'tis better as it is. We never could have been happy again, and she at least is happy now.

Why should I detail more? She died on that evening, and I fled, I know not where or for what purpose. I would have escaped from myself, not from the hands of justice, for life surely could have no charms for me.

I was found in a barn by one of my own men on the following morning, and my trial will have told the world the rest. Of those who read my story, how few, perhaps, will pity, how many will condemn me. Alas! it is not given to man to see the heart of man. From God, at least, I tremblingly hope for mercy and forgiveness, – and I die at peace with all men.

'Only think o' that, now,' cried my uncle, shaking out the ashes of his pipe, when I had concluded the perusal of the document; 'why, I mean to observe, a individual of that natur is worse nor a wild hannimal; but, oh! I say, Jack, blow me,' and he looked at me with an earnest and important face, ''pend on't, Jack, that 'ere piece of writing is o' walley;[407] 'pend on't, this 'ere confession of this 'ere chap is o' walley.' Saying which, he folded it up carefully, and put it away amongst his most precious treasures of that description.

As it now began to wax late, I took leave of the old gentleman and returned home, a little uneasy at the news of which I was the bearer; and for once in my life studied the best means of conveying a piece of disagreeable intelligence without hurting the feelings of the party to whom it was to be conveyed, more than was absolutely necessary.

CHAPTER XV.

IT came across my mind, at the moment that my hand was upon the door-latch of the house in which I resided, that my long absence from home must be a source of much perplexity to Catharine; more especially that the errand upon which I had voluntarily gone, by no means offered any satisfactory explanation of my prolonged stay.

Whether it might be that the confession I had been reading to my uncle oppressed my spirits, and rendered me more alive than usual to melancholy and foreboding impressions; or that the nature of the tidings I had to communicate to my wife was of itself sufficient to depress me, I cannot determine; but certain it is, that when I entered my own room, and beheld her waiting anxiously my arrival, I felt an inward sinking of the heart, and an ebbing of the vital energies which I never before remembered to have experienced.

But, since an unpleasant business cannot be despatched too soon, I made short work of the matter, and satisfied my wife's hasty inquiries respecting the child, by plainly informing her, in few words, of the disappearance of the nurse, and of the ill-success of my endeavours (for I did not care to make known that I had been spending the evening with my uncle) to discover, or even to trace, the whereabout of that extraordinary individual.

Catharine listened attentively to this statement, looking up in my face, and pressing her open and wasted palms upon her bosom. There was a pause of some minutes: – at length, she shook herself with a shudder, as though some sudden remembrance awakened her, and passed one hand over her forehead. 'And so I must never see my child again,' she murmured, with a sickly smile; 'I thought I should have been permitted to see him once before I die.'

'All will be well, I tell you; and you shall see him; I can easily discover the old cat, if she's above ground; be calm, – compose yourself,' for I became alarmed.

'Oh, no, no, no,' she exclaimed vehemently, 'I shall never set these eyes upon him in this world. Oh! John, why did you not let me go to Walworth a month before? I had a presentiment that all was not right; it was cruel of you, – it was, indeed.'

She saw my brow darken, and was silent for a moment.

'You don't know a mother's feelings; indeed you don't,' she continued, more calmly, 'nor what I have suffered here,' pressing her hand upon her heart; 'it is here that I feel it, John.'

'Do you feel pain?' said I; 'what ails you?'

'I don't know; but I do feel pain. I fear, John, I am dying.' I was startled at this; for the emaciated creature before me was too plain an evidence of its truth.

'Come, come,' said I, 'be of good heart, girl, you will be better to-morrow morning; I'll find the child in a day or two; make your mind easy upon that point; and now let us to bed.'

All night long I was troubled with feverish and strange dreams. The circumstances related in the confession of Wilson mixed themselves up with my own immediate affairs; and often, during the night, when some throe of horror or surprise startled me into consciousness, I heard my wife murmuring to herself the name of her child, and repeating the little endearing names by which she had been accustomed to call it; or moaning, with heart-piercing lamentations, the fate to which the phantasy of delirium appeared for the moment to have consigned it. But towards morning I fell into a sound sleep, out of which I was awakened by Catharine, who had arisen, it seemed, some hours before, and who now came to call me to my breakfast.

When I entered the sitting-room, I discovered Mrs. Chadwick officiating at the breakfast-table, apparently endeavouring to persuade my wife to return to her bed; interlarding her discourse, however, with certain dubiously complimentary reflections upon me, which, of course, I had not come too late to overhear.

As I sat down, I could not but remark the extraordinary change that had taken place in Catharine during the night. She appeared, to use a common expressive saying, to be 'struck with death,' and every movement indicated, with a meaning not to be mistaken, that to this world she was about to bid an eternal farewell. I started, but said nothing, and swallowed my breakfast as quickly as possible, intending to proceed in search of the child, as I had promised.

'I'll tell you what it is, young fellow,' said Mrs. Chadwick, suddenly turning her head towards me, as she was holding a round of toast to the fire, 'unless you wish to see this young woman die before your eyes, you will go for a doctor when you have finished your breakfast. Don't you see her peaking and pining in the chimney-corner, scarce able to sit on her chair, – and all your handiworks? you know it is.'

'Silence, you old beast,' retorted I, 'what's the matter with the girl? Why doesn't she speak? How am I to know, else, whether she's ill or well?'

'Speak!' answered the woman, contemptuously, 'a wink's as good as a nod to a blind horse, and neither of much use. You want one like me to speak to you; the poor girl hasn't half the devil in her that her mother had, – have you, girl?'

– here she replaced the toasting-fork and approached the table, – 'Ketch,' she continued, in a more quiet tone, 'go for Drench,[408] the doctor, hard by.'

'No, no, not for me,' interrupted Catharine, 'I had rather not, indeed I would.'

'Nonsense, you foolish woman,' cried the other, 'now, do go, Ketch,' she added in a whisper, 'that's a good fellow, it may be the means of saving her life.'

'Well, I'll go, mother,' said I, somewhat appeased, 'but you know what a hand Drench is at throwing in the physic;' and, to say the truth, this recollection of Drench's doings would have qualified not a little the readiness with which I was about to apply to him, only that I, at the same time, recollected a consolatory circumstance, namely, that I never intended to pay him; and, moreover, that phials could be sold by the gross; so that, after all, in this amended view of the matter, I was, in all probability, to be a gainer by the employment of Drench.

Looking at the thing in this light, I could find no reasonable excuse, even to myself, for delaying any longer to call in the aid of that medical practitioner; and proceeded, accordingly, to his shop, where I stated the case to Mr. Drench, in person, who, casting up an eye, as though in that orb consisted the organ of memory, began to take in mental review the list of his immediate jobs, or rather Jobs,[409] – for by that name the patients of Drench might appropriately be termed. At the expiration of this process, he recalled his eye and put it again into its socket, and at length solemnly assured me (for in no other manner was an assurance to be expected from him, were it of the most agreeable import) that he would wait upon my wife in the course of two hours at farthest.

In the meantime, I deemed it expedient and consistent to call upon Wisp, for the purpose of informing him of his sister's serious illness. Wisp had latterly amended his life, and improved his secular position, by obtaining a situation at a wharf in Lower Thames-street, where, empannelled in a small box, it was his duty to take down the weights of all goods landed at that particular spot; in return for which *weighty* duties, as he, in servile imitation of his friend Gibbon, was pleased to call them, he received a weekly sum, not sufficiently ample for splendour, but predominant over bread and cheese.

To this eastern locality I hastened my steps, and proceeding along, unwittingly found myself in Friday-street, the scene of an adventure, which, to all parties concerned, had turned out so unprosperously. As I passed Marley's door, a sigh escaped me in spite of myself, when I reflected that I had omitted to perform my promise to Haynes on his death-bed; and when I thought of that poor wretch, mouldering in his grave, I could almost have shed a tear over his memory. But my nerves were at that moment unstrung, and human weakness will sometimes overtake the best, – and occasionally the worst of us, – let human wisdom never so manfully strive to resist it.

'Ha! old stick-in-the-mud, what brings you here?' exclaimed Wisp, as I opened the upper half of the door, and looked into the box, wherein his business compelled him to ensconce himself.

I explained in few words the occasion of my visit; and requested him, in case of an accident, to call upon us shortly; for that his sister had expressed a wish to see him once more, before she died; although I had no fear of an immediate calamity of that nature.

Wisp's face underwent a rapid change at this recital, and he leaned his head upon his hands, and presently I saw the tears trickling through his fingers. 'Leave me for a moment,' said he, 'I don't wish you to see me cry like a child; but no. I say, Jack, I can bear anything, d— me, my heart's like this inkstand, hard, and full of black filth; – anything but this. Upon my soul, if anything happens to that girl I don't know what I shall do. Now, – now I remember what my mother said to me on her deathbed; how she implored me to take care of poor Kate – and I've kept my word with a vengeance. How is she? is she dead?'

'Dead! no,' said I, startled not a little by the impetuous manner of my friend, 'she's worth twenty dead ones yet.'

'Ketch,' continued Wisp, 'I fear you've been an infernal rascal to your wife; hav'n't you, now? Make the devil your scapegoat for once, and let him bear your shame; hav'n't you treated her cruelly? hav'n't you beaten her? hav'n't you murdered her?'

'Come, come,' said I, interrupting him coolly, 'Don't rave; don't kick up your heels;' for I was justly incensed at this insolent catechising on the part of a man who would willingly have given his own wife a quietus for a prospective farthing; 'the fact is, Kate is ill, and in low spirits, and wishes to see you.'

'Is that all, eh? sure? – give us your fin,'[410] said Wisp, considerably relieved; 'at all events, I'll look in to-night about seven. The fact is, I'm tied by the leg at this obnoxious receptacle of merchandise. Time and tide wait for no man, they say, and so I'm obliged to wait for them; but be off, Jack; here comes the fat weed that rots on Lethe's wharf'[411] – the governor; hum, good bye.'

As I returned home, I could not but admire the extreme elasticity of my friend's spirits, which enabled him to leap 'from grave to gay, from lively to severe'[412] with equal lightness and despatch; and concluded not unfairly, from the specimen I had just witnessed, that afflictions of whatever nature, would be, by that volatile person, taken to heart, as maniacs are taken to private madhouses,[413] that is to say, not at all.

'Well, sir, you are come at last.' In such language did Drench accost me, as I made my appearance in my room. 'We have been waiting to see you for some time. Now, what is your belief as to the cause of your wife's illness?'

I professed myself (albeit rather astonished at this novel proceeding) entirely unacquainted with the mysteries of medicine, and contented myself, therefore, with giving a meagre outline of the symptoms of her malady, such as general want of appetite, lowness of spirits, constitutional weakness, broken rest, &c.

'Broken fiddlestick!' cried the Doctor; 'I tell you, young man, you're not within a shilling fare[414] of the real cause; broken rest, sir, – broken heart, you mean. I'll tell you what, my friend,' and the Doctor drew me into the passage, 'you may come to me presently for something that I shall make up for her; but you must count upon losing her; she can't live, sir; she can't live; no power on earth can save her.' And with such croakings the Doctor hopped down stairs, like a raven in quest of more congenial carrion.

When he was gone, I retired to the passage window; and, while I picked to pieces a withered shrub, which some former lodger must have left there many years before, I got together my feelings into something like order, and decided upon the course of conduct and behaviour, which, under the circumstances, would be the most decent and appropriate.

I returned into the room, and, with some composure, approached the chair on which my wife was sitting, or rather reclining. Mrs. Chadwick was hanging over her, offering such consolation and advice as women are usually well skilled in dispensing; and I thought I could discover in the faces of both, that Drench had not been much more ceremonious to them, in announcing his opinion of the state of the case, than he had shown himself to me.

'Cheer up, my girl,' I exclaimed, with a painful attempt at gaiety, 'you will be better soon. Come, the Doctor says – '

'Hush!' interrupted Mrs. Chadwick, 'do you know what you are going to say?'

'No, no, let him tell me all,' said Catharine; 'the Doctor says truth. Oh! John, my heart *is* broken, although I never told you before!'

I was about to make some reply to this, but she stopped me, and folded her arms round my neck. 'I could have been,' she murmured, in a stifled tone, 'I could have been a comfort to you, John, and made you happy, if you had let me; but you would'nt. I would have worked for you – slaved for you – by night and by day.'

'You have, my poor girl, you have,' I muttered, for my heart was melting within me.

'Oh, why,' she continued, 'why did you go on as you did? Why did you throw yourself away? With your gifts, what might you not have done? Oh, John! my dear fellow, you have broken my heart!' She shrunk timidly from me, as she said these words, and gazed up into my face, as though she feared that I should strike her; but, no, that memory has been spared me.

'Do not be angry with me,' she resumed, 'for I am very weak and foolish; but, oh! it is a hard thing to die so young, and to leave all I love in this world; and our dear little one, God help it, what will become of my little darling? Oh! mother, tell me, – who will protect it, and take care of it, as I would have done?'

She fell back in her chair and wept bitterly, – such tears as I shall never see again, – for my own eyes were moist; but I turned away ashamed of my manhood.

'Poor thing! poor thing!' sobbed Mrs. Chadwick, 'this was too bad of you, Ketch; but let her alone, those tears will do her good. Come, sweetheart, let me carry you to bed; dear heart, why the child is quite an otomy.'[415]

With observations of this nature did the old woman commune with herself, as she carried my wife through the door that led out of our sitting-room into the bedchamber; and having laid her in the bed, she returned to me.

'Now, Ketch, run for the medicine, will you? She's going to sleep, poor woman – to her last sleep, I fear; she'll never see to-morrow. Goodness, man, how could you have the heart to serve her as you have done? it's your doings; you've killed her, if ever woman was killed by man in this world.'

Yes, Catharine was at length dying. I had looked forward to this event as a release, and I was now about to be requited for my patience and long-suffering; and yet, now that the time was at hand, and my hopes were at projection, I would willingly have recalled my former wish, and felt something that my heart had never recognised before, – of weakness, – of contrition, – and of returning love. And yet, why should I attempt to justify what I can never recal? I have deceived others often enough, but let me not deceive myself; above all, let me abide strictly by the moral consequences of the principle I laid down for my guidance, when I resolved to set pen to paper; let me show both sides of the portrait, although I fear the reader will be puzzled to discover which is the bright side. But this is altogether a matter of taste and of opinion. I shall have some portion of the world, at all events, stirring in my behalf, or their actions belie their feelings mightily.

Acting under the impulse of these better feelings, I hastened to Drench's shop, and requested to see that individual forthwith, purposing to return with him on the instant; but he was gone forth on his daily prowl, and after waiting a considerable time in the forlorn hope that 'the strong rebuff of some tumultuous'[416] patient might, perchance, cause him to hurry back to his shop, I was fain to take the medicines that had been prepared for me, and to put my best leg foremost towards my own dwelling.

Mrs. Chadwick met me on the stairs. 'Ketch' she said, 'it's all of no use; she has had two violent fits since you have been gone, and has been calling upon your name ever since. Will you see her now?'

'I cannot see her yet,' said I, as she took the medicines out of my hand, and was about to enter the bedroom. 'Oh! mother, do keep her calm, that's a good soul; tell her I'm here, and will come to her presently.'

I sat down in a chair, and my heart sank within me. The young creature whom I had once loved, and who had so loved me, through ill-treatment, cruelty, crime, and beggary – without whom I had died of want in the streets; who had never given me a harsh word or a look of unkindness in her life – she was passing away from me, – to leave me for ever, – to damn me with a load of hoarded reproach, which my heart was busy in preparing for me. Every act of cruelty, of meanness, of base and paltry unkindness of which I had been guilty, since my marriage; every endearing word she had ever spoken to me; but, worst of all, that sweet, helpless, timid face, that had so often sought, and sought in vain, to appease my brutal nature; all these came, now that it was all too late to make reparation, like the very retribution of God himself. Bitterly, bitterly did the scalding tears start into my eyes; but it was a mockery – an insult to her whom I had so wronged, and I forced them back again into my bosom. They have never risen since.

At this moment Mrs. Chadwick approached me hastily, her face bathed in tears. 'Go at once to your wife,' she cried, sobbing, 'she's sinking very fast, and wants to see you before she dies. Oh! I cannot bear the sight of the poor thing any longer, indeed I can't,' and covering her face with her apron, she sank into the chair which I had just left.

I entered the room softly, and Catharine, by a mute signal, motioned me to come to her side. I did so, and she made several efforts to speak, but could not articulate a word; but, at length, after I had bent my head towards her lips, she uttered, in a painful whisper, 'I sent for you, John, to see you once more – perhaps you may have something to say to me, – for, John, I am dying. Will you not speak to me?'

I could not speak. Thrice did I strive to move my lips, but I could not speak. She saw my state of mind, for she looked mildly upon me, – but that she had ever done, – and her hand leaned against my cheek. 'Dear John, when I am gone, do not – ' She was silent, and her hand fell upon her bosom.

'Oh! Catharine! oh! my sweet creature, can you forgive me?' Her lips, methought, moved, – but no sound escaped them. Again – and again – but not a word came from her, – and a sudden trembling moved her entire frame, – and all was still.

'Mrs. Chadwick, come here, instantly,' I exclaimed in a voice of terror.

'Hush! hush!' said she, for she was already in the room, and standing at the bedside. She placed her hands between the bedclothes, and felt the feet of the poor creature that lay so still before me. 'Let me come to her,' she whispered, 'it's all over – she is dead.'

'Dead! – it cannot be – it's impossible!' I seized her hand, but it was cold – and looked into her face – alas! it was too true. 'Oh! mother, she is dead – and died without a word of forgiveness!'

'No, no, she forgave you, dear child; and may Heaven forgive you! She told me she had forgiven you.'

I threw myself upon the floor and howled like a wild beast, and beat the ground with my fists – 'Oh, damned, damned, damned villain.'

'Aye, lie there and howl, do, – now you have broken her poor heart,' said Mrs. Chadwick, as she closed the eyes, and bound up the face of the corpse; 'much good that will do – won't it?'

There was a knocking at the outer door: 'Come in.' It was Wisp.

'Why, mother Chadwick, what the deuce is the matter here? Where's Ketch?' He stopped suddenly – the truth had flashed upon him. 'Gracious God! dead!' he exclaimed, and approached the bed, 'and you lying here! Infernal villain! scoundrel! thief! There's not a worm, Mrs. Chadwick, that I would crush so willingly as this,' and he stamped upon me as I lay.

'Aye, I told him what would be the end of his doings,' cried the other, 'but he would not listen to me, and now he feels it. Only come and see her, Mr. Wisp, as she lies now,' she continued, 'pretty creature! pretty creature! what an angel she looks!'

'Angel!' echoed Wisp, 'Oh, yes, she is an angel,' and he went and knelt down by her side. 'My Poor Kate, – my little playfellow, – gone? – gone? Mother Chadwick, do you think there's another world, – is there a heaven, think you?'

'I trust in God there is,' answered the woman, solemnly.

'Then, by heaven, she is there,' and he burst into a passion of tears. 'I would pray for you, if I could, my sweet sister, but I have forgotten our prayers, and they would come with an ill grace from me now.'

'Come, rise, lad, rise,' cried Mrs. Chadwick, in a tone of unusual kindness; 'help me to raise this man, will you, Mr. Wisp?'

'Aye, get up, Ketch,' said Wisp, as he took me by the arm; 'here is a sight that makes us look like villains.'

I arose and tottered to the bed. 'Oh, Wisp, this is no time to quarrel. Comfort me if you can, I beseech you, – for I have need of comfort.'

'Cheer up, then, and let us go down stairs and sit in Mrs. Chadwick's room. Oh, Jack; you have lost more than a world in that girl. Heaven forgive you – for I fear you have been a sad villain.'

The Death of my Wife.

CHAPTER XVI.

THE ice becomes harder and more stubborn, as I have heard (but I leave that to the philosophers to determine), after a thaw; and no sooner was Catharine consigned to the earth than my heart closed up. My feelings were as the bitter waters of Marah, and the coffin of my wife was not of the tree that might make them sweet.[417] I had now become hardened.

As necessity is the mother of invention, so is impunity the nurse of crime, – and I followed my original profession of pickpocket with astonishing perseverance and success; insomuch that I question whether, even at the present day, in this metropolis, or amongst the ancient or modern Greeks[418] (for I believe that Hellenic ingenuity abides by them to this hour) could there be found one combining an equal share of ease, dexterity, and decision, with that which, *I think I may say it without boasting,*[419] I exercised at that period.

Nor was Wisp idle. But as they who write for fame are commonly famished, so also they, whose only claim to fortune is desert, are usually deserted by fortune; and Wisp was now languishing in Newgate.

My friend, it seems, tired of the tedious routine of business of which he had made himself an engine, or instrument, at length found himself laudably anxious to be emancipated from the petty species of wharf-are (as he termed it) in which he had been engaged for so long a period. Towards this end, it naturally occurred to him, that, since he had no fortune of his own, hereditary or acquired, to fall back upon; it would not be unadvisable to march forward upon such funds belonging to others as might certainly and safely be come at. But, seeing that it is somewhat difficult and dangerous

> 'to unhoard the cash
> Of some rich burgher,'[420]

unless you have free and easy ingress to, and egress from, his premises; what could be more likely than that Wisp should turn one eye to his own employer for the means of extricating himself from the unpleasant and irrational position in which he had so long found himself placed, viz. that of getting his own living by his own industry, – a thing too vulgar to be thought of for an instant.

Wisp, accordingly, having collected an infinite variety of wharf dues – which his recent installation to the office of collector enabled him to do – decamped one Saturday evening with the proceeds, leaving behind him in the countinghouse when he departed, nothing but his character, – an old coat, in which he had been accustomed to transact business, – and the solution of this difficult problem to his master, to wit – whether of the two was of the lesser value, or the more threadbare.

But the Governor, as he called him, was a hyperborean,[421] and consequently a great deal too far north[422] for Wisp; and by taking timely and decisive measures, succeeded in discovering his eccentric and flighty assistant at one of the Scotch wharfs in St. Katherine's, from whence he was about to export his newly acquired bullion by one of the Leith[423] smacks; Wisp being, perhaps, of opinion that Scotland was just the last place in the world to which any man could be justly suspected of voluntarily hastening, – not to mention the exceeding improbability that any cash was to be recovered from that country.[424]

Wisp was, therefore, at the present moment in Newgate, awaiting his trial; the result of which, in all probability, would be a seven years' transportation,[425] – a sentence by no means undesirable as a punishment, since it supplies a man with infinitely better opportunities of comfortable existence than diligence and industry could possibly acquire for him in his own country.

My friend, accordingly, although in the first instance somewhat afflicted by the *maladie du pays*,[426] soon recovered his usual spirits, and sent me a polite invitation, through my uncle, to come and have a few minutes' chat, – a summons which in the first instance I chose to disregard, having a shrewd suspicion, although without the skill of a De Moivre, or a Price,[427] in the calculation of chances, that I myself should, in all probability, become an involuntary inmate of that place very shortly. For, I have remarked, that as a field preacher is an abomination in the eyes of a beneficed clergyman, and your patent player cannot away with your peripatetic Punchinello,[428] – so the world generally can by no means permit that to be done openly – I mean the picking of pockets – which, being on the other side of the pale[429] of the law, the world contrives to do so safely, snugly, and respectably. Besides, I had no wish to see my old companion; especially as in all probability I should do myself the pleasure, or rather have the pleasure done for me, of seeing him again in his uncle-land,[430] to which he was now about to repair.

At length, I was so hotly called for by Wisp, who gave me to understand that he had something very particular to relate to me, that I was fain to obtain permission to see him. Being conducted to that portion of the prison set apart for transports, I discovered my friend perambulating the yard in animated conversation with a friend, who seemed by no means backward in contributing his share to the common hilarity; and, indeed, to have observed the general deportment of the prisoners at large – or rather the prisoners confined – a stranger might reasonably suppose that they were persons attached to a projected embassy, instead of victims of offended justice.

Immediately Wisp beheld me he left his friend, and approached the spot where I was standing. 'Well, Ketch, my boy, any commands for your mother? I'm off in a few days.'

'My dutiful respects,' said I, – 'and I'm still unhanged.'

'It's a long lane that has no turning,' remarked Wisp; 'live in hope if you die in despair, – there's plenty of time for that.'

I thanked him for his kind and encouraging assurance, and we entered into conversation; during which I could not but observe the alteration that appeared to have taken place in the manners of my friend. There was a species of flippancy in his discourse, – an artificial carelessness about it that displeased me not a little; and as I occasionally overheard a passing observation made by the other prisoners as they walked to and fro, I discovered that the tone of which I complained was common to them all. Yes, Wisp was an altered man; not in morals – for demoralised he could not be – but in character. He affected to look upon his situation as a species of joke contrived for his amusement, and wondered that I expressed no anxiety to participate in the benefits of an arrangement which to him was so remarkably agreeable.

'Oh! by-the-bye, Ketch,' said Wisp, turning to me suddenly, 'who do you think came to see me yesterday?'

'I cannot guess.'

'Who but little Westminster Abbey; the little man has taken a better three-quarters[431] (as we suspected) in the shape of an old woman with money; he says he has got the right sow by the ear, and has made a silk purse[432] out of it.'

I expressed my gratification at hearing of Gibbon's welfare, and intimated a wish to learn where he resided.

'Oh! he keeps a shop in Westminster, where he sells everything; – there you may buy a tinder-box, and a ton of rags to put into it, if you please, – sand and sugar, separate and together,[433] – birch-brooms and Twankay,[434] ditto; bacon, brimstone, matches, milk, soap, writing-paper, candles, bath-bricks – '

'Stop, stop,' cried I, 'a chandler's shop[435] – I know what you mean.'

'You'll find it,' continued Wisp, and he gave me the direction; 'if you should forget the number,' he added, 'just remember the young lady with a black face and a white petticoat that dangles over the door; but I was forgetting; he has a lodger, and guess who he is.'

'I can't for the life of me.'

'Of all men in the world, Wilmot, whom Snavel chiselled so sweetly. The miserable wretch, it seems, has been looking out after us for years; and reading my trial in the newspaper, was anxious to learn through me what was become of

Jabez; and he despatched his landlord to make himself acquainted with all the particulars I might be able to communicate to him; and so I told Gibbon – '

'What? – why, you know nothing of Snavel.'

'Well, I told him so; Snavel is now comfortably settled in the United States, I have no doubt of that. I say, Jack, if I had not been green[436] as a lettuce, I should never have let him off for two hundred pounds; but bygones are bygones – there's no use talking about that.'

At this moment Wisp was called away by his companion, who wished to speak to him; but he returned presently.

'Jack, my boy,' said he, 'there's a friend of ours here, whom you little expected to see; he remembers you very well, and would have spoken to you, but he thought we might be engaged on business, – Jack Grimes – you recollect Grimes.'

Here Grimes approached, and greeted me with extraordinary cordiality. Grimes had almost grown out of knowledge. Since I had last seen him, he had become an ultra-Grimes in all respects, – an enlarged ruffian, – a complete blackguard. His whiskers had been suffered, or rather encouraged, to grow, till the produce of his jaws would have almost furnished forth a hair mattrass; and the cock of his hat was so adjusted as to communicate to his eye a fierce and mischievous appearance, by no means likely to prepossess the observer with any favourable opinion of his gentleness or amiability.

'Ha! Jack, glad to see you,' he roared, as he took his station opposite to me: 'well, here are Wisp and I about to leave our ungrateful country, and be d— to it, – when are you coming to join us?'

I took the liberty of expressing a hope that many years would elapse before I proceeded on the voyage he referred to; and begged to be informed touching the nature of the business which had brought him to his present condition.

'Why, I'll tell you,' said he, promptly, (and I have observed during my experience, that every man placed in similar circumstances discovers a certain degree of pride in recounting the particulars of his crime to every person, however indifferent to him, who may please to listen to the narrative) – 'you must know,' said he, 'that when I left London with Betsy – you remember how we mizzled[437] – I went down into Yorkshire, – not to catch flats[438] – it's no go *there*,[439] Jack, – but to see my friends, who had done nothing for me for some years; well, they got me into a situation, as overseer in a cloth factory; but I didn't stop very long there, you know, – I left them one day, 'with the broad cloth under my arm,'[440] as the song says, – you twig[441] me, don't you? Well, I run up to London – I lose all my money, – never mind how, – and then, what do you think I do? I draw two bills[442] on the Yorkshire cloth house from which I toddled, and to save time, trouble, and expense of postage, accept them myself in the name of the firm, – ha! ha! ha!'

'Well, but,' said I, a little surprised at his mirth, for which at present there seemed hardly sufficient warrant, 'what then?'

'Why, then I got them discounted, Jack,' said he, in a complacent whisper, 'and shoved the corianders[443] into this pocket,' slapping his thigh, 'and put out these two paddles,' and he stuck out his foot, 'but it was no go – they nabbed me.'

'They talked of making me swing for it,' he continued in a different tone; 'but that wouldn't do at any price. The rum old cove of a governor pattered a great deal about Dr. Dodd,[444] and told us what the king said – that if he spared my life, poor dear dead Dodd was murdered; as though two blacks would make a white! – d— me, that's a good 'un, eh? – and so you knock a man down, and then, to prove that you have done so, you capsize[445] his neighbour, ha! ha! ha!'

'Well, I congratulate you on your escape, at all events.'

'Oh, it makes very little odds to me,' said he, carelessly; 'do you think Jack Grimes cares two pins whether he swings or no? Not he, d— me! After tossing about three days and nights on a tar-barrel, it's not likely that he should snivel when he comes to be tucked up;[446] besides, I've seen the rolls drawn[447] too often for that. There's the sheriff with his gold chain and chalky gills; ordinary looking as though he couldn't help it, with white wig and black book; Ketch, your worthy uncle, curious concerning the raiment; mob – gibbet – noose – eight o'clock – on goes the cap, in goes the head, on goes the parson, down goes the platform, off goes the swell,[448] gentle squeeze, slight caper; – all's over!'

'No *tremor cordis*,[449] Grimes, when the drop falls: no awkward feeling just here, eh?' and I pointed to the place where the heart, like Goldsmith's venison pasty, was – not.[450]

'None in the least, my Jacky: we leave those agreeable sensations to the suddenly converted – the eleventh hour coves. Oh, no! we just lean our heads a little on the left side,[451] and take it easy.'

'But what's to become of poor Betsy,' said I, 'when you're gone?'

'Why, what is *to* become of poor Betsy I don't know,' answered he, picking his teeth with a straw; 'and what's more, Jack, what *is* become of poor Betsy, I don't know; and what's most, what *does* become of poor Betsy, I don't care.'

'How is that? Where did you leave her, then?' I inquired.

'She left me, Jack, when I was in Yorkshire. Toddled with a chap before we had been married six months: a little bandy-legged rascal, with two pieces of round wool stuck on his shoulders, a lobster-salad coat on, and a plaguy long stride of his own. You know the sort of thing I mean – a drummer. Yes,' continued he, 'Betsy went off with the drummer;' and he whistled a military air with much satisfaction: 'queer start, wasn't it, eh? but we were always at it; – cat and dog work – hammer and tongs. Oh! Betsy was a spirited young hussy; and so let the drummer repair his drum with her skin, and make drum-sticks with her elbows – eh?' here he burst into a violent fit of laughter. 'She'll make noise enough then, at all events, ha! ha! ha! d— me.'

The officer in attendance now approached Grimes, and remonstrated with him touching his exuberant vociferation.

'Oh! I say, Clank, you're just the boy I wanted to see,' and Grimes capered towards him after the manner of a seaman; 'any orders from the Home Office this morning: when are we to leave this ugly shop of yours?'

'I don't know,' answered Clank, and walked sullenly away.

'Queer b— that,' observed Grimes, turning to me; 'a good heart, they say; but devilish bad manners.'

By this time I deemed it high time to take my leave, and informed Grimes of my intention.

'Fare ye well, my infant,' said he, waving his hand with a theatrical air; 'now, come and see us soon, that's a good fellow. Wisp tells me you're as likely[452] as any man he knows – good bye!' and he swaggered off to some companions at the other end of the yard, with a nonchalance truly refreshing to behold.

Wisp, during my conversation with Grimes, had been engaged in communion with his wife, who, just as I came up, was launching against him sundry scornful reproaches upon his want of skill and tact, in suffering himself to be so easily captured; and required clamorously to be informed what provision he had made for her, which he well knew was not sufficient 'to satisfy a bee's slight munchings;'[453] telling him at the same time that he ought to be ashamed of himself to go away and leave her without money, food, clothes, lodging, or character. But I believe that Susan would willingly have set the last item out of the account altogether, could she by any means have secured the other four; and it is a marvel to me that she should have insisted upon this point, seeing that (as she well knew), poor Wisp had long ago swopped it for the contingent chance of obtaining those far more essential benefits.

'What's the use of taking a dead eel by the tail, Sue?' said Wisp, 'it's all very true; but what's to be done? Here I am, like the starling, and can't get out;[454] you must fight your way as you can, that's all.'

'Ugh! you paltry villain!' responded Susan, 'what did you marry me for, if you couldn't keep me?'

'For love, Susan, for love,' cried Wisp, winking at me as I drew near, 'all for love, I assure you. But, what! Jack, are you going? well, bye – bye. I say, Jack, I leave my good will to Susan here; if you *should* be able to serve her in any way, think of her – that's all; and think of Will Wisp sometimes, will you? – for his sister's sake, Jack, if not for his own. God bless you!'

Could I be deceived? No; there was a tear in Wisp's eye as he spoke; but he averted his head, and when he turned to me again, the tear was gone; and with a nod and a smile he allowed me to depart.

'Just wait outside for a few minutes,' said Susan, as I passed her, 'I won't be a moment with Wisp.'

'I'll wait at the public-house opposite,' I replied; and thither I went, pondering on the heterogeneous jumble of contrary and opposite feelings and qualities in the man whom I had just left.

Mrs. Wisp soon joined me; and while we regaled ourselves with a small allowance of gin proper to the place and occasion, assailed my ear with complaints of her husband; and thought it very hard that when a woman was placed in her situation, the law did not make some provision by way of compensation for the loss she was about to sustain. 'Not that I ever cared a button for Wisp,' she added; 'not even when I first took him.'

'No?'

'No, Jack, not when he first came cap in hand, as a woman may say, on his marrow-bones, for me to have him.'

'Then why did you marry him?' I demanded.

'I don't know, I'm sure;' and she attempted to imitate a sigh. 'But can't I marry again, now Wisp is transported?'

'I believe you can. I don't know. I think I've heard you can.'

'And so can you, Jack, now your missus is dead. La! how funny, isn't it?' saying which, she skittishly visited my ribs with her elbow, and gazing at me for a moment very earnestly, suddenly turned aside her face, for the purpose of concealing the fact that there was *no* blush upon it.

Ho! ho! thought I, but it won't do. I accordingly observed a grim silence, and, with my hands in my pockets, kept my eyes upon the ground as though in earnest meditation, heedless of certain tender, but rather too emphatic pressures on the foot with her patten.

At length I raised my head slowly, and turning a vacant eye towards her, said with a yawn – 'Where's your mother now?'

'Oh! bother her; what's the odds where she is?' cried Susan. 'You're such a curious man, Ketch: you're a sly dog, a'n't you, now? You know what I mean.'

'Indeed I do not. I say, where's your mother?'

'Why, lad, in the workhouse, to be sure; where should she be? What signifies – '

'Isn't there room for both of you there?' said I, with a sneer; 'but come, I must be off:' and before the storm, which I perceived was brewing, had time to ferment, I snatched my hat, and made the best of my way from the premises, leaving my enamoured companion to shoot after me such verbal arrows as her well-stored quiver of epithets doubtless supplied her with on this occasion.

It was about a week after this, that Wisp and Grimes departed for the vast continent of New Holland;[455] the former for seven years – the latter for life; and, for my own part, I can only say, that if the object of punishment be the prevention of crime, the examples placed before me, in the persons of my friends, by no means tended to deter me from the commission of sundry offences, which, undiscovered at the time, are too minute and unimportant to find a place in a book devoted to more worthy matters.

CHAPTER XVII.

THE growth of time may be appropriately likened to the growth of the aloe, which will not put forth its blossoms on compulsion, or permit its operations to be vexatiously hurried by any absurd attempts to trouble the earth around it. Yet, by waiting patiently, we shall find that many events will inevitably occur, for which we had not only made no preparation, but upon which we never could have calculated. It will not fail also to be remembered by the reminiscent and sagacious reader, that he has frequently gone forth in search of one thing or person, which or whom he might reasonably expect to find, and that, nevertheless, he has not discovered it or him; and that, on the contrary, some other thing or person has made itself apparent to him, which or whom he had no design of seeking, and no expectation, however slight, of having the happiness to meet. Thus, sometimes, an individual goes forth with the express intention of laying a cudgel over the shoulders of his wronger, and is suddenly presented with an unforeseen kicking from a third party, whom he, strange to say, has wronged. Thus, also, the devout cook ascends the area[456] for the purpose of seeking the parish church; and, instead thereof, meets by the way with the dapper groom attached to the adjacent livery stables, whose converse sweet,[457] fraught with the plan of prospective public-house[458] – rendered visible to her mental eye by its fanciful sign of 'The Wooden Spoon and Stomach-ache,' – causes her at once to marvel at the agreeable encounter, and to adopt plans to facilitate its recurrence.

I have thus, at too much length, perhaps, illustrated my meaning, and prepared the reader for what is to follow. When I started out one morning, for the purpose of tracing a clue which had been afforded me to the discovery of Mrs. Adams, and the consequent recovery of my child, I had not the slightest notion that, unsuccessful in that expedition, I should stumble upon a man of all others whom I least expected to behold again in this world; or, in other words, that the retina of my eye would ever again be called upon to receive the inverted and miniature likeness of Mr. Jabez Snavel. But so it was.

Whoever, led by curiosity or business, has had occasion to walk upon the Royal Exchange[459] about noon, cannot fail to have been struck by a distinct class of persons, whom it will doubtless have been his chance to behold, either seated listlessly on the seats, or prowling up and down in pairs or alone,[460] – not, like a certain personage,[461] seeking whom they may devour; but having nobody to seek, and nothing to devour. Were the separate history of these individuals written, there were a calendar of woe,[462] such as would cause the beggar in the streets to hug his rags to his bosom, and thank God for his plenty.

Among these knights of the grasshopper,[463] (for so let me call them, seeing that their precarious and ethereal existence resembles not a little that of the nimble patron of the order); among these, as I idled to and fro, it was my chance to observe one, whose variety of wretchedness appeared to me even greater than that of his fellows. A more particular perusal of this essay on the infinitely miserable, assured me that it was the corporeal presence of Jabez Snavel.

The whole appearance of my former master bespoke – nay, must have bespoken for a long time past, the extremest poverty and want. His suit of black, – let me suppose that it once wore that hue, – was not only what is called seedy, but was of that arid and past-sowing seed, which indicates to a certainty that it will never produce new garments. The neckcloth was folded around his flabby and desponding gills, and pinned over the throat carefully, with a view to conceal that he had, *indeed*, a shirt; or perhaps to hide the fact of its unavoidable absence. On his brow a blighted beaver[464] sat, with which Time appeared to have rudely sported. It was a hat that Chaos might have worn – it spoke of the 'formless infinite;'[465] and its greasy band perspired at every pore, as though it feared lest it should suddenly burst asunder, and suffer the fissured fabric to lapse in ruinous confusion over the ears of its wearer.

Nor did the appearance of Snavel disgrace the unsightly gear. Squalid and miserable, I watched him as he paced up and down the north side of the Exchange. Could this be the scrupulous and neat little man whom I had been formerly accustomed to see; – this thing of shreds and patches? He drew from his pocket a snuff-box; – it was not his former Scotch mull, but a brass receptacle: he took a pinch; – it was not of Rappee, but plain Scotch.[466] And as he replaced it in his pocket, I could discover that he prized it as the most valuable article he possessed in the world.

Moved by curiosity, – there might, perhaps, be another motive, – I accosted him: 'Mr. Snavel, I believe,' said I; 'surely I am not mistaken?'

He started, and turned pale. 'Snavel is my name,' at length he stuttered; 'but no – yes – it must be, I declare. Mr. Ketch, how are you?'

Here we shook hands very cordially, and retired to one of the seats.

'Well, and how is your uncle?' cried Snavel, looking up into my face with an air of interest; 'a very worthy man – a good man. I hope he's doing well.'

'Without his wife,' said I, and closed the sentence. 'Ah! Mr. Snavel – Mr. Snavel.'

'There again,' said Snavel, 'there again I am misunderstood. Mrs. Ketch merely put herself under my protection as a friend; nay, don't laugh, – upon my honour,' – here he laid his hand upon his bosom: 'no, no, no, no, no,' he added, after a pause, taking a pinch of snuff, 'I would not have wronged my friend Ketch for the world; that wouldn't have done at any price.'

'Well,' I inquired, 'and what has become of her?'

'Ah! poor thing,' said Snavel, and he rubbed his chin. 'Why, really, Mr. Ketch, you had grown almost out of knowledge. I heard of poor Wisp's misfortune; it was an unlucky circumstance; it shows how circumspect we ought to be. A clever fellow that Wisp – never knew a sharper lad than Wisp.'

It was evident that Snavel would fain have declined to satisfy me concerning his adventures since the world had lost sight of him; and it was plain that he was far from being at ease in my company. I therefore made a show of friendship, and invited him to partake of a pot of ale in the neighbourhood, a motion which seemed to accord with his wishes exactly; and we accordingly betook ourselves to an adjacent public-house, where the additional luxury of a crust of bread and cheese, created an exercise of Snavel's jaws to which they did not appear to have been recently accustomed, and prepared them for the more easy recital of such things as I might deem it pleasant or profitable to hear.

'Have you heard, Mr. Ketch, what is become of Mr. Wilmot, whom you may remember to have seen, – a client of mine? I have not been able to discover him. I had some communication that I should have wished to make to him.'

Snavel had evidently put forth this speech as a feeler; but I was not so easily to be duped. I also had a game to play.

'Any communication you may have to make to Wilmot,' said I, carelessly, 'must be addressed to the other world. Wilmot is dead.'

'Dead!' echoed Snavel, 'you don't say so – my dear sir, can you vouch for the truth of this statement?'

I instantly invented the time, place, and mode of Wilmot's demise; ascribing that grand result to the agency of a broken heart.

'Then what's to prevent me,' said Snavel, in a transport, 'from returning to my old profession. Dead? died of a broken heart; very foolish – excessively absurd. By the bye, Ketch, is your uncle inveterate against me? Any prejudice existing, eh?'

'Why, no, I think not,' said I; 'you know what a fury *she* was.'

'I do,' cried Snavel, 'therefore, the more easily spared.'

'You speak of Mrs. Ketch in the past tense, Mr. Snavel; where is she? what has become of her?'

Snavel sighed; it was not a good sigh – it was too far fetched; but it passed for want of a better.

'It was an unfortunate business,' said he, 'when I left London. You remember the evening, I dare say. Well, I consented to take charge of Mrs. Ketch, who had a brother in the United States whom she wished to join – eh? why do you fling your thumb over your shoulder? it's a fact, I give you my word. We proceeded to Liverpool, and embarked on a vessel just about to clear out of the docks. Well, sir, we had scarcely got out of port, – hardly made the black rock, when a storm arose – ocean plaintiff, vessel defendant – crew witnesses – impossible to prove an alibi. In a word, we were wrecked in sight of port, and I, with two more, was saved; the rest were lost.'

'And Mrs. Ketch was one of the latter?'

'Just so,' and he took a pinch of snuff. 'But the worst of the thing was, the money – you recollect the money – that also was lost; thrown back upon my native land without a farthing in the world, – without friends; just consider for a moment, – a hard case – a very hard case: how I have contrived to exist until this moment I scarcely know, and you see I am not even now in affluence.' Saying which, Snavel stroked his ancient vestments with the palm of his hand in a singularly lugubrious manner.

There was something in Snavel's mode of relating his disaster at sea, that led me at first to doubt the truth of his narration; but when I began to reflect that Jabez, like myself, had been born and brought up in London, and was entirely unacquainted with nautical phraseology, it appeared only probable that he would adopt such language as came most readily to tongue.

Besides, Jabez was one of that large class of men who, not habitual liars, bear nevertheless no respect to truth when falsehood is at a premium; and it is needless to add, the greater the inducement the larger the lie; and yet, so general a deference do they pay to matter of fact, that to speak charitably of them, it may be inferred, when there is no ostensible motive to the contrary, the truth is in them; unless, indeed, when they *swear* to anything, and then you may safely make affidavit that they have sworn to a lie.

All things considered, there was every likelihood of Snavel's veracity on this occasion: certain it was, that, by whatever means, he was now utterly without present money or resources in prospect; and as for Mrs. Ketch, I threw her overboard out of the present question.

'I am sorry, Mr. Snavel,' said I, 'that you have met with such a reverse of fortune, but it's never too late to mend.'

'Truly, truly,' cried he, 'and Wilmot's death is a great consolation to me, if your uncle could but be brought to pardon my indiscretion.'

'Oh! Don't fear that; my uncle is no Perseus for such an Andromeda[467] as poor Peg; she may stick on the black rock for ever and a day, he'll never think about her; make your mind easy upon that score.'

Snavel was considerably relieved by these assurances, and made an appointment to meet me on 'Change⁴⁶⁸ on the following day at the same hour; for I held out hopes of a small business relating to a recent mistake made by Mrs. Wisp, which I intended to put into his hands, and which we could talk over at leisure in my lodging.

Immediately I left Snavel, who returned to his old haunt, I proceeded on a speculative ramble to Westminster; and by dint of sundry inquiries, – but most particularly through the information conveyed by the black doll over the threshhold,⁴⁶⁹ – was at length enabled to discover the abode of my friend Gibbon.

As I entered the shop, a gentlewoman of pinched and drawn features, well stricken in years, and apparently stricken also by paralysis, was dispensing a minute portion of soap to a ragged and hatless urchin, who appeared for his own part to have washed his hands of that commodity, by never washing them at all, and whose face had lost all its original brightness in a thick layer of mud. 'O cri,'⁴⁷⁰ quoth he, as, with the addition of a ha'porth⁴⁷¹ of pearlash,⁴⁷² he made his exit from the shop, 'what a sight of soapsuds there will be – oh! my eye!'

With much difficulty I gave the ancient gentlewoman to understand that I wished to see Mr. Gibbon, and was ushered into the back-parlour, where my friend sat making conical conveniences of brown paper for the reception of sugar.

'What! Jack,' he exclaimed, starting up, 'you come to shore at last. You see the joke? – jack, a *fish*, come to *shore* – you see it, of course: well, what brings you here?'

I reminded him in few words of his visit to Wisp in Newgate, and informed him that I wished to see Mr. Wilmot, with reference to the anxiety he had expressed to learn something concerning Snavel.

'And so he did, sure enough,' said Gibbon, 'he *was* anxious; but what's the use of hungering after last year's mutton. Snavel has been missing for years, and I would not have you revive the memory of him in Wilmot's breast. When you once get his monkey up, there's a terrible harangue-o'tongue.'⁴⁷³

Here Gibbon rubbed his hands, and looked particularly grave, two evidences by which I discovered that he had succeeded in making a pun. I took no heed, however, of his troublesome annoyance, but inquired how it was that Wilmot had so altered since I had been accustomed to see him.

'O Lord! it's a melancholy affair,' said Gibbon, heaving a sigh; 'robbed of his money by that villain – without food or clothing – rent accruing. Mrs. Gibbon could tell you about that, – but it's all paid now. Daughter dying of consumption – it's a long story: he's a good-hearted creature now, only you mustn't harass him: he's like a bottle of good old port, but it isn't well to disturb him, for he's somewhat crusty.'⁴⁷⁴

'Well, but I wish you'd show me the bin in which he lies at this moment. I have something to communicate respecting Snavel that he will be rejoiced to hear.' And now, being instigated thereto by Gibbon, I informed him in general terms that I had seen Snavel, and that I should have it in my power to consign him to the outstretched hands of justice.

'Come along up,' said Gibbon, briskly, when I had concluded my narration; 'only wipe your feet on the mat. Mrs. G. expects people to go up and down like the angels ascending and descending Jacob's ladder;[475] if you don't walk carefully up to the head of her stairs, you'll find that you'll sink under the stares of her head. Come, that's not so bad, either.'

Talking thus, he conducted me to the door of Wilmot's apartment. He tapped gently. 'A person wishes to see you, sir.'

'Let him enter,' said a voice from within, and I opened the door.

Gibbon now made his way to his own apartment, and left me *tête à tête*[476] with Wilmot.

'What is your pleasure with me, sir,' said he, with a reserved air; 'I must beg you to be brief, I am going out.'

'My name is Ketch, sir, and you will probably remember to have seen me in the office of Mr. Jabez Snavel.'

'Ha!' cried Wilmot, hastily, and as he started from his chair, his eyes sparkled, and the colour mounted from his cheeks to his brow. 'Well, what brings you here?'

'In a word, sir, Snavel is in England, and I can put him into your power.'

Wilmot raised himself from his chair, and presently reseated himself, with his hands upon his knees. 'Snavel in England – in London – here – Impossible!'

'True,' said I, 'quite true. But you need not expect to recover any part of your money; *that* is irrevocably gone.' And I related the substance of Snavel's communication to me.

'It is strange,' muttered Wilmot. 'The money I never expected to recover, nor do I wish it; it is of no service now. But him; let me but have him once more in my grasp. Mr. Ketch, I rely upon you for this; where is he?'

'No soul in England knows that but myself, and we must understand each other before I divulge his retreat.'

'What do you mean?' cried Wilmot, apparently surprised.

'That I must have a consideration.'

'How? a consideration?'

'Yes,' said I, coolly. 'The fact is, I have a certain respect for Snavel, and must not let him go under twenty pounds.'[477]

'Mr. Ketch,' said Wilmot, gravely, 'you are much altered since I last saw you.'

'And you also, Mr. Wilmot; I could hardly have expected so great a change.'

'I did not mean that, young man,' he continued, coldly. 'However, you shall have twenty pounds in three days; will that content you?'

'I know you're a gentleman, sir,' I replied, 'and would trust your word if I could, but – '

'Nay, when you present this paper to the parties to whom it is addressed, they will – they must pay you;' and he showed me a paper which he had written while I hesitated a distrust of his word. 'But, mark me, can you bring Snavel here upon some pretext?'

'I can.'

'To-morrow?'

'Yes.'

'Well then, this paper shall be placed in the hands of Mr. Gibbon below; when you have executed your engagement, it shall be handed over to you; and before the expiration of the three days, we shall have disposed of Mr. Snavel.'

'Yes, by that time we shall have him behind bolt and bar,' said I, to encourage the humour of my employer.

'Or elsewhere,' observed Wilmot, calmly. 'Then you are satisfied?'

I bowed assent.

'Good morning. At this time to-morrow precisely I shall expect you.'

This arrangement having been concluded so entirely to my satisfaction, I joined my friend Gibbon, and made known to him the heads of my discourse with Wilmot; and having so done, returned into the city to chew the cud of sweet and bitter fancy, – the sweetness consisting of the twenty pounds in prospect, the bitterness of regret that I had not demanded more.

CHAPTER XVIII.

MEN are usually sufficiently alert at the discovery of justifying reasons for their conduct upon all occasions; and I believe it is universally acknowledged that every action of our lives may be referred to some motive, – whether in itself sufficiently strong or not is of not much importance, – but at all events so considered during the time of acting.

But yet, when I recal to mind, as well as my imperfect memory will permit me to do so, all the particular bearings of the case, as between Wilmot and Snavel, and the part I had taken upon myself to play between them, I cannot for the life of me hit upon the precise motive which must have weighed with me at that period so strongly, as to impel me to pursue the course I adopted upon that occasion.

In the first place, I had no great faith in the validity of the document consigned to the temporary charge of Gibbon. In the second, I felt no wish to further the ends of justice, or to promote the aim of Wilmot, by delivering Jabez into their hands. And lastly, there was not the slightest animosity existing in my mind against Snavel. Let me then suppose (a common method of untying all Gordian knots[478] in the moral line), let me suppose myself an instrument in the hands of Providence, deputed to work out some hidden end of goodness or justice above mortal ken or human understanding.

Snavel hastened to meet me half way, as with exemplary punctuality I entered 'Change and proceeded towards him; and without hesitation he agreed to accompany me to my lodgings in Westminster, where, as I informed him, the prosecutor of Mrs. Wisp, who had done a little piece of petty larceny, had engaged to meet me, with a view to an amicable compromise.

As we walked along, I fed him with hopes of future employment at the hands of some particular friends of mine, whose hazardous profession occasionally entailed upon them the necessity of applications to the law; and comforted him with the assurance of my opinion, that the transaction with Wilmot, if generally known, would be a point in his favour rather than otherwise; since to defraud the gibbet is the highest glory in the eyes of those whose incessant practice in the arts of fraud is sometimes insufficient to the accomplishment of this last grand manœuvre.

'You will find him up stairs,' said Gibbon, as we entered the passage. 'Why, Jack,' and he took me aside, 'he has sent for no officers, nor will he permit me to do so. What a sneaking scoundrel Snavel looks. However, walk him up into *his* room; I'll take care he shan't come out in a hurry.'

'What is the meaning of this? I really don't comprehend,' remarked Snavel, in a deferential tone, and he treated himself to a pinch of snuff. 'The gentleman you expected to find is up stairs, is he not?'

'He is,' said I; 'my landlord was merely whispering to me some private affairs of his own. Let us walk up;' saying which, I led the way, with a slight feeling of trepidation, to Wilmot's room.

'Wait in the passage for a moment, and I'll prepare the gentleman to receive you,' and I opened the door.

Wilmot was sitting at a table, but when he saw me he started up. 'Have you got him?' said he, in a whisper; but his hand trembled violently, as he laid it on my arm, and his face was as pale as ashes.

'He is here – outside. Shall I fetch him in?'

'Do, do, do,' and he staggered backwards to the wall. 'I am faint; but don't mind me – ' and he waved his hand – 'it will the sooner be over.'

Just as I stepped outside for the purpose of handing Snavel into the apartment, I discovered that cautious person in the act of descending the stairs.

'Hilloah!' said I; 'what are you about, Mr. Snavel?'

'My hat,' said he, in much confusion; 'I left my hat in the passage. I want – I'll be back again in a moment.'

'No, no, the gentleman's waiting,' I replied, and took him by the arm. 'It's nobody you know; don't be a fool – '

'Eh?' said Snavel, in a vague manner. But ere he had time to reflect upon the matter, I had ushered, or rather thrust him into the room, where the first sight that greeted him was the ghastly face of Wilmot, who, with arms folded and a steadfast and searching eye, came slowly towards him.

But if Wilmot's face was colourless and livid, who shall describe the visage of Snavel when he found himself once more in the presence of one whom he had so exceedingly, and out of all reasonable compass deceived? His first impulse was to clutch me by the arm, as a protection, if not from the vengeance, at least from the sight of his victim; his second, to scan the apartment with a view to ascertain whether any one was present, whose immediate employment would be to take him into custody; and his last, to direct a glance of such abject abasement and terror towards Wilmot, as almost caused even me to regret the step I had taken to his prejudice.

'You may go, sir,' said Wilmot, calmly addressing me; 'Mr. Snavel and I can talk over the few matters we have to settle much better alone.'

'Oh! Mr. Wilmot, my dear sir,' exclaimed Snavel, holding up his clasped hands, 'do let the young man stay with us. I have no objection to his hearing all; indeed I have not.'

During this speech, Wilmot, heedless of its substance, had half opened the door, and motioning me to approach, gently pushed me through the aperture. 'I shall see you again, Mr. Ketch,' he said; and as I descended the stairs, I heard him close the door and lock it, drawing the key out of the lock: and presently a murmur of voices in active but not violent discussion.

'Well, of all things in the world,' observed Gibbon, as I took a seat in his back room, curious to know the result of this conference, and accordingly determined to await the issue of it; 'well, of all things in the world, this conduct of Wilmot's is the most extraordinary. He gets a man into his power, – a man who has wronged him in the basest manner, and actually declines taking any steps towards his apprehension. What does the man mean?'

'Why to read him a great moral lesson, I conjecture; to pull his ears, and bid him 'God speed,'[479] after the Christian fashion.'

'But why,' urged Gibbon, 'be at an expense of twenty pounds for so futile a purpose? for Snavel, I should imagine, has left off taking lessons in morality.'

'Um!' said I; 'the waste of the paper and the cost of the ink. The order on Sly and Sharp is not worth a button; it was a labour of love on my part.'

'No, hang it!' cried Gibbon; 'Wilmot's an honourable man, and, I believe, means fairly by you. If you did but know what he has suffered through the villany[480] of Snavel, you would not wonder at his anxiety to lay hold upon him.'

I expressed a wish to hear an outline of that history, especially as, to all appearance, the colloquy above stairs appeared likely to last a considerable time.

'Well, I'll tell you,' said Gibbon, 'in a very few words. Wilmot was formerly a captain in the army, but was dismissed the service for horsewhipping a superior officer, who had insulted his daughter. Now, as pigs do not in this country run about ready roasted, with knives and forks in their loins, crying 'Come, eat me;' but, on the contrary, since without the needful[481] it is hopeless to expect to stick a knife and fork into them upon any terms, – no wonder that Wilmot, when his half-pay[482] ceased, found it difficult to prevent the cessation of his whole vitality. His only hope lay in the successful issue of a chancery suit, which had been pending for a considerable time; and he has told me, that, how he existed so long a period without any ostensible means or plausible expectations, was to him, whenever he looked back upon it, a perfect mystery. For a time, however, one small stream of current coin flowed in a scanty course to his pocket; it was the salary of his daughter, who for two years held a situation as a governess, and was thus enabled, in a much more agreeable and effectual manner than the Grecian daughter,[483] to afford sustenance to her father. About six months, however, before the suit was decided in Wilmot's favour, his daughter was compelled to leave her situation, and returned to her father in a deep and rapid decline. Snavel knew every circumstance of Wilmot's life: his extreme penury; his pride, which forbade an application to friends; the state in which his only daughter was languishing; and yet – but you know all that.

'When Wilmot took our lodgings about a year ago, he brought his child with him. Upon my soul, Ketch, it brings tears into my eyes whenever I think of the poor girl: her patience, her resignation, and the affection that subsisted between the two, the only subsistence, by the bye (a vile pun!) they could count upon. Well, the want, the misery, these two people experienced are beyond my powers of description. We never pressed for the rent, and the score in the shop was a rum one; but Wilmot was as proud as the devil, his daughter as meek as an angel, and Mrs. G. half and half – something between the two. We rubbed on amicably enough, for all that. The daughter at last died. Oh Lord! but I can't talk about it – and Wilmot has never been the same man since. His brains cracked at that moment, and will never be whole again; he'll sit sometimes for hours together, and cry like a child, and will afterwards rise up and walk about the room, laughing like a Merry Andrew[484] – Garrick between tragedy and comedy[485] – but the comedy is the most serious affair of the two. But I'll just go up stairs, and attach my ear to the keyhole, eh? Walls have ears, they say, and doors, also, sometimes. Remain below for five minutes, Ketch, until I return.'

While Gibbon was absent, I pondered over the recital he had just concluded; and more and more, as I took a rapid review of the circumstances, was I perplexed with doubts as to the purpose of Wilmot in requiring a mere interview – for it appeared likely to end as it began – with Mr. Jabez Snavel. Had Wilmot received some secret intimation that the other still possessed part at least of his property, and that he carried about a woe-begone and beggarly exterior with a view to impress a contrary conviction? Had I been deceived by Snavel? it might be so. If, then, any sum worth mentioning were received, should I not be entitled to a fair per centage? And yet – '

Gibbon at this moment returned. 'It was no go,' said he; 'Wilmot heard me on the landing, and put his head out of the door. 'Go away down stairs,' he said, 'I'll call you when you are wanted.' And then a slight struggle took place, for Snavel wished to bolt, but that was no go likewise; and Wilmot closed the door, and locked it after him.'

'Well, I'll wait and see the upshot,' said I; 'if Snavel won't come to terms, Wilmot has him fast, at all events.'

'True,' said Gibbon; 'and so let us make our minds easy. By the bye, Jack,' he continued, 'didn't you think it a rum start, my marriage with the old girl yonder,' and he glanced through the glass door leading into the shop.

'Why, no,' said I, pursing up my lips, and elevating my eyebrows, and endeav-ouring to look as much like a man of the world as possible; 'No. Make hay while the sun shines; strike while the iron's hot.'

'Aye, sure, as St. Anthony did by the devil,'[486] cried Gibbon. 'But you're very right, Ketch; very right. Human life is made up altogether of compromises. We expect a flock of sheep, turn up our noses at a single wether, and at last are too glad to catch hold of a mutton chop, and a handful of wool to stuff into our ears, and so keep out the laughter and contempt of the world.'

'Well said, Gibbon; and without a pun, too.'

'Oh; I've left off puns, except one now and then; it's a bad habit. I've taken to conceits, similes, and all that sort of thing. No, no,' he resumed, 'we can make our own comforts by ceasing to linger over past and unattainable enjoyments, and the first seceder from the board of sentiment usually comes the best off; just as, after a dinner party, the earliest man to leave commonly selects the best hat. Hang sentiment! what will it do? Will it fill my stomach? Environed as we are by appetites, sensations, wants of all kinds – physical for the most part – can we soar out of them on the gnat-like wings of a sentiment? Yes, pigs *may* fly, but they're very unlikely birds. Besides, I knew not what might become of me. Strange things do happen. An acorn falls; it becomes an oak: another descends from the tree, and is eaten up by a sow. One egg is boiled in a pot; another hatched, and turns out a chicken; a third launched at the head of a fellow in the pillory. One tiger jumps about a jungle, another mopes in a menagerie. One – '

'I see, I see,' cried I; 'for mercy's sake forbear further illustrations.'

'Well, well, I won't proceed. What I meant to say was this, that I was decid-edly right in taking unto myself a helpmate. To be sure, she does not kindle my affection, but she keeps the pot boiling; she does not purify my spirit, but she washes my shirts; she does not abstract my mind from baseness and misery, but she makes me acquainted with beef and mutton. When I look upon her, shrivelled and ancient as she is, and then turn an eye towards the multitudinous assortment of vendible articles set out for sale in the shop, I cannot forbear exclaiming with the poet –

> 'Age cannot wither her, nor custom stale
> Her infinite variety.'[487]

At this moment, just as Gibbon was rubbing his hands at the conclusion of this brilliant sally, a piercing scream, followed by several wild and hollow shrieks, to which succeeded a heavy fall and struggling on the floor, proceeded from above.

'Cry matches and burn the bellows![488] what the devil's that?' exclaimed Gib-bon, springing from his chair and running to the door. 'What's the matter, Mr.

Wilmot? was that you?' he called, from the bottom of the stairs. No answer. 'Shall I go up?' said he, turning to me; 'Ketch, will you go with me?'

'I'll wait at the bottom of the stairs,' said I, 'and if you want me, call, and I'll come instantly.'

'Very well,' and he hastened up stairs, while I waited below in the passage, in no small anxiety to learn what had been going on above; but before I could put into shape any probable fancies, nay, even before I could have supposed that Gibbon had ascended to the second floor, I heard him descending in a frantic fashion; and now, with hands extended before, – his coat skirts flying behind him, – his feet unconscious of the staircase, – he came rushing down, like an absorbing bird,[489] with outspread wings and pouncing talons, and threw himself wildly into my arms.

'Oh, God! oh, God! oh, God!' and, as Gibbon caught me with both hands by the collar of my coat, he hid his face in my bosom, and a strong shudder vibrated through every limb.

I drew him into his room and placed him upon a chair. 'What is the matter?' said I; 'my good fellow, tell me at once.'

'I am sick – a glass of water – but no,' and he pointed to the bottom of the door, and his shirt heaved convulsively, 'there was blood, Ketch, running into the passage. Oh, God! what has been done?'

I had heard enough, and called Mrs. Gibbon out of the shop. 'There is something wrong above stairs,' I said, hurriedly; 'look to your husband, while I go for assistance.'

'Run, Ketch, to Triggs, next door, and tell him to step in.' I did so, and Triggs,[490] suddenly twitched from his shopboard, ran in pulling and struggling with his jacket, which at last he succeeded in placing on the wrong side outwards.

Triggs was speedily made acquainted with the horrible event, and thereupon endeavoured to look like a man, who, having been called upon in an emergency, is bound to muster up a superior portion of manhood; but his efforts were vain. All was silent above; and as we huddled close together in the passage, and left Mrs. Gibbon to the private nourishment of a dram-bottle, we looked like men upon whom some common duty is imposed, which each would willingly transfer to the other.

'Shall we go up?' we seemed to inquire, and gazed into each other's faces –

> ' – and each
> In other's countenance read his own dismay; – '[491]

and as we ascended step by step, the immediate object appeared to be, not which should go foremost, but which could contrive to be the last of the party; but at length we reached the landing of the second floor.

Here we halted and again read each other's faces; and, indeed, the sight that had met our eyes, was such as might well appal hearts of sterner stuff than we could boast. The blood had extended over the landing, and was now creeping down the stairs in heavy and purple streams, and clung about our shoes, as though it besought us to be witnesses of the murder just completed.

At length, Triggs, having summoned to his aid a kind of wild fear, which at certain times is mistaken for, and does the work of, courage, levelled his foot at the door with such violence as caused it to burst open without further siege, – and now a sight presented itself to us that struck us motionless with horror.

Wilmot was kneeling on both knees at the head of Snavel, who lay stretched upon the floor, deluged in his own blood; while a wide gash, that had nearly separated the head from the body, revealed too truly the manner by which the unhappy man had been dismissed to the other world. Wilmot, I have said, was kneeling over him, and from between his clasped hands, which were pressed against his forehead, projected the blade of a razor, upon which the blood had yet scarcely begun to coagulate. He appeared unconscious of our presence; but hung over the dead body, as one meditating upon something still to be done, and yet doubtful of the best means of accomplishing it. As we approached, however, he raised his head, and the vacant look with which he for a moment regarded us, was suddenly exchanged for the frenzied glance of a maniac, and, with a hideous grin, he leaned back, sitting upon his heels, and demanded quickly –

'Who comes between me and my vengeance? Who comes between me and my vengeance? – let him not approach me!' and he waved the razor over his head in rapid circles. 'Who are you that wish to snatch him from me? Hah!'

Here, as though some invisible hand had fastened upon him from above, and snatched him to his feet, he arose with a spring, and made one step towards us. This was no time to vindicate our several degrees of manhood, and we all rushed from the room, casting ourselves recklessly from the stair-head, and finding ourselves in the passage in an incredible short space of time.

'For God's sake, Triggs, alarm the neighbourhood,' cried Gibbon, in an agony of fear. 'Mr. Wilmot is mad, and knows not what he does; he may lay violent hands upon himself before you return.'

Triggs was too happy to fly in aid of reinforcement; and presently came back at the head of a miscellaneous concourse of individuals, who, in their collective wisdom, resolved upon proceeding up stairs immediately, with a view to secure the murderer.

When we entered the room a second time, Wilmot was standing with his head leaning on his hand, and his elbow resting on a chest of drawers.

'Come in, gentlemen, come in,' he said, with unexpected composure of voice and manner. 'You are witnesses,' he continued, dropping the razor from his hand,

The Murder of Snavel.

'that I am the murderer of this man. God is just, and has at last delivered him into my power.'

He stooped down, and dipped his finger in the blood of the murdered man, and crossed his forehead with it. 'Here is my sign – here is my confession – I am the murderer of this man!'

As he said this, he cast one look at the wretched and lifeless being beside him, and surrendered himself to the group, who, by no means eager to apprehend the culprit while he retained a weapon of offence, were now exceedingly anxious to make amends by their ultra zeal for their previous cowardice, and very shortly carried Wilmot before a magistrate, whence he was, with all speed, despatched to the secure custody of the Governor of Newgate.

As for me, I was by no means satisfied with the result of this adventure, whether considered in the abstract, or with relation to myself; and returned home that night more than usually impressed by a recollection of certain unpleasant circumstances in my life which had neither contributed to the advancement of my moral worth, nor (what was of far greater importance) had forwarded my secular interests in the slightest degree. But, '*che sarà, sarà*,'[492] and grieving will never help a lame dog over the stile, nor even furnish a plaster by which the aggrieved limb may be made whole again.

CHAPTER XIX.

WERE I not writing a history, and not a fable, my critical reader might, perchance, conceive that there was something unnatural in the conduct of Wilmot towards the ill-fated Snavel; and that although, considering the treatment he had met with at the hands of the latter, he was undoubtedly right in executing this wild justice upon him – yet, that seeing he could be no gainer by his death, Snavel having no power to make restitution, even to the tender of a doit, he was a little imprudent, in bringing his own throat to the squeeze for the momentary gratification of loosening the throat of his enemy.

To this anticipated objection I have no answer. It may be so. Suffice it to say, that as I drive no man's pigs to market except my own, so, while I claim exemption from hindrance for them, I freely permit any species of *Trulliber-ism*[493] to be tried upon the swinish progeny pertaining to other people.

The trial of Wilmot at the Old Bailey excited considerable interest; and the calm and dignified demeanour of the man during the awful suspense attending this lengthened judicial proceeding, together with the gradual knowledge of all the circumstances that impelled him to the act of murder, towards the discovery of which I was an unworthy instrument, caused a sympathy to be felt for him by the crowded court, which people are never so ready to offer as when it appears to be least needed. Nevertheless, and any thing to the contrary notwithstanding, in the shape of pity or compassion, sentence of death was recorded against the prisoner, who, bowing solemnly to the judge, was conducted out of court, to await the execution of a decree which, from the testimony of Gibbon, who saw him frequently before his trial, was a consummation devoutly prayed for by him.[494]

My uncle was in attendance at Court upon this occasion with a prospective eye to practice, and appeared to enter into the spirit of the thing with an eagerness and interest which, in spite of his knowledge of the defunct plaintiff, was to me, who knew his nature so well, by no means a common ebullition on his part. He was wont to be as unmoved at occurrences of this nature as Teneriffe or Atlas;[495] and at one time, like Nero, rather than languish without present employment, would have wished the community at large to be provided with a single neck, that he might dispose of them at once;[496] even though, like the boy with the goose, he thus, for one golden egg, deprived himself of oft-recurring benefits of a similar description.

'I'll tell you what, Jack,' said he, as we retired from the Court, 'I don't half like this 'ere business; that Wilmot's the chap I see when I called at master Snavel's office some years ago; he was a punching his own head in the passage. I don't like the tucking on him up at all, that's what I don't; why, he sarved the varmint right, didn't he now?'

I coincided in the justness of this remark; and, moreover, informed my uncle, as a proof of the superior tact evidenced by Wisp and myself, of the manner in which we had compelled Snavel to disgorge a portion of his plunder.

'No, did you now?' cried he, scratching his ear, 'well, that *was* a good 'un, blow me if it warn't; that Master Wisp was a knowing cove, and you're not much behind him; but, I say, Jack, I wonder what the lawyer did with my old woman; there was a harticle;[497] she was a rum 'un, Jack, afore I knowed her; but that's neither here nor there.'

This, also, was a narrative that I thought it not improbable my kinsman would be well pleased to hear; and I forthwith detailed to him the fatal event communicated to me by Snavel, which had made good the proverb, and had made well the wishes of my uncle, with respect to her ultimate destiny, at the same moment.

'Was she, indeed?' cried my uncle, turning round and looking up into my face with an air of vague perplexity; 'why, you don't say so? and so the fishes ha' got hold on her, have they? Well, I'm blowed;' and as we walked along, he muttered to himself at intervals, 'cantankerous cretur;' 'well, she can't get over that at any price;' 'it's put a stopper on[498] Peg, that has;' 'well, that beats all,' and the like.

When we arrived at his house, he pressed me earnestly to stay with him, a request to which, as I had no particular wish on the anvil,[499] I chose to accede; and the old gentleman smoked his pipe in silence, only broken by an occasional sigh that lifted up his chest for a moment, and then dissipated the fumes of the tobacco through the apartment in fanciful and eccentric wreaths.

It may be, that the most hardened and insensible natures are sometimes visited by a kind of bastard feeling which transports them to the past, and causes them to look upon the accumulation of years, and guilt and sorrow, with something like remorse; but I am not aware that my uncle had much cause of contrition in his early life, his murders having been invariably of a judicial nature; and, if I was rightly informed, he had merely committed some trifling offence in his youth, with a view to qualify him for the office, towards which, as I have before informed the reader, his mind recognised so extraordinary a bias. But no man feels another's toothach;[500] and we are sometimes prone to infer the existence of a perfect felicity in a superb mansion, at the same time that a battle royal is in progress of decision in the drawing-room.

'I'm getting an old man, Jack, and my hand's not so firm, like, as it used to be;' and, as my uncle so spoke, the tears stood in his eyes, and his lips quivered with a nervous trembling, and, for the time, I was struck with the certainty that he was becoming superannuated. 'I don't know how I shall do this 'ere job on Monday morning; blow me, if I do,' he continued; 'I'm gallows shaky about the daddles;[501] I shan't be able to slip a knot next.'

'Come, cheer up, cheer up,' said I, '"faint heart never won fair henroost,"[502] as the fox said to the farmer; let's have another pot.'

'Will you look down on Monday morning, then, and carry my tackle for me?'

'To be sure I will; and do the job myself, if you wish it.'

My uncle gazed at me earnestly for a minute, and then replacing his pipe into his mouth, began to smoke with great perseverance. He pressed down the ashes with his thumb. 'You're a No. 1, Jack; you're a prime piece of goods, s'help me. Well, I'll be blowed if I ever come a near such a cove as you are, Jack.'

With these blushing honours thick about me, I left the old gentleman for the night.

On Monday morning, something induced me – not any particular desire of fulfilling my promise – perhaps a fatality – to step down to my uncle for the purpose of accompanying him to the stage upon which it had been decided that Wilmot should enact his last scene. I was just about to enter Rose and Crown Court, when a ragged urchin pitched himself into my stomach, and was hastening headlong away, when, looking up into my face, he stopped suddenly, and caught me by the arm.

'Ha! Mr. Ketch, I was coming arter you; you're wanted at your uncle's; the lady at No. 7 sent me, – Mrs. Nimblejaw.'

I directed a glance towards my uncle's door, and hastened thither, anxious to learn what possible circumstance could have arisen to justify so peremptory a call upon me. As I approached, I perceived the neighbours in extreme commotion; some stepping in, others hopping out of the house; and, methought, these last carried themselves with the air of people who are carrying something else at the same time, which they would fain conceal from casual inspection. In a word, they had commenced gutting the premises which, had I been ten minutes later would, I verily believe, have been effectually and entirely disembowelled.

I entered and closed the door against these voracious harpies, and found Mrs. Nimblejaw in the lower room.

'What the deuce is the matter, Mother?' I inquired; 'Where's my uncle?'

'Aye, lad, you may well ask. Go up stairs, you'll find him there, in the museum, as he used to call it.'

'Used to call it!' and lingering in the museum at this time of the morning, when his duties called him away; it was very strange; but, without further explanation, I mounted up stairs.

Here the mystery was at an end. Suspended from a beam by a bran-new rope, which he had exhibited to me on the Saturday evening as the particular line he had selected for the suspension of Wilmot, hung my imprudent, and, perhaps, culpably rash uncle; and at the corner of his left ear stuck out a knot which, for intricacy of tie and ingenuity of construction, rivalled that which is termed, par excellence, a true lover's knot. The chair by which he had raised himself to a line with the fatal noose, had either fallen or had been kicked from beneath his feet; and methought, as he hung, surely never had twisted hemp borne so interesting an appendix. He looked like a pair of sugar nippers; but, alas! unlike in this, – that he was never more to nip the sweets of existence in this sublunary world.

I cut him down; but life had, I dare say, been long extinct; and to endeavour to recal him to this lower world, would have been not only a fruitless and unprofitable, but also an absurd, task: – for the debt of nature once satisfied is not easily renewable, – the old lady bearing an antipathy to such proceedings, similar to that of Falstaff, – who 'liked not that paying back.'[503]

In default of any available elixir, therefore, I was fain to set my ingenuity at work to discover some probable or plausible reasons for the commission of so unexpected a climax to my uncle's period of sojourn in the flesh, and was baffled and perplexed at all points. Could any consideration in which Wilmot was included – any unaccountable tenderness on that score, have superinduced this paltry evasion of his professional duties? Impossible! the whole tenor of his life forbade the humiliating conclusion. Could the memory of his wife so distract his sea of troubles[504] as to cause him to run into this unfriendly harbour? If so, he deserved the rope's end to which he had subjected himself, as a hopeless and pusillanimous lubber. No; it was clearly an unsuccessful experiment. I examined the knot again and again; it was a new tie, simple; and yet how complex! admirable for its completeness, and yet, in its negligence, how picturesque! Tyburn had never witnessed such a tie; nor had Newgate[505] hitherto glanced at such a noose. I reserved it as an invaluable work of art. I admired the design while its execution I deplored.

> ' — My uncle,
> My Father's brother, but no more — '[506]

He was indeed no more, – and hereafter could be no less. He was dust in want of a place, – mortality mystified, – mould at most, – dead at least, – gone altogether!

While I thus mused over my relative, Mrs. Nimblejaw approached, and recalled me to this breathing world.

'Ah! poor man,' she said, 'he was bent upon having something to do, I suppose, and so hanged himself. Wilmot is reprieved.'

'Indeed!' I answered, scarce heeding what she said. 'Have you any idea, mother, how or when my uncle took it into his head to put it in this noose?' and I held up the rope for her inspection; 'it must have been an accident, – a craving desire to become a perfect master of his art.'

'God knows what it was, Jack,' cried Mrs. Nimblejaw; 'but I'll tell you all I know about it,' – and she sat herself down on a stool which the ingenious deceased had curiously constructed out of a time-worn gibbet; – 'You must know,' she continued, 'that yesterday arternoon, it might be about two o'clock, Ketch comes to me, and he says, 'Mother Nimblejaw, have you got such a thing as a Bible in the house?' 'Aye, sure,' says I, 'Mr. Ketch, I have; but, worse luck, it's a thing I seldom looks into.' 'Just lend it to me for an hour,' says he, 'and I'll bring it back again.' 'Now, Ketch,' says I, 'you are not a going actually to read it, be you?' 'Yes, but I am,' said he, and away he goes. God forgive me, but I never thought the poor man could read before that blessed day. Well, he comes again in about two hours: 'I've been a reading your book,' says he, 'and I mean to take another spell at it presently.' I won't be sure these were his words; but howsomever, that's what he meant; and says he, 'I'm come to sit with you for an hour or two.' 'Well, do, Mr. Ketch,' says I; and I gets him out the arm-chair, and dusts it nice and tidy, and down he sits. There he sat his body down, if you'll believe me, Mr. Ketch, four hours; and put me in mind, for all the world, barring the hump, of Nimblejaw, when he was alive. Smoke, smoke, smoke, pipe after pipe, and drinking gin and water – that was not his drink, you know – going on about his wife, and that Mr. Snavel, and the unfortunate man he was a going to hang, and you, and such a pedigree. Well, at last he gets up. 'Good night,' says he. 'Good night, Mr. Ketch.' Lord bless me, if he warn't a going without his hat; but at last away he goes. Presently he comes again. 'It's uncommon dull at home,' he says. 'I dare say you find it so, Mr. Ketch,' says I, – for he *was* a lone man, and no one to look arter him; and down he sits again – smokes another pipe – gets up again – goes out – comes in again, – there he was, poor cretur, like a dog that had burnt his tail, – in and out – sitting down – getting up – twisting and turning. At last to make an end of my story, he goes away for good; and I never clapt eyes on him till I see him about half an hour ago, – poor creter!'

At the conclusion of this narrative, Mrs. Nimblejaw had recourse to her apron; some artificial tears she dropt, but wiped them soon, and accompanied me down stairs, whither I went to act in the capacity of residuary legatee of the defunct functionary.

The Bible was lying on the table. A piece of paper stuck out from between the leaves. I opened the volume; my uncle had been reading the Book of Exodus, – typical of his deliverance from this wilderness of life, – and on the paper was a heterogeneous collection of marks, which seemed like the unsuccessful endeavour of a maniac to imitate the Arabic character; but out of which, notwithstanding, after much labour, I succeeded in forming the following epistle: –

'dere Jack, –

'i am a going to go – and i leaves all the things to you xept the chest of draws which i promissed to giv muther Knimblejor – you will fine the stuff in the paper box up stares. Se arter my place will you – you are the man they wonts.

'J. K.'

This laconic production operated as a charm to set me upon the best means of fulfilling the intentions of the testator to the very letter; and I accordingly proceeded to make such arrangements as the peculiar circumstances called upon me to adopt. The conclusion, also, pointed to a consummation devoutly to be wished, and therefore instantly to be looked after; and I lost no time in despatching a letter to Mr. Sheriff[507] Hopkins, in which my qualifications for the vacant office were duly set forth and enlarged upon; – and now the apex of my ambition appeared to surmount the hazy atmosphere of the future with a splendid but, to the philosophic eye, not an insufferable brilliance.

CHAPTER XX.

HAVING religiously observed the injunctions of my uncle, contained in the document, a copy of which I have laid before the reader, not forgetting the bequest to Mrs. Nimblejaw, I proceeded to secure the furniture and all other valuables from the furtive fingers of the neighbourhood; and so arranged the evidence offered to the Coroner's inquest[508] by Mrs. Nimblejaw and myself, as to cause them to bring in a verdict of 'accidental death.' But as there is in human nature a prevailing querulousness, and an unaccountable propensity to lay the fault pertaining, or supposed to pertain to any casualty, upon somebody; or in default of being able to find somebody, upon something; so these grave quidnuncs[509] caused a deodand[510] of five shillings to be levied upon the rope wherewith the unfortunate man had, as they supposed, been trying such hazardous conclusions.

I have heard of some approved instances of individuals who, having lost a leg, nevertheless feel acute physical pain in that particular portion of space which that useful member of the body corporate in fact no longer occupies. Is this a bonâ fide[511] sensation? Undoubtedly. But does it not appear absurd, and in the highest degree ridiculous? No question about it. Now, it seems to me, that to grieve for individuals who no longer exist, though it may be natural in one sense, and proper to do so, is, philosophically to speak, a lamentable defection from reason and common sense. The will may and can repress that grief; whereas, in the other case, no power can prevent that sensation. The senses are arbitrary, but the feeling is a slave. And as a man, by relinquishing his amputated limb to the earth, may thereby supply such nourishment to the ground as will stimulate the growth of some tree, from which in time he may recruit himself with a wooden substitute, – so, by dismissing our deceased friend from our minds, we thereby leave room for the growth of another friendship; and though he be a wooden-headed fellow – the only genuine lignum-vitæ[512] – what matter?

I accordingly thrust on one side all melancholy impressions arising out of the recent calamity, – and my uncle proceeded on his journey, which so many pilgrims have gone before, and so many are still to undertake, with exceeding good wishes on my part, but with no clamorous and indecent lamentations.

On making further inquiries respecting Wilmot, I learned that a representation had been made to the Home Secretary,[513] to the effect that the misguided man was not altogether of a sane mind at the time of his perpetrating the murder for which he had been tried; and that the King had been pleased to command that his execution should be postponed until the truth of that conjecture had been satisfactorily and completely ascertained.

And now my mind was strenuously bent upon attaining that object of ambition shadowed forth in my uncle's testament; and it is surprising with what facility a man, to whom some new and desirable office is, however suddenly, presented, discovers in himself the particular aptitude – the peculiar fitness – the exact degree of capability – which calls upon him, more than upon any other individual in the universe, to occupy, to fill, and to enjoy it. I could never, were I to write or to speak volumes, explain how it happened that I was made to feel, that I, and I alone, was calculated to be, not merely a worthy but, a transcendently worthy successor to my uncle; but, perhaps, the reader, during our short acquaintance, may have gathered enough evidence of my nature to believe that I was marked out, as it were, for the situation at this present juncture vacant.

Pending the negociations between Mr. Sheriff Hopkins and myself – a period of no small excitement on my part – I waited on my old friend Misty, for the purpose of craving his advice, and, if it were available, his assistance, towards the furtherance of my views. Misty was one of those soft, simple-hearted creatures, who, having a strangely overweening faith in their own knowledge of mankind, are so easily deceived, as almost to deprive the cajoling party of the merit, or the disgrace (whichever the reader pleases) of duplicity in any matter in which they are to be made dupes. I had hitherto encouraged a belief in Misty of my integrity and virtue, – a result scarcely to be expected, considering the circumstances under which our acquaintance had recommenced; and now more than ever was he inclined to give me credit for many highly respectable and much to be commended refinements and excesses of feeling, which, although I took some pains at the time to mature into certainty in his breast, I have not been hypocrite enough to affect in this volume. Sufficient for the day is the evil thereof:[514] – sufficient for the purpose was my hypocrisy. I am now sincere.

Acting upon this mistaken notion of my character, Misty had frequently stood my friend, upon occasions – which a perfect knowledge of his nature, and an exact calculation of the depth and measure of his credulity, caused me to make and to find – occasions, for the most part, I mean, which not my circumstances so much as my pleasure incited me to lay before him. It is true that he possessed ample means of supplying my demands; and although the chance or fortune by which he had become so excellently set out and garnished with the wherewithal was to me as yet unknown; still it was apparent, after a very slight scrutiny of the man, that what he held, he held rightly; and that all crooked and indirect measures were as unknown to him as they were intimate with me.

Misty heard me with profound attention; and appeared by occasional inclinations of the head, as I proceeded, to enter into my views and feelings. He paused for some minutes after I concluded.

'Your uncle was a worthy man,' at length he remarked, thoughtfully, 'a very worthy man; I have met him frequently at the house to which we were accustomed to resort, – a single-minded man, indeed, – I respected him much.'

'A slave to his profession,' said I, – 'I may say, a martyr to it; let me hope that I – '

'And why not?' interrupted Misty, with much animation – 'and why not a worthy man, I should be glad to ask? Wherefore should a mischievous and narrow-minded prejudice affix a stigma to a profession, as you justly call it, Mr. Ketch, – calculated, if pursued in a right spirit, and with a philosophical purpose, to elevate and ennoble the nature, to improve the heart, to correct the understanding, to enlarge the mind. – I approve your choice – I envy you the opportunities that will be afforded to you of studying human nature in a particular point of view, and relative aspect, from which the great majority of the world is debarred. You will see the strong and the weak mind, – the highly gifted and the meanest intellect, – the base, the misguided; wretchedness, recklessness, despair: you will behold all these about to pass the threshold of eternity, – you almost hear the gate creak on its hinges, – you almost see them on the other side, – you read in their faces the record of the day of judgment.[515] But the mechanical part, – can you do that? – have you nerve?'

'Oh, yes, that is a simple operation,' I observed, 'practice will doubtless ensure facility.'

'I *could* do it,' resumed Misty, with enthusiasm; 'my heart would let me do it now; but these nerves of mine, – these cursed sensibilities, – a physical infirmity, after all, – for sensibility is merely a physical weakness acting upon the mind, – these would stand in my way, and furnish an insurmountable obstacle to my success.'

'There is *my* fear,' said I; 'it is not every man, Mr. Misty, that can overlay the deep feelings of his nature with the indifference of the Stoic.'[516]

'True, true,' he answered, with a sigh; 'it is not *every* man that can do so, Mr. Ketch. I believe you to be a man of feeling; the sentiments of tender regard, and the expressions of unbounded grief, which fell unbidden from your lips when you made me acquainted with the death of that sweet young creature – your poor wife; these convince me that you are a man of feeling. The appropriate reflections I afterwards heard from you on the transportation of the unhappy Mr. Wisp, assure me that you are a man of principle and virtue. Indeed, they did you honour; nor have you cause to be ashamed of them. Well, then, can you, do you think, thus morally circumstanced, undertake the duties of an office, which has been falsely supposed to be most peculiarly fitted for one utterly without feeling, and entirely destitute of principle and virtue?'

I answered, that my life had hitherto been so attended by want, or by merely transient and swiftly-vanishing glimpses of prosperity, that I should be too happy to secure a certainty even of this nature. I added, also, that no possible situation in life could reflect real disgrace upon him who walked uprightly and honestly in the path of duty; and that I was willing to encounter the odium attached unjustly to the office to which I aspired, confident that prejudice and error must eventually fall harmless from its intended victim.

'As water from the swan's back, or as earth from the glossy skin of the mole,' cried Misty, shaking me by the hand; 'and reflect, Mr. Ketch, upon what I have been impressing upon you. With your talents, which, believe me, are considerable, there will be nothing that comes under your eye in your profession but will furnish an important lesson in ethics and morality to yourself; and through you, digested, matured, and committed to paper, be an invaluable present to the world at large. I will call upon you to-morrow. Anxious and interested, believe me, am I for your success. Good bye!'

I could not repress a smile, as I returned home, at the credulous simplicity of my friend, or refrain from taking some credit to myself for the skill with which I had so long retained his friendship and esteem. This had been chiefly effected by repeating, after long intervals, – when the original announcement of them might naturally be supposed to be forgotten, – certain favourite sentiments and moral axioms of his own, which I took care to disguise so ingeniously as to make them pass for original conclusions. This I have invariably found to be a good and effectual device; since it not only confirms the dupe in a belief of your morality and wisdom, but gratifies him with the fond notion that he has discovered a congenial spirit.

True to his word, Misty called upon me on the following day, and was a little concerned to hear that I had not yet received any definitive answer to my application.

'I am anxious,' said he, 'to see you installed into this appointment. The more I think of it, the more am I persuaded that to the philosophical inquirer it will afford a wide field of interesting – nay, of profound instruction in morals. Believe, Mr. Ketch, men are not to be distributed into moral classes; and that one common nature runs and reigns through all. Tell me not of virtue or of vice; these are but as colours, generated by certain motions, impressed upon the eye, and not existent in the things themselves, that seem to wear this or that particular hue. Be it your task to analyse the human mind – to sift, to weigh, to compare; and it shall be my pleasing duty to aid you from time to time in the selection of such specimens as your daily increasing stock will supply you with.'

'You see, sir,' said I, as I conducted him up stairs to the museum, 'that my late uncle was not altogether unimpressed by a sense of the value of such materials for philosophical purposes; and to these mementos of the departed,' and I pointed to the various ropes that hung in decent and becoming order on the walls, 'to these his surprising memory was accustomed to append many long and touching narratives, which now, I fear, must perish in oblivion. Unhappily, however, my deceased relative was not blessed with an intellect of the highest order, neither was his mind prone to the drawing of any nice moral distinctions; and again, had he committed to paper the results of his experience, I cannot but think that his orthography and style might have rendered his fame as an author at least doubtful.'

'That is a pity,' said Misty, gravely. 'And yet even these relics have their use: you may hang a moral upon them even now;' and he proceeded to examine them with attention. He started suddenly, and a rope which he had taken into his hand fell from his fingers. I read the name attached to it. 'It was a case of forgery,' said I.

'It was; I remember it. I knew him slightly,' answered Misty. 'Let us go down stairs.'

He sat for some minutes in silence. 'Cannot we have a bottle of wine together?' at length he said; 'you must excuse me, Mr. Ketch, if I pay for it.' He drew out his purse, and handed me the money.

'There is no stimulant on earth like this,' said Misty, as, having returned with a bottle of port, I placed it on the table. 'I have tried all – the wines of France and Germany, brandy, rum, Hollands,[517] whiskey, English gin, ale, porter, tea, coffee, tobacco and snuff; they won't do. Port is the *elixir vitæ*, the *aurum potabile,* the nectar of the Gods,[518] the blessing, the comfort of men. Without it, what are friends? – with it, what are they? For a dozen[519] of port I would willingly surrender to any one in want of such articles all the friends I ever had in the world.'

Misty uttered this speech with unaccustomed gaiety; but he was unable to conceal from me that it was a decoy to lure me from a suspicion of the state of his feelings at the moment.

'Pardon me, Mr. Misty,' said I, 'but you have honoured me with your friendship for some years, and at length I am enabled to entertain you under my own poor roof; is it too much to request you to afford me an outline of your history? Let me know to whom I have been indebted for so much kindness; let me participate in the joy of your recovered prosperity; let me sympathise with your former sorrows and distress; let me – '

'My worthy young friend,' – and Misty interrupted a speech which was running from my tongue with a glibness and fluency perfectly enchanting to myself – 'I have nothing to tell that may not be told in ten minutes, a space of time that would be sorrily occupied by myself, and no better spent by you. To you my recital might be tedious; to me it would be distressing. And yet, why not? My story may solve some problem in the science of morals. I also, who never set an example even to myself, may supply a lesson to others.'

So saying, Misty swallowed another glass of wine, and leaning his head upon his hand, thus delivered himself: – 'To be blind, Mr. Ketch, is a bad thing, but to have one's eyes open in the dark is not much better. I have not been blind, but I have been in the dark all my life. I am the only son of a gentleman of moderate fortune in the county of Sussex, of whom let me say nothing that may recal bitter feelings within me, for he is dead. Suffice it, from my infancy he hated me. Shall I surmise the reason of his antipathy? no. He had his reasons, doubtless; if they were valid, they will weigh in his behalf in the other world; if otherwise, it concerns not me. I have outlived my hostilities.

'Now, sir, to be sensitive and to be proud is to be cursed, and to be conscious of it. I was sensitive by nature, and my pride was a garment worn for the purpose of concealing my infirmity. I think no man in my life, now alive, can hug himself with the certainty that he ever wounded my feelings. I took too good care of that. To the world, then, I have ever appeared to be a man entirely without feeling; to myself, my feelings have been a bitter curse. Do you understand me? Yes.

'It was very early in my youth that I discovered that I was not constituted as other natures are. A mellow evening, a tone of voice that struck upon the chord of memory – the tone, I say, and not the thing spoken, whatever it might be – a trait of generosity in others, a word of praise spoken to myself, – all these would bring tears into my eyes, and sometimes, induce a melancholy that preyed upon me for hours. I had been taught to look up to my father as to a superior being; and his invariable harshness and cruelty to me helped, perhaps, to break my spirit and to poison my nature. Do not mistake me; my nature was gentle, but it was not healthy; it was inoffensive because it was weak. I became distrustful of everything – of everybody – of myself. I dare not appear to feel, when not to feel were to be a brute; I was afraid lest I should be made a mockery – lest I should be held up to the world as one upon whom it might exercise its scorn and ridicule with success and impunity.

'But there was one – yes, one whom I *could* trust with a knowledge of my secret nature. I had known Clara Marston from my infancy, and (for the heart is susceptible of the passion of love at a very early age) I had loved her from my infancy. I had been accustomed to spend many an hour, which would otherwise have been wearisome and gloomy indeed, at her mother's house; and as we grew up, in like manner did a mutual love grow between us. Do not laugh, Mr. Ketch, that I talk of love:

> "Old as I am, for lady's love unfit,
> The power of beauty I remember yet."[520]

And, moreover, I speak but truth. Passionately did I love Clara Marston, and with no less ardour did she return my affection. This continued for some years; for I had been brought up at home under the care of a private tutor; and when I went to college, the connexion was for the first time broken off. Just at this period, also, Mrs. Marston settled in London, for what purpose I knew not then, but discovered; if not satisfactorily, at least perfectly, in the sequel.

'In the meanwhile, my father's moroseness, as I approached manhood, increased daily; and my home became unendurable to me. I was overjoyed when the time came round that was to find me again at college; and when at length I left the University, it seemed as though the whole world were now closed against me. Sometimes I would venture to sound my father touching some profession, and endeavour to draw from him an explanation of his intentions, whether in my favour or otherwise; but he uniformly repulsed my endeavours, whether towards a better understanding between us, or a better understanding of my own particular destiny.

'Many things, Mr. Ketch, were they not true, would seem but bungling contrivances of fiction; and this insane antipathy on the part of my father would be of them. No cause assigned, hinted at, or to be surmised; no cause that I ever succeeded in discovering – and yet the most mortal hatred, the most malignant hostility against me. Did he suspect the virtue of my poor mother, who had been long laid in her grave? No. The world at least had recognised her as a pattern of prudence and discretion, – as one fulfilling every duty of a wife and a mother with exemplary strictness and religious fidelity. For such men, therefore, our best apology is silence. There *is* an hour, Mr. Ketch, in every man's life, of bitter reproach, of torturing compunction, for such flagrant acts as these; he felt that hour. I hope he did; for it will lessen his account in the other world.

'At length an uncle of mine died, and left me a legacy of a thousand pounds; it came in good time. I was now of age, and had resolved to endure this degrading life no longer; I would live on no man's reluctant bounty; I would be beholden to no man, who could make the obligation a balance to cruelty and unjust and inhuman treatment of me. I left him, therefore, to gnaw his own heart, undisturbed and at leisure; and came up to London, determined to seek a livelihood for myself in the best way I could, and to apply to and to see him no more. I took chambers in one of the inns of court,[521] and entered into life on my own account, as it were; yet more as a passive observer than as one whose aim it must soon become to play as successful a part in the game as his abilities, opportunities, and ambition, may suffice to bear him through the chances of it. My first impulse, however, was to seek out the residence of Mrs. Marston, which with some difficulty I discovered at the west end of the town,[522] in one of those streets set apart for that particular class of people who are far too refined to mix with the commonly respectable, and at the same time altogether too poor to venture into the world of fashion. These nondescript beings, Mr. Ketch, compound for a servile imitation of the wealthy in all their baser conventionalities, by a profound contempt for those who, having no such qualities as belong to their idols, and no such servility as exists in themselves, are content to rely on their own respectability for that station in society, which their superiors in wealth may pretend to ridicule, but which they dare not even affect to despise.

'I renewed my intimacy with Clara Marston, and the same feelings that had subsisted between us in our earliest youth were renewed, with all the additional warmth which our long separation, and our more legitimate ages, might be supposed to engender. It was not until after many weeks that I discovered, (and then I was willing to believe that it was merely a false impression of my own), that the mother was hardly disposed to encourage an attachment so zealously as heretofore. But as she was silent upon the subject, I also was equally taciturn upon that score; and was content with unrestrained permission to see Clara from day to day. Upon these occasions, I urged my suit with much perseverance and fervour; for I had taken a notion into my head that, once married, the very necessity of applying to a profession would determine me to some particular course; and I was willing to trust to fortune and to my own exertions for the consummation of my hopes in the secondary matter of secular position.

'There was at this time a constant visiter at the house of Mrs. Marston. Mr. Western was a merchant in the city, and a man of the world; that is, a man whose mind is to a soul what chairs and tables are to the universe. His ideas were all mechanical, material, gross; and beyond a good dinner and its concomitants, helped out with a blind cupidity for the comforts of life, this person had no inclination to reach. And yet there was – but I will not anticipate.

'I used occasionally to express my surprise to Clara, that Western should be so constant a visiter at her mother's house; and we have often smiled at the supposed result of this intimacy being manifested by a proposal on his part to join his fortunes with those of Mrs. Marston, – the ages of the two being nearly similar, – and the match not such as, on the lady's side, was to be hastily rejected or capriciously despised. For a time, this was an innocent pleasantry between Clara and myself; but, methought, latterly she smiled less and less at the supposition, and at last was particularly grave whenever the subject was referred to.

'At length, this mystery was cleared up. Mrs. Marston one day expressed a wish to speak to me for a few minutes alone, and drew me to the window. I need hardly explain to you, Mr. Ketch, the woman whom I even now remember with disgust; enough to say, that if Western was a man, Mrs. Marston was a woman, of the world. As we stood together at the window, much did she talk, while she dived her hand into her reticule, of the precarious chances of young people left to the sole care of a mother, as "her Clara" was; much did she lament that she had not "set her face" against an attachment, which she could not but perceive might have led to serious results; happy, however, was she to know that 'her girl' had too much good sense to be led away by false sentiment, and all such stuff. In a word, after a vast deal of preparatory exhibition of prudence and worldly wisdom, she informed me that Western had proposed for her daughter, and that Clara had consented to receive him as a suitor upon trial – that is to say, as a husband so soon as circumstances would allow the marriage to take place.

'I was confounded at this piece of intelligence; but succeeded in stifling my feelings ere they became apparent to the smirking being before me.

'"May I presume to beg," I asked, calmly, "that I may have a confirmation of this unexpected news from the mouth of Miss Marston herself?"

'"Oh, certainly," she answered, with great placidity, "she shall attend you directly;" and she sidled and rustled from the apartment.

'I met Clara half way as she entered the room, and led her to a chair. She was evidently in a state of painful confusion, and kept her eyes fixed upon the ground.

'"Is this true, Clara," I demanded, "that your mother has been telling me? Have you discarded me? Have you consented to receive Mr. Western as a suitor?" She was silent, but bowed her head slightly, as though she meant to confirm the truth of her mother's statement.

'"Have you not been compelled into this match? Answer me, I beseech you. Do you consent to it of your own free will?" Her lips moved, as I leaned my head towards her; a faint "yes" trembled upon them, and they were colourless; and her hand, though it also trembled, was cold.

'"Enough! A few letters have passed between us, Clara, and some trifling presents; you will not keep them, of course. Will you let me have them this evening? I will bring yours with me. It is proper, I believe, to exchange such things at such times."

'I arose and left her without further word, upheld by pride, I suppose, or I know not what, – and proceeded to my lodging, where I collected together all the letters she had ever sent me, without even looking into them again; and with her miniature, which she had given to me but one short month before, made them into a small parcel, and put them into my pocket.

'I returned in the evening to the house of Mrs. Marston. Western was there, as usual, in high spirits, entertaining the ladies with anecdotes pertaining to the class to which he belonged, and making himself as agreeable as it was in his power to be; and far be it from me to deny his merits, whatever they might have been, or were. Mrs. Marston also was in excellent temper, doubtless owing to a complacent review of the ease and success with which she had accomplished her design of putting a stop to my visits to her daughter; and appeared to owe me a debt of gratitude for my readiness to waive any supposed claims I might possess, on the score of priority, to Clara's hand. Accordingly, she took occasion to draw

Western from the room, and to leave Clara and me together, as soon as the tea was removed.

'I handed her the packet without speaking, and she drew from her bosom the miniature I had presented to her in exchange for her own, and some letters which I had addressed to her – more made up of sentiment, Mr. Ketch, than of sense, I dare say; but as sincere and ardent as woman ever received and ever returned. I threw them into the fire, and the miniature followed them with equal promptness.

'She caught me by the arm as I did this. "Oh Henry!" she said, hastily, "even now it may not be too late."

'"To be left a larger fortune than Western possesses. True," said I, sarcastically; "in which case, doubtless, you would choose me in preference to him. I thank you, but I would rather be excused. Perish all, but the memory of all, that has existed between us, Clara."

'I turned, – she was in tears. "Nay, forgive me," said I, and I stooped and took her hand between my own; "I did not mean to insult you, Clara; I hope you may be happy with Mr. Western; I trust you will never regret the step you have taken, – and God bless you!" I pressed her hand and left her, making my way to a tavern, where I, for the first time in my life, got drunk – very drunk; and until the next morning forgot that I had relinquished the only hope of happiness that I had ever entertained in the world.'

As Misty closed this sentence, a letter was delivered to me from Mr. Sheriff Hopkins, requiring to see me the first thing on the following morning; and my visitor having congratulated me on the chance of a fortunate issue to my application, indicated by the contents of the note just received, renewed his story, as follows in the next chapter.

CHAPTER XXI.

'DEPEND upon it, my good friend,' resumed Misty, 'that a wounded spirit must be assuaged, or healed, or got rid of, by some means or the other. Hence drunkenness, desperation, suicide. The first frequently precedes the other two, and sometimes causes a recourse to them; but drinking will suffice to keep out the foul fiend, despair, for many years. I invoked the aid of the benignant spirit of drunkenness; and not a day passed from the evening on which I had relinquished Clara Marston for ever, until the day of her marriage, that I did not drown my senses in forgetfulness and wine.

'Something prompted me to be a witness of the ceremony. I rose at an early hour, and entered the church, which as yet contained but one living creature – an old woman, who was busily employed in sweeping the matting in the centre aisle. I presented her with a shilling, and requested her to place me in a pew contiguous to the altar, from whence I might unobserved behold the solemnisation of a marriage between two persons – so opposite in every respect – so contrary in temper and disposition – so unlike in feelings – so different in age, as to make religion itself appear a mockery. Did God sanction this ceremony? No. Was not His name abused when the minister invoked His blessing on a pair, that might more truly be called a disparity?

'I have told you that I loved Clara Marston. You never can know, however, for she never knew – nor did I myself know, until years of madness and despair taught me that truth at last, *how* I loved that girl. And yet, I saw the marriage – beheld it calmly – listened to every word as the service proceeded – awaited its conclusion, and then retired from the church with the outward indifference of a casual spectator.

'I must see more, too, – I must tamper and trifle with my feelings till they burst asunder, and let madness into my brain. I knew that Western intended to spend the honeymoon at a small villa a few miles from London; no sooner had the carriage departed than I followed thither. In the evening, when it was become dark, I entered the shrubbery. I beheld the festive dance through a window, the blind of which had not been closely drawn. I beheld Clara, – she also danced; and, only that she was somewhat pale and pensive, methought she never looked more beautiful. I waited there for hours, and sucked into my soul a morbid delight, which few could understand, and still less would envy me the possession of. Once, and but once, she approached the very window, and threw it up; and as she sat there for a few minutes, I could almost have touched her with my hand from the spot where I stood concealed.

'But it was growing late; the visiters were departed – the chandeliers extinguished – the whole house, the neighbourhood, in repose. I also retired; but how I reached London, I know not. My first consciousness informed me that I was in a tavern at the west end of the town, – two empty champagne bottles on the table, – candles that appeared to be asleep, – a yawning waiter in the distance, who would fain have been asleep in reality. I ordered one bottle more, which I drank with desperate rapidity; and rushing from the coffee room, reached my own chambers, where the woman found me next morning, extended on the floor of the parlour, raging with a brain fever.

'The six weeks that followed I would not endure again to purchase heaven. I recovered slowly, however; and when I arose from my bed, the former world had passed away from me, and I was left alone to struggle with fortune for a crust wherewith to support an existence which had become hateful to me; for my money was rapidly leaving me. I had no other friend in the world, – there *is* no other friend: to dig I was unable, and to beg I was ashamed.

'I was halting along the park one morning, when an open carriage attracted my attention. It was approaching towards me, and I perceived that Western and his wife were seated in it. Western ordered the coachman to draw up to the side of the path, and accosted me with great kindness, and apparent sympathy.

'"A brain fever," said he, – "a bad thing, – a very bad thing; let us hope you will soon get round; – but you don't see your old acquaintance," – and he turned towards Clara.

'I *had* seen her, though; and I had marked the ghastly paleness that came over her face when her eyes met mine. Could she, then, still love me? Had there been any compulsion on the part of her mother? Oh, no; Mammon is a brisk suitor – it was impossible. I smiled faintly: there might have been a slight curl of pride on my lip, as I said distantly – "I am happy to have the pleasure of paying my respects to Mrs. Western." A few more words of course; a polite invitation – a bow – and they were gone.

'An intimation was some months after this meeting conveyed to me from Western, that he would be happy to serve me in any way that I would point out, as likely to fall within the scope of his influence; and as he feared that I was not so well off in the world as I deserved, he begged that I would accept an enclosure of twenty pounds.

'At this moment I possessed but two guineas, nor did I know any practicable means of recruiting my fortunes, or even of obtaining a subsistence. And yet, had that twenty pounds been twenty thousand, coming whence it did, I would have rejected it, – not with scorn, – for, perhaps, Western had offered it in a friendly spirit, – but in such a manner as should effectually prevent a repetition of the same insult. I did so, and heard no more of him.

'Oh! Mr. Ketch, how dreadful a thing it is to be proud and poor. I felt it, – it was hell to me: not the physical want, – not starvation, – not tramping the streets all night without a shelter for the head, or a resting-place for the sole of the foot, – but the insult – the contumely – the scorn: I felt it until my nature was changed, – until my feelings turned into gall, and burst forth into bitterness. The proudest man must condescend to live; and to do so without means, what must he do? Beg. I could not do that. You may naturally inquire, how a man of my education and acquirements could possibly be suffered to linger in penury, if I made known my capabilities to the world. Alas! I was not the man to blazon my own merits, such as they were; besides, I would rather have broken stones on the road than be at the mercy of men who, aware of the superiority of another in mental endowments, vindicate their actual superiority in secular advantages, by compelling him to feel how dependent he is upon their bounty. For, these men do not feel, or will not acknowledge, that the services you render are the labour for which you ought to be paid; but pocket the advantage, and lay claim to the merit of benevolence. Better for a proud man, Mr. Ketch, to be far below his real station than just under it; it is easier to bear extreme poverty, nay, want, than to endure the unworthy insolence of a patron, or a friend, so called.

'To friends, therefore, I applied but seldom, and never with much advantage to myself; and I was contented to earn a small pittance from a law stationer's occasional employment of me, and to trust to Providence, as the ravens do, – but not with the same success.

'It struck me one night, as I paced up and down Westminster Bridge – for I had no bed to go to – that I would apply to my father in person. It was his duty, at least, to provide for me. I knew too well that his inclination would not keep pace with his sense of duty, however slow of pace the latter might be. In a word, I got together a few shillings with much difficulty, and set out on foot for my native place.

'You have never, perhaps, seen your face in a particular looking-glass after an interval of some years; if you had done so, you would have detected the changes that time had worked upon you in a moment, – a change which your daily looking-glass had failed to discover to you. This is association. In like manner a scene – a place – the home of your youth, familiar to the past, brought before you once more, discloses the altered aspect of the mind within. How different a man had I become since last I had seen my father's house. I almost shuddered at my own former likeness thus presented to me, and was fain, before I proceeded to apply to the bell-rope, to fortify myself with a dram of brandy.

"'What! Master Henry, is that you?" said Higgins, the butler, as he met me in the hall, – "you're come in an ill time, I fear; master won't see you, I'm afraid."

"'Won't is an arbitrary word, Higgins; but *must* will do as well. My father must see me."

"'Lord bless you! he's married again since you left us, – a poor girl out of the village, – and has got a little boy."

"'Well, well, no matter," said I; "tell him his son desires to see him;" and as Higgins entered the library to announce my arrival, I followed in his wake, and stood before my father.

"'Well, what brings you here, sir?" said he, looking up from his writing desk. "Higgins, leave the room."

"'Necessity, sir, as you may perceive – a sorry steed, but a sure one."

"'Which may carry you back again," retorted my father; "I can do nothing for you."

"'Look you, sir," said I; "you do not see the poor tame spiritless boy whom you were wont to spurn beneath your feet; I am now a man, equal with yourself – aye, in all respects your equal. I am poor – I have known want, famine, and desperate distress, and must not be put off as heretofore. I claim something at your hands, – I am your son."

'He appeared surprised at my manner, and looked at me for a minute steadfastly. But he turned away from me on the sudden. "You shall get nothing from me, my good fellow, if you stand here till doomsday."

"'Yes, one thing I will have," said I, calmly.

"'And what is that?" he demanded, in surprise.

"'Your hand; which you shall give me, to prove yourself the vilest creature breathing. Come, confess, what is your motive for treating me thus? Did I ever injure, ever offend you? – and yet from my infancy have you persecuted, and inhumanly persecuted me. Oh, father! father! give me your hand, and prove yourself a villain at once. I will take nothing from you but your hand, – you cannot withhold it from me, I have never wronged you."

"'You *shall* have my hand," said he; and he arose and came towards me. He gazed at me for a moment, and his brow darkened, and he dashed his fist in my face, and would again have done so; – but I stopped his hand.

'I staggered back, for I was weak with walking; and the man before me was powerful, and my father; but I revived suddenly, and sprang towards him, seizing him by the shoulder with my hands. "Father," – I gasped for breath, and every word came with terrible distinctness from my throat, – "when you shall lie dying, you will send for me; do not think that I will come: when you shall lie dead, believe not that I will pollute my eyes with your remains; but when you lie in your grave, – thus, thus, will I spurn you" – and I stamped upon the ground

– "for this your treatment of me," – and dreadful tears burst from my eyes as I spoke; – "curse – curse you, for ever."

'I fell down senseless; I had broken a blood vessel, and was carried up into a chamber which was once my own. My feelings, so long repressed, had burst open beyond human power of control; and when I revived to a consciousness of my situation, I discovered at the bottom of my heart, a bitter contempt and hatred of my father, that I had once thought never to have entertained towards any human being. Ere I was well able to walk, I arose from my bed, and resolved to leave the house for ever. As I passed through the hall, the door of the library opened, and my father came forth.

"'Where are you going, Henry?" he inquired.

"'I am going, sir."

"'But you will see me again?"

"'In another world, perhaps," said I, – "never in this."

"'Well, well," he answered, thoughtfully, – and he drew out his pocket-book, – "this may be of service, at all events," – and he placed a 50*l.* note in my hand.

'I looked at the note for a moment, and turned my eye upon him coldly. "Buy a dog with this," said I; "spurn him well, – don't spare shoe-leather, or hunting-whip, – and call his name Henry." I laid the note upon his hand, and walked from the house.

'If I ever felt anything very acutely, Mr. Ketch, it was the remembrance of that moment; I had cut him to the quick – I had made him feel at last. His look, which never can be described, can never be forgotten.

'I returned to town almost pennyless; and as I traversed the empty streets – for it was early morning when I arrived in London – the spirit that had supported me so long gave way, and I sat down on a door-step, and wept. This passion of tears relieved me; and when I looked up, the sun was rising above the horizon – the market-carts were proceeding to Covent Garden[523] – the watchmen had slunk into their watch-boxes to indulge in secure repose – and here and there a drunkard dotted the long vista of pavement, who, with short pipe, and muttered reminiscence of supposed wrong done to his person on the past night, staggered away into some coach-yard, or stable, to nestle until noon.

'A saloop-stall[524] invited me to partake of its refreshment. I accepted the invitation; and, slightly strengthened by the wholesome beverage, lingered and sauntered about the streets, waiting till the calls of business should awaken the world once more. Yet why should I concern myself with business that, alas! concerned not me? I had nothing to do, but what I was then doing – to wander through a vast and wealthy city without a farthing beyond the coming day to gild the prospect of to-morrow.

'At length, the shops began to open one by one; and it occurred to me, as a small shaving-shop now disclosed its magnetic pole, that to be shaved and washed, even at the expense of three-halfpence (a sum I could ill spare), would not be a waste of money. I accordingly went in, and sat down in the vacant chair.

'"Strange times, these, sir, strange times," said the barber, preparing the lather for my face, – "we are going to have an execution this morning;" – and now for the first time I remarked that I was in the Old Bailey.

'"Who is the unfortunate man?" I inquired, – "of what crime has he been convicted?"

'"Oh! hav'nt you heard all about it, sir?" cried the barber; "but I see by your shoes you have just come from the country, – they hear nothing there. Why, sir," – and he drew the razor across my face, – "it is a Mr. Western, sir, – a large merchant."

'I started up at the hazard of my throat. "Mr. Western! Good Heavens!" – but I checked myself, and lifting the chair which I had overturned, and reseating myself, I muttered an apology for my agitation.

'"Well, I really thought you were ill," said the persevering operator, determined to secure me as an auditor, – "well, sir, this Mr. Western was a large merchant, and reputed rich. But now it all comes out that he has been living in splendour on the money of other people; he has committed such lots of forgeries; you must get the papers and read the whole from beginning to end." The barber added much more; and, indeed, furnished me with a faithful abstract of all the delinquencies of Western.

'The impending fate of the unhappy man was not the first idea that presented itself to my mind, when I left the shaving-shop. I thought of Clara and her mother; and I almost felt a joy to think that their dream of happiness had met with so rude an awakening. "Such be the end," said I, "of marriages like these, – not made in heaven, but perfected in hell. Such be the reward of those who worship mammon: – since they craved the homage that a base world is ever too willing to pay to wealth, let them not repine at the contempt and scorn of a base world, which it is equally prepared to extend to misfortune."

'I mingled with the crowd, and awaited the coming forth of Western. I saw him in the hideous agony of his spirit; I saw him hanged; and I waited till the expiration of the hour, when he was cut down, and delivered to his friends. Poor wretch! And for this haggard, guilty, miserable creature, had I been spurned by Clara. For this wretched counterfeit of wealth had I been set on one side as a thing of no present value, and of no future promise. "Ha! ha! ha!" I laughed – laughed madly; "this is prudence; this is your worldly wisdom; this is your comfortable settlement – your snug jointure; these are your ties, are they? These are your neck-or-nothing[525] expedients? The neck device for your husband, and the nothing for you!"

'I had read from time to time in the newspapers of Western's brilliant parties and splendid fêtes, and of the first-rate actors and professional singers whom he was accustomed to entertain. I had heard of his fine house in Berkeley-square, and his newly-purchased estate, and of his lovely, amiable, and accomplished wife; and all come to this poor foolish swing in the air at last! Well, well, Providence tempers the wind to the shorn lamb![526] And all this was a comfort to me, and a warmth to my soul.

'I left the fatal spot and walked, I know not why, to the fine house in Berkeley-square. I could have wished to see Clara at that moment: I could have cursed her with the mute malediction of my eye; but the family was dispersed, the servants gone, the shutters closed, and a printed bill in the window – "To be sold the Lease, &c., by order of the assignees." This, if I had thought of it, I ought to have anticipated; and I returned at night to the barber who had shaved me in the morning, and took a back garret in his house for two shillings a week: it was a desperate reliance upon Fortune that moved me to this, and my faith was rewarded. In a few weeks I succeeded in obtaining the situation of tutor in the parish school where you first saw me, and where, as you know, I remained for several years.

'It were tedious to detail my course of life at this period; from year to year the same dull round of unthankful duties, which brought me a miserable yearly sum, aided by a few private pupils, whom I instructed in writing. You know how I used to spend my evenings – in pot-houses; sometimes amongst the worst and most dissolute; – drunk – often miserably so: for let philosophy cant as it will, the stricken heart *must* have present relief, or break at once. Mine would not break.

'In the meantime my father died, and I was requested by a solicitor, who addressed me through the medium of an advertisement, to come down and attend the funeral. I did so.

'On reading the will, it was discovered that he had left the whole of his property to his second son; in the event of whose death it was to revert to me. This part of the will was so worded, and the contingency itself was so remote, as to force upon me the conviction that it was meant as a mockery and an insult. But I could bear these insults now; at least, none could discover that they touched me, – which, perhaps, is the same thing.

'"Your father has left you," said the attorney, in a tone of condolence, "a mourning ring. I see nothing more."

'"Enough, sir; I will wear it. I *will* mourn for him. I will mourn his want of charity – his want of human feeling – his want of natural affection – his want of preparation to meet his Maker. These *are* causes of mourning –" and I walked into the garden. Yes, I pitied the poor man who lay above, dead, cold – cold as his own heart while living; gone to his account, leaving behind him a paltry insult to a son who had never given him a moment's cause of offence. How little did he know my nature! How little did he understand me, if he supposed that I should repine at the loss of his rascal money! One pressure of his hand at the last moment – one look of affection – one word of reparation, would have touched me more than all his mistaken and vulgar resentment.

'I sat alone in a small back parlour during the afternoon, for the widow declined seeing me; and on the morrow, after the funeral, I proposed to take my leave.

'Higgins entered the room. "You have not seen master yet, Mr. Henry," said he; "if you wish to look at him once more, will you come now? The men are going to solder the coffin in the evening."

'I arose, and proceeded up stairs to the room in which he was lying. As I passed the drawing room, the door was slightly open. I looked in; my mother's portrait was hanging in its accustomed situation. I approached, and looked upon that face, which seemed to appeal to my earlier feelings, before my heart had turned into bitterness. "Yes, my mother, for your sake I will dismiss these unworthy resentments, that disturb while they debase the heart. There is a gulf between us: in that gulf let me sink all thoughts, save of peace and forgiveness."

'A tear stood in my eye; but I wiped it away, and bade Higgins lead me to my father's room. "Leave me for a few minutes to myself: you will find me in the parlour below should you wish to see me." He retired.

'I lifted the lid of the coffin, and gazed at that face, which time had altered but slightly. The past had trodden lightly o'er that brow; and Death had smoothed its furrows into placidity. I took his hand and said – "Not now, not now, oh, my father! be thoughts of anger remaining in my bosom." I stooped down, and kissed his forehead; "be this the seal of forgiveness between us, and from this hour be the past forgotten for ever."

'Believe me, Mr. Ketch, that I have been a happier and a better man since that day. I hewed away, as it were, the morbid and decayed branches of my nature; and what remains is fresher, and of a greener leaf. Only one trial was reserved for me.

'I returned to town, and soon subsided into the old mill-horse feeling of resignation to my fortune, poor as it was, and addiction to my confirmed habits, such as they were. With me the force of habit was stronger even than the desire of happiness; and I had no wish to run in pursuit of the one to the neglect of the other.

'One evening the son of the landlady at whose house I lodged, came to me to the Magpie and Punchbowl, and informed me that a lady wished particularly to speak with me. I took my hat, and followed the boy, wondering not a little, and conjecturing who it might be that had taken such extraordinary trouble to discover my abode.

'As I entered the room, the lady rose from her seat, and advanced towards me. It was twilight. I could not see her face. "Pardon me, madam," said I, "but some mistake, probably –"

"'Oh, Henry! you do not know me," said a voice which I remembered too well; and, with a flutter of agitation, Clara placed her hand in mine.

"'Will you bring a candle," I said to the woman of the house, "and permit me to occupy your parlour for half an hour? Pray, Mrs. Western, sit down."

'We were silent for a few minutes, until the candle was brought in, and the woman had retired. At length I said – "You are much altered, Clara, since I saw you last."

"'And you, too, are changed," she answered, in a tone of meekness that softened my heart at once, and brought the tears into my eyes.

"'My fortunes, Clara, have made me what I am, and have been for years. You, also, I fear, have not been happy – you –"

'I paused, for she was weeping bitterly. She arose silently as I ceased speaking, and came softly towards me and knelt at my feet; and leaning her head upon my knee, continued to weep in silence.

"'Rise, Clara, for God's sake, rise!" I exclaimed in anguish; "what is the meaning of this emotion – you distress me."

"'Let me be," she whispered; "it will ease my heart of a weight which has long oppressed it, and I shall then be able to tell you all. Oh, Henry!" and she raised her streaming eyes to mine, "can you forgive me? – ought you to forgive me? No. But you shall hear me. I have sought you for three years, and have never, until now, succeeded in discovering your lodging. Let me tell you all, that I may die in peace. My mother compelled me to marry Western. She placed before me her own precarious income; she told me that I should save her from destruction and ruin, by consenting to receive him for a husband; she showed me her debts, and the clamorous demands of her creditors; and I knew that she had not sufficient to discharge one tithe of them. She forced me into this marriage –"

"'Where is your mother, Clara?" I asked, with a calm voice.

"'She is dead, Henry."

"'Enough; the dead have their reward. Rise, my poor creature, and calm yourself. Wherefore explain these things to me? I absolved you from your engagement. I relinquished you for ever. I knew it was to be for ever. I am content."

'I raised her from the ground, and placed her in a chair by my side.

"'Oh, Henry! can you forgive me?" she asked, and looked into my face piteously. Those eyes were still the same, and I pressed her hand, but replied not for some moments: I was unable.

"'No, Clara, I cannot forgive you," I said, at length; "I cannot forgive you; for you have blasted your own happiness. Heaven be my witness, that I never sought you but to make you happy; if my love would have made you so, you would have been happy indeed; but now, what is left? the day is gone by – it is too late."

'I turned towards her; she had fainted. Once, and but once, as I pressed her to my heart, I touched her lips with mine; and that one kiss repaid me for all my years of misery – but she revived.

"'Can we never again be happy, Henry?" she exclaimed, in a faint voice, and she averted her head from me; "we are yet young."

"'Never – never – never, Clara," said I, interrupting her. "You know me not if you think I can join together, by some painful mockery, the shattered hopes of my youth, and call it happiness; let it go; it *is* gone. I can bear to live without it."

'I arose and opened the door. "Let us part, Clara, for this meeting afflicts and unnerves me." She sighed but once, and placed her hand in mine.

"'You will see me to a coach, Henry?"

"'I will."

'As we walked together, she gave me her card, and made me promise to see her again, and I left her.

'Do not smile at me, Mr. Ketch, when I confess that I closed not my eyes that night, and that the pillow was wet with my tears. I have learned too late to let Nature have her way – and this weakness was but for once.

'I wrote to Clara on the following morning, and told her that we had parted for ever. It was a kind and a proper letter; and expressed the sentiments I at this instant feel. Should I have seen her again? No. To what might that meeting not have led? I should have despised myself had I yielded. It is better as it is. She died shortly afterwards.

'Why should I proceed? aye, there was another death; the boy died – my younger brother, whose life had been impiously set up in the face of the Almighty to reverse the decrees of justice and of nature. That boy died, and to me reverted the property of my father. It came not too late. There is a time for all things; the game's never won till it's lost. What remains? Nothing.'

Misty arose from his chair as he concluded, and shook himself. 'I will begone,' said he, and he buttoned his coat. There was more upon his mind at that moment than he could bear, or desired me to discover, and as he caught my eye, he turned his head from me.

'Cannot we have some brandy, Ketch?' he said, reseating himself; 'the wine sits cold upon my stomach: go for a bottle.'

I acceded to the request, not the less willingly because my guest insisted upon paying for it; and we proceeded to open the bottle as soon as it appeared, with the gusto of impatient connoisseurs.

'Next to the exhilaration of drunkenness,' cried Misty, tossing off a bumper, 'give me the melancholy of music: after this, a lovely air of Mozart, or the rapturous tenderness of Gluck;'[527] and here Misty rambled into a wild eulogium upon music, which, as I understood not a word of it, I forbear to inflict upon the reader.

Misty left me at a late hour, with best wishes for my success, and the empty brandy bottle before me; and I retired to bed, in a state of elevation induced not more by what I had drunk, than by the anticipated fulfilment of my hopes on the morrow.

CHAPTER XXII.

NEVER did placeman awake in greater eagerness for the premiership[528] – never did demagogue arise with more sanguine hope of a pension[529] – never did tuft-hunter sally forth with brisker alacrity to the dinner of a Marquis,[530] than I awoke, arose, and went forth, eager, sanguine, and alert for the vacant Ketch-ship.

The house of business, of which Mr. Sheriff Hopkins constituted the head and front, was situate in Mincing Lane. Thither I hastened, arrayed in the best apparel I could muster, worthy of receiving the visual rays poured from the highly respectable orbs of Hopkins. And my dress, succinct,[531] and of becoming sable, tended, I am disposed to believe, to create for me the favourable impression which, as I have before observed, good woollen, well made clothes, never fail to awaken. And, indeed, I may as well add, with reference to the woollen manufacture, that with respect to applications for vacant offices, where a suit is wanted, the suit is not granted:[532] and again, even if a man's life depend on the success of his application, it may no less certainly be affirmed, that if the coat of his shoulders have taken its leave, farewell to the coat of his stomach.[533]

Therefore, I have been ever inclined to view a certain class of men whom we see daily perambulating the streets, in the light of amiable peripatetic philosophers,[534] whose warning voice exhorts the community to get rid of its old clothes as speedily as may be, seeing that rags can never by any possibility bring grist[535] to the mill, – unless, indeed, it be a paper-mill,[536] – in which case, undoubtedly, they may be converted into best foolscap[537] for the heads of the original wearers.

But to leave for the present all further reflections upon a subject which, were I to enter upon it, would probably detain me a considerable period of time, and occupy as considerable a portion of space, let me at once intimate, that I arrived at the warehouse door of Mr. Sheriff Hopkins in due time, and that I waited there for a minute or two for the purpose of plucking up my courage, and the frill of my shirt; and while I arranged the outward man, of collecting and putting together the man within me also.

Mr. Sheriff Hopkins was a sugar-broker, as I conjectured from certain small samples of that commodity, placed at equal distances from each other on square black boards, and which appeared not unlike ingenious models of the Egyptian pyramids formed out of the sand of the desert. I passed through the warehouse, however, without further scrutiny of its contents; and, having been announced to the great half representative of the Shrievalty,[538] through the medium of a clerk, was ushered into the august presence of that personage, who, in his private counting-house, was holding converse with no less a functionary than the Ordinary of Newgate[539] himself.

'Well, young man, and so you are ambitious to succeed your uncle in his office?' said Hopkins, turning at the same time to the Ordinary; 'an onerous and important duty, Mr. Kilderkin,[540] is it not?'

'No doubt – no question,' said Kilderkin, taking a pinch of snuff out of his waistcoat pocket, and drawing it into his nostrils with a hissing sound; 'it *is* a very weighty office, Mr. Hopkins.'

'You are very young,' remarked the Sheriff.

I confessed that I was not a Parr or a Jenkins[541] in point of longevity, but trusted that my youth would be no serious objection to my attaining the dignified employment to which I aspired.

'Well, sir, we think it not unlikely that your application may be granted,' said Hopkins; 'what say you, Mr. Kilderkin?'

'I say nothing,' quoth Kilderkin, 'it rests not with me.'

'Well, sir,' cried the other, 'you were observed the other day in court: you were a witness, I believe, in a case of murder – one Wilmot – I think the name was Wilmot.'

'It was, sir.'

'Well: he was a friend of yours, was he not? He had been friendly to you, I mean; he had employed you. Now, sir, suppose for a moment, that that person had not been reprieved by his Majesty, and were now to suffer, – could you hang him, think you?'

'Certainly,' said I, with alacrity; 'certainly, sir, I could.'

'Um,' said Hopkins, gravely.

'Um,' echoed Kilderkin, with a grunt like that of a well pleased hog, who, experimenting on the contents of his trough, finds that it is good; and he took another enormous pinch of snuff; and now these worthy gentlemen laid their heads together, and conversed in whispers for a considerable time.

'He'll do,' I heard Hopkins observe. 'Just the man we want,' said the other.

'Now, Mr. Ketch,' resumed Hopkins, addressing me; 'let me see – hum – ha – what was I going to say? oh! you must know – ' but here Hopkins foundered, and rubbed his chin ruefully, in all the agony of extreme non-plusage. 'By the bye, Mr. Kilderkin,' said he, at length, 'I wish you would examine Mr. Ketch touching his capacity and skill in his profession. I have some Muscovados[542] here,' and he

My Desire to take Office.

pointed to a board of sugars, 'which I can just look over while you put the several questions to the young man.'

'That thing I'll do,' replied Kilderkin, blowing his nose with a pocket hand-kerchief, which, from the report it caused, might have been thought to contain a pocket pistol; and while the ordinary prepared himself for the examination, I looked upon him with reverential awe.

And, indeed, the appearance of this extraordinary ordinary was well calculated to excite that feeling in the breast of a novice. He was a great fat man, whose physical energies were of the most intense and vigorous description. It might be imagined by a fanciful Pythagorean[543] that, not the souls but, the animal functions of every individual whose execution he had attended, had passed into his one economy,[544] and there subsisted in congregated vital force. Judge, then, as he sat before me, and I gazed upon his vast rotundity, whether such a substantial son of the church were not likely to be alarming to one about-to-be-catechised limb of the laity.

But he now fixed his noticeable eyes upon me.

'Can you hang?'

'I can, sir; I studied under my late uncle, by whom I was considered – '

'Silence! Are you fully alive to the particular duties which the important office you will occupy calls upon you to discharge. Hold your tongue, and don't interrupt me. Do you know that you may be required to hang your own father, mother, grandfather, grandmother, – nay, every relative you have in the world; and that you will be called upon to swear that you will do these things if occasion demands?'

I answered, that I was perfectly aware of these contingencies, and quite willing to take the required oath.

'Good,' said the ordinary. 'Are you aware,' he continued, 'of the responsibility and the respectability of the office?'

I looked blank at this question. Was Kilderkin serious? He was.

'Consider,' said he, encouragingly, – 'consider for a moment. You are performing an operation properly belonging to the sheriff – you are the representative of the sheriff – you are equal with the sheriff.'

'Equal with the sheriff?' cried Hopkins, turning suddenly round, 'nay, Mr. Kilderkin, not exactly so, surely.'

Kilderkin nodded his head.

Hopkins scratched his. 'Eh?' said he, 'do you class us together? Do we go abreast like horses in a curricle, *passibus equis*,[545] as we used to say at Merchant Tailors'?'[546]

'*Passibus asinis*,'[547] cried the ordinary; 'stuff – nonsense – fudge. I say, Mr. Hopkins, that for the time, mark me, for the time, Mr. Ketch fills your situation. He is your *locum tenens*[548] – he does your work. *Qui facit per alium, facit per se*

– he who does a thing through another, does it virtually himself. If you pick a man's pocket with a dead man's fingers, I'll warrant you won't get dumby to hold up his hand in the dock: *you* suffer in *propriâ personâ.*'[549]

Here Kilderkin chuckled amazingly, while a no less amazing gravity drew down the visage of Hopkins.

'Do you understand all that I have said to you,' resumed the ordinary; 'do you subscribe to it; are you willing to undertake the situation, and to perform everything that shall be required of you, proper and peculiar to it?'

I expressed my readiness to do all these things, and manifested my gratitude by many broken sentences of thankfulness and respect, and slidings of the foot behind me; and every other ceremony proper to the occasion.

'Very good,' said Kilderkin, 'very good. Now then, take one word of advice. Never hang the wrong man – never fail to hang the right one; and never hang yourself, as your poor simple uncle did. And now,' and he rose and approached Hopkins, 'I think we may say that this young man may take it for granted, that he is to succeed his kinsman in his duties, and that he may prepare to get his hand in, at all events, forthwith.'

'I think so,' said Hopkins. 'You may prepare, young man, to get your hand in forthwith; and in due time you will be sworn into your office.'

Again I mumbled the same sentiments of gratitude and respect, and with many profound bows retired from the presence.

Like Mr. Sheriff Hopkins himself (to compare small things with great), who some years subsequently carried up an address to the king, and going before him in an unchivalrous fright, came out a puissant knight; so I, who presented myself to Hopkins in a great funk,[550] left him a great functionary. I had become hangman in ordinary[551] to the people of England.

And here I drop the pen, in defiance of a principle which has been laid down for me in the best works, not only of fiction but of history.

And as in comedies it is usual to dismiss to happiness the several parties concerned, – the lovers to the immediate service of hymen,[552] and the uncles and guardians to the pleasing recollection of their obstinacy and folly throughout the piece, and the sudden light that has so instantaneously converted them into amiable and complying individuals; and as all these great and surprising changes are suffered to take place to supply the exigencies of the last scene; and as, moreover, the spectators are contented to leave them to the happiness which they all and each appear so confident of attaining: so I, having brought my autobiography, not down, but up to a particular epoch – a glorious consummation beyond which I could hope for and expect nothing, save to be permitted to enjoy my honours unenvied and at peace – have nothing further to do but to make my best bow, and to retire from the hubbub of applause and admiration, which I cannot but think my appearance, even for so short a space, most discriminating readers, must inevitably cause amongst you.

I must confess, that when I began this volume, I had proposed to myself to give to the world a history of my life and adventures, brought down to the very moment at which I dipped my pen into the ink for the inscription of the last sentence. But many objections presented themselves to me as I proceeded, which effectually dissuaded me from pursuing this course. In the first place, it would have destroyed the wholeness, the integrity of a work, which in its present shape, I am fondly disposed to look upon as complete, so far as it goes. I have purposely omitted, accordingly, many passages in my earlier life of singular interest and beauty which, not immediately conducing to the great climax of my fortunes, however indirectly they might possibly be supposed to aid and assist, would have been in point of fact out of place, and irrelevant to my great design.

Again: tied down as I have been since my attainment of the Ketchship, to the performance of the arduous duties and routine of a most difficult profession, much that I should have laid before the reader must necessarily consist of the adventures of other people, in which I myself have performed a distinguished, indeed; – but, after all, a subordinate part. I should have lost myself as one of the characters of the piece – I should have been degraded below the dignity of a Greek chorus[553] – I should barely lay claim to the merit of a scene-shifter.[554]

Besides, I could not have connected these various and distinct scenes – independent of each other as they necessarily must be – so closely and implicitly as, a stickler for the unity of action, I could have reconciled it to my own sense of propriety to do. The rope being the only ligature to bind them to each other, they might not inaptly be compared, by the facetious and critical wag, to a rope of onions, which, strung together might perhaps draw tears from the eyes of the public, but should not be suffered to come before them in so raw a state.

Another weighty and important reason moved me to ground my pen at this particular crisis. It has been notified unto me, that the world is grown so much wiser of late – so intolerant of trifles – so impatient of prolixity – so eager, nay, so ravenous after knowledge of all kinds, whether political, philosophical, or literary, that it is well that the discreet author should beware how he present the absorbing monster with counterfeit gingerbread; lest he not only engulf the offering of a sudden, but swallow the hapless writer also with the like despatch.

In fine, under the advice, and subject to the revision of my friend Misty, I may one day, perhaps, be prevailed upon, should the present volume meet with due favour from the public, to lay before them 'The Ketch Papers;' a title which at once indicates the scope and matter of the book, and exempts the author from the necessity of adhering to those epic rules to which he has voluntarily subjected his pen in the present volume.

BRADBURY AND EVANS, PRINTERS, WHITEFRIARS.

EXPLANATORY NOTES

1. *MEADOWS*: Joseph Kenny Meadows (bap. 1790–1874), engraver, illustrator, and caricaturist; born in Wales, moved to London in 1827, illustrated various works, notably an edition of Shakespeare (1839–43), early issues of *Punch* magazine, children's books, and humorous books.

2. *Priscian's head*: Priscianus Cæsariensis (AD *c.* 500), Latin grammarian; to break or injure Priscian's head is to violate the rules of grammar.

3. *flower*: figure, trope, rhetorical device.

4. SMITH AND BRANSTON: Smith: probably Edward Smith, a Scot who worked in London from about 1823 to about 1849; Branston: one of the second generation of the Branston family of engravers, perhaps Robert Edward (baptized 1803–77) or Frederick William (baptized 1805).

5. '*No book ... learned from it*': widely attributed to Samuel Johnson (1709–84).

6. '*small deer*': Shakespeare, *King Lear*, III.iv.134: 'mice and rats and such small deer' (deer: beasts, animals, as distinguished from birds and fishes).

7. *trunk-maker ... pastry-cook*: Unsold books were torn up and used to line trunks and pastry dishes.

8. '*the great sublime he draws*': Alexander Pope, *An Essay on Criticism* (1711), l. 680, describing Longinus, the supposed author of an ancient treatise on the sublime.

9. *benefit of clergy*: In earlier times, clergymen could claim exemption from jurisdiction of secular courts and be tried by the more lenient ecclesiastical courts; in time the privilege was extended to anyone who was literate, and then to all first-time offenders; Parliament abolished it in 1827.

10. *Hippocrates ... Babel*: Hippocrates (*c.* 460–*c.* 380 BC) famous Greek physician; Hippocrene: in ancient legend, a fountain on Mount Helicon, home of the Muses, with power to inspire poets; Elysium: in ancient myth, a paradise inhabited by the virtuous and heroic after death; Babel: in Genesis 11, humanity, at that time speaking one language, tries to build a tower to heaven but God confounds their plan by making each speak a different language, so they cannot understand each other.

11. *La Rochefoucauld*: François de La Rochefoucauld (1613–80), nobleman and author; his widely read *Maximes* (1665) expressed a view that people are motivated by self-interest.

12. '*pours out all himself*': perhaps echoing Alexander Pope, *Satires of Horace Imitated*, Satire I, l. 153: 'I love to pour out all my self ...'.

13. *Jack Ketch*: proverbial nickname for an official hangman.

14. *coup de grace*: literally 'mercy stroke' (French): finishing blow delivered to a wounded or executed person.

15. *'marriage ... destiny'*: Shakespeare, *The Merchant of Venice*, II.ix.83: 'Hanging and wiving goes by destiny'.
16. *hymeneal*: of marriage, from Hymen, ancient Greek god of marriage.
17. *original sin*: The Christian doctrine of the first sin, marking humanity's flawed nature, depicted in Genesis, where Adam and Eve disobey God's command not to eat the fruit of the tree of knowledge (i.e., knowledge of sexuality) and are banished from the Garden of Eden and condemned to toil and to mortality for the rest of history, until the last judgment at the end of time.
18. *so many laws ... death*: At its greatest extent in Britain, the death penalty, or 'Bloody Code', could be inflicted for some 220 crimes, but a reform campaign reduced these in the early nineteenth century, the 1832 Punishment of Death Act cut the number by two-thirds, and the death penalty was abolished in 1969.
19. *'he who is born ... hanged'*: echo of François Rabelais, *Gargantua and Pantagruel* (1532–64), ch. 4.24.
20. *bed of honour*: grave of a soldier on the battlefield.
21. *Some ... greatness thrust upon them*: echoing Malvolio's speech in Shakespeare, *Twelfth Night*, II.v.145–6.
22. *chamber practice*: practice of the law in chambers, or the legal office, rather than in court and in public, with a play on words referring to committing suicide in private, in one's own chamber or room.
23. *certain ... world*: echoing William Cowper, *The Task*, IV.88–9, with several plays on words: 'loopholes' are small round holes in fortress walls allowing defenders to shoot at attackers, hence any small aperture, with a play on 'loop' for 'noose'.
24. *debt of nature*: the inevitability of death.
25. *'stand ... Calendar'*: Shakespeare, *Macbeth*, IV.i.134, said of the witches by Macbeth; a calendar is a list, as of saints, or those condemned to execution.
26. *three ... mutes*: 'Mutes' were professional mourners, here hired at three shillings and sixpence.
27. *'the drop'*: trapdoor in a gallows through which the hanged person dropped, but also a small drink, as of a cordial, or tonic.
28. *'good wine ... bush'*: Shakespeare, *As You Like It*, V.iv.200–1; a 'bush' was a crown-like frame hung outside a tavern advertising wine for sale.
29. *coffin ... earth*: According to legend the coffin of the prophet Mahomet at Medina was suspended magically above the earth.
30. *'do unto others ... me'*: adaptation of Christ's words to his disciples in his 'Sermon on the Mount', Matthew 7:12.
31. *ordinary*: tavern or public house.
32. *chamberlain ... up*: A chamberlain is a bedchamber attendant, and so could be said to 'tuck up' or tuck in his employer, but in colloquial language the executioner also 'tucks up' or hangs the condemned
33. *locusts ... Moses*: In Exodus 10:12–15, God commands Moses to stretch his rod over Egypt to bring a plague of locusts that darkens the sky; Cimmerian: in legend, the nomadic Cimmerians lived in a land of perpetual darkness.
34. *executive government*: the branch of government that executes or carries out the laws, with a pun on 'executes' as 'puts to death'.
35. *three volumes*: At this time novels were commonly published in three volumes.
36. *'fleshy nooks'*: Milton, 'Il Penseroso' (1645), l. 92: 'fleshly nook'.
37. *fleecy hosiery*: wool stockings.

38. *bay or laurel*: leaves used to make garlands to crown a victor or poet.

39. *hemp*: Ropes were made from hemp fibres.

40. *Phalaris*: sixth-century BC tyrant of Agrigentum in Sicily who killed his opponents by roasting them in a bronze bull; when he was overthrown the same fate was dealt him.

41. *'Tis not ... deserve it'*: Joseph Addison's tragedy *Cato* (1713), I.ii.45.

42. *insatiate archer*: death; quotation from Edward Young, *Night Thoughts* (1742–5), 'Night I', l. 18.

43. ex gratia: without compulsion or obligation (Latin), but perhaps intending *exemplum gratia*, 'for example'.

44. *'She ... laughing'*: Sarah Catherine Martin, *The Comical Adventures of Old Mother Hubbard and Her Dog* (1805), ll. 7–8.

45. *Actæon*: In ancient legend, the hunter Actaeon spied on the goddess Artemis while she was bathing and in revenge she changed him into a stag and set her dogs to kill him.

46. *at his Majesty's pleasure*: at the discretion of the king.

47. *fatal tree*: the gallows, but also the tree of the knowledge of good and evil in the Biblical garden of Eden.

48. *'Youth ... helm'*: Thomas Gray, *The Bard* (1757), l. 74.

49 *tabernacle of jumpers*: possibly a Methodist meeting; Methodists were sometimes called 'Jumpers' from their agitated movements while worshipping; a tabernacle is a tent or meeting-house of religious Dissenters, such as Methodists.

50. *'you ... drink'*: proverbial.

51. *'books ... brooks'*: Shakespeare, *As You Like It*, II.i.16.

52. *sin from the head of Satan*: as represented in Milton, *Paradise Lost* (1667, 2nd edn 1674), book II.

53. *Jason*: In ancient Greek legend, Jason and his companions undergo a variety of adventures in their quest for the golden fleece, recounted in the third-century BC poem, *Argonautica*, by Apollonius of Rhodes; in one adventure Jason is required to sow a field with dragon's teeth, which spring up as soldiers, whom he defeats by a trick.

54. *the devouring flames*: In folklore, an extracted tooth must immediately be put in the fire.

55. *Rose and Crown Court*: There were such named locations in Gray's Inn Lane and in Bishopsgate, in the City of London.

56. *Newgate*: the historic prison of the City of London, originating in a fortified gate which was used, among other things, as a temporary jail; it was altered and expanded over the centuries to become the most infamous prison in the English-speaking world, so that prisons everywhere were named after it; it was demolished in 1902 and replaced by the Old Bailey courthouse.

57. prima stamina: origins (Latin).

58. *fortress*: Newgate prison.

59. *Gazette*: the *London Gazette*, an official semi-weekly periodical publishing lists of public appointments, names of bankrupts, and public notices.

60. de facto ... de jure: in fact or reality; in law (Latin).

61. *Plutarch ... professors*: Plutarch (AD *c.* 47–127), Greek biographer whose *Parallel Lives* of famous Greeks and Romans was widely translated; according to Plutarch's life of the Athenian leader Pericles (*c.* 495–29 BC), the Sophist philosopher Damon, who believed in arbitrary power, taught Pericles politics under the guise of music instruction.

62. *Colley Cibber*: Colley Cibber (1671–1757) controversial actor, dramatist, and Poet Laureate, author of *An Apology for the Life of Colley Cibber* (1740), where 'apology' means 'self-vindication'.
63. *quintain*: a post used as a target for lances, spears, or darts.
64. *tilt*: combat, of two armed knights in medieval chivalric tournaments.
65. *pearlash*: potassium carbonate, used in making soap and glass.
66. *handing off the plate*: conveying (surreptitiously) the silverware.
67. *dustman*: paid refuse-collector; also a personification of sleep.
68. *magpie*: bird famed for carrying shiny objects to its nest.
69. *as the laws … protection*: proverbial: possession is nine-tenths of the law, meaning that the law heavily favours the actual possessor of a contested property.
70. *laying wait for*: robbing.
71. *black cap*: hood placed over the head of someone just before he or she was hanged.
72. *tie*: no winner, but also play on 'tie' as hangman's noose.
73. *sea of troubles*: echoing Shakespeare, *Hamlet*, III.i.59.
74. *many … lip*: proverbial.
75. *many a goose … noose*: play on 'goose' as fool, victim.
76. *myrmidons*: unquestioning followers, after the soldiers led by Achilles in Homer's *Iliad*.
77. *suspicious character*: someone known to police as likely a criminal.
78. *distraining broker*: dealer in confiscated goods, here a euphemism for 'thief'.
79. *sojourn*: 'soujorn' in original.
80. *no part … leaving of it*: echo of Shakespeare, *Macbeth*, I.iv.7–8, Malcolm's description of the execution of Cawdor.
81. *ordinary*: clergyman assigned to counsel and console the condemned.
82. *ceremony … leave-taking*: At this time executions were held in public.
83. *Surgeons' Hall*: By law, bodies of executed criminals were made available for dissection in anatomy schools – an arrangement much resented by the lower classes.
84. *cub … shape*: According to popular lore, she-bears licked their newborn into appropriate shape.
85. *Curtius*: In ancient legend, an oracle declared that a gap in the Roman forum could only be closed by Rome's most precious thing; Marcus Curtius leapt into the gap and it miraculously closed.
86. *'a flag … sign'*: Shakespeare, *Othello*, I.i.154, said by Iago about how he will deceive Othello.
87. *sent over the water*: Condemned criminals could be transported to an overseas penal colony, such as Australia, for terms ranging from seven years to life.
88. *unneccessary*: probably a misprint, but in the past an accepted variant of the more usual 'unnecessary'.
89. *perquisites and vails*: Servants were legitimately permitted to receive cast-offs and left-overs from their employers, though in this case they were stolen.
90. *Parnassus*: In ancient legend, Mount Parnassus was home to the muses.
91. *Apollo… Mercury*: respectively, ancient gods of the arts and of communication.
92. *bowels*: mercy.
93. *'unhoused free condition'*: Shakespeare, *Othello*, I.ii.26.
94. *Cornaro … Hygeian*: Luigi Cornaro (died 1566), Venetian nobleman who wrote trea-tises on dieting and advocated temperance and moderation; Hygeian: from Hygeia, ancient Greek goddess of health.
95. *scrip*: bag in which mendicant clergy used to keep food they received.

96. 'very *like a whale*': Shakespeare, *Hamlet*, III.ii.373.
97. *blubber*: another pun: blubber is whale-fat but also means 'to weep noisily'.
98. '*Waft ... Pole*': Alexander Pope, *Eloisa to Abelard* (1717), l. 58; Indus is a river in India, in the tropics, and the 'pole' refers to the north or south pole.
99. '*That ... wisdom*': Milton, *Paradise Lost*, VIII.193–4.
100. *Misty*: obscure, unintelligible, of impaired mind.
101. *spirits*: ghosts but also alcoholic drinks; vaults: cellars used as burial places but also wine-cellars.
102. *judge ... fruit*: echo of Luke 6:44.
103. '*idea ... shoot*': echo of James Thomson, *The Seasons*, 'Spring' (1728), l. 1150.
104. *lay-figure*: a dummy or wooden figure used by artists to practise drawing, but also a nonentity or person of no consequence.
105. *mill-horse*: horse harnessed to a mill for grinding grain into flour by plodding in a circle.
106. *pothooks and hangars*: joking terms for strokes made in writing, but also hooks for hanging pots over a fire for cooking.
107. *running hand*: cursive script, but also deft manual move by a pickpocket.
108. *organ-loft*: As a pupil in a parish charity school, Jack had duties including operating the bellows which forced air through the church organ for Sunday service.
109. swopped: or swapped: 'exchanged' but also 'struck a blow'.
110. *cushion*: cushion placed on the book-holder in the pulpit to support the Bible or other book, and pounded by the preacher for emphasis during a sermon or service.
111. *abduced*: abducted, stolen.
112. 'the nick of time': precise moment; but 'nick' is also a nickname for the Devil.
113. *Saint Monday*: a holiday, official or – more usually – unofficial.
114. *nine points*: referring to the proverbial wisdom that the possessor of a property has the advantage in a legal dispute over possession of it.
115. *potential*: powerful, convincing.
116. *black sheep*: bad character.
117. *bred ... flesh*: what is inherited from parents cannot be purged from the body or character; proverbial phrase, also used in Daniel Defoe's very popular novel, *Robinson Crusoe* (1719).
118. *made ... vanished*: from Shakespeare, *Macbeth* (Malone Boswell edn, 1821), I.v.5.
119. *betaken herself to water*: possibly a joking circumlocution for having her death sentence commuted to transportation to a penal colony.
120. *turn ... myself*: walk around; turn (to): take up, as a trade or profession.
121. JOHN KETCH: John (or Jack) Ketch, had been the proverbial name for the public hangman in England from the seventeenth century.
122. *fell upon his neck*: embraced him (the usual sense), but also, here, participated in hanging him by pushing on the hanged person's shoulders to hasten death.
123. *Katterfelto*: Gustavus Katterfelto (died 1799) was a celebrated quack doctor, conjurer, public lecturer, and skilled self-publicist who travelled around England.
124. *let ... take, me*: let: rent or lease, but also allow or permit; take: rent or lease, but also apprehend, arrest.
125. *premises ... fell in*: premises: building, rooms, but also assumptions in a logical argument; lease: agreed term of rental, but also lease or length of life; fell in: expired (ran out its term, as with a lease) but also expired (died).

126. *rope walk*: stretch of ground for making twisted ropes, but also profession (walk of life) involving use of the rope (hangman's noose).

127. *Montague … Tyaneus*: Montague on Hanging: possibly Basil Montagu, *Hanging Not Punishment Enough* (1812); Ure on Dyeing: Andrew Ure and others, *Elements of the Art of Dyeing* (1824), i.e., dyeing cloth; Strype's Memorials: John Strype, *Memorials of Thomas Cranmer* (1694), Protestant martyr, with a pun on 'stripes' or lashes and 'memorials' as 'remembrances' or 'physical traces'; Apollonius Tyaneus: first-century AD Greek philosopher who supposedly performed miracles, here with a pun on 'Ty' and 'tie,' and '-neus' pronounced as 'noose'.

128. *Roscommon … destroyed*: said of the poet Wentworth Dillon, fourth earl of Roscommon (1633–85) by fellow poet John Dryden.

129. *Newgate Calendar*: a widely read collection of accounts of criminals, republished often in the late eighteenth and early nineteenth centuries.

130. carte-blanche: full discretionary power, from the blank sheet (French, *carte blanche*) on which a person could write his or her own terms and conditions.

131. *Sessions*: periodical sittings of magistrates to try cases.

132. *tying … up*: hanging.

133. *classical taste*: knowledge of Latin classical literature and culture.

134. *lares*: with the penates mentioned earlier, figures representing the protecting deities of the household in ancient Roman culture.

135. *quicksilver*: mercury, as in a thermometer.

136. *Talus*: or Talos; In the ancient Greek legend of the voyage of Jason and the Argonauts, Talos is a metal statue that attacks two of Jason's men.

137. upsides *with*: even with, equal to.

138. *sea-coal*: coal brought to London by sea.

139. '*nods … smiles*': Milton, 'L'Allegro' (1645), l. 28.

140. *squint*: looking obliquely or sideways.

141. *Hamlet … Easel*: Shakespeare, *Hamlet*, V.i.271. Easel, or eisel: vinegar.

142. *sophisticated*: altered from her natural state, i.e., inebriated.

143. *dromedary*: 'drumedary' in the original.

144. *dromedary*: a camel used for riding; the pun by Jack and his uncle may refer to being 'ridden' in the sense of 'dominated', and 'hump' as a 'burden'.

145. *queer*: drunk.

146. *tucking … up*: hang (slang).

147. JABEZ SNAVEL: In 1 Chronicles 4:9–10, Jabez (the name means borne with sorrow) is more honourable than his brothers and prays to God to enlarge his territories and keep him from evil; snavel means to steal or snatch (slang).

148. *attorney … solicitor*: An attorney is someone appointed to act for another in matters of law, or more particularly someone who so practises in courts of civil law; a solicitor is someone who practises in courts of equity; both attorneys and solicitors prepare the cases for barristers, who enjoy higher professional status and actually plead or argue the cases in court.

149. *platform*: basis of the legal argument, but also the platform of the gallows where Snavel's clients usually ended up being hanged.

150. *expectations*: of a legacy.

151. tout ensemble: everything together (French).

152. *Brutus*: Titus Brutus, son of the founder of the Roman republic in the late sixth century BC, was executed for plotting to restore monarchy to ancient Rome.
153. *French ... prose*: A character in Molière's comedy *Le Bourgeois gentilhomme* (1670) learns that he has been speaking prose all his life without realizing it.
154. *Fortune*: goddess of chance.
155. *mull*: snuff-box, originally one of Scottish design which also ground the tobacco into snuff powder.
156. *napt it*: or napped it: caught it, or received severe punishment, as in a boxing match.
157. *succabus*: properly 'succubus', a demon in female form.
158. *account*: 'acount' in the original.
159. *by goles*: a euphemistic substitution for 'by God'.
160. *found*: supplied to.
161. *East Indiaman*: large ship trading on the long voyage to the East Indies.
162. *initiation*: 'iniation' in the original.
163. *Mammon*: spirit inspiring avarice.
164. *calculating my destiny in a tea-cup*: foretelling my future by 'reading' the pattern left by tea-leaves in the bottom of a cup.
165. *Jonathan Wild*: famous thief catcher and criminal (died 1725) who became a figure for working both sides of the law.
166. *Cheapside*: a major thoroughfare in the City of London.
167. *term*: one of the three or four periods of the year during which certain courts were sitting, or in session.
168. *Will Wisp*: A will-o'-the-wisp is a thing or person that deludes or misleads.
169. *rip*: worthless person, perhaps an abbreviation of 'reprobate'.
170. *deuce*: devil.
171. *Horatian*: after the Roman poet Quintus Horatius Flaccus (65–8 BC), who wished for just enough income to enjoy a simple and quiet life.
172. *cameleons*: In legend, the chameleon, a small lizard, was supposed to live on air.
173. *sanctified*: sanctimonious.
174. *skurrick*: a halfpenny (slang).
175. *wages ... death*: echoing Romans 6:23: 'For the wages of sin is death'.
176. *mizzled*: disappeared suddenly, i.e., died.
177. *Wizen*: wizened: shrivelled, withered.
178. *do out*: clean out.
179. *three-quarter grog*: a drink of one-quarter spirits (usually rum) and three-quarters water, and so more likely to freeze in the cold.
180. *rushlight*: a cheap candle made by dipping the pith of a rush in tallow or grease.
181. *chance*: accident, occurrence.
182. *Merry-Andrew*: clown.
183. *short ... pie-crust*: The phrase 'short and sweet' means 'brief and to the point', but short crust is made with butter or fat to make it tasty and crumbly.
184. *chancery suit*: a lawsuit, over disputed property, in the Court of Chancery, or equity; at this time such lawsuits were notorious for their length and cost, at times devouring the property that was disputed.
185. *buck*: dashing fellow.
186. *guinea*: one pound and one shilling – a substantial tip.
187. *worldly*: original text: wordly.

188. *chequers*: A checker-board pattern was the sign of an inn.
189. *Malkin*: name meaning 'little Maud' but signifying a lower-class, untidy woman.
190. *rhumatis*: or rheumatiz: colloquial form of 'rheumatism'.
191. *sine die*: indefinitely (legal Latin).
192. *significant*: 'signficiant' in the original.
193. *limb of the law*: derisory term for any official of the law.
194. *little*: 'litle' in the original.
195. *Westminster Abbey*: a large solemn church in the Gothic style, formerly the church of an abbey in Westminster, to the west of the City of London.
196. *persuing*: perhaps a misprint for perusing.
197. *Monument*: a 61-metre column topped with a metal crown, erected between 1671 and 1677 to commemorate the Great Fire of London of 1666.
198. *mushroom Ketch-up*: pun on 'mushroom ketchup', a sauce made from juice of mushrooms, walnuts, tomatoes, etc., 'mushroom' as a social upstart, and 'up' as rise in social status.
199. *rum*: slang for both 'fine' and 'odd, strange, spurious'; also a play on rum the drink, suggesting Gibbon's proclivity for it.
200. *great historian*: Edward Gibbon (1737–94), author of *The Decline and Fall of the Roman Empire* (1776–88).
201. *killing dog*: killing: extremely attractive, but also causing death; dog: jovial fellow.
202. long *home*: grave.
203. *plain*: both 'homely' and 'smooth' or 'unmarked'.
204. *rum one ... Roman*: Gibbon's nose is not 'rum', or attractive, because a 'Roman nose' with its prominent upper part was considered unattractive.
205. *clearly*: original text: clealy.
206. *score*: money owed.
207. *hum*: humbug, hoax.
208. *nutmeg-grater chaps to grinding grins*: jaws resembling a nutmeg-grater to unwilling grins made while grinding the teeth.
209. *attic rooms*: rented as cheap lodgings.
210. *Die ... pain*: punning echo of Alexander Pope, 'Die of a rose in aromatic pain', *Essay on Man* (1733–4), epistle 1, l. 200
211. *villanous*: an alternative to the more usual 'villainous'.
212. *proctor in Doctor's Commons*: practitioner from Doctor's Commons, a college of ecclesiastical lawyers licensed to practise civil and canon law.
213. penchant: leaning towards, amorous interest in.
214. *mopusses*: mopus: coin of small value, but also a simpleton.
215. des*kant*: descant: to discourse, to enlarge upon; i.e., Jack's work as legal copyist, at his *desk*.
216. *deformity ... position*: perhaps referring to the peculiarity of his position in the world, perhaps to his crooked posture while writing at his desk.
217. 'things as they are': the (unreformed) state of the world, alluding distantly to William Godwin's widely read political novel, *Things As They Are; or, The Adventures of Caleb Williams* (1794), which critiques the differences of power and oppression in the unreformed state of society.
218. *fanciful ... changes*: Writers such as Godwin were often criticized for the supposedly impractical nature of their proposals for social and political reform.

219. *Italian Opera*: frequented by the upper and upper-middle classes, who disdained popular theatrical entertainments.

220. *excercise*: a variant of the more usual 'exercise'.

221. *rags ... bank notes*: a mild pun: bank-note paper was made from rags, and more durable than other papers.

222. *scape-sheep*: play on 'scapegoat', a person who receives blame or punishment due to others; here the substitution of 'sheep' for 'goat' seems to support the following puns on kinds of cloth made from the wool of sheep.

223. entrée to Almack's: *entrée*: admission (French); Almack's: exclusive London club devoted to gambling, balls, and socializing.

224. *superfine ... broad cloth*: superfine: cloth woven of very fine threads; broadcloth: fine wool cloth used for men's garments.

225. coterie: French, adopted into English, for a circle or association of people, informal club, with a pun on coat-erie.

226. ex-cathedrâ: Latin for 'from the chair', i.e., with official authority, though Jack seems to mean 'unofficially'; here used with a pun on Westminster Abbey, a church that is cathedral in size, though not a cathedral in status.

227. 'memento mori': reminder of (the inevitability of) death (Latin).

228. *Gothic*: barbarous or uncivilized, after the ancient Germanic tribe of Goths, who rampaged through the Roman empire.

229. *aristocratic novelist*: 'aristocratic' is 'asistocratic' in the original; the novelist may be Edward Bulwer Lytton (1803–73), or Marguerite, Lady Blessington (1789–1849), or some other author of the so-called 'silver fork novels' depicting fashionable life and pronouncing on fashions and proprieties.

230. parvenus: French for 'newly arrived', or social upstarts.

231. *board*: table.

232. *consummation ... prayed for*: echoing Shakespeare, *Hamlet*, III.i.63–4.

233. *2286l. 16s.*: worth about £ 137,000 in today's money, using the retail price index.

234. *party*: legal jargon for person.

235. *such ... parsnips*: proverbial: fair words butter no parsnips, i.e., are of no material benefit.

236. '*soft nothings*': James Cobb, *The Strangers at Home: A Comic Opera* (1786), I.i, 'Air', l. 2.

237. '*more ... ear*': Milton, 'Il Penseroso', l. 120.

238. '*sagacious ... afar*': echo of Milton, *Paradise Lost*, X.279, describing Sin.

239. *Alcestis ... grave*: In Greek legend, Alcestis agrees to die in place of her beloved Admetus, but Hercules retrieves her from the underworld and she is re-united with Admetus.

240. *drawing in ... drawing out*: drawing in: closing in; drawing out: withdrawing (the money from Snavel).

241. *devil's tattoo*: tapping, as with agitation.

242. *business*: 'buisness' in the original.

243. *law-list*: list of practitioners or cases.

244. *St. Anthony's fire*: burning sensation in the limbs caused by a fungus in grain.

245. *Hockley in the hole*: Hockley-in-the-Hole was a place of resort and entertainment on the outskirts of London.

246. *Hercules ... laughing philosopher*: Hercules: adventurous strongman of ancient Greek legend; Democritus (460–370 BC): the historical 'laughing philosopher', so called for his constant mocking of human follies.

247. *gammon*: deceive.

248. *bender*: possibly 'whopper', i.e., a lie (slang).
249. *your's*: at that time an accepted variant of 'yours'.
250. mizzle: disappear (slang).
251. *Laocoon*: Laocoön and his sons were crushed by a serpent as a punishment by the gods, an event depicted in a famous ancient statue.
252. *perspiration*: 'perspiation' in the original.
253. *devil's dancing hour*: midnight.
254. *cut our stick*: depart, supposedly from cutting a branch to serve as a walking stick before setting out on a journey.
255. *thumb to it*: reference to the custom of licking one's thumb to seal an agreement.
256. *mother*: familiar address to any old woman.
257. *screw ... shakes*: screw: a small measure of tobacco wrapped in a twisted paper; brace of shakes: two shakes (of a lamb's tale), i.e., quickly.
258. *twig*: understand.
259. *comb*: In legend, mermaids spent much time combing out their wet hair.
260. *paid ... 'through the nose'*: paid exorbitantly.
261. *Seven Dials*: so called from the seven sundials in the centre of an intersection of several streets, in what was then a poor and teeming quarter of London, now a theatre and restaurant district near Leicester Square underground station.
262. *Jew ... asses*: In 1 Samuel 9:3, Kish sends his son Saul to find the lost beast of burden.
263. *Jew*: Jews were stigmatized at the time as money-lenders and also as dealers in used clothing.
264. wool-gathering: collecting fragments of wool left by sheep on bushes and brambles, but also day-dreaming.
265. Fleecing: shearing the wool from sheep, but also cheating.
266. *gave ... sack*: dismissed (slang).
267. *ha'porth*: halfpenny's worth.
268. *sack*: sherry, echoing Shakespeare, *2 Henry IV*, II.iv.528.
269. *eyes-in-glass*: isinglass, a gelatinous substance obtained from fish and used to make jellies, clarify liquors, and so on.
270. *stand* Sam: pay for.
271. *colloguing varmint*: flattering vermin.
272. *toddled*: strolled off, went.
273. *vally*: value.
274. *daddles*: fists.
275. *arter*: after.
276. coup de main: bold stroke (French).
277. *bang ... goles*: as well as it can be done, by God.
278. *Garrick*: David Garrick (1717–79), shrewd theatre manager and versatile actor.
279. *gemman*: gentleman (Wilmot).
280. *knowledge box*: head.
281. *Haman*: In Esther, Haman tries to persuade the king to kill all the Jews but is foiled by queen Esther and hanged with his ten sons.
282. *turned off*: hanged.
283. hump higher: hump: fit of vexation or the sulks.
284. *infant ... Solomons*: In 1 Kings 3:16–28, king Solomon resolves a dispute between two women claiming to be mother of the same child. He offers to cut the child in two and assign each woman a portion, whereupon one woman relinquishes her claim, thereby

disclosing that she is the actual mother, unable to bear seeing her child killed, and Solomon assigns the child to her.

285. *blood*: bold fellow.
286. *crib*: house; literally, a hovel.
287. *great house*: Newgate prison.
288. *culls*: fellows.
289. *clean a hand*: without a criminal record.
290. *on*: of.
291. *salt-box*: cell in Newgate (slang).
292. *squaring the circle*: an insoluble problem, from the long-standing quest by mathematicians for a formula to construct a square equal in area to that of a circle.
293. *fly to*: clever at.
294. *gammon*: humbug, rubbish.
295. *not ... from*: near to.
296. *exalted*: noble, but also elevated, as when hanged from the gallows.
297. *mantua-maker's twist*: Mantua-makers were notoriously underpaid dressmakers; a twist is a small measure.
298. *souchong*: fine (i.e., expensive) black tea.
299. *alderman ... turtle*: alderman: civic official, usually a wealthy middle-class person, proverbially fond of delicacies such as turtle soup.
300. *jointure*: legal provision for a wife to possess a particular property on her husband's death.
301. *bourne ... returns*: death; echo of Shakespeare, *Hamlet*, III.i.79–80.
302. *wainscot ... bar*: A customer's accumulating debt would be marked in chalk on the wall or wainscot.
303. *newspaper ... sphere*: Announcements of marriages were recorded in newspapers between announcements of births and deaths.
304. *sanded*: sprinkled with sand to absorb spills, etc.
305. *pop*: pawn.
306. *'much pondering on these matters'*: perhaps echoing Shakespeare, *King Lear*, III.iv.24–5.
307. *Hymen*: ancient Greek god of marriage.
308. *man of straw*: someone who undertakes something without the means to accomplish it.
309. *Augean stable*: In ancient Greek legend, one of the twelve labours assigned the strongman Hercules (or Herakles) was to clean the large and long-neglected stables of king Augeas in a single day; he did so by diverting rivers through the place.
310. *keep ... up*: stay alert.
311. *thumb ... shoulder*: apparently a dismissive gesture.
312. *'how awful goodness is'*: Milton, *Paradise Lost*, IV.847, describing Satan's sensation on first beholding Eve; here 'awful' means 'awe-inspiring'.
313. *short*: strong drink, drunk in small or 'short' measure.
314. *Marley*: also the name of the kindly partner of Ebenezer Scrooge in Charles Dickens's *A Christmas Carol* (1843).
315. *stumpy*: money (slang).
316. *Old Bailey*: London's central criminal court.
317. *Recorder ... corder*: Recorder: magistrate with criminal jurisdiction, appointed by the City of London; corder: hangman.

318. *watchman ... box*: Watchmen were a form of police, patrolling from sunset to sunrise, and sheltering in watchhouses in various locations; they were notoriously ineffective and in 1839 were replaced in London by a more organized and specially trained force.

319. *Oliver ... Museum*: A silver watch once belonging to Oliver Cromwell (1599–1658), former Lord Protector of England, was displayed in the Ashmolean Museum, Oxford.

320. *being 'down on your luck'*: experiencing hard times.

321. *'beautiful ... not'*: echoing S. T. Coleridge, *The Death of Wallenstein: A Tragedy* (1800), V.i.68.

322. *man ... Abbey*: Britons excelling in various fields, such as literature, were sometimes buried or memorialized in Westminster Abbey, especially in the so-called Poets' Corner.

323. *diamond cut diamond*: Turnabout or tit-for-tat is fair play because it takes a diamond to cut a diamond.

324. *tossed ... nose*: in the action of drinking, excess of which eventually causes a red nose.

325. *right ... cunning*: echoing Psalm 137:5.

326. *outward shows*: echo of Shakespeare, *The Merchant of Venice*, III.ii.73.

327. *'hypocrisy ... virtue'*: see note 11.

328. *letter ... spirit*: the literal or surface sense, as opposed to the spirit or deeper significance, as in the letter rather than the spirit of a rule, law, or contract.

329. *child*: a term of endearment.

330. *certain ... intentions*: proverbial: the road to hell is paved with good intentions.

331. *galvanic eruptions*: after Luigi Galvani (1737–98), Italian physician who experimented with passing electricity through a dead frog, causing it to move, and concluded that a form of electricity animated living creatures.

332. *'hung fire'*: literally, delay in discharge of a gun.

333. *'Honour ... thieves'*: i.e., the proverb, 'There is no honour among thieves.'

334. *land of Van Diemen*: in Australia, site of a penal colony.

335. *Styx*: In ancient legend, the Styx separated the land of the living from the land of the dead.

336. *right trim*: literally, ready to sail.

337. *take ... ear*: proverbial: easily perform something difficult.

338. *don't ... hatched*: variation on the proverb, 'Don't count your chickens before they're hatched', i.e., don't anticipate good fortune, with the raven, a bird of ill omen, substituted.

339. *creter*: creature.

340. *mull*: muddle.

341. *capital ... exactions*: alluding to Shakespeare's *The Merchant of Venice*, IV.i.99, where the Jew Shylock demands fulfilment of Antonio's bond to forfeit a pound of his own flesh should he fail to repay Shylock's loan.

342. *cock's eye*: possibly a small measure or tot; possibly cock's egg ('eye' or 'ei' was an earlier form of 'egg'): a yokeless egg, high in protein, and presumably used as a tonic, here mixed with brandy.

343. *'cute*: acute, sharp.

344. *coup*: stroke (French).

345. *whistle*: with relief.

346. *Rubicon*: In 49 BC, Julius Caesar with his army crossed the Rubicon river in northern Italy, breaking a Roman law forbidding this and thereby precipitating civil war; 'cross the Rubicon' became proverbial for 'take an irrevocable step'.

347. *China*: fragile, like fine earthenware of the kind originally manufactured in China.

348. *split*: inform (slang).
349. *dead take in*: absolute deception.
350. *Plutus ... Fortune*: Plutus, ancient Greek god of wealth, depicted as blind because he dispenses his gifts without prejudice and by chance, lame because he arrives late, and winged because he departs quickly; also confused with Pluto, Roman name for the god of the underworld, as Neptune was the god of the ocean; Pluto was the god of wealth because he presided over the subterranean realm, which concealed gold and silver.
351. quid ... smoked ... pro-quo: *quid pro quo*: Latin meaning something for something, or tit-for-tat; but a quid is also a sovereign or pound in money, or a piece of tobacco suitable for chewing; 'smoked' refers to a way of consuming tobacco, but also means 'detected', 'understood', or 'exposed to (justified) ridicule'.
352. *'unsphere the spirit'*: Milton, 'Il Penseroso', ll. 88–9.
353. *Rochefoucault*: see note 11.
354. *fig ... raisins*: fig: a fruit, but also something valueless or unprofitable, giving rise to Jack's pun on 'raisins', which are dried grapes but also 'raisings' or 'raisin's' – i.e., children, who have to be raised with effort and expense.
355. *consols*: consolidated annuities or government stock, in this case expected to return three per cent. interest a year.
356. *settlements*: contracts drawn up before marriage assigning certain property and interests to the respective partners.
357. *lays*: puts to rest, buries.
358. *'With ... head-shake'*: Shakespeare, *Hamlet*, I.v.182.
359. *'rights of the thing'*: legal phrase meaning the issues involved in the matter or object in which a person has a concern or interest.
360. *Medes and Persians*: ancient peoples of what are now Iraq and Iran.
361. *'When ... war'*: echoing Nathaniel Lee's play *The Rival Queens* (1677), act IV (p. 48, 1677 edition), spoken by Clytus, meaning that it is difficult to predict the outcome of a contest between rivals of equal strength or bravery.
362. *jawbones ... Philistines*: In Judges 15:15, the Jewish strongman Samson slays a host of Philistines, armed with but an ass's jawbone, here with a play on 'ass' as 'fool'.
363. *thrasonical*: boastful, after Thraso, a braggart soldier in Terence's second-century BC Latin comedy, *The Eunuch*.
364. *'Brag ... better'*: proverb meaning action is better than talk.
365. *perdue*: hidden, from French *perdu*, lost.
366. *motes ... beams*: echo of several passages in the Bible, e.g., Matthew 7:3: 'And why beholdest thou the mote (dust particle) that is in thy brother's eye, but considerest not the beam (large timber) that is in thine own eye?' – i.e., as Jack says below, 'men generally are much more prone to discover blemishes in others than to detect faults in themselves,' with 'beam' allowing Jack to build a pun on gallows, which is constructed of beams.
367. *lynxes ... moles*: Lynxes are proverbially sharp-sighted, moles blind.
368. *Pythoness ... inspiration*: priestess at the ancient Greek sacred site of Delphi, so named from a prophesying serpent there; the Pythoness's utterances while in an agitated trance were construed as prophecies from the god Apollo.
369. *heterogenous*: variant of the more usual 'heterogeneous'.
370. *thumb*: from the custom of licking one's thumb to seal an agreement.
371. *grizzling*: fretting.
372. *Polite Letter Writer*: one of the numerous published manuals for letter-writing, with sample letters for various occasions, such as the often reprinted *Universal Letter-writer;*

or, Complete Art of Polite Correspondence (1779), 'polite' here meaning 'polished, elegant, genteel'.

373. *Peter Grievous*: proverbially any fretful or whining person.

374. *nonplus*: inability to proceed, from Latin *non plus*: no more, no further.

375. *eccentric*: deviating from normal paths.

376. *drawing a long bow*: literally, pulling on the longbow; figuratively, making exaggerated statements.

377. *wolf* at the door: imminent poverty or starvation.

378. *foster-mother of the Roman twins*: In ancient legend, the orphaned infant twins Romulus and Remus, later founders of Rome, were saved from death by being suckled by a she-wolf.

379. *ignis fatuus*: from Latin meaning 'fool's fire', referring to flitting flames caused by gas or vapour emitted by rotting vegetation in swamps, and chased by fools to their destruction; also known as Will-o'-the-wisp.

380. *Antony ... gipsy*: the love of the Roman general Marcus Antonius (83–30 BC) for the Egyptian Cleopatra (69–30 BC) caused his destruction, as depicted in histories and Shakespeare's play; gipsy: fickle woman – before her affair with Antony, Cleopatra was the lover of Julius Caesar.

381. *Helen ... weight*: Helen, wife of the Greek king Menelaus, eloped with Paris, son of the king of Troy, precipitating the Greek war against Troy, celebrated in Homer's epic poem the *Iliad*, here with a pun on the 'troy' system of measuring weight (from the system once used at Troyes, France).

382. *Diana ... moonshine*: The moon goddess Diana fell in love with the mortal Endymion and asked Zeus to make him immortal, which Zeus did by putting him into an eternal sleep, here with a pun on 'moonshine' as something attractive but insubstantial.

383. *Latmos ... lunatic*: Endymion was a shepherd on Latmos and a 'lunatic' because he fell in love with the goddess of the moon (Latin *luna*); according to folklore and poets, lunacy or insanity was caused by the influence of the moon.

384. *Pincher ... Dobbin*: Pincher was a common name for a dog (pincher means biter), Dobbin for a horse.

385. *Walworth*: a lower-class neighbourhood in Southwark, on the south side of the river Thames facing the City of London.

386. *cloven hoof*: a trait of the devil.

387. *means ... at*: probably prostitution.

388. *sheep's eye*: shy or sly oblique glance.

389. *Banstead Downs*: sheep-grazing area in Surrey, southeast of London.

390. *patent*: open, obvious.

391. *menace*: At that time wife and child abuse were regarded by communities as serious crimes, even when not illegal, and often punished by communal action.

392. *black box*: coffin.

393. *guy*: grotesque person, from the 'guys' or crude effigies made to be burned every year on 5 November to celebrate foiling the attempt by Guy Fawkes (1570–1606) and his accomplices to blow up Parliament in 1605.

394. *turned off*: hanged.

395. *nor*: than.

396. *snuffed the candle*: trimmed the burnt portion of wick away, enabling the candle to burn more brightly.

397. sine quâ non: Latin for 'absolutely necessary'.
398. *apprehensive*: perceptive.
399. *mortal*: extremely (slang).
400. *Dispenser of events*: God, divine providence.
401. *lenth*: possibly a misprint for 'length', but also an alternative spelling in the past.
402. *thick-coming fancies*: echoing Shakespeare, *Macbeth*, V.iii.38.
403. *outside ... coach*: The cheap seats were on the outside of the coach.
404. *pigeon-livered*: meek.
405. *'Thou ... murder'*: Matthew 19:18, spoken by Jesus to the Pharisee, based on the ten commandments handed down to Moses by God, Exodus 20:13.
406. *her's*: at that time an accepted variant of 'hers'.
407. *walley*: value.
408. *Drench*: In medical terminology of that time, a 'drench' was a potion causing sleep or death.
409. *Jobs*: sufferers; in the eponymous book of the Bible, Job is subjected by God to a succession of physical and mental afflictions as a test of his faith.
410. *fin*: hand.
411. *fat ... wharf*: echoing Shakespeare, *Hamlet*, I.v.32–3, in ancient legend, Lethe is the river of forgetfulness.
412. *'from ... severe'*: Alexander Pope, *An Essay on Man*, Epistle IV (1734), l. 370.
413. *maniacs ... madhouses*: At that time, asylums for the insane were private businesses, but a series of scandals revealed that they were often used to imprison and abuse sane people for various purposes, such as a husband wishing to dispose of his wife, or relatives to obtain control of a person's property.
414. *shilling fare*: a fare that would take a person a long distance; the first public buses, or omnibuses (literally 'for all', from Latin), charged the relatively high fare of one shilling, and so were in effect mainly for the well-to-do.
415. *an otomy*: figuratively, a skeleton, from colloquial misapprehension of 'anatomy', meaning emaciated body or skeleton.
416. *'the strong ... tumultuous'*: Milton, *Paradise Lost*, II.936.
417. *bitter ... sweet*: In Exodus 15:22–5, Moses leads the Jews to the oasis of Marah, but the waters are too bitter to drink; God shows Moses a tree which he throws into the waters, making them drinkable.
418. *ancient or modern Greeks*: The ancient Greeks were legendary for their cleverness and ingenuity, exemplified by the figure of Odysseus in Homer's epic the *Odyssey*.
419. *I ... boasting*: a formula phase used so often as to become empty; here, the ironic use of the phrase is indicated by its being put in italics.
420. *'to unhoard ... burgher'*: echoing John Dennis, *Appius and Virginia: A Tragedy* (1709), II.i.28–9.
421. *hyperborean*: far northerner, i.e., a Scot – Scots were known for canniness.
422. *too far north*: too clever, probably from the preceding association of Scots with cleverness.
423. *Leith*: the harbour serving Edinburgh in Scotland.
424. *last place ... country*: The English regarded Scotland as an unpleasant place and Scots as stingy.
425. *seven years' transportation*: At this time, many criminals, especially first-time offenders and those committing lesser crimes, received a sentence of transportation to a penal colony such as Australia, with a ban from returning to England for seven years.

426. maladie du pays: homesickness (French).
427. *De Moivre ... Price*: Abraham de Moivre (1667–1754) and Richard Price (1723–91), famous mathematicians.
428. *field ... Punchinello*: Field preachers were unlicensed and so often had to preach in fields, but their popular style was supposed to take congregations away from licensed or beneficed clergy; patent players or actors were those in the 'patent' or licensed theatres of London, and the stars of the theatrical world, and so disdained or refused to tolerate ('away with') itinerant or 'peripatetic' actors who relied on slapstick and comedy of the popular or street theatre, represented by the famous character of Punch (Punchinello).
429. *pale*: fence, border.
430. *uncle-land*: Australia, site of a penal colony to which Wisp would be exiled.
431. *better three-quarters*: joke on 'better half', i.e., wife.
432. *sow ... purse*: conflation of two proverbial expressions: get the sow by the ear (come to the right conclusion or understanding), and make a silk purse out of a sow's ear (transform something homely into somethin beautiful, i.e., do something difficult).
433. *sand ... together*: suggesting that Gibbon sells sugar and sand separately and also adulterates the sugar with sand.
434. *Twankay*: green tea.
435. *chandler's shop*: selling candles, but also many other things, i.e., a general store.
436. *green*: naïve.
437. *mizzled*: disappeared.
438. *catch flats*: swindle fools.
439. *no go* there: Yorkshire people were famous for canniness.
440. '*with ... arm*': Grimes means he absconded with his employers' money; the line is from a popular ballad: 'Oh the miller he stole corn, / And the weaver he stole yarn, / And the little tailor ran away, / With the broadcloth under his arm' – tailors being entrusted with the cloth to make suits of clothes.
441. *twig*: understand.
442. *bills*: notes promising to pay, like cheques.
443. *corianders*: money (slang).
444. Dr. Dodd: William Dodd, clergyman, hanged in 1777 for forgery, a few years after he had published a pamphlet opposing capital punishment; George III rejected a petition for clemency on grounds it would be a bad precedent.
445. *capsize*: knock over.
446. *tucked up*: hanged (slang).
447. *rolls drawn*: rolls: perhaps 'the lists of those to be hanged on a certain date', or 'those so listed'; drawn: perhaps 'set forth in due form', or 'taken to the place of execution'.
448. *swell*: fine fellow.
449. tremor cordis: heart flutter (Latin).
450. *Goldsmith's ... not*: An echo of the comic poem, 'The Haunch of Venison' (l. 84) by Oliver Goldsmith (1730?–74), in which a friend invites Goldsmith to dinner and then inveigles him out of a piece of venison on pretence of using it in a pasty for the dinner; when Goldsmith shows up, the pasty is not to be seen.
451. *lean ... side*: anticipating the position of the head after he has been hanged.
452. *likely*: capable.
453. '*to ... munchings*': echo of Byron, *Don Juan*, canto 11 (1823), l. 516: 'to gratify a bee's slight munchings'.

454. *starling ... out*: referring to an episode in *A Sentimental Journey* (1768) by Laurence Sterne.

455. *New Holland*: Australia.

456. *area*: sunken, railed off courtyard connecting a basement, its kitchens, etc., with street level.

457. *converse sweet*: a phrase found in numerous authors.

458. *public-house*: Supposedly servants who had saved enough would, on retirement, become proprietors of a public house.

459. *Royal Exchange*: at that time the stock exchange in London; it burned down three years after this novel was published.

460. *persons ... alone*: bankrupts or those who have lost their own fortunes and hope to benefit from someone else's.

461. *personage*: the devil.

462. *calendar of woe*: Charles Whitehead, *The Solitary* (1831), II.27.

463. *grasshopper*: In fable, the grasshopper failed to provide for winter and perished, while the ant put aside a store and so survived.

464. *beaver*: hat made of beaver pelt.

465. *'formless infinite'*: Milton, *Paradise Lost*, III.12.

466. *Rappee ... Scotch*: Rappee: coarse snuff; Scotch: a kind of snuff.

467. *Perseus ... Andromeda*: In ancient Greek legend, one of Perseus's adventures is to rescue Andromeda from being a sacrifice to the Gorgon, a sea-monster ravaging the coast of her parents' kingdom; Perseus then marries her.

468. *on 'Change*: an area at the Exchange where people met to make deals, investments, and so on.

469. *threshhold*: a variant of the more usual 'threshold'.

470. *cri*: perhaps short for 'crimini', an exclamation of astonishment.

471. *ha'porth*: halfpenny worth.

472. *pearlash*: or pearl ash, potassium carbonate used in making soap and glass.

473. *get ... harangue-o' tongue*: get his monkey up: anger him, with 'monkey' giving Gibbon the chance to pun on 'harangue-o' tongue' (i.e., orang-utan, a kind of ape).

474. *port ... crusty*: reference to crust acquired by old port in the bottle and to 'crusty' meaning 'irascible'.

475. *Jacob's ladder*: In Genesis 28:11–19, Jacob has a vision of angels going up and down a ladder between earth and heaven.

476. *tête à tête*: in intimate conversation, literally 'head to head' (French).

477. *twenty pounds*: about £1,500 in today's money, using the retail price index.

478. *Gordian knots*: In legend, king Gordias of ancient Phrygia devised an intricate knot and an oracle declared that he who could undo it would rule Asia; the young Alexander the Great attempted to do so but after a time simply cut the knot with his sword; he went on to conquer lands from Greece to Persia and Egypt.

479. *'God speed'*: good luck.

480. *villany*: accepted variant of the more usual 'villainy'.

481. *needful*: money (colloquial).

482. *half-pay*: Military officers not on active service received half their normal pay.

483. *Grecian daughter*: In Arthur Murphy's play *The Grecian Daughter* (1772), Euphrasia suckles her father Evander when the latter is confined in a dungeon, thereby saving him from starvation.

484. *Merry Andrew*: clown, buffoon.

485. *Garrick ... comedy*: Sir Joshua Reynolds's portrait (1760–1) of the versatile actor David Garrick depicted him undecided between the muses of comedy and tragedy.
486. *St. Anthony ... devil*: According to the biography by Athanasius, the devil long afflicted St Anthony (251–356) in various ways but was defeated by Anthony's prayers and ridicule; the subject was depicted in several well known paintings.
487. *'Age ... variety'*: Shakespeare, *Antony and Cleopatra*, II.ii.244–5, said of Cleopatra by Enobarbus.
488. *'Cry ... bellows'*: apparently from a seventeenth-century ballad, 'Old Rose', in which to sing 'To burn the bellows and sing old rose' initiates merrymaking.
489. *absorbing bird*: The word 'absorbing' here may mean 'imbibing' or 'drinking', or possibly 'intently engaged in', as when descending on its prey, which seems to be the posture Jack is describing.
490. *Triggs*: 'trig': 'faithful', as well as 'alert' – good things for a shop assistant to be.
491. *'and each ... dismay*: Milton, *Paradise Lost*, II.422, describing the consternation of the fallen angels.
492. *che sarà, sarà'*: 'what will be, will be' (Italian).
493. *Trulliber-ism*: Parson Trulliber, in Henry Fielding's novel *Joseph Andrews* (1742), raises his own pigs.
494. *consummation ... him*: echoing Shakespeare, *Hamlet*, III.i.63–4.
495. *Teneriffe or Atlas*: Teneriffe (or Tenerife): a mountainous island in the Canaries, off the coast of Africa; Atlas: a number of mountains and ranges have this name.
496. *Nero ... once*: According to the Latin historian Suetonius in his *Lives of the Twelve Caesars*, the infamously cruel Roman emperor Caligula (12–41), rather than Nero (37–68), wished that the people of Rome had but one neck that he might execute them all at once.
497. *harticle*: article, thing (derogatory).
498. *put a stopper on*: put an end to (slang).
499. *on the anvil*: in hand, in preparation.
500. *toothach*: variant of the more usual 'toothache'.
501. *daddles*: hands.
502. *faint ... henroost*: Jack adapts the proverb, 'faint heart never won fair lady'.
503. *Falstaff ... back*: Shakespeare, *1 Henry IV*, III.ii.179.
504. *sea of troubles*: echo of Shakespeare, *Hamlet*, II.i.59.
505. *Tyburn ... Newgate*: Public hangings were held at Tyburn near present-day Marble Arch in London until 1783, when they were moved to Newgate prison.
506. *'My uncle ... more'*: echo of Shakespeare, *Hamlet*, I.ii.151–2.
507. *Sheriff*: The City of London annually elected two sheriffs, or law officers responsible for custody of prisoners, summoning jurors, executing writs of the courts, and executions.
508. *Coroner's inquest*: The coroner was a law officer charged with holding an inquiry, or inquest, into any violent or accidental death.
509. *quidnuncs*: gossips, from Latin *quid nunc*, 'what now?' or 'what's new?'
510. *deodand*: from Latin, meaning 'given to God', in English law a thing forfeited to God or the monarch for having been the cause of a person's death.
511. *bonâ fide*: authentic, genuine, from Latin meaning 'in good faith'.
512. *lignum-vitæ*: a kind of tree used in medicines, from Latin meaning 'wood of life'.
513. *Home Secretary*: member of the British government responsible for domestic affairs and public order, including execution of the laws.

514. *Sufficient ... thereof*: Matthew 6:34, from Christ's sermon on the mount, or advice to his followers.

515. *day of judgment*: that is, the final judgment of all sinners by God.

516. *Stoic*: in general, one who displays no emotion; more particularly, a follower of the ancient Greek philosopher Zeno of Athens (late 4th century BC), who advocated self-control and indifference to pleasure or pain.

517. *Hollands*: Dutch gin.

518. elixir ... *Gods*: drink of supposedly supernatural powers: *elixir vitæ*: literally, potion of life, from Latin, a potion with power to prolong life; *aurum potabile*: literally, drinkable gold, from Latin, a suspension of gold in liquid, supposedly a powerful restorative; nectar of the Gods: or ambrosia, in ancient legend the food of the gods.

519. *dozen*: dozen bottles.

520. *'Old ... yet'*: slightly misquoted from John Dryden, 'Cymon and Iphigenia', ll. 1–2, in *Fables Ancient and Modern* (1700).

521. *inns of court*: institutions like colleges, in the City of London, housing students of law, but also others; they included Lincoln's Inn, Gray's Inn, Inner Temple, and Middle Temple; they now house law firms.

522. *west end of the town*: The 'town', or genteel and fashionable quarter of London, extended westward from Charing Cross, and was outside of and contrasted to the City of London, extending east of Temple Bar and considered to be more mercantile and bourgeois than genteel, typified by Mr Western, two paragraphs down.

523. *Covent Garden*: formerly the fruit, vegetable, and flower market of London.

524. *saloop-stall*: stall opened at night till early morning, selling saloop, a hot drink of powdered salep, milk, and sugar.

525. *neck-or-nothing*: ready to venture everything.

526. *Providence ... lamb*: echo of 'God tempers the wind to the shorn lamb', from Laurence Sterne, *A Sentimental Journey*, chapter titled 'Maria' and referring to a young madwoman.

527. *Mozart ... Gluck*: Wolfgang Amadeus Mozart (1756–91), popular Austrian composer of concertos, symphonies, operas, etc.; Christoph Willibald Gluck (1714–87), popular and prolific opera composer.

528. *placeman ... premiership*: placeman: official of a sovereign or state, usually in a derogatory sense, or Member of Parliament who has sold his vote to the current regime; premiership: office of Prime Minister, or head of the government.

529. *demagogue ... pension*: demagogue: popular or influential orator, especially against the government; in Parliament, such a person might agree to desist from speaking out in exchange for a pension, or regular payment.

530. *tuft-hunter ... Marquis*: tuft-hunter: toady, from university slang for someone who sought the company of aristocrats, who were distinguished by a 'tuft' or tassel on their caps; Marquis: nobleman below a duke but above a count in rank.

531. *succinct*: close-fitting.

532. *where ... granted*: play on 'suit' as 'outfit of clothes' and as 'request, application'.

533. *coat of his stomach*: hunger was supposed to cause the stomach to consume its own lining ('coat').

534. *peripatetic philosophers*: followers of the ancient Greek philosopher Aristotle, from their practice of discoursing while they walked up and down the public square of Athens; here, itinerant buyers of used clothing.

535. *grist*: corn or grain to be ground into flour by the mill, but also business, generally.

536. *paper-mill*: Such mills ground rags into fibres so they could be made into paper.
537. *foolscap*: a size of paper, but also a cap made of such paper, placed on the head of a dunce or fool.
538. *half ... Shrievalty*: one of the two Sheriffs elected annually.
539. *Ordinary of Newgate*: see note 81.
540. *Kilderkin*: a half-barrel cask.
541. *Parr or a Jenkins*: Thomas Parr died in 1635, aged 152; Henry Jenkins died in 1670, aged 169.
542. *Muscovados*: unrefined sugar.
543. *Pythagorean*: believer in the transmigration of souls, after the Greek philosopher Pythagoras (sixth century BC).
544. *economy*: (physiological) structure.
545. passibus equis: at a horse's pace or stride (Latin).
546. *Merchant Tailors*: a famous London grammar school founded in 1561 by the guild of merchant tailors.
547. 'Passibus assinis': at an ass's pace or stride (Latin).
548. locum tenens: place holder, substitute; from Latin.
549. *in* propriâ personâ: in your own person (Latin).
550. *funk*: panic.
551. *in ordinary*: in official capacity.
552. *hymen*: see note 307.
553. *Greek chorus*: in ancient Greek drama, a group of singers and dancers who commented on the play's action.
554. *scene-shifter*: person who moved the scenes, or painted flats depicting settings, during a play's performance.

For Product Safety Concerns and Information please contact our EU
representative GPSR@taylorandfrancis.com Taylor & Francis Verlag GmbH,
Kaufingerstraße 24, 80331 München, Germany

Batch number: 08153780

Printed by Printforce, the Netherlands